MANUSCRIPT AND MANUSCRIPTOLOGY IN INDIA

MANUSCRIPT AND MANUSCRIPTOLOGY IN INDIA

Edited by

Subodh Gopal Nandi
Projit Kumar Palit

Kaveri Books
New Delhi-110002

First Published in 2010
Edition 2025

ISBN 978-81-7479-105-4

Front cover visual : Indigenous Methods of Preserving Manuscripts

Back cover visual: Collected from Department of Medieval Studies at Central European University, Budapest (http://web.ceu.hu/medstud/manual/MMM/index.html)

Kaveri Books
4832/24, Ansari Road
New Delhi - 110 002 (India)
Tel.: 011-4707 2321
e-mail: kaveribooks@gmail.com
info@kaveribooks.com

Laser Typesetting by : Aarati Computers, Delhi - 110 009

PRINTED IN INDIA

Dedication

To

Arati Nandi
Susmita Palit

प्रो. तपोधीर भट्टाचार्जी
Prof. Tapodhir Bhattacharjee
M.A. (Triple), Ph.D.

कुलपति
Vice-Chancellor

असम विश्वविद्यालय
(केन्द्रिय विश्वविद्यालय)
ASSAM UNIVERSITY
(A Central University)
सिलचर-७८८०११ असम (भारत)
Silchar 788 011, Assam (India)

Foreword

I am delighted to introduce 'The Manuscript and Manuscriptology in India', edited by two eminent scholars of the region namely Dr. Subodh Gopal Nandi who is the Librarian of Visva-Bharati, Santiniketan while Dr. Projit Kumar Palit is the Reader in the Department of History at Assam University, Silchar. As many as twenty-eight contributors have shed illuminating light on various aspects of manuscript and manuscriptology as practised in India. The readers would be immensely benefited from the learned exposition of manuscripts as primary sources of our rich cultural heritage. It has been preserved for the posterity through manuscripts on variety of media. The authors have commented upon the religious, philosophical, literary, historical and scientific nuances of the manuscripts. The strength of this volume rests on the wide variety of the subjects as well as projects of the learned discourses.

I am confident that the scholars of the coming generations would accept this volume as reliable references for embarking upon new projects on the study of manuscripts and manuscriptology. I congratulate the editors for their sincere and successful effort.

Tapodhir Bhattacharjee

(Prof. Tapodhir Bhattacharjee)

Acknowledgement

We are happy to announce that our endeavour for the publication of a volume on 'Manuscripts and Manuscriptology' which has come out finally for the participation of thirty-four distinguished scholars from India.

We are expressing deep regards to Prof. Tapodhir Bhattacharya, Vice-Chancellor, Assam University for his valuable 'Foreword'. We are sincerely grateful and indebted to all authors who have contributed their research papers for this volume. We are thankful to Mr. Rakesh Goel of Kaveri Books, New Delhi for publishing this volume within a very short time. Thanks are due to Mr. Achintya Kumar Mandal for his sincere co-operation. We are also thankful to Visva-Bharati Library and all staff members for helping us during this work. We acknowledge our family members for their encouragement and assistance for completing this work. We are immensely grateful to the Department of Medieval Studies, Central European University, Budapest for using the plate as 'Cover Page'.

Subodh Gopal Nandi
Projit Kumar Palit

Contents

Diacritical Marks

System of Transliteration

Roman equivalents of Deva-nāgarī Letters

a	अ	ka	क	da	द
ā	आ	kha	ख	dha	ध
i	इ	ga	ग	na	न
ī	ई	gha	घ	pa	प
u	उ	ṅ	ङ	pha	फ
ū	ऊ	ca/cha	च	ba	ब
ṛ/ri	ऋ	cha/chha	छ	bha	भ
e	ए	ja	ज	ma	म
ai	ऐ	jha	झ	ya	य
o	ओ	ñ	ञ	ra	र
au	औ	ṭa	ट	la	ल
		ṭha	ठ	va	व
		ḍa	ड	śa	श
		ḍha	ढ	ṣa/sha	ष
		ṇa	ण	sa	स
		ta	त	ha	ह
		tha	थ	ṃ/ṁ	ं
				ḥ	:

Common words and modern names are usually written without any diacritical marks.

List of Plates

Contributors

A.I. Rahmathullah
Professor, Department of Arabic
University of Calicut
P.O. Calicut University
Kerala-673 635

Abhijit Banerjee
Reader, Department of
Chinese Language and Culture
Visva-Bharati
Santiniketan-731235, West Bengal

Ajit Kumar Baishya
Reader, Department of Linguistics
Assam University, Silchar - 788 011
Assam

Alakananda Banerjee
Professor (Retired)
Department of Sanskrit, Pali and Prakrit,
Visva-Bharati
Santiniketan - 731235, West Bengal

Amalendu Bhattacharjee
Lecturer (Selection Grade)
Department of Bengali
G. C. College, P.O. Silchar-788004
Assam

Anita Bagchi
Reader, Department of History
University of North Bengal
P.O. North Bengal University
Siliguri-734013, West Bengal

Aarti Sharma
Assistant Librarian
Punjab Agricultural University,
Ludhiana-141001, Punjab

Buddhadev Acharya
Associated with Lipika
(Manuscript Centre of Visva Bharati)
Santiniketan-731235, West Bengal

Deepak Agarwal
Librarian, DAV College, Malout-152107
Dist. Muktsar, Punjab

Dipendu Das
Reader, Department of English
Assam University, Silchar - 788 011
Assam

G. S. Khwaja
Assistant Superintendent
Arabic and Persian Epigraphy Branch
Archeological Survey of India
Nagpur - 440 001, Maharashtra

Harekrushna Mishra
Senior Lecturer
Department of Sanskrit, Pali and Prakrit
Visva-Bharati
Santiniketan - 731235, West Bengal

J. Lalitha
Librarian
The Kuppuswami Sastri Research Institute
Chennai - 600 004, Tamil Nadu

Jagat Ram Bhattacharyya
Professor
Department of Sanskrit and Prakrit
Jain Vishva Bharati University
Ladnun - 341306, Rajasthan

Jagatpati Sarkar
The Asiatic Society, Kolkata-700016
West Bengal

Jahar Kanti Sen, HOD (Retired),
Department of English, G.C. College
P.O. Silchar-788 004, Assam

Kh. Dhiren Singha
Lecturer, Department of Linguistics
Assam University, Silchar-788 011, Assam

Lata Mahesh Deokar
Research Assistant, Dictionary Unit,
Central Institute of Higher Tibetan Studies,
Deemed University
Sarnath, Varanasi-221 007, Uttar Pradesh

M.N. Krishnakumar
Lecturer in Sanskrit Government College
Chittur-678104, Dist. Palakkad, Kerala

Mitali Chatterjee
Librarian, The Asiatic Society,
Kolkata-700016, West Bengal

Muhammad Ismail
Associate Professor
Department of Islamic Studies
Aligarh Muslim University,
Aligarh-202002, Uttar Pradesh

Naba Gopal Roy
Research Fellow
The Asiatic Society, Kolkata-700016
West Bengal

Pranabananda Jash
Professor (Retired)
Department of Ancient Indian
History Culture and Archeology
Visva-Bharati
Santiniketan - 731235, West Bengal

Pranati Mohapatra
Lecturer, Department of Sanskrit
Purnidevi Chaudhury Girls' College
Bolpur - 731 204, West Bengal

Projit Kumar Palit
Reader, Department of History
Assam University, Silchar - 788 011, Assam

Rani Syamalamba
Librarian, Maris Stella College
Vijayawada-520008
Andhra Pradesh

Rupinder Singh
Assistant Librarian
M M Central State Library, Patiala-147001
Punjab

S. Y. Wakankar
Deputy Director, Oriental Institute
M S University of Baroda,
Baroda - 390001, Gujarat

Sailen Kumar De
Deputy Registrar (Retired)
Visva-Bharati, Santiniketan-731235,
West Bengal

Sanjeev Kumar
Assistant Librarian
M S Randhawa Library
Pantnagar Agricultural University
Pantnagar-263145, Uttarakhand

Sanjib Deblaskar
Teacher in English, Mainul Haque Chaudhury
HS School Cachar-788013, Assam

Subodh Gopal Nandi
Librarian, Visva-Bharati
Central Library
Santiniketan - 731235, West Bengal

Suniti Bala
Assistant Librarian
Punjab Agricultural University
Ludhiana-141001, Punjab

Suniti Kumar Pathak
Professor (Retired)
Indo-Tibetan Department
Visva-Bharati
Santiniketan - 731235, West Bengal

Introduction

The word 'Manuscript' has been derived from the Latin word '*manuscriptus*', This Latin term actually consists of two Latin terms '*manu*' plus '*criptus*' which literary means 'hand' and 'written' respectively. The Latin term "*manuscriptus*" has been used for "a document written with a person's own hand". The Oxford English Dictionary defines 'Manuscript' as "a book, document, or the like, written by hand; a writing of any kind, as distinguished from printed matter". The term manuscripts are used in various Indian languages as: hastalekha, pandulipi, matrka, pustaka, pustika, pusta, potha, pothi, pothaka, mulakosa, adarsa and so on.

Manuscripts are of great interest to the learned scholars throughout the world. The Manuscript is considered as one of the main knowledge resource of humankind. Each and every Civilization has its own particular type of culture. Manuscripts have the pivotal role to focus of that Civilization. Indian Civilization has rich cultural heritage. Manuscripts are primary sources of such heritage knowledge.

It is also noticeable that various medium have been used for Indian manuscripts such as clay tablets, stones, metals, ivory, tortoise shell, tree barks and leaves, animal skins, cloths, papers, etc. In case of tree barks mostly used are: Papyrus, Sanchi bark (Aguru tree), etc. Mostly used leaves are Palm Leaves, Bhurja-patra, Terata-leaves, etc. The animal skins are used like: deer, sheep, goats, calves, cows, asses, buffalos, etc. Silk and cotton cloths are also used. As a medium of writing material tulat paper and hand made paper are very popular item in later time.

Manuscripts are available throughout India and those are in many languages and scripts, which cover religious, philosophical, historical, literary and scientific subjects. As per the present available source we may estimate that there are 50 lakh manuscripts scattered over the country of which 67 per cent are in Sanskrit; 25 per cent in other Indian languages out of which Arabic, Bengali, Hindi, Kannada, Malayalam, Oriya, Pali, Persian, Tamil, Telugu, Urdu, etc. are major and rest 8 per cent are of non-Indian languages. These huge collections of manuscripts cover various subjects on ancient Indian thoughts viz., Jainism, Buddhism, Hinduism, Vedas, Upanishads,

Ramayana, Mahabharata, Ancient Indian Science, Ayurveda, Indian Philosophy and Literature, etc. They are written in different scripts such as Brahmi, Sarada, Modi, Newari, Grantha, Kutila, Sanskrit, Tamil, Telegu, Malayalam, Arabic and Persian, Bengali, Oriya and others.

Manuscripts have their own texts or contents and other illustrations, which are the combination of mathematical calculations, maps, and explanatory figures. Manuscripts are found in the form of scrolls, in book form, and codex format. Illuminated manuscripts are enriched with pictures, border decorations, elaborately engrossed initial letters, full-page illustrations and decorative binding.

Manuscript has comprised of main body where the scribe used to display the text. It has also some other parts, viz. Pre-amble or *Bhonita*, Colophon or *Pushpika,* Binding, etc. Pre-amble or *Bhonita* describes the name of the manuscripts. Colophon or *Pushpika* is a composite work made of a brief autobiography of the writer, the name of the manuscript, the date of writing/copying and the name of the writer/ copyist. *Pushpika* contains the names of the scribe, generally found on the first leaf, at the end of the chapter or act, and on the last folio of the manuscript. *Pushpika* also contains the names of the scribe and the former content of the manuscripts in last folio, along with the dates of writing or copying in last folio.

The binding or outer covers of these Manuscripts are generally made of wood of birch trees, sal and other teaks, parchment or dyed skin etc. Deluxe covers of the manuscripts were made of ivory or brass, ornamented with carvings, precious stones, and cut and uncut. Manuscripts are found in various sizes, the smallest one having a dimension of 6 inches × 3 inches and the biggest one measuring three and half feet in length and one and half feet or 18 inches in breadth.

In case of writing or copying manuscripts in middle Ages the writer / copyist have used chiefly black ink, *incaustum*, composed of a mixture of gall nuts and vitriol. Red ink has been reserved from ancients times for titles. Gold and silver inks have been used for making manuscripts deluxe. The ink has been made instantly at the time of writing of the manuscript from the available ingredients. The best quality ink has prepared from the items: sesame, three kinds of myrobalan, bark of the silk cotton plant compounded with goat milk. All the items are to be grinded by lac in an iron pot. For writing purposes feathers of the peacock or the feathers of the vulture or branches of the bamboo tree are also in use as pen. The metal nibs are also in use for writing manuscripts.

It is important to note that till recent past manuscripts were a great interest of Kings, Priests, Scholars, etc. and that were kept under their custody, i.e. organizations like palaces, temples, monasteries, museums, archives, libraries and other similar repository institutes. These organizations have always taking care to add manuscripts into their collection. Now-a-days, Manuscript Centers, Libraries, Museums and Archives store and preserve the collection of manuscripts scientifically. Manuscripts are generally wrapped up in a piece of cloth, preferably red in colour, or enclosed in wooden box. The boxes are painted in different colours with the picture suitable to the text of the manuscript.

For serving the interest of the users manuscripts are catalogued in seven different types such as: i) Manuscript search report, which provides general account of availability of manuscripts in a particular area with list of titles. ii) Simple list contains author and title of manuscripts. iii) Alphabetical catalogue by author or title, which includes author title, commentator, script, date, extent etc. along with corresponding accession number. iv) Catalogue in tabular form is arranged in classified order with information in tabulated form under separate column /heads. v) Descriptive catalogue in tabular form, which includes tabular description consisting of eleven vertical columns of additional particulars of a manuscript, i.e. beginning and ending lines, colophons of select manuscript, etc. vi) Descriptive catalogue provides full physical description, post colophons, select portions from the text, notes on authors and works. vii) General register of works contains short information on author and title with source of availability of manuscripts.

Preservation of manuscripts is a serious issue for the Librarians, Information Scientists and Archivists ever since human beings acquired the knowledge of writing. The manuscripts have the chances to be damaged by insects or due to tearing by use of rough handling; so it is most essential to repair these damages at the moment of identification. The preservation of manuscripts follows traditional as well as modern methods, which are scientific and preserve documents for further use. In traditional system of preservation herbals are used such as neem leaves, aswagandha leaves, dried ginger, kumkum fruit powder, sandal wood, termaric powder, garlic, etc. In case of modern methods suitable chemicals are used for preservation.

This volume contains twenty-eight research papers in different areas of manuscripts and manuscriptology which includes the following facets like: Manuscript as heritage document; Manuscript and society; Manuscript and religion; Manuscript writers; Manuscript research; Manuscript typology; Manuscript and use of colophons; Style of writing Manuscript; Manuscript editing; Manuscript centers; Manuscript collection; Manuscript storage and preservation; Manuscript conservation; Manuscript catalogue and cataloguing; Manuscript case studies.

Buddhism and Indo-Tibetan Literature:
A Survey Linked to Manuscripts and Xylographs in India

1

S.K. PATHAK

Indo-Tibetan

A brief elucidation of the term 'Indo-Tibetan' may be relevant in this context. Fr Hermann had used the term in the ethnic context to refer the Himalayans of Tibeto-Mongoloid origin. Probodh Chandra Bagchi however used Indo-Tibetan with its historical reference India and Tibet. The two neighbouring countries have extensive cultural affinity since the seventh century A.D. The Buddhists from India crossed the snowy mountain passes of the Himalayas and those from Tibet also came to Arya-desha' phags *yul,* the land of Buddha for pilgrimage and education.

In the context of literature, Indo-Tibetan may be of two varieties. The Indian literature in Tibet and in Tibetan, The Tibetan literature in India and in the Indian languages. The Indo-Tibetan literature therefore has contributed greatly in the Buddhist literary heritage of India and that continues up till date. A large number of xylographs (= Xylo) and manuscripts (= Manus) are available in multiple repositories in India. A survey of those literary materials in manuscripts and partially in xylographs may speak about the Indo-Tibetan cultural legacy through centuries.

Literary materials in Xylo and Manus.

In fact, the Indo-Tibetan Literature as they have been preserved may be of four dimensions either in Xylo or in Manus are enumerated below:

(1) Xylographs of Ka-Tan *bka' 'gyur* and *bstan 'gyur* carried from the Trans-Himalayan regions like Peking, Snar thang, Sde dge, Co ne, Li thang, Phug brag, and other (Appendix A). Taishun Mibu prepared a comparative list of *bka' 'gyur* edition of the first three editions along with that of Co ne (*Memoirs of Taisho University* 1959). Some Ka-Tan mss are available in the repositories and in monasteries like Stok in Ladakh, Tabo in Himachal Pradesh, Gilgit in Pok and in the National Museum, Government of India, New Delhi.

(2) Ka-Tan-genous materials with ritual manuals and other in Xylo have been available in Indian repositories like SRIT, Gangtok, Calcutta University, the Asiatic Society, National Library, National Archives CIHTS, Central Institute of Higher Tibetan Studies, Sarnath etc.

(3) Moreover, the MSS of Buddhist thematic compositions contributed by the Indo-Tibetan authors, critic literati and poets are available in the Indian Himalayas and in Tibetan Buddhist monasteries scatteredly.

(4) MSS on gnomic *bstod pa,* liturgy, didactions *man ngag* by eminent Buddhist teachers, also spontaneous out bursts in songs like *guima* by the personal experience through introspection and meditations are available in MSS with the laities and recluses in Indian Himalayas.

Ka-Tan from Manus to Xylo

The Ka-Tan, are available in three different successive stages :

(1) The establishment of the School for Translation *Sgra bsgyur grva* tshang inside the *Bsam yas* monastery of Tibet in the eighth century A.D. had been a unique instance of the Indo-Tibetan academic mission. After the Bsam yas debate, Shantaraksita, a notable Ācārya of Nālandā in Tibet was entrusted to spread the Indic Buddhism instead of that from the then China. The Ācarya was epitheted as Bodhisattva for his dedication in the cause of the Tibetan peoples. *Sad mi mi bdun,* seven novice scholars were commissioned by *Khri srong Ide btsan* to be well-versed in Buddhism. Later on, the Translation Methodology was innovated how to transmit the connotation of each Buddhist term into Tibetan faithfully. It was not a lay-men's task. Because the genesis of the Indian languages is not the same with that of Tibetan. By strenuous efforts of the band of Indian Sanskrit veterans from Kashmir in collaboration with the Tibetan language experts the *Bye brag tu rtogs par byed pa* Mahāvyutpatti and *Sgra sbyor Nighaṇṭu* could be prepared. Those were the guide manuals for maintaining uniformity in the standard of renderings. 11 may be noted that all the translated Buddhist texts in Ka-Tan were not out of the Indic languages carried from India and Nepal. A sizeable number of Ka-Tan texts had been rendered in Tibetan from the Chinese Buddhist source materials and those carried from Central Asia, like *Li yul* Khotan, Kucha, Turfan etc. The methodology in rendering of the Buddhist

literary materials developed from the 8th century A.D. downwards continued upto the 15th century A.D. uninterruptedly in Tibetan. A bilingual glossary was prepared joint collaboration of the Indian pandits and the Tibetan translator *lo tsa ba*. The drafts after rendering were generally placed before the revisors (hsudakpa *Zhu dog pa*). In the case of important texts like the *Yum* i.e. *Aṣṭ asāhasrikā Prañāparamita Sutra* seven instances of revision were followed to ensure the best standard in rendering.

The Kanjur *bka' 'gyur* referring to the *Buddhavacana* and the Tanjur *bstan 'gyur* to *shastra,* the works other than the Buddha's sayings amounted to preservation of various branches of the Indo-Tibetan Literature. Their broad divisions as found in xylographs are in the Appendix-B. While the manuscripts of Ka-Tan available, now in India may not agree in toto. That requires separate discussions. With reference to the mss Kanjur of O rgyan Ling family temple of the Dalai Lama VI (1683-1708) in Mon-Towang, Arunachal Pradesh, Jampa Samtan dealt briefly.

(2) Again, the codification of each draft translation was rigorously followed. The said procedure was taken over the manuscript(s) of each text to be entered in the *dkar chag*, prescribed catalogue for preservation. The items of the bibliographic catalogue were generally manifold. 1. category, 2. title, 3. author, 4. number(s) of chapters if any, 5. number(s) of volumes, if required, 6. numbers of pages, 7. whether the translated work is completed or not, 8. name(s) of the team for revision of the said text, where revised once or more.

After completion of those measures, those Tibetan translated works were preserved either in an important temple or in a royal palace. For example Ka ba Dpal brtsegs rig bdag and Dpal gyi Ihun po were directed to preserve sacred translated *Bka' 'gyur* texts in *Bka*' smad temple of 'phang thang. That catalogue with relevant works was called *Bka' 'gyur rin po che'i dkar chag mgon pa*, the primary catalogue of the jewel-like Buddhavacana rendered in Tibetan during the first phase of translation *sgra bsgyur.*

(3) The wooden block or copper plate prints otherwise 'xylograph' printing of those manuscripts together with the *dkar chag* index of the translated works of the *Bka' 'gyur* appeared in Peking during reign of the Chinese Emperor Yan li in 1549. Thereafter the *Bstan 'gyur* in 42 volumes was published. Gradually xylographs of the Ka Tan by different monastic centers like Snarthang, Sde dge Ba rgya bi thang temple under the patronage of some benovalent chieftains and rulers of Tibet promoted the cause of disseminating Buddhism. Again, the portions of the Kanjurs, partially or completely had been copied in Tibet as one of the meritorious deeds. Its latest recension was printed from Lhasa zhol. About the arrangement of the *dkar chag* classification of the subject matter, variations in numbers prevail. A band of scholars in Europe has already undertaken a long term project for preparing their standardisation. Despite the socio-political unrest in the Trans-Himalayan region upto the Mt. Kailash *tishe*

and Mansarovar *Mapham tsho* during the tenth-century A.D. the rigors in respect to the Ka-Tan were faithfully maintained. Thereafter, a band of U-tsang pa from Central Tibet ran away and entered in the West Sector of Indian Himalayas in the 10th cent. A.D. Fr. Hermann's apposition of Indo-Tibetan for the Himalayan inhabitants of the Tibeto-Mongoloid ethinicity began historically in India. Prior to them, the Totos claim their entry since the 7th cent. A.D.

The Indian literature in Tibetan translations got an open access among the Buddhist Indo-Tibetans named Bhotia, Bhutia, Bhote or Bhoti, Budi other than the Khu nu wa. In the course of time many immigrants from Tibet crossed the Himalayas *gangs ri* on foot and had settled in through generations ancient Indian Himalayas. They profess also Bon, Islam or Christianity, though the Buddhists claim majority. Among the Buddhist Indo-Tibetans the Ka-Tan are regarded as their Holy Scripture. Above that, they have contributed in developing Buddhism in the areas in which they reside. In that respect the Indo-Tibetan Literature holds a wider scope for extending their heritage to sustain.

The categories of the Kanjur Buddhavana has been arranged under twelve heads as enumerated in the Mahāvyupatti. In the Theravada tradition the Buddha's sayings are ninefold. But the Sarvastivadins enlarged the classification. The Sutras are classified in different headlines like *Prajñāpāramitā Sūtra*, Ratnakūṭa Sūtra Avatamsaka Sūtra and so on. The Tantra texts numbering 446 according to the Derge recension are placed in the order of *Anuttarayoga Advaya tantra* like Kalacakra tantra, *Yogatantra*, *Caryā tantra* and *Kriyātantra* including *Dhārani* coilections. Again the last section of Tantra may be distributed according to the Kulas as Buston Rinpoche distributed in *Rgyud sde spyi'i rnam par bzag* (*Gsung 'bum* vol.II). Slob bzang 'phrin las in *Thab yig gsal ba'i me long* followed the same outlook among the Tibetans after Shantaraksita's demise. Nalanda had been demolished but Nalanda shaped a new monastery named Na len dra in vicinity of Lha sa in Central Tibet (U-tsang *dbu-tsang*). The Tibetans could witness the life style and daily routine. Cultural adoptability prompted the creative Nalandan literati and poets to promote Tibetan Buddhism vigorously in a new mode.

Ka-Tan-genous Literature

Apart from the translation literature out of the Indian source materials, a vast Ka-Tan-genous literature had been composed in last millennium. Shantaraksita framed out the master plan very widely to introduce the Nalandan, academic dimensions. As far as the materials available up till now, Nalanda had the syllabi of five major subjects for learning *rig gnas chen mo nga* and several subsidiary subjects like lyrics, drama, rhetories, prosody, lexicon, polity, social mannerism, mathematics with reference to astronomy and astrology, etc. The Ka-Tan preserve authoritative source materials to promulgate the educational curricula, as the Buddhists require (Appendix-B).

In due course the erudite in Indo-Tibetan literature endeavoured to contribute in various fields for the advancement of knowledge. In this connection, Atisha Dipankara's visit in Tibet and his contemporary Rin chen bzang po's massive monastic service in the Western Sector of Himalayas, particularly in Ladakh, Kashmir and Khu-nu (upper Kinnaur of Himachal Pradesh), Lahul and Spiti paved a path for the Ka-Tan-genous Indo-Tibetan Literature since the eleventh century A.D.

The Tripitaka *sde snod gsum,* as preserved in Tibetan enumerate Sutra, Vinaya and Tantra. Because, an Indo-Tibetan Buddhist follows the Mūla-sarvastivada-vinaya. Seven Abhidharma treatises of the Sarvāstivādins are not similar to those of the Theravadins. Also the Sarvāstivādin Abhidharma treatises had developed out of *Sutranta*, aphoristic teachings of the Buddha. That was, later on, commented in the *Mahāvibhāsa*. The eminent exponents like Vasubandhu, logician Diṅnaga, Dharmakiriti had their separate views as regards the Abhidharma concerned. Again the critical exposition of the Prajñapāramitā Sūtra promulgated Abhisamaya literature as those are preserved in the Tanjur *Bstan 'gyur* collection.

Tantra is regarded as the epitome of the Buddha's teachings. In this respect Advayavajra's analysis of Buddhism in multiple dimensions may be late, but significant (Chart). Resultantly, Padmasambhava, a contemporary of Shanṭaraksita visited Tibet and introduced Tantra practices with numerous rituals, Vimalamitra followed him vigorously to generate the Old Tantra *rnying rgyud.* Later on, diverse opinions about *Rnying rgyud* grew among themselves as Bu-ston rin chen grub disclosed. Marpa had not been satisfied with the Old Tantra. He had rushed to Nalanda and the around repeatedly in search of an efficient Tantra teacher. He could meet Siddhas like Naropa, Maitripa and learnt from them *ṛgyud gsar ma* the New Tantra. Meanwhile, Kālacakra tantra was translated in Tibetan by Gyi jo lotsa ba (Agni-shashaka varsa c. A.D. 1027) according to Sum pa mkhan pol (born 1704 A.D.).

Again, 'Khon dkon mchog rgyal po (b. 1035) founded Sa-skya monastery (1073) after being initiated by Birupa of Bengal, who visited Tibet after Atisha Dipankara. In due course the four major Tantric schools flourished and those continued till date among the Indo-Tibetans of Himalayas; Such as, *Rnying ma, Bka' brgyud, Saskya, Bka' gdams.* The last is reformed as *Dge lugs* to which the Dalai Lama belongs.

The patrons and advocates of the above Tantric schools claimed their direct lien to what the Buddha had taught. Several monastic hierarchs and eminent teachers composed Ka-tan-genous works indigenously in order to probe their respective position. Likewise, the disciples of Atisha Dipankara, like Brom ston and others did not sit idle. They interpreted the teachings of their masters respectively without deviating from the Ka-Tan. In this connection the Terton teachers of *Rnying ma* declared that hidden texts had a lien to what Padmasambhava and Vimalamitra had disseminated during the Early spread of Buddhism *snga dar,* pre-Atisha period.

About a couple of centuries or more during the Later Diffusion of Buddhism *phyi dar* after the advent of the Indian Buddhist pivots like Birupa, Atisha, Smritijnanakiriti and others. Some important literary works were contributed in Indo-Tibetan Studies. Such as, *Bka' gdam 'phags chos, Sa(s) Kya bka' 'bum, Gams ngag mdzad* referring to the collected works of Jam dgon 'Khong sprul Zangs dkar 'phag pa shes rab (b.1060), contemporary of Rin chen bzang po, 'Bri Khungs skyab rgon of La dwags (c.14th cent.A.D.) etc.

In this connection two socio-religious factors became significant (1) Downfall of the Buddhist monasteries like Nalanda, Odantapuri, Vikramashila, Valabhi, Somapuri. Jagadtiala, Rangarnrittika, Ratnagiri in Magadha, Bangala and Odivisha and other parts of India. Many learned Buddhist erudites had crossed the snowclad Himalayas and entered in Trans-Himalayan regions for asylum. They carried some of their treasures like the important works of the Indian Acharyas alongwith their own writings. Their presence in Tibet could built up then a new image among the Tibetan Buddhists what the then Indian Buddhists had had. (2) Secondly, the new Buddhist monastic installation in Indian Himalayas as enumerated encouraged a big generation to be involved in a rational understanding in spite of various shortcomings for living in the hill tracts. The Indo-Tibetan literature thereby has got a new dimension. That continues till date uninterruptedly.

Creative agility through competitions

In the development of Indo-Tibetan Literature, schisms in the Buddhist monasteries *dge 'dun* played an important role. On the basis of four eminent teachers namely, Pudmasambhava, Naropa, Birupa and Atisha four major Tibetan Buddhist schools flourished like Rnying ma, Bka' brgyud, Sa skya and Bka' gdams respectenely since the 11th century A.D. in Tibet. Schisms in the Buddhist organizations were not decried. In India, eighteen Buddhist schools developed. In this respect the socio-cultural aspects became always significant for organizational growth. Because, the founder left none to succeed him. That amounted to generate collective responsibility in the *dge-'dun* culture of the Indian Buddhists in particular, and Shramanas in general.

Since the Sa (s) Kya monastery had been favoured by the Yuan emperors of China, particularly Kublai Khan and his successors, a new turn in the socio-culture among the Tibetan intellectuals prompted to be agile enough. A new socio-economic structure was firmly set up to compete each faction with practical means *thabs* upāya. That led their creativity to compose in literatures, to develop arts, and to build architeral models.

Many creative writings among the Buddhist authors came out through their personal experiments and logical reasoning along with their relevance to the scriptural interpretations. Those may be of diverse directions.

(i) Doctrinal works belonging to the aforesaid schools of Buddhism in Tibet to differentiate one another with some historical account of theirs.

(ii) Critical expositions on the major Buddhist thoughts like Madhyamika, Abhidharma Vaibhasika, 'Yogacara Vijnaptimatrata and Tanta manuals with the individual esoteric experiences by the eminent literati.

In fact, a separate dimension of the Indo-Tibetan Literature was innovated towards an unparallel path of the awakening for humankind. That is not limited to respective sectarian doctrines, like the marge-phala *lam 'bras* of the Sa(s) kya pas, the marga krama /*lam rim* of the Dge lungs pas. Again, the *Gsung 'bum* collected work of the eminent teachers like Sa (s) kya Panchen (1192-1251 A.D.) O rgyan Ling pa, 'Brom stong (11th Cent) Bo dong 'phags las rnam rgyal (1375-1451), 'Brug chen Pad ma dkar po (1527-92), Rmor chen Kun dga' than grab (1654-1726), Gang thang Dkon mchag bstan pa'I sgron mc (1762-1823)). Tsong kha pa, (1375-1451) Rgyal ba Nga ba (1617-1682), Dar ma rin chen, Mkhas grub rje dge ligs dpal (15th cent. A.D.) 'jig bral ye shes rdo rje (15th cent.) may be referred here.

Moreover, several Buddhist poets; in spite of their monastic discipline preferred to compose verses to elucidate their understanding of the views they followed. The Tibetan rendering of a rhetoric text *Kāvyādarsha* ascribed to Acarya Daṇḍin nurtured their poetic style to excel. Several commentaries were written by the Tibetan rhetoricians. The mundane nature of metrical composition by the Dalai Lama VI was however not thoroughly Buddhistic in spite of its rhetoric splendour.

In this connection, the contributions of the Mongolian Qutuqto literati deserve a special mention with their indigenousness. Many Mongolian inquisitive learners used to be in Tibet for higher studies in the monasteries of Sa(s)kya, Sera, 'Bras spung. Among them Spyan sha rin po che otherwise named Lean skya Qutuqtu (1390-1448 A.D.) was a forerunner. Their contributions were not always scriptural, nor restricted within to the paradigm of the Buddhist sects to which they belonged. Their writings on Tibetan grammar, rhetorics, arts, crafts medicine deserve mention. Their contributions covered the doctrines, philosophy, logic, esoteric methods. Moreover many indigenous works on Buddhist Tantra rituals, arts, paintings iconometry, metallic iconmaking, etc. had been contributed for their requirement. The early improvised technology developed in the cis-Himalayas along with Nepal and Bhutan. Nālandā is said to have metallurgic' crafts of icon-making with excellent polish. That could make the Mahavihara economically self-sufficient. Also, the *thanka* scroll painting art with its herbal and mineral colours had prevailed there and those were the part of the

Buddhist ritualistic art in which the monastic members and house holders used to be engaged.

Literary expressions of spiritual experience

Some Buddhist esoteric practitioners occasionally experience their spiritual joy. They occasionally burst out in course of psycho-somatic joyous vibrations spontaneously, Buddhist Siddhacaryas left numerous songs with such spiritual outburst in Apabhramsa. Some of them had been rendered into Tibetan, Numerous prayers and benedictory verses have enriched the Indo-Tibetan literature. Among them Milarapa's *gur ma* spiritual songs may also cited for instance. Many excellent spiritual outbursts in metres *glu bshes*, devotional prayers *tro pa* are available in manuscripts. Again, the didactions *man ngag* by the eminent spiritual persons in Tibetan may be taken in account. Those are traced in the *gsung 'bum* Collected Works as dealt above.

Catalogues of Mss & Xylo

The Tibetan materials came to the notice of the Europeans through the Russian soldiers by the end of the 18th century. Several endeavours to focus on the contents of the vast Tibetan literature prompted to prepare many catalogues for the academicians at different levels. I.J. Schmidt's attempt might be the earliest in the 19th century (*Index des Kangur*) and that was followed by analyses in the *Bulletin historico-philologique de L'Academic Imperial des Secenecs de St. Petersburg*, tome iv, nos 6, 7.8.(1846).

In India, Csōma de kötös pioneered in preparing a narrative information of the contents of the *Bkah hgyur* in the Asiatic Society and that was published in the *Asiatic Researches* (1836-39). The Library of the Tibetan Works and Archives have been engaged in preservation of the Tibetan literary culture. Jampa Samtan prepared the catalogue of Phug brag edition of Kanjur. The author had studied the Tibetan collection of the catalogue in the Towang (NEFA) monastery together with Ven. C.R. Lama from Visva Bharati in 1958.

Again, a joint venture in compilation of a Union Catalogue of the Tibetan materials in India has been programmed for last three decades in collaboration with the National Archives New Delhi, National Library, Calcutta, Indira Gandhi Centre for Arts, New Delhi and Central Institute of Higher Tibetan Studies. In its first phase the materials preserved in 'Calcutta and the Around' have already catalogued and is being ready for publication. That catalogue covers not only the Ka-Tan texts of different recessions but also the indigenous works. Nava Nalanda Mahavihara prepared a Sectional Catalogue of the Lhasa edition Kanjur.

After the study of the Kanjur mss preserved in Tabo monastery by Paul Harrison, Christiana Scherrer Schauh under the guidance of Stunkellner, a band of European scholars are engaged vigorously to prepare a standardized critical edition of the Kanjur and the Tanjar for the use of international academicians. Helmut Eimer, Michael Hann, Paul Harrison, Peter Skilling, Jekrey Schoening, Jonathan Silk, Jens Braarvig, Johannes Schneider and others are engaged in the program.

The Kanjur mss collected from Gilgit monastery (now in Pok) by N. P. Chakravarti in the forties of the last century were catalogued by Durga Charan Chatterji under the instruction of the Archaeological Survey of India. Again, that was re-appraised by Lokesh Chandra in 1998.

In China, the Tibetan Tri pitaka had been collated critically after basing upon the Peking recessions of Ka-Tan. A catalogues note on the Kanjur editions with reference to the *Dkar chag* appended to each recession has been done by Helmut Eimer in Bonn of Germany.

It may be relevant to add that a Descriptive catalogue of the Ka-Tan texts is a long felt need for the advanced Indo-Tibetan Studies in spite of the English rendering of the Kanjur in America. A catalogue of the Indo Tibetan works in Indian Buddhist Himalaya is yet to come. In order to understand multiple dimensions of the Indian history and culture the Ka-Tan texts are regarded as the immense resources. Also, that may be more useful to study their spread in the Trans Himalayan regions upto China in East Asia and in Central Asia.

A sizeable number of bilingual (Tibetan-Sanskrit) editions of the Tanjur texts, as compiled out of the Indian Buddhist treatises have been restored or retranslated for the promotion of higher academic pursuits. That was initiated by Mm. Vidhu Sekhar Bhattacharya Shastri in Visva-Bharati by the twenties of the last century. That trend has been followed up by the Central Institute of Higher Tibetan Studies under the guidance of K. N. Mishra vigorously. Again some scholars are engaged in utilizing the relevant Buddhist Sanskrit mss of the Asiatic Society Calcutta (collected by Hodgson, Rajendralal Mitra and Haraprasad Shastri) and the comparative bilingual Tibetan-Sanskrit editions with collations and emendation, where necessary. That venture opens a new vista in studying the manuscripts and their respective Tibetan renderings with different recensions.

Manus-making materials and Calligraphic art

Pt. Rahul Sankrityayana dealt about the materials of Indian Buddhist in mss, followed in the Trans-Himalayan region. In different Himalayan monasteries the base materials are found. The Kagate Bhotias of Darjeeling district, claim that the parched paper-making business is their Community trade and that developed in Nepal and Tibet. China invented the paper-making process out of the paperus grass and that was one of Bagdad-centered Sino-Persian trade commodities in olden times. The writings in golden and silver fluids require their base materials made of leather dust, ragged cotton parched by improvised chemical processing for black surface. Again the ordinary black and red ink writing's need the handmade thick papers with plane surface. The materials of ink are locally prepared out of burnt corns mixed with bitter salt and herbal juice in order to safeguard from worm eating.

The professional scribers of golden and silver colours are employed for designing valuable mss with calligraphic art usually in Ucan *dbs can* scripts, U-can scripts in Tibetan are similar to the late Gupta script, sprouted out of the Later Brahmi (Appendix-A). The *lancha* ornamental scripts *rgyan* yig holds close affinity to the Lanchana lipi. That entered Tibet through Nepal and Garwal. Again the Siddham scripts used for writing the Dharani rnantra belonged to Madhya-desha and that entered into Tibet. Later on, that script spread in East Asia upto Japan, through Central Asia. Besides them, the paintings and drawings on xylo and manus deserve mentions.

The Tibetan u-me *dbu med* scripts are said to have sprouted out of Vartula lipi, round letters *wartu*. Numerous u-me scripts in manuscripts are found mostly in the ducha cereallike design *'bru cha*. Scriptural Mss in u me tsukti *dbu med 'khyag bris* are not uncommon. Those scripts are used for documents. Moreover, *hor yig* scripts are used in Indo-Tibetan scriptural writing.

Buddhistic imports used in the *Ka-Tan*

The principle of bilateralism of culture migration may be observed in the Indo-Tibetan Literature led by the Buddhists. That may be traced clearly in understanding the import an Indian Buddhist scripture through its Tibetan version. Some instances from the Ka-Tan may be sorted out.

(i) The dictions as well as the style of presentation used in the Indian Buddhist mixed languages, Pali, Sanskrit, Prakrit or Apabhramsa do not always prone to the standard grammatical rules. The pre-Paninian usages with the Vedic language dictions are occasionally traced. The Pali texts which are in the Kanjur focus more light to clarify. The Buddhist Prakrit scriptures promoted by the Mahasanghikas have not come down other than their Chinese version. The fragments of Prakrit mss remains and the Dhammapada in Gandhari Prakrit hold difference than the grammatic formulae enunciated by Vararuci and Hemacandra. P.C. bagchi referred to their instances of Culika and Paishaci Prakrits used by the Buddhists in some cases. So those were distinct from Maharastri, Saurasemi Prakrits of Central and Central West India. However, Prakrits had been once the local dialects of many ethnic groups. The Buddhists used them what the Buddha had granted to preserve his speech.

Again, the Sammatiya / Sammitiya Apabhramsa scriptures are partially preserved in the Chinese version. Some specimens of the Buddhist Apabhramsa used by the Siddhacaryas of Magadha, Bangala and Odivisha and those of Nepal are available. P.C. Bagchi and Shanti Bhiksu Sastri worked out their Tibetan renderings. Similar attempt was done by Pt Rahul Sanskrityana as Munidatta's commentary does not always bring out appropriate import. As regards the *Vaipulya Sutras* in the Indian Buddhist Mixed Languages similar problems appear to the academicians to find out significance. In that respect the Tibetan renderings may be better instrumentation than their speculative presumption on the basis of the Prakrit and the Apabhramsa grammars available now.

Hermeneutics of the Indo-Tibetan Scriptures

Especially, the compilation of the Buddhist Sutra and Vinaya scriptures had been processed through stages. What the founder of Buddhism had said was not laid down in writing, as that was not the usual practice in the Indian culture then. Traditionally, after the demise of the founder, the prominent personalities like Ānanda, Upāli and Makakassapa are said to have come forward to reproduce what the founder had said, as far as they could hear and recollect. With such background the hermeneutic peculiatics and semantic variations are occasionally observed. For instance, dhamma/ dharma has been interpreted with multiple connotations in the Buddhist thought. Particularly, dhamma in the sense of phenomena is enumerated by the Theravādin. Abhammikas differently than that was done by the Sarvastivādin Abhidharmikas. Again, the Prajñapāramitā Sūtra, which presumably belonged to the Prajnaptivadin Buddhists enlisted dharma(s) separately. Above that, the significance of some items of the dharma phenomenon had been interpreted separately by the subsequent Buddhist authors like Vasubandhu and Buddhaghosa. The interpretations of Yashomitra and Shantaraksita, margined by about four centuries, did not agree. Again the Mahāyana Abhisamaya treatises with their lien to Prajñāpāramitā Sūtra vary in this regard.

The Buddhist hermeneutic problems are also experimented in course of rendering those texts while translated. In order the overcome those intriques, the authorities of *Sgra bsgyur grva tshang* endeavoured to compile the bilingual Sanskrit-Tibetan lexicon *Bye brag rtogs par byed pa* Mahāvyutpatti after the First Tibetan Buddhist Assembly held during the centuries 8-9 A.D. Some instances of their method of compilation may be referred. Eight synonymous words regarding the 'rays of light' were rendered in Tibetan differently with their varied derivative connotations,

prabha	*'od*
rashmih	*'od zer*
alokah	*snang ba*
marici	*mun sel lam*
archih	*gsal ba / 'od zer ba*
tejas	*gzi brjid*
jvāla/ jvala	*'bar ba*
dyutiḥ	*gsal ba / 'od zer*

It does not mean that Lo tsa bas confined themselves with these specific terms only. They had option to change and alternate, while translating a text according to the context.

Again, subtle differences in connotation of technical terms like manas *yid / thugs,* citta *sems*, vijñapti *rnam par rig pa* and vijñāna *rnam par shes pa* become explicit in Tibetan renderings. The enumeration of twenty prefixing particles upasarga in Sanskrit had been rendered by the Indo-Tibetan translation unit *Sgra bsgyur sde tsang* and those were included in *Bye brag rtog ba* Mahavyutpatti accordingly. In due course several Indian grammatical texts were translated in Tibetan.

Apart from particular care in rendering the Sanskrit dictions with Buddhistic significance and the contextual relevance of the text under translation, the style of original composition as well as its subject matter according to the tradition in particular were always kept in view by the translators. Those may be traced from many texts. For example, Nāgārjuna's *Prajñā-nāma-mula-madhyamaka Kārika* may be specimened here. *Dbu ma rtsa ba'l tshig le'ur byas pa shes rab ches bya ba* was translated by Jñānagarbha and Lo tsa Klui rgyal mtshan (c. 11th cent. A.D.). That was revised twice by Pa tshab Nyi ma grags in collaboration with Hasumati of Kashmir and thereafter with Kanaka (or Bangala) in the 13th cent. A.D. The final shape, as it had been codified and was preserved in the Bstan 'gyur collection, reads thus:

> I prostrate to the perfect Buddha
> The best of all teachers, who taught that
> That which is dependent origination is
> Without cessation; without arising.
> Without annisulation; without permanance;
> Without coming; without gaing;
> Without distinction, without identity
> And peaceful—free from all fabrication.

(*Ocean of Reasoning*: Rje Tsong Khapa'c commentary on Nagarjuna's *Mulamadhyamaka-Karika*. Translated by Geshe Ngawang Samten and Jay L. Garifield, 2006).

gang gis rten cing 'brel bar 'byung/
'gag pa med pa skeye med pa//
chad pa med pa rtag med pa/
'ong ba med pa 'gro med pa//
tha dad don med don cig min/
spros pa nyer ni zhi bstan pa//
rdzogs pa'i sangs rgyas smra rnams kyi/
dam pa de la phyag 'tshal lo//

anirodhaṁ – anutpādaṁ – anucchedaṁ – ashāshtwataṁ/
anekārthaṁ – anānārthaṁ – anāgamaṁ – anirgamaṁ//
yaḥ pratītya samutpādaṁ prapañcopashamaṁ shivaṁ/
deshayāmāsa sambuddhastaṁ vande vadatāṁ varam//

Appendix - A

(i) Repositories of Indo-Tibetan Literature in India (Xylograph and Manuscripts)

I. Kanjur *bka' 'gyur*

i. Peking Xylographs (1737) now available in photographic edition (168 Volumes) are preserved in Visva-Bharati, Santiniketan, the Asiatic Society, Calcutta, Nava Nalanda. SRIT Gangtok Mahavihara. Delhi University, Delhi. Library of Tibetan Works & Archives, Dharamsala, H.P.

ii. Peking edn. (1168 -92) patronized by Kanshi Emperor of China reprinted in PRC.

iii. Mongolian edn. of the Kanjur in mss: ed. Lokesh Chandra Saraswati Vihara, New Delhi.

iv. Urga mss. of the Khu Lun monastery (Mongolia) are now renamed Ulan Bator Dga' ldan bshad sgrub gling mss. preserved in Central Institute of Higher Tibetan Studies (CIHTS) Sarnath.

v. Snar thang Xylo. edn. (100 vols), preserved in the Asiatic Society, Calcutta, Sanskrita Sahitya Parisad Kolkata, Visva-Bharati Santiniketan, Bihar Research Society (BRS) Patna, Missionary College, Srirampur (?) CIHTS (Central

Institute of Higher Tibetan Studies), Sarnath Library of Tibetan Works and Archives (LTWA), Dharmsala.

vi. Mongolian translation of the Ka-Tan printed in India by Raghuveer, Saraswati Vihar, New Delhi.

vii. Sde dge xylo edn. (103 vols), preserved in University of Calcutta, Kolkata, CIHTS, Sarnath, Sikkim Research Institute of Tibetology (SRIT). Gangtok (?) LTWA, Dharmsala, (Reproduced in India New Delhi 1975-80)

viii. Co ne Xyio edn. preserved in Bhutan house, Kalimpong. LTWA. Dharmsala,

ix. Phug brag monastery Kanjur mss edn. (119 volumes), in Library of Tibetan Works and Archives, Dharmsala

x. Stog palace Kanjur mss belonging to Stg palace, Ladakh, J & K

xi. Rta pho Kanjur mss (incomplete), a rare edition

Rta pho (Tabo) monastery temple, Himachal Pradesh

xii. O rgya ling Kanjur mss, in the Family Temple of the Dalai Lama VI (1683-1706) Towang Mon, Arunachal Pradesh

xiii. Li thang 'jang sa tham (Eastern Tibet), Xylo edn (103 vols) preserved in Thup bstan smin gcol gling monastery, Candragiri, Orissa. Microfiche available in Nepal and Japan

xiv. Lha sa zhol xylo edn. (100)

The Asiatic Society, Calcutta, LIWA, Dharmsala, CIHTS, Sarnath, Bihar Research Society (BRS) Patna, Nava Nalanda Mahavihar, Nalanda, Bihar.

xv. Gilgit monastery mss (incomplete) Catalogued by Durga Charan Chatterjee (preserved in National Museum New Delhi, and reveiwed by Lokesh Chandra-1998).

II. Tanjur *bstan 'gyur*

i. Peking edn. Tanjur: Photographic print published from Tokyo, The Asiatic Society, Calcutta Visva Bharati, Santiniketan, Nava Nalanda Mahavihara, Delhi University, Delhi.

ii. Snar thang Xylo edn.

The Asiatic Society, Calcutta, Visva-Bharati, Santiniketan, University of Calcutta. Kolkata.

iii. Sde dge Xylo

ClHTS, Sarnath, SRIT, Gangtok (?), LTWA, Dharmsala.

iv. Co ne. ClHTS, Sarnath, LTWA, Dharmsala.

(ii) Compilation of the Ka-Tan Manuscripts and Xylographs

8th Century A. D.

'phang thang Kanjur *bka' 'gyur* manuscripts (8 volumes) had been preserved in Bka' smad tempie in 'phang thang. Its *Dkar Chag* was edited and collected by Dpal brtsegs and Dpal gyi lhung po during the reign of Khn srong Iden btsan.

9th Century A. D.

Ldan dkar palace Kanjur (30 sections) with *dkar chog* by Dpal brtsegs, Khong yid dbang po srung during Ral pa can's rule.

13th Century A.D.

'phag pa'l gser bris ma bka' 'gyur golden lettered Kanjur prepared by 'Gro mgon 'phag pa blo gros rgyal mtshan (1235-1280 A.D.) is said to have been preserved at Sde dgon near Sgral ma Iha khang in Ldeng Khong of Khams.

(Ref. *Central Asiatic Journal* XII, 1 -2. 1988 Helmut Eimer; A Note of the History of Tibetan Kanjur).

In Indian Himalayas Rin chen bzang po (11th century A.D) devoted to generate a general awareness of Buddhism in the Western Sector and the Middle Section of Himalayas. An incomplete specimen of Lahul mss (?) probably appeared by the centuries 11-12 A.D Again Rta pho mss (incomplete) were compiled before cent. 13 A.D.(?)

14th Century A.D.

i. *Mchims 'Jam pa'i dpal byung* The local Chieftain, took initiative to collect the translated Indic-Tibetan texts by the earlier Tibetan Lo tsa bas from different monasteries and temples under the instruction of Lo tsa ba Bsod names, od zer. That collection became the nucleus of *Snar thang bka' 'gyur* after revision. That was named Mchims phu palace collection.

ii. *Tsal pa* Kanjur mss edited by Bu ston Rin Chen grub (1290-1360 A.D) as that collection was compiled by Tsa pa Kun dga' rdo rja the chieftain of Tsal pa. The *Tsal pa Kanjur* was thereafter preserved in Tchingwa taktse (*'Phying ba stag rtse*) castle which was otherwise named Tchyongya ('Phyong rgyas) at Ra-sa where the early Tibetan had ruled before Srongtsangampo (Srong btsan sgam po d. 650 A.D). It was moved northward to *Lha sa* (abode of the divine beings).

iii. Again Kublai Khan alias Ren Tsong of the Yüan Dynasty of China collected translated the Tibetān materials of the Indic texts from Central Tibet. A separate index volume *dkar chag* was prepared at Peking.

iv. The Nar thang *Snar thang bka'gyur* mss were pepared after 1310, according to H. Eimer. Two separate traditions of that set of the Kanjur (*bka' 'gyur rin po che*) developed in the 14th century, (i) The Tsal pa mss of Eastern (Khams) of Tibet and (ii) The Nar thang mss of Western (Khams) of Tibet.

15th Century A.D,

i. Yang li Xylographs in 141 volumes with copper plate print (1410 A.D.) may claim to be an early xylograph during the Ming emperors of China. Its mss are said to have been brought to Nanjing from Snar thang.

ii. Rab Kun bzang 'phags pa managed to copy the Kanjur in golden colour out of the Snar thang mss in Tibet also. That was named Thems spang ma (confidential) recension 1431 (c. A.D.).

iii. Ne wak Sba' thang (Eastern Kham) mss of this period prepared after thorough revision of the Snar thang mss (?) require further information.

16th Century A.D.

i. Another venture of printing the xylographed editions of the Kanjur and the Tanjur was done by the Ming emperor Wang li at Kang.

ii. *Stog pho brang* (Stok palace in Ladakh) Kanjur was a recension of *Thems spang* ma in collation of its Bhutanese '*Brug pa bka' 'gyur* edition (c. 14th cent. A.D.).

17th Century A.D.

i. *Li thang* mss collated from *Tsal pa* Kanjur mss in 107 volumes were prepared between 1608-1614 A.D. as sponsored by Kar ma bka' brgyud teachers of the eastern Tibet.

ii. *Phug brag* rnss in 119 volumes were compiled by an anonymous disciple of Gter bdag gling pa (1646-1714 A.D.).

18th Century A.D.

i. *Sde dge* xylograph wood blocks *par shing* in 102 volumes were prepared after collation of the first Narthang recension and the *Li thang 'Jang sa tham* recension as that was initiated by Btson pa tshe ring.

Sde dge bstan 'gyur xylograph recension was printed also after basing on the Bstan 'gyur mss revised by the Dalai lama V Ngag dbang blo bzang ngya mtsho at Mdo stod Lho dzong.

ii. Co ne Xylograph printed from Amdo between 1721-31 out of the collated edition by Co ne rje btsun Grags pa zhabs grub.

iii. In China Quin long (Ching long) Kanjur xylograph edition was printed as a revised recension of Li thang recension earlier.

iv. Pho ilha nas Bsod names stobs rgyas arranged to revise *Bstan 'gyur* and copied in gold. That is named *Bstan 'gyur gser bris ma.*

v. The Mongolian version of the Tibetan Kanjur was under preparation for about three hundred years and that was printed in Xylograph *pothi* format by A.D. 1717-20.

19th Century A.D.

i. *Ba rgya Bka' 'gyur* printed on the basis of Sde dge edition was kept in the Ba-rgya monastery of Ching hai in China with *dkar chag* catalogued by Panchen Lama VII Bstan pa'l nyi ma.

ii. Uighur version of the Kanjur came forth from the Quin long Chin long Kanjur in Uighur scripts.

20th Century A.D.

i. Lhasa zhol Xylograph of Kanjur block printed claimed to be revised edition of the Sde dge Kanjur. The said collection is reprinted from Shes rig par khang, Dharmsala.

ii. Khu Lun monastery (Dga' Idan bshad grub gling) of Ulltan Bator reprinted the Kanjur in 108 volumes out of !he materials preserved in the Urga monastery of Mongolia. The Kanjur in Mongolian drafted in the 14ll* cent. A.D. Lcan Skya Rol pa'l rdo rje revised again with the help of several scholars between 1741-49. He also translated 228 volumes of the Tanjur in collaboration with Dga Idan siregetu qutuqta Blo bzan bstan pa'l ni ma. (1689-1746) during the reign Manchu king Kao tsung (K'ien lung).

(iii) Indo-Tibetan mss and Xylo repositories in India

Arunachal Pradesh : Ancient Indo-Tibetan repositories

Towang Gonpa, Towang Town; Ogyam ling Gonpa. Towang District Ro par (Rupa) lhakhang Rupa (near, Bomdila); Sengezong Lhakhang, (after crossing the Shela peak); Pema Choling monastery; Tantric rgyud stod Gyuto monastery, Bomdila.

Bihar

Karma Shedup Dhargye ling monastery Bodhgaya; Gaden Phyegye ling monastery Bodhgaya; Thuptan Shedup Dhargya ling. monastery Bodhgaya.

Delhi

Tsangchub Lkakhang Temple, Delhi; Kargyu monastery, Majnu Ka Tilla; Dro ngak pa Dratsang monastery Majnu Ka Tilla; Delhi.

Karnatak (Resource Centres Since 1960's)

Nying ma pa monastery, Mundgod; Urgyan ling Gonpa monastery Hunsur; Dzongchen Rudham Samtan monastery Kolleged; Orgyan Samtan Choling monastery Kolleged; Palyul Namdrol ling monastery Bylakuppe; Karnataka Nying ma monastery; Thupten Shedup Jangchub ling monastery. Bylakuppe; Thupten Samphel Ling monastery Mundgod; Rigon Samdup Chockthor, Kallegal; Palsa Ngar tsar sum monastery Mundgod; Phureng Shedphel ling monastery Bylakuppe; Gaden/Ganden monastery, Mundgod; Sera monastery (with Sera je and seramē) Bylakuppe; Drepung monastery Mundgod; Tashilhunpo monastery, Mundgod; Gurmey rgyad smad Tantric college monastery Hunsur.

Himachal Pradesh

Dgung rang Gonpa (Bhaga river valley), Lahul; Zholing (Jholing Bhaga river valley) Gonpa, Lahul; Rang rigrtse Gonpa Spiti; Dkyil / Skyid Key Monastery Kaza, Spiti; Lha lung Gonpa; Brag mkhar / Brang mkhar (Drankar) Gonpa; (S)na sgo (Nako) Lha Khang, Upper Kinuar; Bka' rnam (Kanam) Gonpa, Kinnaur; Srib hren (Ribba) Gonpa, Kinnaur; Ro Pag (Ro-pa) Gonpa, Kinnaur; Spu (pooh) Gonpa; Spin Nyingnaa Gonpa (Pin valley); Ti yak (north of the Sutlej) Gonpa; Mi yang (Mayon) Gonpa; Dril chung Gonpa; Ril sgang Gonpa; Pangi Lo tsa lha Khang; Tang gi Nran Monastery; Mone lha Khang (Baspa Valley India China border).

Resource centres since 1960s

Palyul Chokhor monastery Bir, Drukpa choling (Bhutanese) monastery Bir; Evam Cholgan Gurme Ling monastery Bir; Thuptan Dorje Drak monastery, Shimla; Dorje drag monastery, Shimla; Nechung Drayanling monastery, Dharmsala; Namgyal monastery Dharmsala; Gadong monastery, Dharmsala; Himalayan nying ma chos gling Manali; Kham Kathok monastery, Sataun; Dzonsar Institute, Bir; Tso Padma Nying ma pa Gonpa Rewalsar Mandi;

Sherab ling monastery, Upper Bhattu, Kangra; Chime Drupe Gatshel monastery Kullu; Zilnon Dhargye lhakhang (retreat temple) Meleod Ganj, Dharamsala; Zigar Drukpa Institute Rewalsar, Mandi; Sherab ling monastery, Bir; Phuntsok Chokhorling Center, Bir; Samdup Dechen chockhor rnon, Bir; Drongsar rime Institute Bir; Tsechen ling monastery, Kumrao; Ngor Awang Institute Bir; Saskya Chokor Lab da (monastic school) Bir; Namgyal monastery, Dharmsala; Sangye Choling, monastery Shimla; Phuntsok ling nyen sampa monastery Dalhousie.

Orissa

Dadul Raptan ling, monastery Gajapati District; Urgan Thekchok Chokhor ling monastery Gajapati; Dechen Chokhorling Gajapati.

Ladakh: Ancient repositories of the erudites

Phe yang Gompa; Dkar lha (Zangskar) Gompa; Gsum da (Sumda) Gompa; Dpe thub (near Leh) Gompa; Gyung drung (lamayuru) Gompa; Sa spo la (saspal) Gompa; Wang la Gompa; Ba sga / Ba mgo (Basgo) Gompa; Krigtse (Thikse) Gompa; Ling snyed (lingsha) Gompa; Stog pho brang (Stok) Gampa; Hemis Gonpa; Likir Gonpa; Leh monastery; Nubra Gompa; Matho Gompa.

Maharashtra

Drukgyu Chopheling monastery Bandara; Thekchen ling monastery, Bandara.

Sikkim: Ancient repositories under royal patronage

Guru Kubum monastery Gangtok; Rumtek monastery, Rumtek. Ganglok; Dharma Cakra monastery Centre Gangtok; Tirkey Jang Gompa monastery Gangtok; Gaden Chokhorling monastery Gangtok.

Uttaranchal

Mindolong monastery Clement Town Dehradoon; Srontsen Library Dehradun; Jangchub ling Drikhung Institute, Dehradun; Sakya Lab da thowo, Dehradun (branch at Mundgad Karnataka Phureng shedphei ling); Lhabrang Tashikyi Gomang monastery college, Dehradun; Gomang Omang Tashikyil monastery Clement Town, Dehradun.

Uttar Pradesh

Haldibardi Buddhist temple tha khangla branch of Pithoragara Gompa.

West Bengal

Palyul Namdrol gling monastery Darjeeling; Phuntsok Pema Chokhor ling monastery Darjeeling; Gepheling monastery Kalimpong; Sang ngag choling, monastery Darjeeling; Samdup Dhargye ling monastery Darjeeling; Goom Guru Gonpa, Darjeeling; Samtan Chaeling monastery Darjeeling; (Arndo) Ganden Tashi Choling monastery Darjeeling; Kurseong Tashi Choling monastery, Kurseong; Sed gyu Datsang monastery Kalimpong; Gaden Tharpa Choling monastery, Kalimpong.

Appendix-B

Contents of the Kanjur & the Tanjur
(According to the Derge recension of Tibet)

The Kanjur:

1. *'dul ba* Code of discipline *Vinaya*. 2. *Sher phyin molo* different *Prajnaparamita sutra(s)*. 3. *dkon mchog* multiple sutras of excellence *Ratnakuta sutra(s)*. 4. *Phal chen mdo* Avatamshaka sutras depicting the merits of the Buddha(s). 5. *mdo sde* various groups of the *sutra* aphoristic sayings. 6. *rgyud sde* manifold Tantra groups like *Kalacakra tantra, Yoga tantra, carya tantra, kriya tantra*. 7. *gzhungs* cryptic methods of the mantra applications Dharani.

The Tanjur:

1. *bstod tshogs* liturgy collections of prayers *stotra-samgraha* 2. *rgyud 'grel* commentaries of the Tantra stated above and indigenous treatises on Tantra 3. *indo 'grel* commentaries of the sutra as treatises of the Indian Buddhist sutra experts. 4. *'dul ba'i 'qrel* commentaries of books on discipline 5. *dbu ma* treatises on the *Madhyamika* doctrine 6. *mngonpa* treatises on *Abhidharma* doctrine dealing the Buddhist phenomenology 7. *tsha ma* treatises on epistemology by the Indian Buddhist authors. 8. *sems tsam* treatises on the Buddhist concept of ideation in psychology *Vijnaptimatrata* 9. skyes rabs the birth stories of the Buddha 10. *lugs kyi bstan bcos* treatises on moral maxims and polity *nītishastra* 11. *sprin yig* classic letters and didactions *lekha mala* 12. *sgra rig* treatises on the science of language 13. *sman rig* treatises on medicine and health management. 14. *bzo rig* treatises on arts and crafts. 15. *thun mongs kyi bstan bcos*. miscelleneous treatises *samanya shastrani*.

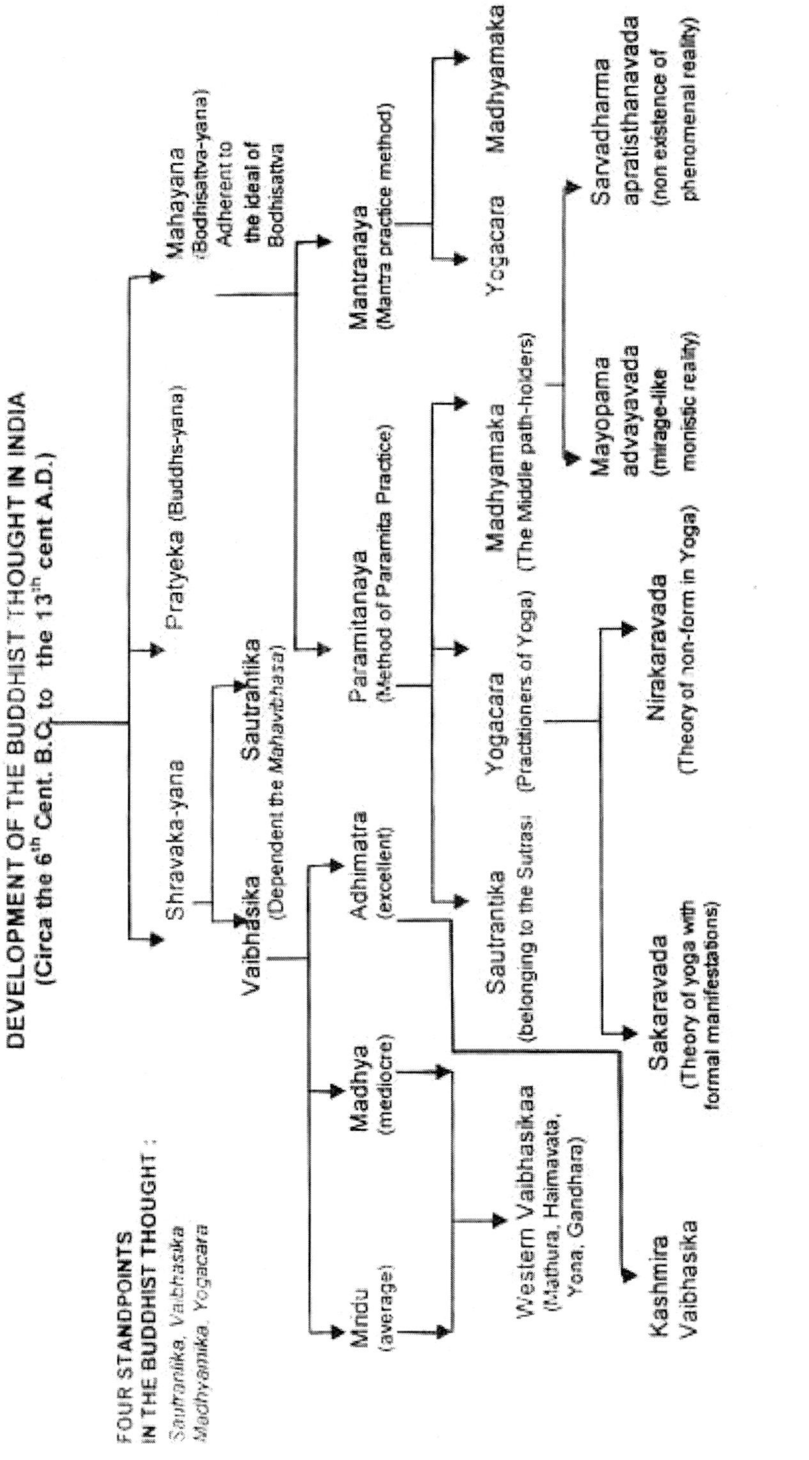

(Divisions as mentioned in the Tatva-ratnavali ascribed to Avadhuta-Advayavajra-pada Circa, late 9th Cent. – 10th Cent. A.D. of Magadha)

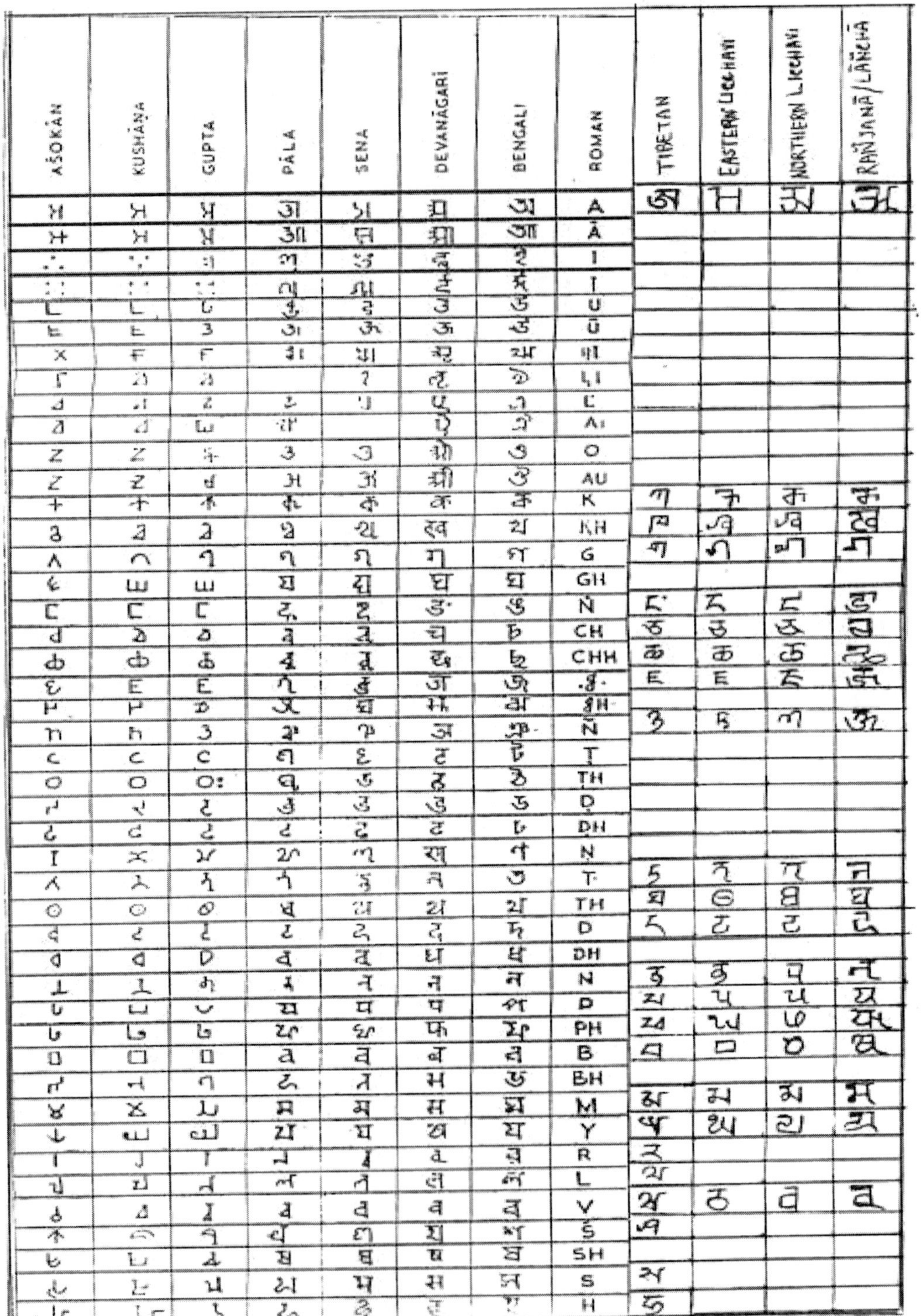
AŚOKAN
KUSHĀṆA
GUPTA
PĀLA
SENA
DEVANĀGARĪ
BENGALI
ROMAN
TIBETAN
EASTERN LICCHAVI
NORTHERN LICCHAVI
RAÑJANĀ/LĀÑCHĀ
A
Ā
I
Ī
U
Ū
ṚI
Ḷ I
E
AI
O
AU
K
KH
G
GH
Ṅ
CH
CHH
J
ÑH
Ñ
Ṭ
ṬH
Ḍ
ḌH
Ṇ
T
TH
D
DH
N
P
PH
B
BH
M
Y
R
L
V
Ś
SH
S
H

References

Abu Bakar Amunuddin (1989) : *Tibet and Tibetan Muslims* (Tibati Wadu).

A.K. Jha (ed) : *Catalogue of the Tibetan works collected by Rahul Sankritayana*, Bihar Research Society, Patna.

Csoma de Koros (1836) : Analysis of the Dulva, a Portion of the Tibetan Work entitled the Kah-Gyur : *Asiatic Researches*. XX 1, No. 2, pp. 41-93.

(1838) : Analyses of the Sher-Chin-P'hal-Ch'hen-Dkors-Seks-Do-De-Nyang-Das and Gyut. Being the second division of the Tibetan Work entitled the Kah-Gyur in : Asiatic Researches. XXII, No. 12, pp. 553-585.

(1839) : Abstract Contents of the Bostan, 'gyur, *As. Res*. XX, Pt. II pp. 553-585.

(1856) : A Brief Notice of the Subhasita Ratna-nidhi of Saskya pandita, with extracts and translations. *Journal of Asiatic Society of Bengal* XXIV; pp. 141-165; XXV (1856) pp. 257-294; (posthumus).

David Jackson (1987) : The Miscellaneous series of Tibetan texts in the Bihar Research Society, Patna, A hand list of Tibetan and Indo-Tibetan Studies, 2 Franz Steiner Veriag Wiesbadan (Stutigart).

E. Denison Ross (1912) : Tibetan Studies ; A collection of the contributions in the Journal of Asiatic Society of Bengal, The Asiatic Society of Bengal, Calcutta.

Egon von Etekstedt (1926) : *Man in India* Vol VI, 7. V.

Gene Smith (1969) : *Tibetan Catalogue* Pt.-I, University of Weshington (Sea Hie).

Geza Bethlenfalvy 1980 : *A Catalogue of the Urga Kanjur*, New Delhi.

Guiseppe Tucci (1949) : *Tibetan Painted Scrolls*, 3 Vols., Institute Italiana per it Medio ed Estreme Oriente, (IsMEO), Rome.

(1980) : *The Religions of Tibet* (tr. From German and Italiana by Geoffery Samuel), Routledge & Kegan Paul, London.

Helmut Eimer (1972-78) : *Handlists der Tibetsofen texts de Sven-Hedin Stiftang and des Ethnigraphischen Museums Zur Stockholm* (Zentralasiastisch Sfudien 6-12).

T. D. Lesing & A. Wayman (1978) : *Introduction to the Buddhist Tantric System* (Molilal Banarasidass New Delhi).

Hugh Richardson (1949) : Three ancient inscriptions from Tibet *Journal of the Royal Asiatic Society of Bengal*, Letters, Vol. XV, No. 1. pp. 45-64).

(1952) : *Ancient Historical Edicts at Lhasa*, London (1952-53); Tibetan inscription at Zva' Ida khan (Journal of the Royal Asiatic Society London 1952, pp 133-54; 1953 pp 1-12) London.

(1957) : A Tibetan Inscription from Rgyal Lha-khan and a note on chronology from A.D. 841 – A.D. 1042 *Journal of the Royal Asiatic Society* London pp. 57-78).

(1964) : A new inscription of Khri srong Ide Btsan *Journal of the Royal Asiatic Society*, London.

(1993) : *Richardson Papers* (Sikkim Research Institute of Tibetology, Gangtok, Sikkim).

Laufer, Berthhold (1916) : Loan words in Tibetan *Toung Pao* pp. 403-552.

Lokesh Chandra (1963) : *Materials for History of Tibelan Literature*, 3 Vol. Saraswati Vihar, New Delhi.

(1964) Tibetan Buddhist texts printed by Mdsod dge sgar gsar monastery *Indo-Indian Journal*.

Nebesky-Wojknowite (1956) : *Orades and Demons in Tibet*, the Hagne.

Peter PF and T (1968) : Mahayana texts Translated into Western Languages (*Kommission* bei E. J. Brill Koln).

Pathak, Suniti Kumar (1990) : Classification of Buddhist Literature in Tibetan *Principles of Editing and Instrumentation*, Central Institute of Higher Tibetan Studies. Sarnath, Varanasi.

(1995) : The Perspectives of the Mongolian (Hukuqtu) Teachers. *Buddhist Literature* : Its Perspective 'Proce of Indouhan Nipponji', Bodgaya.

Radhakrishna Sarvapalli (1957) : *Contemporary Indian Literature* (Foreword), Sahitya Akademi, New Delhi.

Singh, Bireshwar Prasad (1991) : *The Chronology of Tibet according to the Re'u mng of Surnpa mkhan* po (Bihar Research Society, Patna).

Stien, R.A. (1956): *L'Epoise tibetaine de Gesar dans sa version lamaique* de ling Paris.

Verma, Siddheswar (1920): *The Puruski Language*, Hoshiarpur.

Manuscript Catalogue and Cataloguing

2

ALAKANANDA BANERJEE

The term 'Manuscriptology' is derived from two Latin words and one Greek word. Latin words-'Manus' and 'Screbere' or 'Screpte'. 'Manus' means hand and 'Screbere' or 'Screpte' means scrateh. The Greek word is 'Logos'. 'Logos' means science. So 'Manuscriptology' means a science relating to the study of documents or text written by hand. For writing documents or texts birch barks and palm leaf were used in Ancient India. The first example of a palm leaf Sanskrit Manuscript belongs to sixth century A.D. According to Hiuensen Tusang, the Chinese pilgrim, the use of palm leaf was common all over India in seventh century A.D. At the time of Mohmmedan kings paper was introduced for writing Manuscripts. The oldest known example of a paper Sanskrit Manuscript in India is one from Gujrat which belongs to the early part of the thirteenth century. Perhaps at that time ink was employed for writing Manuscripts. After the introduction of paper palm leaf went out of use. Sanskrit Manuscripts are usually kept between the strips of wood with cords round them. Those are wrapped in coloured sometimes embroidered clothes. They have been still preserved in the Libraries of Temples, Monasteries, Courts of Princes, Educational Institutions as well as private houses.

According to recent survey conducted by Prof. Biswas and M.K Prajapati, it is estimated that there are about 5 million Manuscripts of Indian origin preserved in public and private collections in India. In addition about 60,000 Manuscripts are preserved in Europe and North America. The catalogue should be prepared keeping in mind various types of users like text finder, palaeographer, artist, historian, etc. There are seven type of Manuscript found:

1. Manuscript search reports.
2. Simple list (contains author and title or sometimes only title lists).

3.Alphabetical Catalogues: author or title.

4. General informative tabular catalogues.

5. Descriptive Catalogues in tabular form.

6. Descriptive Catalogues in descriptive form.

7. General Register on basis of the Manuscripts.

For cataloguing purpose Manuscript materials include works in handwriting, inscriptions on clay tables, stones, etc. and works in type script.The cataloguer faces many problems. In most cases the Scribes are anonymous and title pages, indices, table of contents are absent. In cataloguing Manuscripts the cataloguer should investigate the correct or conventional title, the beginning of the text, and the ending of the text.The date, character, material, collection, etc. should be examined and recorded.The technical description of a Manuscript should include the following: the title, language of the text, date or approximate date, actual number of leaves, number of columns and average number of lines to the page. New findings include informations on the country or place and style of writing, on the scribes and annotators, binding, boards, opening words, closing words, subject, name of the donor, substance, etc.

The most suitable method for editing Manuscript is by applying the principles of textual criticism. To make a proper critical edition more number of manuscript of a work is required.The most desirable number is to have at least five manuscripts. If there is one manuscript only on the subject then it is difficult for the editor to clear the doubts found in the manuscripts. Scribal errors and interpolations may not be identified.The editor faces additional problems while editing Sanskrit manuscripts written in other scripts. Special care should be taken by the editor.

Manuscript Centres

Visva-Bharati

Visva Bharati preserves a huge collection of Sanskrit, Prakrit Manuscripts. The Manuscript section has a great heritage. From the very conception of Visva Bharati it had been the nucleus of Research. Visva Bharati concentrated mainly in researches in oriental subjects, particularly Sanskritic studies under Vidya Bhavana. Original researches were undertaken by Indologists like Sylvan Levain (1921), Lesny (1908), Stenkonow (1923), M. Winternitz (1922), G. Tuchhi (1924), Prabodh Chandra Bagchi (1921), Kshitimohan Sen Shastri (1908), Vidhushekhar Shastri (1905), R. Anantakrishna Shastri, Nityananda Binode Goswami, Dharmadhar Rajguru, Haridas Mitra, Manimoy Babu, Bhim Rao Shastri, N. Aiyarswamy Shastrigal (1924), Kapileswar Mishra (1939), Amarendranath Tarkatirtha, Sukhamoy Saptatirtha (1937), Siddheswara Bhattacharya and others on the basis of Manuscripts deposited in the

Vidya Bhavana. It may be noted that in 1923 Gurudeva realised the importance of Manuscript Library. He wrote a letter to the Editor, Behar Herald, Patna in quest of rare Manuscripts. R. Ananta Krishna Shastri of Baroda Library rendered his sincere service to Visva Bharati for collection of Manuscripts.

The Sanskrit Manuscript section is one of the oldest Manuscript Research Institute in India and a sister Institution of Bhandarkar Oriental Research Institute, Poona, Adyar Library, Madras, Varendra Research Institute, Rajasahi etc. and is likely the next to Asiatic Society of Bengal in credit in the eastern zone of India. In 1957, Visva Bharati transferred a good lot of Sanskrit Manuscripts nearly about 2500 to the Adyar Library, Madras. Those Manuscripts were written in South Indian scripts. But only 1225 manuscripts were perhaps received by the Library. In exchange of our Manuscripts the Adyar Library transferred 270 Manuscripts approximately to Visva Bharati.

From 1923 the work of collection of Manuscripts started. R. Anantakrishna Shastri of Trivandrum helped much in collecting Manuscripts. A good number of Sanskrit and Bengali Manuscripts were collected by him from different villages of Birbhum and Burdwan. From South India approximately 2500 Manuscripts were collected at that time. Photocopics of some Manuscripts were brought from the Royal Manuscript Library of Nepal. N. Aiyarswami Shastrigal made catalogue of 3137 Manuscripts in 1924 Samvat 1981 Saka 1846. Haridas Mitra performed a notable work in the Manuscript section. In 1946 Prof. Prabodh Chandra Bagchi submitted a new plan for collection and preservation of valuable Manuscripts to the then Registrar Sj. Rathindranath Tagore. This new plan contained three parts; (1) collection of Manuscripts, (2) preparation of Descriptive Catalogues and (3) editing the old rare Manuscripts. Shri Panchanan Mandal collected a good number of Manuscripts including ten Sanskrit Manuscripts from South Burdwan and North East Bankura during the period 23rd November to 2nd December in 1946. Some Manuscripts including two Sanskrit Manuscripts were collected by him from West Burdwan to North West Bankura during the period from 28 Jan, 1947—3 Feb. 1947. Again Shri Mandal collected some Manuscripts including three Sanskrit Manuscripts from Keshia, a village of Bankura District during the period from Summer vacation to 03 July, 1947. Prof. Shibnarayan Ghoshal collected 48 Manuscripts from different villages of Burdwan and of Birbhum within 1980-81. Dr. Alakananda Banerjee and Dr. Arun Kumar Mondal collected 395 Sanskrit Manuscripts from Dakshinkhanda, Shrikhanda of Burdwan, Moutor of Purulia, Bipratikuri, Bolpur, Suri, Bihira, Bangachatra, Domra, Dwaraka, Ghurisha, Milonpur of Birbhum and Calcutta during the period from 1983 to 1999.

The notices of the twenty point Descriptive Catalogue of Visva Bharati Sanskrit Manuscripts approach to fulfil general requirements of Research students. It seems both the purposes — the Library purpose as well as the research purpose. The fourteen point tabular catalogue of Manuscripts as chalked out in the report of UGC Manuscripts committee, serve more the Library purpose than the research purpose of a scholar. For the benefit of research scholars we have added exhaustive reference to each Manuscript along with the immediate new findings of the Manuscript concerned. The twenty points of Descriptive Catalogues are —name of the Manuscript, subject, author, commentaries and commentators, script, substance, accession number – old and new, condition, complete or incomplete, number of folio missing, extent–number of leaves, number of lines, number of letters, size, date, description, beginning line, ending line, colophon, post–colophon (if any), reference. Fourteen points of tabular catalogues are– accession number, descriptive catalogue number, title, subject, author, collection, language, date, size, script, lines, scribe, folio, letters. Sanskrit Manuscripts have been catalogued into 19 subjects with 67 sections. As for example–subject Veda with four sections–Samhita, Brahmana, Aranyaka and Upanisad.

Number of Manuscripts —6000 approximately. There are old collections. This was reported by Prof. Shibnarayan Ghoshal who was in charge of the Manuscript section upto February, 1983. Local collection–443. Total number of Manuscripts upto 1999 is (6000 + 443) 6443. Accession number of 3478 Manuscripts has been made upto March, 2005. Accession number of (6443—3478) 2965 Manuscripts is yet to be done. The following table shows the number of Manuscripts which have been catalogued upto this date.

Name of the book: A Descriptive Catalogue of Sanskrit Manuscripts —Visva Bharati.

Part	Subject	Number of Manuscripts catalogued	Year
I	Vyakarana	242	1975
II	Sahitya	167	1983
III	Sahitya	192	1988
IV	Epic and Purana	186	1993
V	Kosa and Sahitya	92	1993
VI	Paddhati and Prayoga	194	2005
	Total number	1073	

Number of Manuscripts which have not yet catalogued is (6443—1073) 5370.

The part I was published by Prof. Shibnarayan Ghoshal from Visva Bharati. The part II was published by Prof. Shibnarayan Ghoshal and Dr. Alakananda Banerjee jointly from Tara Printing Works, Kamachha, Varanasi. The III, IV, V, VI parts of the book mentioned above were published by Dr. Alakananda Banerjee and Dr. Arun Kumar Mondal jointly from Srilaksmi Press, Bolpur, Birbhum.

Substance of the Manuscripts — palm leaf, paper, birch, tulat etc.

Script — Devanagari, Newari, Bengali, Sarada etc. One Microfilmed Manuscript belongs to the section.The Department has a plan to publish Descriptive Catalogues volumes VII and VIII containing Manuscripts on Smriti and Alamkara soon.

Two very rare documentary Manuscripts of good extents on Indian Aesthetics have been edited by Prof. Shibnarayan Ghoshal and published by Visva-Bharati and the Chowkhamba Sanskrit Series, Varanasi—2. The Rasachandrika of Madhusudana Kavindra (1695 A.D.) with Sanskrit Commentary entitled Chakora by the Editor himself has also been published by Prof. Ghoshal. The book has two volumes. The first volume contains the text of Rasachandrika and the second volume is studies in Divine Aesthetics in two parts. The Kavyaprakasha with the commentary entitled Rasaprakasha by Shrikrishna Sharman (1650 A.D.) in two parts has been published by Prof. Ghoshal. The Vritti-Vallabha of Laghu Vyasa edited by Prof. Gourisvara Bhattacharya was published in Visva-Bharati Annals, 1955. The Pingalamata and Pichumata, parts of the Brahmayamala and the Jayadrathayamala were edited by Prof. Ghoshal. Shrikalachakra-tantra critically edited by Prof. Biswanath Banerjee was published by the Asiatic Society, Calcutta. Researches on the Manuscript of the drama entitled Jagannathaballava and of the Yamala Texts, of the Nagarajashataka have been done. Research works on the Manuscripts of the Pratinatakam and of the Gitagovindam are in progress.

To keep up with the tradition in Sanskritic studies set up by the eminent scholars as mentioned at the beginning of the paper, the Department of Sanskrit, Pali and Prakrit would like to conduct its research activities mainly with the help of Manuscript materials available in Manuscript section of the Department. There is a great possibility in the Department to organize pioneering researches on the basis of Manuscripts in Sanskritic studies dealing with such subjects as Philosophy, Chemistry, Physics, Architecture, Music, Grammar, Veda, Vyakarana, Sahitya, Alamkara, Prakrit, Politics, Zoology, Ayurveda, Tantra, Mathmatics, Geography, History, etc., Valuable unpublished texts are available in the section but these treasures will soon be lost to us if immediate attention is not paid to them. Unclassified and unidentified Manuscripts are heaped up in a corner and those classified are kept in the most unscientific manner at the total mercy of insects and climate. Publication of Texts and studies in Manuscripts have been suffering continuously because the existing opportunities for publication of research works are not sufficient.

Some teachers of the department have long been engaged in critical editions and Textual studies of highly important unpublished and little known Manuscripts. Inspite of the serious constraints on the working condition as indicated above it has been possible for the Department to publish six volumes of Descriptive Catalogues of our Manuscripts during last thirty years. The process for the next volumes is in progress. Volumes prepared by the teachers with materials available in the University are waiting for publication.

In order to bring to light such valuable but unknown materials promptly it is proposed to start publication series under some appropriate title like "Rare Sanskrit Texts/Study Series".

Manuscript Case Studies

Pratinatakam: A rare unpublished drama

The Manuscript of the drama entitled Pratinatakam is preserved in the Manuscript section of the Department of Sanskrit, Pali and Prakrit in Visva-Bharati. It is an old rare unpublished drama. It contains 40 pages. The story of the drama is based on the Ramayana. There are seven acts and 532 verses in this drama. From its colophon we know that it was written by Pandit Jagatdurlava Bhattacharya. He was the son of Pandit Ramakanta Vidyalamkara Bhattacharya of village Nanoor near Santiniketan in the District of Birbhum in West Bengal. The composition of the Manuscript was complete on the 21st day of Falgoon of 1239 B.S.(Saka 1754 i.e. 1832 A.D.). The author also wrote a commentary on this drama. The Manuscript of this commentary is also preserved in the same section of the department. It consists 53 pages. In the colophon of the commentary we see that the composition of the commentary was complete on the 23rd day of the month Chaitra of 1239 B.S.(Saka 1754 i.e. 1832 A.D.).

From the concluding verse of each act of the drama it is known that the present Mahanataka is not a complete work. Mahanataka traditionally known as the work of Hanumat, the follower of Ramachandra, was long lost. It is told that Valmiki was afraid of hearing of the composition of Mahanataka. He thought that the charm of this poem would completely overshadow his Ramayana. Since divine ape was generous and without egoism he laughed at Valmiki and threw into the ocean the stone — slabs on which he had written this drama. After a long time, certain parts of the poem were recovered and brought to king Bhoja. The king entrusted to Damodar Mishra the task of bringing together those parts of the poem to fill the lacunae and to make from them one unified work. The West Indian recension attributed to Damodar Mishra is styled as Hanuman-natakam. It has fourteen acts and 581 verses. The East Indian recension arranged by Madhusudana is styled as Mahanatakam. This work has ten acts and 720 verses. At the end of this recension it is found that this sublime Mahanatakam was composed by well-known Hanumat and was recovered by Vikramaditya. According to commentators, once Hanumat wrote these verses on rocks and sunk them into sea-water. Vikramaditya, however, got them taken out with the help of fishermen. According to Winternitz, there are 730 verses and 9 acts. Of these two recensions, mentioned above, Hanuman-natakam seems to be the earlier as analysed by Kilson.

However, the Mahanataka, arranged by Madhusudana was not still a complete work. We have already mentioned that Vikramaditya got some stone slabs on which Hanumat, the son of Vayu, wrote the drama. As the task of bringing together the stray parts of the drama was not complete, so our author Pandit Jagatdurlava Bhattacharya tried to fill the lacunae and to make them a complete unified work. He composed 532 verses in seven acts and the drama was styled as Pratinatakam.

Pandit Jagatdurlava Bhattacharya, the author of the drama, lived at Nanoor near Santiniketan. Nanoor is a famous place where Chandidasa a famous Vaishnaba poet was born. His love towards a washermaid Rami and devotion to the goddess Vishalaksmi, another form of Mahasaraswati have been described in details in Bengali literature. Perhaps our author was also a priest of the temple of the Vishalaksmi in his life time. She is the main deity of the whole village. Like Chandidasa Sri Bhattacharya was a devotee to Lord Visnu. In the beginning of the drama the author showed respect to the desired deity. He wrote Pratinatakam and its commentary, also a commentary on Padankadutam and on Harischandra-charitam and some stotras.

This drama Pratinatakam has not yet been published. To bring prominence the importance of the work it is urgently necessary to publish the drama.

Arabic Manuscripts of Kerala

3

A.I. RAHMATHULLAH

Kerala, as is well-known, falls on a long maritime route stretching from the north-westernmost regions of the orient to the eastern and south-easternmost ports and harbours thereof, allowing regular flows of heavy and hectic commercial traffics among countries, located at stupendous distances from each other, since the most ancient times. The ramification of this region with the influence of the communities of Arabia has been especially significant, since Arabia in particular and Western Asia at large, kept since the earliest times having their interests enter in a very vital way into these international interactions. Such, in course of time, might, in all probability, have caused a quite warm relationship to develop between the natives of Kerala and the peoples inhabiting the lands falling right across the mass of water that extends beyond the western coastline as seems inferable from the fact that no sooner had a Great Monotheistic Dispensation, launched through the Agency of an Arabian Prophet started sending its tides sweeping across the sandy terrains that would have neighboured Kerala but for the sea, than the natives of this Indian region, hailed the creed into their very midst by sending a member of their own highest nobility, king Cheraman Perumal of Samoothiri dynasty, amongst its adherents. The Arabs and their language having already left some marks on the ethnicity and the culture of the region, come thus to be initiated in a fuller way into its affairs, having now the force that propelled them redoubled through the addition of a spiritual mission to the usual mundane ones. And it is in this way that there came to be augured the beginning of a tradition of cultivating the letters of the Arabs among the native populace, a tradition destined to evolve uninterrupted through the subsequent centuries.

The beginning of the development of the Arabic literature in Kerala having thus had a religious motive underlying itself, the earliest compositions that made up the bulk of Arabic literary output here, had without doubt a colouring characteristically religious...sermons and exhortations, denouncing and discouraging forbidden practices and promoting a love for and a commitment to the Holy Law. A number of couplets and small pieces of poetry composed to promote such ends must have been in currency in those earliest days of Islam in Kerala though none seem to be available today in its original form. The oldest poetical works available today belong to the kind of poetry classified as 'Mukhammas' and they are barely any more than six centuries old. The first Keralite poet writing in Arabic with works surviving to our day is El Qadi (shari'a judge) Abu Bakr bin Ramadan ash-Shaliyati (d. 885A.H/ 1480 AD). Out of the works attributed to him, only two 'Mukhammas' have been saved from getting lost, a fortune, which they owe probably to the significant religious value attached to them. Such Mukhammas are commonly sung among the local Muslims on religious occasions but the physical shape their composer originally chose to put them into, continues to be unknown or have they not been published till date.

Another poet of Kerala from these early times to have composed his verses in Arabic was the famous Zainu'd Deen bin 'Aliy al Ma'bari (d.928AH/1521 AD) who was a student of El Qadi ash-Shaliyati and imbibed, owing to his long exposure to the influence of the latter, a keen interest in composing poems. He is a writer in Arabic of great renown and left behind many a valuable work relating to subjects other than poetry but as to the evidence of his genius in the field of Arabic poetry, we have access today to no more than two qaseedahs the themes of them both being religious, one of them being the famous Hidayet ul Adhkiya fi Tareeqi el Awliya' (A guidance for those with minds incisive traveling in the way of the spiritually exalted) and the other being 'Tahreed Ahli' el Iman ala Jihadi Abdati es-Sulban' or 'urging on the community of the faithful the course of waging war on the worship of the crucifix' (the Portugals and the English). This latter work, though basing itself upon a theme historical, bears obvious marks of having flown out of a mind most thoroughly imbrued with a religious fervour and is venerated as such today more as a religious than as a historical work. In what original shape did the two works appear are unknown today, a condition that owes itself partly to the issue of an order by the British government demanding the destruction of all the manuscripts containing this second work. And no published forms of the two are known to have been in existence.

Among such early poets, a very high rank has to be ascribed to Muhammed bin 'Abd elAzeez, the illustrious Qadi of Calicut, the span of whose life is known to have extended from 985 AH/1577 AD to 1025 AH/1616 AD. Among the numerous works authored by him, one should make mention especially of an elegy or 'marthiyya' he wrote on Shaykh 'Othman Labba el Qaaelee', his teacher, in which he praises his qualities in superlative terms. This poem has not survived except for a few of its verses and could as such, be probably given a place among the unpublished Arabic works of the kind being dealt with here.

The Age of Re-awakening

This is the name generally given to the stage of evolution that the Arabic poetical literature in Kerala came to attain in the 19th century. A great many of the works authored during this period have survived to our own time, a fact that contrasts the period remarkably to the ones preceding it. The subjects dealt with by the poets from this age are diverse and the styles used are marked as much with variety as, on occasions, with brilliance and splendor. It is worthy to note that many of the poems written in this age distinguish themselves through a simultaneous conformity with literary modes and ideals both old and new. All the poetical works written in this period are, however, preserved in the forms of manuscripts available with various persons or at multifarious libraries spread over the province with the exception of a few of those authored by 'Umar bin Aliyy al Balankoti' who later was known as Umar Qadi el Balankoti.

In what follows, one would seek to furnish a few particulars about the works penned during this period as well as some others available in the forms of manuscripts.

'Risalat ila Ba'adhil 'Ulama': Authored by Shaykh bin Muhammed al Jifry (1139 AH - 1222 AH). A noted scholar born at Hadramawt, (a city of Yemen) who migrated to Calicut and settled there with the help of the Zamorin and the Muslims of Kerala. He devoted himself to the writings of poetry and participation in religious discourses as well as preaching. The present poetical work is intended to serve as a reprimand directed at certain religious scholars and jurisprudents from the region of Calicut for their having failed in the task of curbing the popularity of Muhammed Shah, a certain Sufi migrant to this region whose views struck the orthodox as bearing a flavour of heterodoxy. This is complete in 23 verses.

'Risalat Ileyhima Aiden': A work by the same author. A message in the form of a qaseedah addressed to two of the scholars to whom the author had spoken through the first poem meaning to serve as an answer to the reply written by them on receiving that first epistle. Through the present qaseeda the Shaykh seeks to establish the view that the pretender is neither a shaykh nor a sufi nor a faqir as he and his followers claim but his preoccupation is to darken the counsel by spreading words of evil among the populace and by performing deeds whose merits have not been attested to anywhere in Islam. He earnestly exhorts the addressees to keep the evil company of him and his disciples at an arm's length.

'Al Irshadaat ul Jifriyyeh Fi arRaddi Ala adDalalat inNajdiyyeh': A work by the same author. The author, himself hailing from Arabia, had a direct insight into the circumstances surrounding the emergence of Wahhabism, a creed whose tenets had few appeals for him. He was the first literary voice to raise itself from this part of India in open defiance and criticism of this system of belief. In the work in question he expresses the view that Wahhabism's is a dispensation of such a nature that it hardly pays any one even to do so much as to attempt a polemical venture aiming at its confutation.

'Al Qadi 'Umar bin 'Aliyy alBalankoti' (1179 AH/1757 AD - 1273 AH/1852 AD) one of the most prolific composers of poems in Arabic in the soil of Kerala, has brought forth so far he penned, the following works most of which are available in the form of manuscripts, an important exception being however the Eulogies of the Divine Messenger (one or a few of which appear to have found their way to press):

1. **'Al Qaseedat ulUmariyyeh fi lMadaaih inNabawiyyeh'** (Whether this or the other praises to the Holy Messenger written by the author was published). This is also called Qaseedatu Salla al Ilaah. A plaintive devotional song, sung in the praise of the Holy Prophet of Allah. (Published from Egypt?):

2. **Qaseedatun fi Madhi nNabiyy:** A versified description of the circumstances under which the Holy Messenger of Allah was born entailing a bestowal of profuse praises on his Exalted Person. The language used here is ornate and eloquent and the ideas reflected should not fail to be marked for their elegance.

3. **Qaseedatu Alfi elAasi ; Also authored by al Qadi 'Umar.** It is linguistically delicate, producing an effect musical on the reader. This elaborates deep and mystical meanings of the Faith. It is sung widely, especially in religious assemblies. As to its genre, it must also be deemed classifiable with the Eulogies of Last Divine Messenger ascribed to the author.

4. **Marthiyyatu Aliyy ilQadi Muhiyy udDeen bin Aliyy:** A work by the same author. The poet mourns deeply through the verses the loss of his dear brother Muhiyy udDeen who used to accompany him to Calicut whenever he would undertake a trip to there on some or other errand. It bestows high praises in the deceased.

5. **Marthiyyatun alayhi aidhen:** Another elegy written by the poet on Muhiyy udDeen, his brother, describing qualities he had found in him but had omitted to enumerate, however, in the first elegy.

6. **Marthiyyatu 'Aliyy asSayyid 'Alawi bin Muhammed:** An elegy written on the occasion of the death of 'Aliyy asSayyid 'Alawi bin Muhammed, a great scholar and one of the close acquaintances of the poet who took part with him in preaching against the rule of the British.

7. **Nufaisu adDurar:** By the same author. A long qaseedah composed in praise of the last Holy Messenger of Allah containing the explication of many a secret meaning pertaining to the Faith. Explains in full the meanings contained in the

Basic Credo of the Faith. It has two parts—one devoted to a delve at the significances of some esoteric features of the Faith and the other to the praise of the Holy Messenger.

8. **Maqasid unNikah:** A long qaseedah by Al Qadi 'Umar devoted to the enumeration of diverse commandments in Islam relating to the institution of marriage. The subject is, for its most part, jurisprudential, but bears, for all that, an obvious mark of the poet's innate inclination for the subtle and the abstract and for the beatific and the spiritual. A Sharah (interpretation) for this detailed enumeration of Muslim rules of marriage using versified form of narration was written conjecturably by some author from Kerala, and it is available in a manuscript form with one of his descendents at Chaliyam in the district of Kozhikode.

9. **Dhau ul Hilaal:** Authored by Al Qadi 'Umar. The intention of the author here again is to extol the attributes of and to bestow praises on the Last Divine Messenger, Muhammed. The script chosen here is of a special kind known as the 'Muhmalah', dispensing with the dots which occur in several letters of the Arabic alphabet. The method is considered effective in serving the end of underscoring some subtle significances inhering in the words.

10. **Qaseedah fi Mad hihi aidhen:** Author: As in the preceding. Subject: Praising the Final Messenger of Allah.

Al Qadi Muhiyyud Deen bin Aliyy el Kaalikoti: Born at Calicut in 1186 AH/ 1787 AD hailing from a famous family of Qadis of Calicut. A contemporary and acquaintance of AsSayyid Shaykh bin Muhammed al Jifry. He was appointed by the British to preside, in the capacity of a Qadi, over the Islamic law court of the city. Not many events are known out of his life as a judge. It is well known, however, that Qadi 'Umar bin 'Aliyy used to be a close friend of his, with whom he shared many views on poetry and literature. His poems themselves are distinguished by a certain delicateness of style and a fine peculiarity of wording. He breathed his last in 1251 AH.

His works:

1. **Qaseedatu Bushrat il ameemah fi Qissat inNasrat ilAdheemah:** A long qaseedah commemorating the war that took place between the armies of Sultan Mahmoot Han II of Turkey and those of the Russian Tsar, the theatre of the same comprising the Danube region and Bessarabia. The news of the Turkish forces' having become successful in one of their campaigns reached India and was greeted by the Muslims here through grand rejoining, with the poet also joining the celebration. The poet speaks exultingly of the personal qualities of

the sultan and the extraordinary virtues having been displayed by his armed forces in winning that difficult campaign. It speaks also of the happiness of the Arab world over that victory. This shows the concern of the Muslims of Kerala for the goings on elsewhere in the Muslim world.

2. **Marthiyyatu 'Aliyy asSayyid Shaykh bin Muhammed elJifry:** An elegy written on the death of the illustrious Awliya an event, sings the poet, which would cause the departed to attain the proximity of his Lord, and couldn't yet but occasion mourning among the dwellers of the earth, who are doomed to remembering with bitter lamentation, the evaporation, from their midst, of a great source of fulfilment to their spiritual needs. This comprises 74 verses.

3. **Fi anNahsi wa asSa'ad:** A qaseedah (Ode) which enumerates the ominous and auspicious days occurring in every month, and how Muslims in Kerala, aspiring for felicity, spend their time on these days.

Al Qadi Abu Bakr bin Muhiyyu dDeen el Kaalikoti: Come of a line of Qadis of Calicut. Grew into a scholar with a profundity of knowledge in diverse fields, especially the sciences of Islam and the affairs of the society, and as such, the Zamorin of Calicut (King Saamoothiri) would consider it appropriate to discuss matters of royal concern with him. He used to be a source of guidance to the ordinary Muslims as well who would frequently consult him with regard to their affairs, but would regret very much their internal differences over issues related to sects, which became very rife during his days. He died in 1301 AH/ 1883 AD. He is also famous for his extraordinary command over the nuances of the Arabic language and to him is attributed the authorship of a number of prose and poetical works. A famous work of his is entitled 'Masaabih ulKawakibi dDurriyyeh' and another is the explication of the book 'Naseehat ulekhwan'. He also authored 20 qaseedahs on different themes. All of these are available in manuscript forms.

1. **'El Hamziyyat unNabewiyyeh':** A qaseedah comprising 58 verses with the commencing letters of the lines being so ordered as to conform to the order of letters in the Arabic alphabet. Each line's termination has been marked with a Hamzah with the poet's intention being here to extol the virtues of the Last Messenger of Allah and herein lies the reason for the verses for the poem's being so entitled.

2. **El Tashawwuq ila Ziyarati rRawdhah elMusharrafah:** A qaseedah of 41 verses describing the aspiration of the poet to visit the Tomb of the Holy Messenger of Allah. He embellishes his poetry with ideas fine and a language delicate and entrusts it to the morning wind to take it to the Presence of his Exalted Addressee.

3. **Marthiyatun ala Abeehi elQadi Muhiyy idDeen:** An elegy of 72 verses dedicated to the memory of his father and teacher Qadi Muhiyy udDeen bin Aliyy.

4. **Marthiyyatun ala Walidihi Aidhen:** A qaseedah of 80 verses dedicated to the memory of his father but while the elegy aforementioned commemorates his death, the present one contains the mention of many such virtues as used to distinguish him during his lifetime.

5. **Marthiyyatun ala Ustadihi:** An elegy commemorating the virtues of his illustrious teacher Al Fadhil Al 'Alim Abdul Qadir bin 'Umar Labba elQaeli: a qaseedah of 59 verses.

6. **Marthiyyatun ala Akhihi:** An elegy comprising 29 verses on his brother al 'Alim Muhammed bin Muhiyy idDeen from whom he had learnt the fundamentals of the Islamic sciences. He describes in it his beloved brother's death and the difficult polemical interaction he had with the contemporaneous 'Ulema.

7. **Risaalatun Ila Ahmed Dahlan:** A versified letter addressed to Ahmed Dahlan, a resident of the Holy City of Meccah, whose name was well known to the Muslim scholars of Kerala. The poem begins with a praise sung to the memory of the Holy Messenger of Allah, describing, in its later lines, the extraordinary attributes of the addressee.

8. **Risaalatun Ileyhi Aidhen:** A versified letter addressed to al Shaykh Dahlan, the lines of which confer high encomiums on the addressee, and seek his consent, to the writing, by the author, of a biography of the last Prophet of Allah.

9. **Risaalatun Ukhra:** A versified letter addressed to asShaykh elFaadhil asShaykh Muhammed Shamsu'dDeen elMakki. The letter shows how deep a relationship used to exist there between the author and the foreign scholars of Islam living contemporaneously. The purpose of writing it was to show deference, to confer compliments, to communicate information and express friendly affection.

10. **Risaalatun Ila Ustadihi:** A tribute, comprising 21 verses, to the memory of his professor AsShaykh Abdu elQadir bin Umar Labba elQaaeli. The poet here confers lofty praises on the high qualities he had found in his teacher.

11. **Ma'ariju asSalik ila Maaliki elMulk Wa elMamalik:** A long qaseedah comprising 1130 verses, conferring high encomiums on the salutary nature of

the Sufistic ways as well as the orders of the Sufis, while describing also the characteristics and other peculiarities of this particular department of Islam. Sufistic orders used to be fairly common in this part of India in those days the most worthy of mention among them being perhaps the Qadiriyyeh and the Shadhiliyyeh orders. Composed in 1276 AH. Uses lofty terms of praise and fine similitude.

12. **Fi dhikri Abaaihi elKiram:** A qaseedah comprising 55 verses through which the author's own ancestors, gracing the office of the Qadi of Calicut and maintaining themselves in a station of honour so as to attract the praise and the respect of the entire community of the local Muslims, are commemorated.

13. **Qasidatun Fi Widai elRamadan:** A qaseedah composed in the closing days of a certain month of fasting, bearing the marks of the ecstatic feelings awakened in the heart of the writer through the Influence of the Holy Season as well as the sadness he felt at its departure. The language is delicate and the similitude used is magnificent.

'Abdu'r Rahman bin Muhammed elMaaturi: Nothing is known about the life of this poet except that he breathed his last in 1312 AH. His style as a poet bears a certain resemblance to those of alQadi Umar bin 'Aliyy elBalankoti and alQadi Abu Bekr bin Muhiyyi dDeen, as demonstrated by the lone piece of poetry that has come down to us out of his works, and that is an elegy written on the occasion of the death of alQadi Umar bin Aliyy elBalankoti. The poem is as distinct with regard to its linguistic style as also to the depth of its significance, calling it futile to mourn the bereavement, which is great, and proceeding then to praise the deceased in the choicest of terms and remember his literary achievements.

A new Renaissance in the Field of Arabic poetry in Kerala in the 20th Century: A new renaissance come to unfold itself in the field of Arabic poetry in Kerala in the 20th century which reflected from both the styles employed and the choice of subjects the range of which become wide enough to encompass and a great variety of human interests. The greatest poets from this age, known collectively as 'Fuhoolu' sShu'ara' have their foremost ranks filled by 3 outstanding figures — those of Abu Layla Muhammed bin Meeran, Muhammed elFalaki elJamalee and Abu rRahmat Muhammed elFai'i. Of them Abu Layla developed the habit of jotting his poetry down into his diary while he was away to Pakistan and some while later, to Saudi Arabia and it is this diary, conserved in the collection of some relative of his that serves one's purpose as the manuscript of his literary works. Of the works of Abur Rahmat Muhammed elFai'i (1322 AH/1901 AD - 1363 AH/1942 AD) quite a few are available in the form of manuscripts e.g. 'Al Fawaaid ul Faraid', 'Gharaaib Shatta', 'Tahdheeru nNas 'Ani elwaswasi elKhannas', 'Taaleeqatu elFai'i', 'Fathu elMala'ikah', 'Urdu Min Shayy' and 'Tahneek elBanat wa Baneen bi Ahadeeth Arba'een'.

Al Faraaid al Multaqat: Author: Qadi Muhammed ibn 'Abd elAzeez (d. 1025 AH/1516 AD) Subject: Inheritance, which, the author says, should be ranked among the branches of religious knowledge related to the life to come. It discourses through verses. It is an unpublished work, the manuscript being available with Qadi N. Muhammed Koya of Calicut.

AlFiyah elFaraaid: A poetical work on inheritance composed by Ahamed al Faruri. It was completed in 1346 AH/1927 AD not published. The manuscript is available in a mosque constructed by the author.

Qaul al Haqq Wa elSalaameh: Author: Qadi Muhiyy dDin ibn Ali, the judge of Calicut. Subject: Some jurisprudential commandments related to the Muslim call to prayer. Available in a manuscript form with Qadi N. Muhammed Koya of Calicut.

Al Fatawa elAzhariyeh: Author: Ahmed Koya ibn 'Aliyy of Chaliyam 1302 AH/ 1884 AD—1374 AH/1954 AD. The work: A compilation of religious edicts issued by the author himself on various occasions. It is comprised of 154 Fatawas relating to subjects like inheritance, marriage, divorce, prayer, business and so forth. Few of them are in Arabic Malayalam, available in the form of a manuscript in the Library at Chaliyam.

Al Qaseedah al Azhariyyeh fi Hukmi attaqleed bi elKalimati elMalaibariyyeh: A poem by Ahmed Koya of Chaliyam. It discusses the nature of the work which would make the utterance of divorce effective. It disapproves the use of Malayalam words for that purpose as less than sufficient as substitutes for corresponding words in Arabic. However, he says marriage bonds could be invalidated through them in a manner less than final than is signified by a decisive declaration of divorce. Unpublished and kept in manuscript available in the author's own personal library at Chaliyam.

Qaseedah fi Bayan al Tasawwuf Author: Shaykh ibn Muhammed al Jifri. Born in Hadramaut in Yeman and migrated to Calicut in 1159/1795 AD. A poem elaborating the meanings represented by every single letter contained in the Arabic word 'Tasawwuf', and describing the qualifications of a true Sufi. Manuscript available with N. Muhammed Koya, at one time one of the 2 Qadis of Calciut.

Ma'din al Falah : Author: Ahamed al Faruri (d. 1383 AH/1983 AD). The date of completing it 1328 AH/1910 AD. It deals with sins committed by the limbs of the body and bears on the personal morality which is exposed to severe trials on the occasions of diverse private dealings. Published by the Bayaniyya press, Parappanagadi. But the original and very famous manuscript is available in a mosque constructed by the poet at Parur near Attappuram in the district of Trichur.

Qaseedah fi Bayan al Faqeer : A poem written by Shaykh ibn Muhammed al Jifri (d. 1222 AH/1807 AD) Subject: The qualities that should be possessed by a faqeer (which term is supposed to designate a spiritual rank higher than that of a Sufi). It elaborates the spiritual significance and the implications contained in each of the letters constituting the Arabic word faqeer. Not published. Manuscript available with Qadi N Muhammed Koya of Calicut.

Siraj al Quloob wa I'laj al Dhunoob : Author: Zaynu'dDin Ibn 'Aliyy. Subject: Exhorting obedience to God and prescribing remedies for sins committed. It quotes liberally from the Koran and the Holy Traditions. Manuscript available, albeit in a rather delicate condition, in the library of Ahmed Koya at Chaliyam.

'Umdatu'l As-haab wa Nuzhatu elAhbaab : Author: Qadi ZaynudDin Ramadan ibn al Sheykh Sharaf al Deen Musa, the Qadi of Calicut. He flourished most probably about the middle of the 14th century AD. Discusses knowledge and devotion in a theological perspective as well as ways of invoking the Mercy of the Lord and of attaining fortune in regards temporal and spiritual. Manuscript available in the library of Ahamed Koya at Chaliyam.

Ḥidayetu'rRasi ala Ghawayati elQasi : Author: Qadi Muhammed ibn 'Aliyy (d. 1346 AH/1927 AD) Subject: A criticism of the exploitative attitude and errant practices of a certain Sufi, castigated as an impostor, named Mohammed Salih who came to Calicut in 1285 AH/1868 AD. Manuscript is available with Qadi N. Mohammed Koya of Calicut.

Al Burhanu'l Muneer : Author: Qadi Muhammed ibn 'Aliyy of Calicut (year of completion 1346 AH/1927 AD) Subject: Versified criticism of a Sufistic practices in Kerala known as 'Ratib', involving the infliction self injury by the participants. Manuscript is available with Qadi N. Muhammed Koya of Calicut.

Sharah elRazanah : Author: Al Shaykh ibn Muhammed al Jifri. A commentary of al Razanah, said to have been authored by a Keralite. Written on 17th Muharram 1211 AH (1796 AD), Manuscript available with Qadi N. Muhammed Koya, Calicut.

Nasihatu'l Ikhwan : Author: Qadi Abu Bakr bin Muhiyyi'd Deen of Calicut. It is an explication of the poem 'Ila Kam Ayyuha el Insan by Qadi Muhammed. Completed on 30th Shawwal 1270 AH (1853 AD), Manuscript available with Qadi Ahmed Shihabu'd Deen of Calicut.

Tanweeru'l Fuad : Author: Qadi Abu Bakr Ibn al Qadi Muhiyyi'd Deen of Calicut (d.1291 AH/1874 AD). Subject: Reference to and explication of the verses occurring in the Book of Allah focusing on the exaltedness of the Prophet and a believer's obligation to respect him and his Illustrious Family. Manuscript is available with Qadi N. Muhammed Koya of Calicut.

Mawlid an Nabiyy : Author: Muhiyyi'dDeen Ibn Kunhi Moideen Kutty (d. 1309 AH/1891 AD) of Nediyiruppu near Kondotty (a town in Malappuram district of Kerala). Subject: A mystical interpretation of certain features of the Spirit and the Person of the Holy Prophet. Manuscript available with Haji. T. Muhammed ibn Muhiyyi'd Deen of Nediyiruppu, the grandson of the author.

Mawlid al Muhmalat Wa al Mu'jamat Author: As in the preceding, Subject: Mawlid (verses glorifying the Birth and the Attributes of the Holy Prophet of Allah). The lines exemplify the mastery of the author of the Arabic language. The scripts used in writing are peculiar, most being in the Muhmilat form (letters without dots). Manuscript is available with Haji. T. Muhamed ibn Muhiyyi'd Deen, the poet's grandson, of Nediyuruppu (in Malappuram Dt.).

Manaqib al Shaykh Muhammed al Kaalikoti : Author: Ahamed Koya of Chaliyam Subject: Mawlid of Sheykh Muhammed ibn Alaau dDeen of Calicut whose death anniversary is celebrated at Calicut every year.

Shu'ab al Imaan

Jami'e elFawaaid

Jawahir fi nNathr

The author of the first: Al Shaykh Zain al Deen ibn 'Alyy ibn Ahmed al Ma'bari (928 AH/1521 AD). Abridged form of Shu'ab al Iman by al Beyhaqi. It discusses the aspects of Imaan (Faith) with frequent references of the Book of Allah and the Tradition of the Holy Prophet. Also contains verses in praise of the Holy Messenger and his miracles.

The second, by the same author, is a small treatise of scholastic Theology written in 1311 AH.

The author of the 3rd is Valiya Purayil Mayin Kutty of Chovva in Cannanore (d. 1270 AH/1853 AD). It is a poem comprising 120 couplets. Praises God and His Messenger (ﷺ). Describes special features of the Holy Book, the Last day, and the Destinations after death. Contains many theistic observations and statements about the fundamental articles of the Faith.

Al Fathu'l Mubeen Author: Qadi Muhammed ibn Qadi Abd al 'Azeez of Calicut. (1025 AH/1505 AD) A long poem comprising 537 couplets. It describes the conditions of Muslims under the Zamorins and the war between the Portuguese and the Muslims. Resembles somewhat the subject matter elaborated in the famous Tuhfatu'l Mujahideen by al Shaykh Zainu'd Deen. The manuscript is available in the India Office Library in London and with Qadi N. Muhammed Koya of Calicut.

A'ayan Malaibari : Author: Al Shaykh Abdu'r Rahman ibn 'Aliyy of Tanur. Subject: The lives and the works of the 'University 'Ulama of Malabar. Manuscript is available.

Al Minhat al Harfiyyeh: Author: Moulavi al Hajj Muhammed Sa'id ibn Ibrahim (of Talangara in Kasargod, 1323 AH/1905 AD—1392 AH/1972 AD). Subject: A verified treatise aiming at simplifying the grammar of the Arabic language.

Tasheel al Huffaz bi Tafasiri elAlfaz: Author: 'Aliyy Hassan Musliar of Tirurangadi. Completed in 1352 AH/1933 AD. This is a short dictionary containing 700 common words. Manuscript is available with M.P. Kunhi Muhammed Moulvi, the author's son.

Alfiyyah fi'llugha: Author: Ahmed al Faruri. Written in 1367 AH/1947 AD a dictionary in which words, with their meanings, have been arrayed in the form of verses. Manuscript is available in the mosque founded by the author at Attapuram.

Muthallathatu el lugha: Author: M.V. Kunhi Ahmed Moulavi of Trichur. Written in the year 1969 AD. A dictionary showing how entirely do changes in vowel marks alter the meaning of a word constituted by the same set of letters. Meanings are given in English. It contains more than a thousand words, manuscript available with the author.

Hadiyyatu'l Ikhwan: Author: Ahmed al Faruri (Parur Kunhi Ahamad Musliar). Written in 1336 AH/1917 AD. Subject: In the main, a versified explication of Tuhfat al Ikhwan of al Imam Dardir (d. 1301 AH/1786 AD). Manuscript available at the author's own mosque at Attupuram in the district of Trichur.

Tarikh al Nahw wa Tetawwurah: Author: Al Sayyid Abdu'r Rahman (b. 1344 AH/1926 AD) Subject: The origin and the development of the grammar of the Arabic language written in 1388 AH (1968 AD). Has not have been published.

Marthiyyatun 'Ala al Sayyid 'Alawi bin Muhammed: Author: Muhiyyu'd Deen ibn Fareed ibn Muhiyi'd Deen al Bariree of Bangalore. Elegy on al Sayyid 'Alawee (written in 1260 AH/1944 AD), who is described here as the full moon of guidance and a source of succour to humanity. Manuscript is available at the Muhiyyu'd Deen Mosque at Quilandy, Calicut District.

Marthiyyatun 'Ala Abdir Rahman bin Shaykh bin Ahmedi'l Hamadani: Author: As in the preceding. It is elegy on 'Abdu'r Rahman ibn Shaykh (d. 1259 AH/1852 AD) whose pedigree, character, scholarship and deportment are praised here. Manuscript available at Muhiyyu'd Deen Mosque, Quilandy.

Marthiyatu'l Qadi Muhiyyi'd Deen ibn 'Aliyy: Author: Qadi Abu Bakr Kunhi of Calicut Subject: On elegy commemorating the death of his father Qadi Muhiyyu'd deen ibn 'Aliyy (d. 1266 AH/1849 AD). Manuscript is available with Qadi Muhammed Koya of Calicut.

Marthiyyatun 'Ala' sh Shykh Abdul Qadir Bin Umar: Author: Qadi Abu Bakr Kunhi, Subject: Commemoration of the death of Al Shaykh Abdul Qadir bin 'Umar of Kayalpatnam of Madras State, a teacher of the poet (d. 1272 AH/1855 AD). Manuscript is available with Qadi N. Muhammed Koya of Calicut.

Marthiyyatun Ala Inkadh 'Umar bin 'Aliyy: Author: Muhiyyu'd Deen ibn Fareed of Bangalore. Date of composing 1274 AH/1857 AD. Subject: An elegy commemorating Qadi 'Umar bin Aliyy (d. 1273 AH/1852AD) of Valiyankode of Malappuram district. Manuscript is available in the Muhiyyud Deen Mosque at Quilandy.

Marthiyya ala elJifri: An Elegy Composed by Ahmed Koya of Chaliam on Al Sayyid Ahmed al Jifri (1349 AH/1930 AD). Included in Diwan of the poet, a manuscript of which is available in his library at Chaliam.

Rethaun 'Ala Abi's Sabah: Author: Mawlawi Muhammed Abu Salah (born: 1338 AH/1919 AD) Date of composing 1390 AH/1970 AD. Subject: An elegy written on Abu Sabah Ahmed 'Aliyy, the founder and one time head of the 'Rawdatu'l 'Uloom' Arabic College at Feroke. The presentation marks itself with eloquence and clarity. Manuscript is available with the poet's family.

Masha 'ikhu Kondotty: Author: Shaykh Muhammed al Jifri. Subject: A satire directed at the evil practices of certain shaykhs of Kondotty. Manuscript is available with Qadi N. Muhammed Koya of Calicut.

Muslimu'l Asri elHaadir: Author: Muhammed Abu Salah, Subject: A satirical description of the factionalism that divides the Muslims of the modern age. Manuscript is available with the poet's family.

Zilzal 1251: Author: Qadi 'Umar bin 'Aliyy. Date of composing 1253 AH/1835 AD. Subject: A versified description of the earthquake at Ponnai in 1251 AH/1835 AD. Manuscript available with Prof. V. Muhammed Sahib of Farook College.

Zilzal 1317: Author: Al Shaykh 'Abdu'l Azeez. Subject: Poem describing the earthquake that occurred at Ponnani in 1317AH/1899 AD. Manuscript is available with the family of late Prof. V. Muhammed Sahib of Farook College.

Hawja 1941: Author: P.V. Muhammed Moulavi. Subject: Long poem describing the cyclone that struck Malabar, 26th May 1941 (1360 AH). Manuscript is available with Ibrahim Moulavi, head of the Madeenath'ul 'Uloom College, Pulikkal.

Diwan al Azhari: It is collection of 40 poems by Ahmed Koya of Chaliyam. Manuscript is available in his library at Chaliyam.

Diwan Abi Salma: Collection of poems by P.V. Muhammed Moulavi, also called Abu Layla (in the second half of the 20th century). It contains nine poems only. Manuscript is available with K.N. Ibrahim Moulavi, Head, Madinatu'l 'Uloom Arabic College Pulikkal, Malappuram.

Jainism and Jain Manuscripts

4

Jagat Ram Bhattacharyya

The history of writing is not as old as the verbal tradition is. In India from the time immemorial the wisdom through intellectual exercise have been flowing with the verbal tradition. Naturally the sacred literature was kept alive in verbal tradition. People in ancient India had tremendous capacity in memorising the scripture. It was considered to be sin to reduce the scripture to writing. So education in ancient India was imparted verbally from generation to generation. It was in practice of both the *Brāhmaṇic* and *Śramaṇic* (Jain and Buddhist) tradition. The other name of the Veda is *Śruti*. It means the oral tradition. In the beginning, the Vedic literature was not in written form. Appropriate tools and mechanism were evolved to enhance the memory power. Right pronunciation, accent, punctuation were taught as primary requisite of memorising the sacred texts. And these had been enlivened through *Guru-śiṣya-paramparā*.

According to Jain Canonical texts and *Jaina Purāṇas* the religous doctrines and sermons, beginning from the time of Lord Ṛṣabha, the first Tīrthaṅkara up to Lord Mahvīra, the twenty-fourth Tīrthaṅkara were preached only orally. The literary document whatever available today was compiled as written from the the fifth century A.D. As time goes on the sermons preached by Lord Mahāvīra get voluminious. A group of eleven *Gaṇadhara*s was he first messenger of the teaching of Mahāvīra. Later on Ācāryas have taken the great responsibility to spread that message. By that time, due to intellectual exercises the original canons were explained with *bhāṣya*, *niryukti*, *ṭikā*, *cūrṇi,* etc. And realised to be mutialated with secondary thoughts. And it was found necessary to compile the canons in its own form.

The Digambara does not believe the restoration of the canons in such a way that the Śvetāmbara does. The fourteen *Pūrvas*, the foundation of Jain ethics in particular and the philosophy in general have been claimed to be lost by both the sects. According to the Śvetāmbara, a meagre portion that have been preserved in the canons in scattered manner, where as the Digambara believes that these are preserved in the *Ṣaṭkhaṇḍāgama, Kasāyaprābhṇa,* and *Mahābandha* etc. in the same way.

After the *nirvāṇa* of Lord Mahāvīra, 527 B.C., famine occurred in India very frequently. At the time of Maurya Chandragupta famine lasted for twelve years. So the continuous process of natural calamity was the cause for the declination of retentive power of sacred texts, as people were starving. Owing to these series of devastating famines many Jain monks also died. And that was the cause, Ācārya Bhadrabāhu, who was known as the knower of the complete sacred texts, migrated to the south with a large group of monk disciples. Even quite a substantial number of monks of this group also died. The sacred text was found to be lost with the death of Bhadrabāhu.

As Bhadrabāhu migrated to south India, Sthūklabhadra was representing as the head of the community in the north with a large group of monks and stayed in Magadha region. There was fear that the knowledge of the sacred texts might lapse into obvilion. And for that reason a council was convened at Pāṭaliputra (Patna) for the restoration of the sacred texts. The monks who were in north India, compiled the 11 Aṅgas and the remnants of the 14 Pūrvas in the 12th *Aṅga*, *Dṛṣṭvāda* in that convention. This was the first ever attempt to reduce the sacred texts to writing. By that time the disciples and adherents of Bhadrabāhu returned to the north and saw a big change in doctrine propunded by Mahāvīra was compiled in the 12 *Aṅga*s. They even saw a big change in the life-style of the sādhus. That was the period when Jain monks were clearly identified with two sects — Digambara and Śvetāmbara. The Digambara monks refused to acknowledge the canons compiled by Sthūklabhadra and his disciples. They were of opinion that the *Pūrva*s and *Aṅga*s, taught by Lord Mahvīra were lost to a large extent.

After the Pāṭaliputra conventions several conventions were held in subsequent times in different parts of northern India. Two of these conventions, one of the Digambaras and the other of the Śvetāmbaras were famous. Dharasenācārya, the last Ācārya, being the representative of the Digambara tried to restore the original and is believed that he could retain a meagre amount of scriptural knowledge, that is the *Pūrva*s and *Aṅga*s. The remaining scriptural knowledge is considered to be lost. He taught a few portion of the fifth *Aṅga* - *Viyāhapaṇṇatti*, and *Diṭṭhivāya*, the twelfth *Aṅga* to his disciples, Puṣpadanta and Bhūtavalī. These two texts, afterwards were reduced to writing by these two disciples. Both of them have written the scriptures in first or second century B.C. Puṣpadanta composed *Satprarūpaṇā* in 177 *gāthā*s where as rest of the knowledge has been composed by Bhutavalī by the name *Ṣaṭkhaṇḍāgama*.

According to the Śvetāmbara, the last conference was held at Vallabhī, Gujarat in 4th/5th century A.D. (*Vīr saṃvat* 980) in the leadership of Devardhigaṇi Kṣamāśramaṇa where it was the first time that the scriptures were attempted to reduce into writing. It was a large gathering of learned Jain monks who compiled the *Aṅga*s and *Upāṅga*s. *Dṛṣṭivāda*, the 12th *Aṅga*, however, here also considered to be lost.

As the earliest ever script is believed to be the inscriptions of Aśoka of 3rd century B.C., it is to be understood that the Jain scriptures as composed by Puṣpadanta and Bhutavalī in 1st/2nd century B.C. were the source of compilation of Śvetāmbara canons. So the compilation of the scriptures held at Vallabhī was partly based on the scriptures written earlier and partly by the verbal knowledge. The art of writing was amply developed even in 1st or 2nd century B.C. and onwards the Jain *Rāmāyaṇa*, *Paūmacariyaṃ* was composed by Vimalasūri in 1st century B.C. The dramatic Prakrit of Bhāsa and Aśvaghoṣa's compositions were also available in early Christian era. Even the commentary literaure of Jain canons came into existence before the compilation of the canons. So the tradition of writing of the scriptures was in vogue before the Vallabhī conference. On the basis of the compilation of Śvetāmbara canons, the history of Jain manuscripts believed to be started. As the tradition of writing sacred literatures came into practice, efforts from every corner of religious sects were made to register all religious documents into writing. Within a short span of time the practice of writing became so popular, the religious heads and Ācāryas started preserving those manuscripts in the temples that all these scriptures would be easily accessible to the scholars. Mainly the temples were the store-houses of manuscripts which were called as *Granthabhāṇḍār* or *Śāstrabhāṇḍār*.

Beginning from Bhadrabāhu, 2nd century B.C. and onwards up to 16th / 17th century A.D. there were number of learned monks and Ācāryas in Jain community who have great contribution to the literary works. They not only preserved the old canonical texts, enormous number of sacred literatures were composed through out the ages. Monks used to travel in and accross the country on foot and propagate the scriptural knowledge among the masses. Some of the prominent names are — Ācārya Kundakunda, Ūmāsvāti, Siddhasena Divākar, Samantabhadra, Devanandī, Devardhigaṇi, Haribhadrasūri, Jinasena, Guṇabhadra, Hemacandra, etc. They not only taught the scripture but inspired the followers to preserve manuscripts. It was a noble duty to copy the sacred literature and propagate more and more to the masses. It was said that doing so one can earn merit (*puṇya*). The Ācāryas preached how to preserve manuscripts. They also taught the art of writing and copying of old manuscripts. They took initiatives to establish *Śāstrabhāṇḍāra*s. The *praśasti*s which are written at the end of the manuscripts clearly indicate that most of the manuscripts have been copied out due to the teachings of the monks. People who were in the mission in distributing manuscripts to others for the sake of spreading knowledge were considered highly respectable and noble. In most of the cases, at the end of the manuscripts it is written – 'one who writes or makes individuals to write, one who hears or one who makes others to hear, one who gives or make others to distribute, is noble one and sharer of *puṇya*. He will certainly attain *nirvāṇa* some day'. Jain teachers always emphasized on regular reading of manuscripts and recorded reading scriptures or self-study (*svādhyāya*) is one of the six essential duties of layman.

Jainism, although, has been originated in the eastern part of India (Bihar) as the birth palce of Lord Mahāvīra, it has been spreaded over the other parts, central, western and southern parts of India. *Śāstrabhāṇḍāra*s or *Granthabhāṇḍāra*s were established basically in the temples. Jain manuscripts are highly adorable to the Jain people. As these are the sermons of the *Tīrthaṅkaras* recorded in the written form. Jain people consider these of great esteem. Jains used to visit the *Śāstrabhāṇḍāra*s at the time of visiting temples. They pay obeisance to these sacred scriptures. Usually these manuscripts are kept in the custody of scholarly hands who had knowledge and authority on the subject matter as well as the script. But they were directly guided by the learned monks. Later on, in the 13th century and onwards the noble duty of preservatiopn of manuscripts were laid upon the *Bhaṭṭāraka*s, *Yati*s and their disciples called *Maṇḍalācārya*s, *Pāṇḍāras* and *Brahmacārī*s. They were idenfied as *Caityavāsī*s — the temple dwellers. The *Bhaṭṭāraka*s along with their other duties and responsibilities to the Jain community have shouldered upon the establishment of *Śāstrabhāṇḍāras*. Maintaining asceticism in life they also used to travel through out the country and where ever they stay in the rainy season, they establish manuscript libraries. They kept vigilance over the condition of the manuscripts. They used to take a number of manuscripts with them at the time of their travelling. They used to take care of every leaf of the manuscripts and replace it, the cover and even the wooden plates from time to time. They often sold the extra copies to the *Śrāvaka*s for its preservation in other *Śāstrabhāṇḍāras*. Gradually it comes again under the control of the house-holders. There were number of house-holders through out the ages who bacame very good scholars. The *Śāstrabhāṇḍāras* have come under their control. Substantial development in increasing manuscripts had been found. The other side of the picture was that in some places in some periods the management of preservation of manuscripts had come under the control of so called illiterate persons and on the name of preservation they used to keep those manuscripts under lock and key and not make available to the keen readers, that results the manuscripts to be reduced to ashes.

Modern system of preservation in and issuing books from the library is the developed system of those of the traditional *Śāstrabhāṇḍāras*. Even in earlier times manuscripts were preserved with cataloguing systems and were issued after maintaining register. Generally part of the manuscripts were issued, mainly for two reasons—other part might be issued to other and if it is lost, other part might be restored. In most of the cases there are clear instructions written at the end of the manuscripts that it was written with great difficulty so it should be preserved with great care.

bhagnadṛṣṭi kaṭigrīvā vakradṛṣṭiradhomukham
kaṣṭena likhitaṃ śāstraṃyatnena paripālayet /

baddhamuṣṭi kaṭigrīvā mandadṛṣṭiradhomukham
kaṣṭena likhitaṃ śāstraṃ yatnena paripālayet //

Not everybody was allowed to copy out the manuscripts. The writer should have good hand-writing with ample knowledge of alphabets and the language. He should be genious, good in talking and having control over senses.

sarvadeśākṣarābhijñaḥ sarvabhāṣāviśāradaḥ /
lekhakaḥ kathito rājñaḥ sarvādhikaraṇeṣu vai //

medhāvī vākpaṭurdhīro laghuhasto jitendriyaḥ /
paraśātraparijñātā eṣa lekhaka ucyate //

The writer should follow the strict principle in writing. The art of writing was developed that a writer should be very attentive and careful that how long the letters should be, and of which size, the place where the letter to be curved and where they should be written in plain way. It is said thus—

akṣarāṇi samaśīrṣāṇi vartulāni ghanāni ca /
parasparamalagnāni yo likhet sa hi lekhakaḥ //

samāni samaśīrṣāṇi vartulāni ghanāni ca /
mātrāsu pratibaddhāni yo jānāti sa hi lekhakaḥ //

There are also the prescribed instruments by which the manuscript should be written. Different types of inks are also found to be described in many manuscripts, such as —

maṣyardhe kṣipa sadgundaṃ, gundrāhe bolomeva ca /
lākṣā bīyārasenoccair mardayet tāmrabhājane //

bolasya dviguṇo gundo gundasya dviguṇā maṣī /
mardayed yāma yugmaṃ tu maṣī vajrasamā bhavet //

Five kinds of books are mentioned in the *Vṛhad Kalpasūtra*. Those are, *gaṇḍī*, *kacchapī*, *muṣṭi*, *sampuṭaphalaka* and *chedapāṭī*. All these five kinds of books are written mainly on palm leaves. Although the palm leaves were one of the oldest material on which manuscripts were written, later on manuscripts were written on *bhoja patra*, cloth, paper and on copper plates. Before 13th century A.D. the manuscripts were mostly written on palm leaves. The oldest ever Jain manuscript we have is in the Jaisalmer *bhāṇḍār*. The manuscript of the Śvetmbara commentary literature is *Ogha niryukti Vṛtti* of *saṃvat* 1117, that is, 1060 A.D. It is written on palm leaves. Palm leaf manuscripts are presently available in many manuscript libraries in south India and the libraries in north India, such as, Paṭṭan, Karṇāvatī, Jaipur, Jaisalmer, Nagaur, Jodhpur etc. Different types of inks are used in these manuscripts. Some of the palm leaf manuscripts are written in golden ink also.

Cloth was also used by the Jain monks as the material of manuscripts. These types of materials were used mainly for illustrations, drawing, paintings, etc. The earliest manuscript on cloth is found in the *bhāṇḍār* at Paṭṭan. It was written in 1361 A.D. Some other contemporary cloth manuscripts are also found in the same *bhāṇḍār*. *Saṃgrahaṇī Ṭīppaṇakam* was written in 1396 A.D. In the cloth manuscripts mainly the life sketch of the *Tīrthaṅkara*s are illustrated in a beautiful manner. Geography as mentioned in the scriptures and contemporary social and political issues have also been illustrated in the Jain manuscripts.

As it is mentioned that we don't have any evidence of availability of paper manuscript before 13th century A.D., a good number of paper manuscript came out right from the use of paper in that period. Rajasthan and Gujarat have always been the best repository of Jain manuscripts. Rajputana was one of the paper manufacturing industry and with the growing atmosphere of paper manufacturing, the availability of paper gave enough space to the manuscript writers. Manuscripts written on paper are several size and also of vaious kinds. Pagination marks are in one side. These leaves are in many cases decorated in red and blue colours. Some of the manuscripts are found written in golden and silver ink. The Śvetāmbara canon *Kalpasūtra* is written in golden ink with beautiful illustrations. Some of the manuscripts are written in wooden and copper plates. Jain yantras are mostly illustrated either on the copper plates or bronze plates with the illustrations made of golden and silver ink, are preserved in the temples.

There is scarcely any province of Indian literature to which the Jains have not contributed. Along with the religious aspects Jain scholars have contributed a lot to the narrative literature, epics, didactic and scientific literatures. There are number of manuscripts on novels, prayer and short stories. Language used in these manuscripts are Prakrit, Sanskrit, Old Rajasthani, Old Hindi and some local dialects in northern India where as in south India along with Prakrit and Sanskrit there are number of manuscripts are written in Kannada, Tamil, Telugu and Malayalam languages. Manuscripts on logic and philosophy are also in good number. In different repository of Jain manuscripts, the works of Samantabhadra, Vidyānandī, Akalaṅka, Haribhadrasūri and Hemacandra are preserved. Apart from all these there are number of general literatures on which the Jain Ācāryas and monks have great contributions.

All the Śvetambara canons are written in Prakrit, especially known as Ardhamāgadhī. These are divided into *Aṅga*, *Upāṅga*, *Chedasūtra*, *Mūlasūtra*, *Āvaśyaka*, *Prakīrṇaka,* etc. Some of the names are — *Āyāro, Sūyagaḍo*, *Ṭhāṇaṃ,*

Samavāo, Bhagavaī, Nāyādhammakahāo, Uvāsagadasāo, Aṃtagadaḍasāo, Aṇuttarovavāio, Paṇhavāgaraṇāiṃ, Vivāgasuyaṃ, Jambuddīvapaṇṇattī, Caṃdapaṇṇattī, Sūrapaṇṇattī, Uvavāia, Paṇṇavaṇā, Uttarajjhayaṇa, Dasaveyliya, Nandī, Āvāsayaṃ, etc. Apart from Canonical literatures of the Śvetāmbaras and other canonical and philosophical literatures of the Digambaras, there are number of *Purāṇic* literatures written by the Jain Ācāryas, although the aim of writing of this kind of literature was not the same as that of Hindu scholars. Jaina *Purāṇa* covers the lives of the sixty-three great personalities. So the name of the Purāṇas are based on the names of the *Tīrthaṅkara*s or named as *Padma Purāṇa, Harivaṃśa Purāṇa, Pāṇḍva Purāṇa* etc. In these *Purāṇas*, along with the lives of the *Tīrthaṅkaras*, *Rāma, Kṛṣṇa, Pāṇḍvas* and so on are also given. Ācārya Raviṣeṇa wrote the *Padma Purāṇa* in 678 A.D. Ācārya Jinasena II composed *Harivaṃśa Purāṇa* in 8th/9th century A.D. In this work the life sketch of Neminātha the 22nd *Tīrthaṅkara* has been given. Naturally the characters like *Kṛṣṇa* and Balarāma have come. It is a Jain *Mahābhārata* dealt with Jainistic view where as the *Padma Purāṇa* is a Jain *Rāmāyaṇa* where Rāma is identified with sixty-three great personalities. In the 12th century, Hemacandra wrote *Triṣaṣṭi śalāka puruṣa caritra* in the pattern of *Mahāpurāṇa*. *Purāṇas* are not only written in Sanskrit and Prakrit, these are also written in Apabhraṃśa and in Old Hindi.

Besides the *Purāṇas*, there are enormous number of literatures on *Kāvya*, *Carita* literature, *Rāsa* literature, *Adhyātma* literature, Philosophical literature, *Kathā* literature, Didactic literature, such as, *subhāṣita*, *nīti*, *pūjā*, *stotra,* etc., Scientific literatures, such as, *Jyotiṣa*, *Mathematics*, *Astrology*, *Āstronomy*, *Ayurveda*. Grammar, Drama, Lexicography, Prosody and Metre, sexuology, Literature on songs and dances all have been dealt with a great extent by the Jain scholars.

Some important repositories of Jain manuscripts are in Delhi, Agra, Sonipat, Indore, Karanja (Gujarat), Patan, Arrah, Surat, Mumbai, Khamvat. In south India there are number of places in Andhra, Karnataka, Chennai and Kerala known as the Jain *Śāstrabhāṇḍāras*, some of them are, Mudabidri, Karakal and Aliyoor etc. In the state of Rajasthan there are many repositories of Jain manuscripts, some of these centres are in Jaipur, Ajmer, Jodhpur, Jaisalmer, Nagaur, Sikar, Jobner, Godha temple, Alwar, Fatehpur (Shekhawati), Jain Vishva Bharati (Ladnun), Dausa, Jhunjhunu, Rajmahal, Mozamabad, Malpura, Bharatpur and in many places and Jain temples. Jain Ācāryas have enriched the Indian culture through their literary excellence. Thousands of manuscripts are still unpublished. It is difficult to imagine about its hidden treasure.

References

Aṃgasuttāṇi Synod chief Ācārya Tulsī Ed. Ācārya Mahāprajña, Jain Vishva Bharati, Ladnun, 1974.

Bhagavatī Ārādhanā by Śivārya. Ed. Kailash Chandra Shastri, Sholapur, 1978.

Dhaky, M.A. The Date of Kundakundācārya, Pt Dalsukhbhai Malvania Abhinandan Grantha, Parshvanath Vidyashrama Shodh Sansthan, Varanasi, 1991.

Ghosal, Sarat Chandra – The Digambara Saints in India, Cooch Bihar Digambara Jain Muni Raksha Committee, 1932

Kasliwal, Kastur Chand — Jain Grantha Bhāṇḍārs in Rajasthan, Shri Digambar Jain Atishay Kshetra, Shri Mahavirji, Mahavir Bhawan, Jaipur, 1967.

Mūlācāra — Ed. Pt. Kailash Chandra Shastri, Bharatiya Jnanapeeth, Delhi, 1986.

Pravacanasāra of Kundakunda. Ed., A.N. Upadhye, Raychandra Jaina Shastramala 9, 1935.

Sen, Amulya Chandra – School and Sects in Jaina Literature, Vishva Bharati Book Shop, Calcutta, 1931.

Ṭhāṇaṃ — Synod chief Ācārya Tulsī Ed. Ācārya Mahprajña, Jain Vishva Bharati, Ladnun, 1976.

Uvaṃgasuttāṇi - Synod chief Ācārya Tulsī Ed. Ācārya Mahaprajña, Jain Vishva Bharati, Ladnun, 1988.

Bhakti as Gleaned from the Manuscript of Chaitanya Charitāmṛita of Krishṇadāsa Kavirāja

5

PRANABANANDA JASH

The study of manuscript is one of the invaluable source materials for reconstructing the history and culture of the country. The *word 'manuscript',* according to the *New Webster's Dictionary,* has its origin in two Latin words – *manus* meaning hand and *scribe or scriptum* denoting the written character, i.e. script, etc. The term thus bears the meaning of a book or a written document, prepared by hand either by the author himself or copied by a competent scribe who is loyal in copying the original writings–

Yadṛiśam pustake dṛishṭam, tādṛiśam likhitam

This kind of statement is usually found in post-colophon of numerous manuscripts from Bengal during the mediaeval period. The present volume of the Basumati publication,[1] Calcutta, is doubtlessly an important one portraying devotion *(bhakti)* of the mediaeval period both as the philosophical as well as poetical levels.

The concept of *bhakti* (devotion) plays an indomitable role for making an egalitarian socio-religious order, irrespective of any caste, colour and sex in the mediaeval period especially during the time of Śrī Chaitanyadeva (c.1485/86-1533 A.D.). Śrī Chaitanya was one of the foremost personalities who took the cause of the common and divergent elements in the society and made them relevant to the *bhakti* phenomenon for a sort of social resuscitation. It was thus a spiritual idea as much as a social movement. In fact, adoration to Krishṇa-Rādhā and the doctrine of *bhakti* are woven round the texture of the *Chaitanya's School of Vaishṇavism,* popularly known as the *Gauḍīya Vaishṇavism.* The rudimentary principles of this faith centre round the spirit of sincere devotion (*bhakti*) of worshipper and the worshipping object and thereby growing into a deepening consciousness of the Infinite and Eternal. It added a new impetus to the Vaishṇava theogony.[2] Side by side, it had also remained concerned with the task of organizing his followers through the *Saṁkīrtana* and *Mahatosavas.*[3]

The followers as well as philosophers of this School, especially the six Gosvāmīs (Rūpa-Sanātana-Raghunātha Bhaṭṭa-Raghunātha Dāsa-Gopāla Bhaṭṭa and Śrī Jīva) of Vṛindāvana, have discussed *bhakti* in an exhaustive manner in their works like the *Bhaktirasāmṛita-sindhu,*[4] *Ujjvala-nīlamani*[5] and *Saṁkshepa-Bhāgavatāmṛita or Bhāgavatāmṛita-kaṇikā* by Rūpa Gosvāmī; *Bṛihad* Bhāgavatāmṛita by Sanātana; *Sandarbhas (Tattva, Bhāgavat, Palramātma, Śrī Krishṇa, Bhakti and Prīti)* by Jīva Gosvāmī; *Haribhakti-vilāsa* by Sanātana and Gopāla Bhaṭṭa[6] and those words were followed by the writings of Vṛindāvana Dāsa, Krishṇadāsa Kavirāja and others. A close scrutiny of these works will reveal that the theology of the Gauḍīya Vaishṇava School founded by Śrī Chaitanya is characterized by certain distinctive features which distinguish it from other Vaishṇava Schools of thought. Besides, its concept of *Achinta-bhedābheda* to explain the nature of Brahman, its ontology of Rādhā, its ideas on the values of human life of *Purushārtha,* the doctrinal exposition of *bhakti* accompanied by the *rasa* theory gives it a unique position in the realm of religious history. They evolved a system of partial religious emotionalism and explained to intricate classifications and nomenclature. Again, the *rasa* theory in relation to *bhakti* and its various categories with special emphasis on the *madhura-rasa* not only exhibit the profound philosophical knowledge of the āchāryas, but all these new and fresh ideas taken together amply demonstrate the exclusiveness and originality of the Gauḍīya Vaiṣṇavism. Thus the word *bhakti* has a special bearing upon the Gauḍiya Vaiṣṇavism, though the idea of *bhakti* is rooted in the far off antiquity.

To have a proper understanding of the role of *bhakti* as reflected in the *Chaitanya Charitāmṛita* of *Krishṇadāsa Kavirāja,* it is a prerequisite to apprise briefly about the origin and evolution of the history of *bhakti-vāda* upto the time of Śrī Chaitanyadeva. A.B. Keith long ago suggested that the thought of India started from a religion which had in Varuna a god of decidedly moral character and the simple worship of that deity with its consciousness of sin and trust in the divine forgiveness is doubtless one of the first roots of *bhakti.*[7] But this is not acceptable to all the scholars. Subsequently, J.N. Banerjea remarks that 'in the Upaṇiṣads, on the other hand, the mental attitude of the thinkers to the one supreme entity, viz, Brahman-Ātman, gets a character which is in not very uncertain manner, reminiscent of *bhakti*. The growth and development of monotheism, a direct result of the pantheistic conception of the earlier Upaṇiṣads, was the certain background on which *bhakti* was to develop among the intellectual section of the composite population of India.[8]

The term *bhakti* occurs probably for the first time in the Śvetāśvatara Upaṇiṣad.

Yasya deve parā-bhaktiryathā deve tathā gurau/
Tasyaite kathitā hyarthā prakāśante mahātmanaḥ//[9]

But it is to be noted that the idea of the God of Grace, the doctrine of *bhakti*, which form the salient feature of Vaiṣṇavism are not very conspicuous in the Viṣṇu worship of the Vedas and the Brāhmaṇas is more closely associated with *yajña* than with *bhakti* or *prasāda*. Yet from the time of the *Śvetāśvatara Upaniṣad* onward *bhakti* became an indispensable term for using the sense of faith and devotion.[10] The *Ashṭādhyāyī* of Pāṇini and Buddhist works speak of this in the sense of the 'love directed to God'. By the time of the composition of the *Bhagavad-Gītā* (c. second century B.C.), it is established as a technical religious term. Like *Jñāna-Karma-Yajña, Bhakti* is also considered as one of the powerful avenues for realizing the ultimate reality. Nārada defines *bhakti* as of the nature of intense love for God. It is of the nature of love (*premam*) which reaches its acme of perfection (*parama*).[11] It is of the nature of *amṛta* (nectar or immortality) or 'it also means that it is undying in nature'.[12] Śāṇḍilya explains the term as 'absolute devotion to God' (sā parānuraktirīśvare),[13] and Svapaneśvara illustrates the devotion by describing it as a function of the mind with reference to the supreme being similar to what is evinced in regard to worldly objects under particular circumstances.[14] In the later devotional literature, a distinction is drawn between *bhakti* and *premam*. Bhakti is the spontaneous attachment for the desired object, God, being entirely possessed by and absorbed in Him. *Premam* is the most concentrated love for God which is full of the most intense attachment, and which purifies the heart completely. Divine love (*prema*) is the completion and perfection of devotion-*bhakti*.[15]

In order to create popular interest of the concept of *bhakti*, the *Purāṇas* looked at the ideas of devotion (*Bhakti*) with a new dimension in addition to its earlier bearings. The Purāṇas introduce emotional joy and ecstatic flavour into it. *Bhakti* is now loving, joyous and voluntary homage. The *jīva* by means of *bhakti* realises his intrinsic nature of partnership with god which is but kept in obscuration by *māyā* which represents the principle of Illusion.

The *Bhāgavata Purāṇa* states that if the persons to whom God shows his grace shake off all hypocrisy and take refuge in Him with all their hearts, they transcend His *māyā,* and are purged of egoism.[16] However, emotional *bhakti* charged with a feeling of intense love for a God who fulfilled the yearning of his devotees and reciprocated their love finds expression, at a later stage, in the hymns of the twelve Ālvar and sixty three Nayanmars, saints of Tamil land and still later in the School of Gauḍīya Vaiṣṇavism when Vaiṣṇavism had reached nearer to the masses and assumed a popular character. Some have even explained away the *bhakti* movement as an attempt to respond to and come to terms with the arrival of Islam in India. But this argument may not be quite valid even in terms of history, for Islam came to Kerala long before the Afghan invasion, and this did not precipitate any religious upheaval at that time. Perhaps the Sufi tradition had its origin in early contact between Persia and North West India. The twelve Ālvars and sixty three Nayanmars—as the traditional accounting goes—of south India wrote out of inner urges, not necessarily in response to external stimuli. Impact of Sufi tradition can not be denied altogether in shaping the *bhakti* phenomenon of Śrī Chaitanya. In fact this kind of admixture in the religio-cultural scenario of this land happened time and again because of its heterogenous characters in cultural and ethnical behaviour. Periodic attempts at reformation from within can take place in any culture, and have happened in India from time to time, the great Jaina and Buddhist enlightenments being the most important in the ancient period. Similarly, the inclusion of *bhakti* along with the earlier forms of worships, viz., Yajña-Jñāna-Karma during the period of *Bhagavad-gītā* is a new factor/form of worship in Indian religion. With the full dawning of the mediaeval ages there was an efflorescence of devotional poetry in almost all major languages in India. In those days of difficult communication channels, the whole of India throbbed with one passion, as if possessed by the divine spirit, Basava (12th century A.D.), Mahādevī, Jañeśvara (13th century A.D.), Nāmadeva (13th-14th century A.D.). Ekanātha, Tukārāma (17th century A.D.), Kabir, Nānak, Tulsidās, Chaitanya, etc., were among those who breathed a fresh awareness of the immanence of the divine in the human in India. Although they may be said to belong to the same broad movement, each one had his own idiom and manner, feelings and experiences, urges and emotions, etc. Mīrā (15th-16th century AD) bhajans express powerfully the twin aspects of the *bhakti*, namely, the personal and the public, the human and the divine, experience and transcendence. The longing for union with the absolute is deeply felt and sweetly sung. The Rajasthani poems of Mīrā are even more poignant. The expression becomes the cry of the soul: *Īśvaraviraha* or separation from God, causes excruciating agony, and the *bhajana-kīrtaṇa* is a source of relief for the disconsolate *Jīvātmā*.

While comparing the concept of *bhakti* propounded by Madhavāchārya (1197-1276 A.D) the upholder of Dvaitavāda doctrine,[17] and the *bhakti* of Chaitanyadeva it is clear that both of them placed importance on *bhakti* as a path, but the forms of *bhakti* are different. Madhva followed the *dāsya-bhāva* (attitude of a servant towards the deity), while Chaitanya accepted all the five attitudes connected with *bhakti* (*Śānta*, *Prīta* or *Dāsya, Preya, Vātsalya* and *Madhura*) with special emphasis on the *madhura-bhāva*. Moreover, *bhakti,* according to Madhva, is a means for the attainment of salvation (*mukti*); while for Chaitanya it is an end in itself, the ultimate goal of life. It is thus interesting to note that the Gauḍīya Vaiṣṇavas do not explain *bhakti* as devotion in a general sense only but make classification into *sādhanā, bhāva* and *prema*. Before interpreting these nomenclatures, it is to be remembered that *bhakti* has been distinguished from the *Uttama-bhakti*, i.e., the best type of *bhakti*. It denotes whole-hearted service to Kṛṣṇa, for His satisfaction alone, without being in any way influenced by the desires for philosophical knowledge, *karma* and while remaining disinclined to worldly matters.[18]

There are six specific characteristic features of the *uttama bhakti*. They do good and cause happiness; capacity to produce indifference to *mokṣa* or liberation, identifying with a particular mood of complete happiness; and ability to attract Kṛṣṇa Himself.[19]

According to the Gauḍīya Vaiṣṇavas, *bhakti* has broadly been classified as *Sādhana-bhakti, Bhāva-bhakti* and *Prema-bhakti*; and each of these three is the representation of different stages of realisation.

Sādhana-bhakti is attainable by the senses like hearing the Lord's name, singing His *kīrtana* seeing His beauty. It can be practised under some given circumstances when the devotee completely disregards the obligations of the *Varṇāśramadharma* (*Sammatambhaktivignanām bhaktvāngatvam na karmanām*)[20] and does not covet sensual enjoyment and liberation.[21]

The Vaiṣṇava *āchāryas* ordain sixty four rites and rituals for a devotee to attain *Sādhana-bhakti* like submitting to the *Guru,* accepting *mantra* or initiation and learning *bhakti* from him; serving the *Guru* faithfully, performing *nāma-saṁkīrtaṇa*, etc.[22] *Sādhana-bhakti* is also of two kinds—*Vaidhi-Bhakti* and *Rāgānuga-bhakti*. When a *bhakta* practices *Sādhna-bhakti* being inspired by the procedures of the scriptures, it is called as *vaidhi*;[23] but it is called *rāgānuga* when such a *bhakti* flows spontaneously, without any scriptural injunctions or procedures.[24] The *rāgānuga-bhakti* is again of two *types—Prema* or *Karma-rūpa* and *Sambandha-rūpa*. The source of the former is the passionate desire to be Kṛṣṇa's beloved like the Gopīs while the latter seeks establishing relationship with Kṛṣṇa as his servant, friend or parents.

Bhāva-bhakti is the direct outcome of inner emotion for Kṛṣṇa, but this is something different from love. *Bhāva-bhakti* which is the ultimate stage of *Sādhana-bhakti* has been described by Rūpa Gosvāmī as follows :

"When the *bhāva* for Kṛṣṇa develops in one's mind, he becomes impatient, no one does waste his time unnecessarily. His begins to sing His name constantly and eulogises Him. He then longs for union with Him and starts loving His abode. Outward calm is followed by modesty and indifference to the sensual enjoyments. Yet, he remains firm in his hope of attaining Him."[25]

On attaining *Prema-bhakti* which is considered as the final stage of devotion and the culmination point of all forms of *bhakti*, the devotee feels that Kṛṣṇa is something like his own possession which he would like to keep with love. This form of *bhakti* reveals gradually in line distinct succeeding stages with the cultivation of the following deeds, like faith (*śraddhā*), holy company (*sādhu-saṁgata*), spiritual practice (*bhajana-kriyā*), removal of constraints in the spiritual path (*anārtha nivṛttih*),

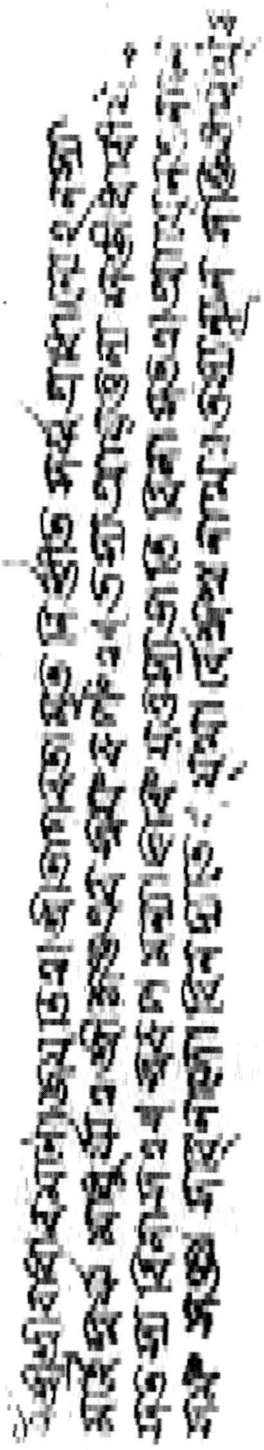

Opening folio of the *Bhāgavatāmṛita-Kaṇikā* of Rūpa Gosvāmī

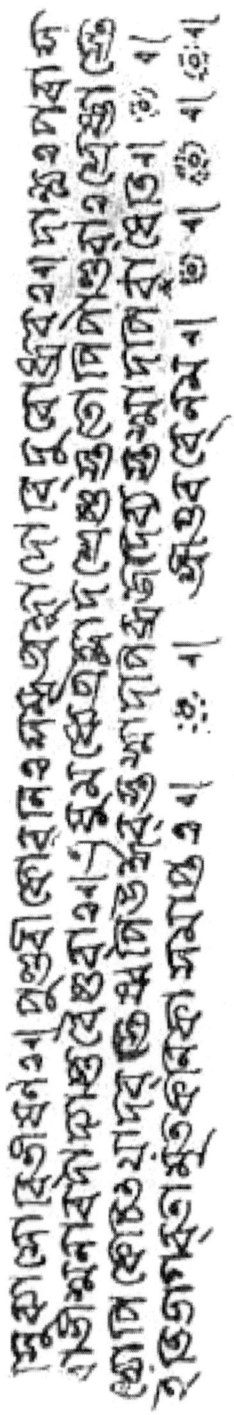

Concluding page of the Manuscript – ***Bhāgavatāmṛita-Kaṇikā.***

devotedness (*syattate niṣṭhā*), the taste for the state of devotedness (*rucistatāḥ*), attachment to that state (*athaśakti*), emotional feeling (*bhāva*) and *Premam.*[26]

As we have already mentioned that the Gauḍīya Vaiṣṇavas regard Lord Kṛṣṇa, the ultimate ideal, as an object of love and devotion. The devote considers Him as the beloved. The exchange of loving reciprocation between the lover (devotee) and the beloved (Kṛṣṇa) is called *bhakti-rasa* (love sentients). The combination of the term '*rasa*' with *bhakti* is a new phenomenon and it is, in fact, the creation of the Gauḍīya *āchāryas*. *Rasa* is the revelation of the highest reality in its undifferentiated blissful nature.[27] Chaitanyadeva considers 'love for god' as the fifth or *pañcama-pūrushārtha* instead of traditional four, viz, *Dharma, Artha, Kāma* and *Moksha*. And this *Pañcamapurushārtha* is the superior of all goals aspired for, and for that matter, they ignored the importance of *Varṇāśrama-dharma* when compared to love for God.

Any way, the full flegdged conception of *bhakti* as *rasa* finally emerged in the fifteenth and sixteenth centuries AD in the compositions of the Gauḍīya Vaishṇavas. It is to be noted that Vallabhāchārya (11th century AD) earlier distinguishes between *maryādābhakti* and *pushṭibhakti*—the former being subject to rules and descriptions, the latter being the result of divine selection and grace.[28] *Maryādā bhakti* functions between *Karman* and *Jñāna*. *Pushṭi-bhakti* is an endless flow of love for God of which the archtype is the love of the gopis for Krishṇa. The love of the soul for God is romantic at its highest and is part of the eternal play (*nitya-līlā*) of God.[29]

The soul was conceived by Vallabhāchārya not as an emotionless and self sufficient spirit as in Nyāya Vaiśeshika, Sāṁkhya or Advaita but as a living spark out of the divine substance seeking to return to it and pulsating with this transcendental attractions. Love of God instead of becoming something metaphorical becomes a fundamental *bhāva*. Hence love for God is not an imaginative imitations of human erotic love but on the contrary human erotic love is but a faint image of the souls longing for God.[30]

The role of imagination of spiritual love is confirmed to meditational practices, which has symbolic aspect. The real love of God arises from pure grace of God. The gopis illustrate this highest kind of love or *Prema* which arises as *sneha* and culminates as *rasa* in the vision of *nitya-līlā*. Hence *sneha* is the *sthāyī bhāva* of love according to Vallabhāchārya.

While Vallabhāchārya had spoken of *Jñāna-karma-samuccaya* at various places, the Gauḍīya *āchāryas* believed that the highest *bhakti* is unmixed with *Jñāna* and *Karma*. *Bhakti* in its highest aspect as *Rāgatmika bhakti* is the eternal sport in the various *dhāmas* (sacred centres). Love is established as a spiritual mode rather than a mental mode. Since *bhakti* was regarded as the essence of the *Hladini Śakti* of the Lord, it acquired a transcendental character and was regarded as *nitya-siddha.*[31] It was the *summum bonum* of perfect freedom and not the result of temporal process. The Gauḍīya *āchāryas* believed that whereas other *rasas* give transcient pleasures *Kṛṣṇa-rati* gives pure and permanent pleasure. In this *mādhurya* is exemplified by the love of *gopis* for Kṛṣṇa specially by Rādhā. This experience of *prema-vilāsa-vivarta* is the *ujjvala-rasa* or the highest state of relish. The *alambana* or determinent is Kṛṣṇa as the object and devotee is the locus of emotions. Rādhā is the embodiment of *mahābhāva* or *Hladini-śakti*. The Gauḍīya *āchāryas* developed the concept of Nimbārka (12th century AD) who had brought the concept of Rādhā and Līlā into prominence in his system.

An exhaustive account of the *bhakti-rasa* is reflected in the Vaiṣṇava scriptures and the number of the *rasa* is of the following twelve kinds:

i. Śānta-rasa (quiet devotion);
ii. Prīta-rasa (devotion as His faithful);
iii. Preya-rasa (devotion is a friend);
iv. Vātsalya-rasa (devotion as parents);
v. Madhura-rasa / Ujjvala-rasa (devotion with erotic);
vi. Hāsya rasa (comic);
vii. Adbhuta-rasa (marvellous);
viii. Vīra-rasa (heroic);
ix. Karuṇā-rasa (pathetic);
x. Raudra-rasa (furious);
xi. Bhayānaka-rasa (terrible); and
xii. Vībhatsa-rasa (ghastly).

Of these, the first five are *mukhyas* (primary) while the remaining seven are considered as *gauṇa* (secondary).[32] According to the Gauḍīya Vaiṣṇavas, Lord Kṛṣṇa can be realised by practicing these twelve kinds of *bhakti-rasa* (love sentients). However, the primary *rasas* remaining constantly within the heart of the devotees whereas the seven others appear and disappear. A devotee adopts a particular devotional attitude according to his inclination and leaning. But *madhura-bhāva* (an attitude of conjugal love) is the best sentient (*rasa*) for realising Lord Kṛṣṇa.[33] The expression of *madhura-bhāva* is distinctly projected in the concept of Rādhā and her love for Kṛṣṇa. Her love for Kṛṣṇa transcended all barriers of this mundane world. Śrī Chaitanya introduced Rādhā as the idealised representative of bliss. From the philosophical perspective it may be said that it is the Gauḍīya Vaiṣṇavism which presents the concept of Rādhā-

Kṛṣṇa-*tattva* in its most mature and developed form. A supramundane (*paramārthika*) is transferred semantically to empirical reality (*Vyavahārika*).

Such a form of all-absorbing love advocated by the Chaitanya School of Vaiṣṇavism through *madhura-bhāva* has been expressed in the following :

Yuvaker ārti yathā yuvati dekhiyā /
Sei rūpa ārti ār nā dekhi bhāviyā //
E kāraṇe bhaktagaṇa bhaje Yadupati /
Patnībhāva tār prati sthir kari mati //[34]

i.e, "as a young man yearns for his sweet-heart, in the same manner, the human soul may yearn for Kṛṣṇa. In order to imbibe the same yearning, the Vaiṣṇavas worship (Kṛishṇa) with an attitude of conjugal love." But it is very difficult to perform this kind of worship,[35] because the love sentient entertained by Rādhā towards Kṛṣṇa was entirely different from the ordinary earthly passion.[36] *Premam* (love for god) and *Kāma* (lust or earthly passion) characteristically differ from each other as iron from gold, in colour and element. Earthly passion (*kāma*) denotes sensual enjoyment of one's self while *preman* devotes to make Kṛṣṇa happy.[37] In order to practise *madhura-rati* (conjugal love-attitude to Kṛṣṇa) the devotees have to undergo a series of succeeding stages, such as, *rati, preman, sneha, māna, praṇaya, rāga, anurāga, bhāva* and *mahābhāva*. *Mahābhāva* is regarded as the supreme form of the realisation of love for Kṛṣṇa. In fact, there are many other stages in between these succeeding stages, but we have hardly any scope to analyse them in an amplified form.[38]

Thus while dealing with the evolution of *bhakti* it may he said that earlier *Vaiṣṇava āchāryas* had extolled *bhakti* as a religious attitude, but it is the contribution of Mahāprabhu Śrī Chaitanya and his disciples and/or followers to present *bhakti* not only as a path but they interpreted it also as a *rasa*. They accepted *bhakti* as a doctrine and a part of theology. The Gauḍīya Vaiṣṇavas thus evolved system of practical, religious emotionalism and explained its intricate classifications and nomenclature. Śrī Chaitanya transformed the *bhakti* form of ritualistic procedure into a devotional (*bhakti*) movement which for a long time overflooded Bengal its neighbouring regions and ever touched the far off southern soil. To him love and devotion to Kṛṣṇa would lead to the illumination of the mind and to ultimate salvation. He recommended dance and music to produce a state of ecstacy in which the *bhaktas* could have a vision of god. No doubt, several Vaiṣṇavite *āchāryas* like, Mādhavendra Purī, Advaitāchārya, Śrīvāsa and others flourished before the advent of Chaitanya, "but the advent of Chaitanya" as observed by S B Dasgupta, "was something like a fruition of all their devotional penances, and it was an event which was really epoch-making in the religion and literature of Bengal.

Chaitanya, as he is interpreted by his followers, embodies in him the quintessence of both Rādhā and Kṛṣṇa, and is both realiser and the realised in the same personality."

References

1. *Chaitanya Charitāmṛta* by Krishnadasa Kaviraj. Basumati Publication, Calcutta.
2. Jash, Pranabananda, *History and Evolution of Vaiṣṇavism in Eastern India*, Calcutta, 1982, p.202.
3. It is well known that Chaitanya adopted effective, though simple, methods to strengthen his movement by performing *Saṁkīrtana* and *Mahotsavas* for the propagation of his faith, and also for holding the community of his followers together. *Saṁkīrtana* is an informal mode of group-singing to the accompaniment of musical instruments reciting the name of Kṛṣṇa loudly with devotion. *Mahotsavas* (grand festivals), also popularly known as *macchavas* helped Chaitanya to keep in touch with the Vaiṣṇava devotees. Such festivals were generally organized at the time of the inauguration of temples of when wealthy devotees volunteered to arrange them for purpose of community gatherings. These *Mahotsavas* were preceded and followed by *Kīrtanas* and attracted large crowds.
4. It expounds systematically the theory of *bhakti-rasa* and its emotionalism. It is divided into four *vibhāgasPūrva. Dakṣiṇa, Paścima* and *Uttara,* and each of these *vibhāgas* and subdivided into two *laharis*. Any way, the Pūrva-*Vibhāgas* explains different types of *bhakti*, the dakṣiṇa treats *bhakti* as a *rasa,* the *paścima* describes the five *mukhya* to unfold the history of the seven secondary *rasas*.
5. *Madhura-rasa or Ujjvala-rasa* is explained separately because of its prime importance in the *bhakti-rasa*. The text consisting of fifteen *Prakaraṇas* (divisions) deals with Kṛṣṇa as a hero and his eternal consort *Rādhā* (*Rādhā-Prakaraṇa*) exhaustively. The succeeding stages of *Madhura-rasa* are also mentioned in an elaborate manner.
6. For all these textual information please consult S.K. De, *Early History of the Vaiṣṇava Faith and Movement in Bengal,* Calcutta, Second edition, 1961. Also see B.B. Majumdar, Chaitanya Caritera upādāna, were best possible details are provided regarding the literary works of the Gosvāmis.
7. Keith A.B. *Journal of the Royal Asiatic Society*, 1915, p. 834.
8. Banerjea, J.N., *Development of Hindu Iconography,* pp. 73-74.
9. *Śvetāśvatara Upaṇiṣad,* VI, 23.
10. Jash, Pranabananda *op.cit*.pp.203-204.
11. *Narada Bhakti Sūtra* (Swami Bhuteshānanda) 2: *Sātvasmin Parama-Premarūpā*.
12. *Ibid.,* 3: *Amṛta-Svarūpā ca*.
13. *Śāṇḍilya-sūtram,* I. 1.2
14. Svapneśvara on *Śāṇḍilya-sūtra*
15. *Cultural Heritage of India*, Ramakrishṇa Mission, Calcutta, vol. IV.
16. *Bhāgavata-purāṇa*, II 29.50. In the *Bhagavata Gītā* VII. 14 we find a similar expression "They alone can cross it (*māyā*) who take refuge in me."
17. It may be mentioned that the four pre-Chaitanya Vaiṣṇava āchāryas like Rāmāṇuja (Viśiṣṭa Advaita). Nimbārka (Dvaitādvaita), Madhvāchārya (Dvaita) and Vallabhāchārya (Śuddhādvaita)

had propounded the *bhedābheda* doctrine (unity in difference) in one way or the other, in sharp contrast to the Advitavāḍa of Śaṅkara. Chaitanya also accepted this doctrine of identity in difference, with the modification that he described the nature of Brahman as something beyond the reach of human thought, calling it *achintya* (incomprehensible). Brahman is qualified by his qualifications which are different as well as non-different from Him. This apparent contradiction in the nature of Brahman is known as *bhedābheda-vāda* or difference. This contradiction was reconciled by Chaitanya and later theologians through the concept of *achintya* (incomprehensible). The *Achintyabhedābheda* of Gauḍīya Vaiṣṇavism is described as "an incomprehensible difference-non-difference." (S. Radhakrishnan, *Indian Philosophy*, London : George Allen & Unwin, 8th impression, 1966, vol. II. p. 762).

18. Rūpa Gosvāmī *Bhaktirasāmṛta Sindhu,* Murshidabad, 1925 Bangali era (1888 AD), Second edition, Purva-I, pp. 8-9.

    Anyābhilāsīta Śūnyam Jñānakarmādyanāṛtam /
    Aṇukulyeṇa Kṛṣṇānu Śīlanam bhaktiruttamā //

19. *Ibid.*, p. 13: In fact, the text also mentions certain factors that make obstructions in the way of performing *bhakti* such as, over-eating excessive efforts, unnecessary talks, anxiety for too many regulations, restlessness, etc. Interestingly enough, there are also six qualities, like enthusiasm, belief, patience, suitable action, detachment and good conduct, which consider the supplementary factors that lead to *bhakti.*

20. Rūpa Gosvāmī. op. cit. Pūrva II, p. 151.

21. Ibid., p.44 :

    Bhukti mukti spṛhā yāvat piśācihṛdi vartate /
    Tāvat bhakti sukhasyātra katham abhyudaya bhavet //

22. Ibid., pp. 73-77.

23. Ibid., p. 33;

    Yatra rāganavaptatvat pravrtirūpajayata/
    Śāsananaiva Śastrasya sa vaidhi bhaktirūpeyate//

24. Ibid., pp. 162-63;

    Iste svarasiki rāgaḥ Paramaviṣṭara bhavet /
    Tanmayi ya bhavedbhakti satra rāgātmikodita//

25. Rūpa Gosvāmī. op. cit, Purva III, pp. 196-197.

26. Ibid., Pūrva-IV. p. 218.

27. *Bhagavata bhakti rasāyanam,* 3rd ullāsa, verses-71.

28. Anubhāshya, 3.3. 38; On Kṛshṇa as the Embodiment of *Rasa* of Redington, Vallabhācārya and the Love games of Kṛishṇa, pp. 7-8.

29. Rūpa Gosvāmī. *Bhaktivasanṛtasmdha.*

30. Anubhāshya, 3.357

31. *Bhaktirasāmṛta Sindhu,* 1.2.2

32. Rūpa Gosvāmī. op. cit., Dakṣiṇa-V. p. 601;

    Mukhyastu Pañcadha Śāntaḥ Prītaḥ Preyanissa Vātsalaḥ/
    Madhurascatyami jñeya yathā Pūrvamanuthamaḥ//

Hāsyadhutastalaḥ vīraḥ Karuṇe raudra ityapi/
Bhayānaka savibhatsa iti gauṇaśca saptadhā//

33. Rūpa Gosvāmī in his *Ujjvala-nilamaṇi* (Navadvipa, 1st edition 469 Gaurābda 1955 AD), Verse-2, p.2) designated it as '*bhakti-rasa rāja.*'
34. Govinda Dāśer Kaḍocā, p. 10.
35. Ibid., p. 13;

Prem Prem kare save prem jāne kevā/
Premer ki tattva haya ramanira sevā//

Abhede puruṣe-nārī jakhana jānive/
Hṛdaye Premer tattva āpani sphurive//

36. Kṛṣṇadas Kaviraj in his *Chaitanya Charitāmṛta* (Madhya II, p. 68) mentions that love for Kṛṣṇa is as the water of the Ganges and it is clearly distinguished from earthly love.
37. Ibid., Ādi, Chapter-4;

Kāma Prema domhakara vibhinna lakṣmaṇa/
Hauna ār hema jaicne svarūpe vilakṣaṇa//

38. For details, See Ujjvala-nīlamaṇi of Rūpa Gosvāmī, pp. 225-291.
39. Dasgupta S.B. Obscure Religious Cults, Calcutta pp. XV-XVI.

Haracandra Tarkapañcānana: A Little-known Scholar from Calcutta

6

S.Y. Wakankar

The two states of Maharashtra and Bengal have been in forefront in almost all fields of activities—social, academic, political, etc. As the luck would have it, many of the names have been almost forgotten in course of time. One such scholar who was a staunch supporter of Hinduism and who vehemently answered a Britisher who made an attempt to prove the superiority of Christianity and denounce Hinduism has, so to say, gone into oblivion. This paper is an attempt to bring to the notice of the scholars, especially, Bengalee, the small rejoinder sent by this Bengali Brahmin, to the British Civil Servant, working in different places in North West Provinces in the British period. Before, I actually turn to the proper topic let me give a small introduction regarding the background of this academic battle.

Faith or Devotion to a particular religious principle is a main source of happiness of a human being. Hence, Religion is the unifying force to bind a set of people to a particular Divine Entity. It may be said that if the religious faith is attacked or challenged, then the concerned people react to it very forcefully. This is proved by history also that religious wars or Crusades destroyed nations also when the followers of different religious faiths fought with each other to impose their religion on others. Fortunately, the preachers and followers of Hinduism never believed in imposing or thrusting their religion on the followers of other religious faiths, neither did they believe in the nefarious activity of converting some non-Hindus to Hinduism. This tolerant tendency of the Hindus was able to accommodate followers of all the religious faiths and India gladly accepted them throughout the centuries. This strength of the Hinduism could not be digested by the followers of Christianity and Islam, who were interested in turning the Hindus to their religious faiths, by trying to prove the superiority of their religious faiths over Hinduism. Thus started the religious quarrels, culminating into wars which devastated the lives of millions of people.

In this paper, I intend to put before the scholars/researchers one such attempt made by a British Civil Servant during his tenure in India. That attempt was thwarted by three intellectuals—one Maharashtrian scholar, named Subājī Bāpu, the other is Haracandra Tarkapañcānana—a poor Bengali Brahmin from Calcutta and the third was a very young nineteen year old Maharashtrian Brahmin Pandit from Varanasi, whose name was Nīlakaṇṭhaśāstrī Gore.

A brief note on the works of the Britisher and the Indians' response to him follows. At the end of the paper, the full text of the work of Haracandra Tarkapañcānana (which was composed in Sanskrit, but printed in the Bengali script) will be given.

Before I do that, let me clarify one thing. I do not want to enter into any controversy, especially, religious faiths, because, it divides the children of the God and secondly, no true religion preaches hatred towards others. It is the misled and mischievous followers of the religious faiths who exhibit their arrogance and so-called sense of superiority—due to the false notions of their greatness—who indulge in such deplorable and divisive activities for the propagation of their religious faiths. Such a mischief was played by a British Civil Servant, of course, with the backing and full supports of his fellow-preachers and the then rulers, viz. the administrators of the East India Company, with their base at Calcutta. My only intention is to put this historically important event before the modem scholars, especially. Bengalee, most of whom must not have even heard the name of Haracandra Tarkapañcānana who vehemently refuted the claims of the Britisher and who unfortunately seems to have been forgotten by the present generation. Now, I turn to the proper topic.

1. John Muir (1810-1882 A.D.): was a Civil Servant of the East India Company and occupied many positions in the administration of the North West Provinces in India. He was almost a Christian Missionary in disguise who took to the idea of spreading malice against Hinduism in a very novel way, viz. through the medium of Sanskrit, the Language of the Hindu Gods. He composed a work in Sanskrit and termed it as *Mataparīksā : A Sketch of the Argument for Christianity and Against Hindus*. It is in the form of a Dialogue between a Guru and his Śiṣya. The work couched in Anuṣṭubh metre contained five chapters, termed as Adhyāyas as under: Īśvaraguṇavarṇanam (34 verses); Aiśanityāvaśyakatā (15th vs); Satyadharmalakṣ-aṇavarṇanam (38 vs); Khṛṣṭīya-mat-apramāṇadarśanam (103th vs) and Bhāratīyaśāstravicāraḥ (189 verses). Total 379 verses. The first edition of this work was published in 1839 A.D. from Calcutta. In 1840, he expanded the bulk of this work to 1032 verses by profusely quoting from many Sanskrit works. The third and final edition was published in 1854 A.D. Immediately after the publication of the first edition, three Hindu Sanskrit scholars attacked the work in Sanskrit verses only, as per the challenge of Mr. Muir.

2. Pandit Subaji Bapu : a very sound Maharashtrian scholar of Sanskrit, especially, Jyotiśśātra, who helped Mr. Lancelot Wilkinson in his works on Indian Astronomy and Astrology, ways the first to send his rejoinder to Mr. Muir. He composed the work known as *Matapariksaśiksā*, containing 107 verses, divided into three chapters, known as Upadeśas, viz. Mataikyasankṣepopadeśa (9th verses); Sarvamatāvirodhasthāpanopadeśa (51 vs) and Tṛtīyopadeśa (47 vs.).

3. Haracandra Tarkapancanana : No authentic information about this Bengali scholar is available. He composed his *Matapariskottara*, in KS/ 159 verses, divided into two Paricchedas, containing 76 and 83 ślokas. He wrote a two-page English Preface to this small book which was printed in 1840 A.D. Though the Text is couched in Sanskrit, the script is Bengali.

4. Nīlakaṇṭhaśāstrī Gore (1825–1885A.D.): A brilliant Maharashtrian young Pandit of only 19 years of age and hailing from Varanasi, reacted very sharply and vehemently to the *Matapariksā* of John Muir and composed his treatise, named, *Śāstratattvavinirṇaya,* containing 786 verses, divided into six chapters. In this work, the Pandit controverted the claims of superiority, as stated by John Muir in his *Mataparīksā*. Incidentally, this happens to be biggest work, that too, by a youngest scholar from amongst the three Sanskrit scholars who tried to refute John Muir's arguments, in favour of Christianity and against Hinduism.

In this paper, we are concerned with only the work of the Bengali scholar. Haracandra Tarkapañcānana.

John Muir composed his *Mataparīksā*, stating three characteristics (lakṣanas) of a True Religion, viz. (1) The power of the Founder of a Religion to work wonders/ miracles. (2) The One True God being the source of everything and (3) The Universality (sāmānyatā), i.e. equal validity for every race on the surface of the earth.

Since I have given the full Sanskrit text in Devanāgarī as well as the Bengali script of the *Matapariksottaram* by Haracandra Tarkapañcānana, I think, I need not dilate on any specific aspect, because, the Text is very simple to understand.

Acknowledgement

Since the text is printed in Bengali, my two Bengali colleagues, viz. Ms. Sasvati Sen and Dr.Mrs. Sharmila Chatterji Bagchi copied down the entire text in Devanāgarī script. Ms. Sen helped me while getting the text composed on DTP in Devanāgarī – a work, which was nicely carried out by Shri Manoj Upadhyaya—a budding young scholar and a Ph.D. student in Sanskrit. I express my gratitude to all these three young and energetic colleagues of mine. I must also mention and thank two other scholar-friends of mine. viz. Dr. Mitali Chatterji, the Librarian of the Asiatic Society of Calcutta, for supplying to me a Xerox-copy of the Bengali text of this work and to

Prof. Dr. Richard Fox Young, for sending a copy of his Dissertation, viz. Resistant Hinduism-Sanskrit Sources on Anti Christian Apologetics in early nineteenth Century India, published from Vienna in 1981 A.D.

मतपरीक्षा

"A Sketch of the Argument for Christianity and Against Hindus" in Sanskrit verse by J Muir, Esq. Bengal Civil Services Calcutta, Bishop's College Press, 1839.

Preface

The principle of "becoming all things to all men" is not only sanctioned by human reason, but, enforced by Apostolical authority; and can, therefore, never be neglected by any Teacher without detriment to the legitimate effect of his instructions. Individual tastes are for the most part susceptible of being converted by a judicious and dexterous preceptor into the instruments of intellectual and moral benefit to their possessors. There is, doubtless, some one particular avenue by which the understanding and heart of every being may be more certainly and readily reached than by any other way; and what is true of individuals, is also true of nations, or of large bodies of men, similar in their natural character, situated in similar circumstances, and exposed to the action of the same influences. In their case, some particular scheme of instruction, formed on and adapted to their natural and adventitious peculiarities, must be above all others effective. But where truth has to contend against interest, prejudice, and the oppositions of sciences, which though "falsely so called" is yet the deeply revered object of a not altogether unintelligent devotion, it becomes more than ever necessary to call in every auxiliary force which can aid in undermining or beating down obstacles so formidable.

It is plain that this course is very necessary to be pursued with the learned Hindus. Their lofty ideas—springing (we may charitably hope) far more from delusion than from craft—of the antiquity of their nation and national institutions, of the particular dignity of their own priestly order, and of the sacredness of their Scriptures, handed down and interpreted, as they believe, by successive generations of inspired sages, conspire with baser suggestions of interest, and the fear of shame and worldly loss, to render them deaf to the voice of truth. If then this voice, by uttering the accents of their own venerated and polished language, can acquire any additional potency to charm and to persuade, the neglect of such a soothing medium of instruction appears to be nothing less than the needless abandonment of an important instrument of success in the most momentous of all enterprises. This argument acquires additional force if the Pandits are found to have a prejudice against the use of the vernacular tongues as the vehicles of religious and philosophical discussions; and if, as is the case, the knowledge of Sanskrit, thought (=though) limited to a small class in each province, is yet common, to the learned throughout whole continent of India.

These considerations appear to be sufficient to justify the attempt which has been made in these pages to follow (hauel passibus aequis) the example which has been set by the Rev. Dr. Mill, in his "Christa Sangita", of moulding the instruction intended for the learned men of India into a form congenial to their national models. A sketch of the argument is all that has been attempted, which ought undoubtedly to be followed by a more detailed statement. But until the subject has begun to be viewed with attention and interest, a brief abstract will probably be found as serviceable as an elaborate discussion.

The following is the plan of the tract:

Section I. Introduction; Being and character of God.

Section II. The need of Divine Guidance, or the necessity of Revelation.

Section III. Statement of the tests of a Divinely-revealed Religion.

Section IV. Proofs of Christianity.

Section V. Examination of Hinduism.

I should mention that, I am indebted to the works of Rev. Dr. Wilson, and the Rev. Mr. Mundy on Hinduism, for some ideas and quotations.

मतपरीक्षोत्तरम्
or
An Answer to
"A Sketch of the Argument For Christianity and Against Hinduism"
(मतपरीक्षा of, John Muir)
By
Hurachunder Turkapunchanun,
Calcutta, February, 1840. Printed at the Sumachu Chundrica.

Preface

My attention has been directed to an argument by Mr. Muir, in favour of Christianity and against Hinduism, in Sanskrit Metre. As a Hindu, I think, he has not proved that the Christian Revelation is true, nor that the Hindu Revelation is false. Entertaining this opinion, I have attempted an answer in the annexed verses. I would have chosen a more popular means of disquisition, but, as the learned gentleman has courted the contest is shlokas, I must not decline the challenge.

I am aware of the inutility of discussions on this subject and that it is impossible to prove the truth or falsity of any scheme of faith. Revelation itself implies a miracle. The first votaries must believe in humble reverence, the person really or falsely designating himself us the chosen of God. Each succeeding race of believers yields a blind and more pious acquiescence. A Moslim asserts that Muhammad was the Prophet of God, because he has asserted his divine missions and his assertion is recorded in the Koran. If I must break the silence, which is most prudent on such occasions, I reply, that I admit that Muhammad made these pretensions, but that, I consider him to be an imposter or insane—at least, on this subject—I have no pious prejudice in favour of the Koran, and reply without hesitation. The Moslim makes equally short work of the Christian or the Hindu faith.

I cannot find in Mr. Muir's shlokas any argument in favour of the truth of Christ's divine mission, which may not be used in support of the Hindu or Moslim revelation. In a word, asserted miracles have only the force of argument, when the mind is predisposed to a pious belief which dispenses with proof. The inference of a god from the works of nature is open to every reasoning being and common to all religious systems.

The truth of a revelation cannot be proved by an appeal to the beauty of its perceptive morality, nor can its falsity be established by imputing deformity to its institutions. The standard of beauty and deformity is arbitrary and a man with his limited reason is not able to scan the objects of the precepts, which he believes to have been divinely revealed.

In the annexed shlokas, I have met the cavils and arguments of Mr. Muir, in a mode, which will be perhaps more convincing to the Hindu than to him. But, using his own weapon, I have put questions to him in regard to Christianity, his satisfactory solutions of which would greatly serve the cause, he advocates and shakes the skepticism of those who pretend that belief should be preceded by conviction.

॥ मतपरीक्षोत्तरम् ॥
हरचन्द्र–तर्कपञ्चाननः।

मतपरीक्षोत्तरम्

मियुराख्येण अर्थात् केनचिदिङ्ग्लण्डीयेन हिन्दुधर्मद्वषाणखृष्ट–धर्मस्थापनपुरःसरं प्रकाशितस्य मतपरीक्षा नामकग्रन्थस्य उत्तरं हिन्दु–धर्मस्थापनखृष्टधर्मदूषणपूर्वकं मियुरसम्मतरीत्या गुरुशिष्यप्रस्तावेन श्रीहरचन्द्रतर्कपञ्चानेन विरचितम्।

अत्र सर्वसुगमार्थं हिन्दुपृष्टकबरादिशब्दानां संस्कृतानामपि व्यवहारः।

॥ श्रीगुरुः ॥
प्रथमः परिच्छेद ।

शिष्यः

नानाविधानां धर्माणां श्रवणे चञ्चलं मनः ।
जायतेऽत्र विशेषेण खृष्टधर्मप्रवर्तकाः ॥१॥

नगरे वापणे राजमार्गे क्रोशन्ति सर्वतः ।
अस्माकं धर्ममालम्ब्य चिरं व्याप्य सुखीभव ॥२॥

साम्प्रतं मियुराख्येण हिन्दुधर्मातिवैरिणा ।
खृष्टधर्मस्य माहात्म्यमुच्यते च मुहुर्मुहुः ॥३॥

तन्मे संशयकूपारबृहद्वीचिनिपातिनः।
यथार्थयुक्तिभिः सम्यगुध्दारः क्रियतां गुरो ॥४॥

गुरुः

शिष्य त्वद्वाक्यजातेन सन्तोषो मे महत्तरः ।
नेदृशः क्रियते प्रश्नः प्रायेण केनचित् क्वचित् ॥५॥

केवलं धूर्त्तपृष्टानां मायाजाले पतन् जनः ।
मद्यमांसादिलोभेन पृष्टकन्यादिरूपतः ॥६॥

मोहितो भोगलाभेच्छुरविचार्य स्वकं मतम् ।
खृष्टधर्मस्य दोषं वा नावेक्ष्य खृष्टिको भवेत् ॥७॥

तस्मान्मदुक्तिषु श्रद्धां विधाय श्रूयतां त्वया ।
तत्त्वतश्च स्वयं बुद्ध्वा मनसैव विचार्यताम् ॥८॥

ईश्वरोऽस्तीति केचिच्च केचिन्नास्तीति वादिनः ।
परलोकं न मन्यन्ते धर्माधर्मौ तथापरे ॥९॥

सर्वैः सह विवादेऽत्र नास्ति किञ्चित् प्रयोजनम् ।
केवलं वाक्यबाहुल्यं तस्मात्तत्त्यज्यते मया ॥१०॥

मियुरस्य मतेनैव मनस्ते चञ्चलीकृतम् ।
तस्मात् खार्ष्टञ्च वेदोक्तं धर्ममेव विचार्यते ॥११॥

यदि ग्रन्थेऽस्ति विश्वासो वेद एवावलम्ब्यताम् ।
यतोऽसौ सृष्टिकालादि चलितोऽस्ति महीतले ॥१२॥

ईशः सूर्येन्दुनक्षत्रप्रभृतीनां स्थिरां गतिम् ।
तथा वृक्षादिसस्यानां नियतं कालरूपकम् ॥१३॥

जीवानाञ्चैव सर्वेषामन्नस्थाननिरूपणम् ।
सृष्टिकाले विनिश्चित्य न धर्मं किञ्चिदुक्तवान् ॥१४॥

याते बहुतरे काले खृष्टद्वारा स्वकं मतम् ।
ज्ञापयामास केनात्र विश्वासो विदुषां भवेत् ॥१५॥

तस्मात् सृष्टिं समारभ्य यो धर्मश्चलितो भुवि ।
स एव सत्यो नान्योऽस्ति धर्मः कालान्तरोत्थितः ॥१६॥

शिष्यः

सृष्टिकालादिचलितो वेदोऽसावत्र का प्रभा ।
मूर्खाणां वञ्चनाथं चेत् कृतः स्याद्वञ्चकोत्तमैः ॥१७॥

गुरुः

श्रुतिस्मृतिपुराणेषु लिखनं दृश्यते सदा ।
सृष्टिकाले स्वयं ब्रह्मा तान् वेदान् व्यक्तमुक्तवान् ॥१८॥

लिखने चेदविश्वासः का प्रमा खृष्टधर्मके ।
युक्तिमात्रं समाश्रित्य वक्तव्यं नास्तिकं प्रति ॥१९॥

लिखनं मन्यमानस्य मियुरस्य मतं यतः ।
प्रकृतं तत्र वक्तव्यं नास्तिकं प्रति किञ्चन ॥२०॥

तथात्वे वाक्यबाहुल्यं केवलं निष्फलं भवेत् ।
इति निश्चित्य मनसा संक्षेपः क्रियते मया ॥२१॥

शिष्यः

वेदोऽस्तु मान्यः सर्वेषां मानवानामबाधतः ।
पुराणस्मृतितन्त्रेषु परस्परविरोधतः ॥२२॥

अप्रामाण्यस्य सन्देहो जायतेऽत्र पदे पदे ।
तथैव सृष्टिकालादि चलितं नैव किञ्चन ॥२3॥

तत्तच्छास्त्रं निर्मितञ्च सृष्टेः पश्चाच्चिरे गते ।
कुत्रचिद्विष्णुमाहात्म्यं घृणा विष्णोस्तथा क्वचित् ॥२४॥

शक्तिरुद्रादिदेवानामेवंरूपेण भूरिशः ।
प्रधानत्वाप्रधानत्वे वैपरीत्येन वर्णिते ॥२५॥

गुरुः

वेदानुयायि यच्छास्त्रं तद्ग्राह्यं विदुषां भवेत् ।
वेदार्थविपरीतं यत् सर्वैस्तत्त्यज्यते बुधैः ॥२६॥

वेदार्थस्य दुरूहत्वात्तस्य टीकास्वरूपतः ।
श्रुतिस्मृतिपुराणानि निर्मितानि महर्षिभिः ॥२७॥

अतो वेदप्रमाणत्वात्तेषां प्रामाण्यमुच्यते ।
गतेऽपि सुचिरे काले निर्मितावपि मान्यता ॥२८॥

आपाततो यद्विरुद्धं दृश्यतेऽत्र परस्परम् ।
विश्वेशचित्तयोगेन तन्निवार्यं सुबुद्धिभिः ॥२९॥

इतिहासवर्णनायां न तात्पर्यमृषेः क्वचित् ।
पुरावृत्तच्छलेनैव धर्ममार्गः प्रदर्शितः ॥३०॥

वर्णनायामतो यद्यदलग्नमिव दृश्यते ।
तद् गृहीत्वा विवादोऽत्र न कर्तव्यःसुबुद्धिभिः ।।३१।।

वर्णनायामसंलग्नं खृष्टशास्त्रेऽपि लक्ष्यते ।
प्रस्तावे तत् प्रपञ्चस्य मया वक्तव्यमेव तत् ।।३२।।

ब्रह्मोपासनमेवास्ते मुख्यं शास्त्रेषु दर्शितम् ।
तस्य दुःसाध्यता हेतोर्मूर्खाणां दुर्लभा गतिः ।।३३।।

अतः साकारदेवस्य भजनं क्रियते भुवि ।
तेन मूर्खस्य लोकस्य मोक्षप्राप्तिः शनैर्भवेत् ।।३४।।

यथा समुद्रो गन्तव्यो नानानद्यादिवर्त्मना ।
तथा ब्रह्म समासाद्यं शिवविष्ण्वादिसेवया ।।३५।।

यो यो यत्पथमातिष्ठेत्तस्य श्रद्धाविवृद्धये ।
तत्पथस्य प्रशंसास्ति निन्दा चापरवर्त्मनः ।।३६।।

एवं क्रमेण हे शिष्य देवानां स्तुतिनिन्दयोः ।
प्रवृत्तिः सम्मता लोके न तु सा पारमार्थिकी ।।३७।।

शिष्यः

वेदे न तावत् प्रस्तावो दृश्यते रामकृष्णयोः ।
पुराणादिषु नैवास्ते तयोश्चेष्टितमद्भुतम् ।।३८।।

मियुरेणेति यत् प्रोक्तं तत्र किं कथ्यतां गरो ।।३९।।

गुरुः

मियुरस्य भ्रमस्तत्र पक्षपातोऽथवा पुनः ।
जातिभ्रंशार्थमन्येषां प्रवृत्तस्येच्छयान्धता ।।४०।।

अथर्ववेदशेषांशे वर्णनं रामकृष्णयोः ।
दृश्यते दृश्यतां ग्रन्थं बहिष्कृत्य बुभुत्सुभिः ।।४१।।

कृष्णः स्ववामहस्तेन त्राणाय व्रजवासिनाम् ।
धारयामास विपुलं शैलं गोवर्द्धनाभिधम् ।।४२।।

रामस्य पादस्पर्शेन पाषाणो नरतां गतः ।
इत्याद्यद्भुतवृत्तान्तं दृष्ट्वा नास्तीति वादिनः ।।४३।।

कीदृशः पक्षपातोऽस्ति वक्तुमेतत्र शक्यते ।
स्वीयजातीयधर्मेषु बद्धवा विश्वासमुत्तमम् ।
परकीयेषु विश्वासं कुर्वतोऽत्यन्तमूर्खता ।।४४।।

शिष्यः

कृष्णस्य राधागमनं ब्रह्मणोऽप्यात्मजागतिः ।
इत्यादिदेवचरिते ज्ञाते भक्तिः कथं भवेत् ।।४५।।

गुरुः

ईश्वरस्य न दहोऽस्ति पूर्वमुक्तमिदं मया ।
केवलं लोकसिद्ध्यर्थं देहस्तेन समाश्रितः ।।४६।।

न देहधारिणां शक्यः कर्तुमिन्द्रियनिग्रहः ।
सहजेनेति लोकानां शिक्षार्थं विदधे तथा ।।४७।।

न जातु देववाण्यस्ति प्रवृत्ताविन्द्रियार्थके ।
तस्मान्मनः प्रयत्नेन स्थाप्यमिन्द्रियनिग्रहे ।।४८।।

तथा यो येन भावेन भजते परमेश्वरम् ।
तं प्रतीशस्तथामूर्तिर्भवेदेव न संशयः ।।४९।।

यतो व्रजाङ्गनाः सर्वाः स्वामिभावेन भेजिरे ।
परमेशं तथा सोऽपि तासां काममपूरयत् ।
न तु तेन समादिष्टमेवं कार्यं नरैरिति ।।५०।।

शिष्यः

केषुचितन्त्रशास्त्रेषु दुष्कर्माप्युपदिश्यते ।
कथं तत्तादृशं शास्त्रं माननीयं मनीषिभिः ।।५१।।

सर्वत्र त्रिविधा लोका उत्तमाधममध्यमाः ।
धर्मोऽपि त्रिविधो ज्ञेयस्तेषां सेव्यो यथार्हतः ।।५२।।

उत्तमस्य हि धर्मस्य कठिनत्वात्र मध्यमैः ।
सेवां कर्तुं सुशक्यास्ति तथा नीचैर्न पूर्वयोः ।।५३।।

एवं यदि कृतं न स्यात् कथमल्पधियस्तदा ।
धर्मे प्रवृत्तिर्जायेत सुखसंलग्नचेतसः ।।५४।।

यथैव मधुलोभेन बालस्य कटुकौषधे ।
प्रवृत्तिस्तादृशी वृत्तिर्मूर्खाणां धर्मकर्मणि ।।५५।।

शिष्यः

गङ्गास्नानेन चेत् सर्वं पापं नश्यति तत्त्वतः ।
निवृत्तिः कुत्सिते कार्ये कथं स्यात् पापचेतसाम् ।।५६।।

गुरुः

शृणु तात्पर्यमेतस्य न हि केवलशब्दतः ।
पूर्वापरञ्च नावेक्ष्य कर्त्तव्यो धर्मनिश्चयः ॥५७॥

ये सदा धर्मकार्येषु रताः संशुद्धमानसाः ।
दैवात् कृते कुकार्ये तैर्गङ्गास्नानं विधीयते ॥५८॥

उत्साहभङ्गो नैव स्यात्तेषां सत्कर्मकारिणाम् ।
न तु ये पापकार्येषु रता निन्दितचेतसः ।
तेषां शुद्धिविधानार्थं गङ्गास्नानं नियन्त्रितम् ॥५९॥

शिष्यः

मियुरस्य मते मुक्तेर्यादृग्रूपं प्रपञ्चितम् ।
तादृशं वा ततो भिन्नं किं गुरो कथ्यते त्वया ॥६०॥

गुरुः

नित्यानन्दस्वरूपत्वं मुक्तेर्यत्तेन दर्शितम् ।
कथं तत् समभवेच्छिष्य त्वयैवात्र विविच्यिताम् ॥६१॥

शरीरेण विना नैव सुखं लोकेऽनुभूयते ।
मुक्त्यवस्थासु चेद्देहो दुःखं तत्राप्यबाधकम् ॥६२॥

अपरं यच्च तेनोक्तमात्मानो विभुना कृताः ।
तत्रेयं जायते शङ्का किं विभोः पक्षपातिता ॥६३॥

अन्यथात्मा सुखी कश्चिद्दुःखी कश्चित् कथं भवेत् ।
सुकृते दुष्कृते वापि सदृशीच्छा न वा कथम् ॥६४॥

शिष्यः

भारतीयेषु शास्त्रेषु चातुर्वर्णविभागतः ।
धर्मस्य पन्था निर्दिष्टः कथं सेव्योऽन्यदेशजैः ॥६५॥

गुरुः

चत्वार एव वर्णाः स्युः सृष्टिकाले विनिर्मिताः ।
तेषां कृते सुधर्मस्य लक्षणं ब्रह्मणा कृतम् ॥६६॥

दुष्टाचारेण ये भ्रष्टाः स्वधर्माद्यवनादयः ।
कथं तैः सेव्यमानोऽस्तु वेदधर्मः सनातनः ॥६७॥

धृतिः क्षमा दमोऽस्तेयं शौचमिन्द्रियनिग्रहः ।
धीर्विद्या सत्यमक्रोधो दशकं धर्मलक्षणम् ।।६८।।

एवं साधारणैर्धर्मैर्यापिताशेषजीवनाः ।
परजन्मनि हिन्दुत्वं प्राप्य धर्माधिकारिणः ।।६९।।

शिष्यः

भारतीयेषु शास्त्रेषु विप्रस्यैव प्रधानता ।
वर्ण्यत फलतः कश्चिद्विशेषो नोपलभ्यते ।।७०।।

यथा विप्रस्तथा शूद्रा मलमूत्रविसर्जन ।
भोजने कान्तया योगे विशेषो नास्ति कश्चन ।।७१।।

गुरुः

यथा प्रजा तथा राजा यथा मूर्खस्तथा बुधः ।
पूर्वोक्ते विषये किन्तु विशेषः कर्मयोगतः ।।७२।।

विप्राः सदा देवकार्ये नियुक्ता धर्मतत्पराः ।
परेषां धर्मतत्काराः कुकर्मपरिपन्थिनः ।।७३।।

तपः क्लेशसहाः शान्ता निर्जितेन्द्रियशक्तिकाः ।
यत्र कुत्सितकार्येऽस्ति प्रायश्चितं तु यादृशम् ।।७४।।

शूद्रस्य ब्रह्मणस्तस्मादधिकं शास्त्रचोदितम् ।
अतो लोकैस्तु मन्यन्ते ब्राह्मणा उत्तमा इति ।।७५।।

पूर्वोक्ताचारशून्यास्तु ब्राह्मणाः शूद्रवत् स्मृताः ।
शास्त्रे लोकेऽपि दृश्यन्ते मानभाजो न ते तथा ।।७६।।

द्वितीयः परिच्छेदः

शिष्यः

सम्यक् शास्त्रानुसारेण धर्ममुक्तं त्वया गुरो ।
यदि जानासि तद्ब्रूहि खृष्टधर्म तु कीदृशम् ।।१।।

गुरुः

माहात्म्यं खृष्टधर्मस्य प्रोच्यते पृष्टसंज्ञकैः ।
तस्मान्मया न वक्तव्यं सर्वैस्तच्छ्रूयते यतः ।।२।।

न दोषः संशयो वापि पृष्टवर्गैः प्रकाशते ।
तस्मात् स एव वक्तव्यस्तेन विज्ञैर्विविच्यताम् ।।३।।

मेरिनाम्नी खृष्टमाता बहुभिर्याजकैर्वृता ।
एकदेवालयेऽतिष्ठत् षोडशाब्दवयोऽवधि ।।४।।

तत्र गर्भान्विता भूत्वा जनयामास संशयम् ।
स्वामिनो निश्चयं वापि ततः सोऽचिन्तयत् सदा ।।५।।

स्वप्ने चिन्ताकुलत्वेन तेन दृष्टः समागतः ।
देवदूतो जगादोच्चैर्मा चिन्ता क्रियतामिति ।।६।।

ईश्वरेणैव धर्मात्मा जनितोऽस्ति स्त्रियां तव ।
न शङ्का व्यभिचारस्य तस्मात् कार्या त्वयानघ ।।७।।

एवं स्वप्नस्य वृत्तान्ते सर्वत्र प्रकटीकृते ।
स्वीयदोषापहारयत याजकास्तेऽपि सम्मताः ।।८।।

तदानीं याजकादीनां प्राधान्यं सर्वथा स्थितम् ।
तन्मतेन मतं जातं प्रजानामप्यरोषतः ।।९।।

विचारयन्तु विद्वांसो युवत्याः पुरुषैः सह ।
वासो गर्भस्य हेतुः स्यात् स्वप्नो वा स्यात् प्रमात्मकः ।।१०।।

स्वप्नो यदि प्रमाणं स्यात् पुत्रदारादिनाशतः ।
बहुशो जायते स्वप्ने कथं संस्थितदर्शनम् ।।११।।

स्वप्ने दृष्टं यथार्थं स्यान्नवेति ज्ञायते बुधैः ।
स्वप्नः प्रमाणं युद्धर्मे ग्राह्यता तस्य किं भवेत् ।।१२।।

लिउकेनोच्यते किन्तु स्वप्ने मेरी निबोधिता ।
न तद्भर्ता कथं तत्र विश्वासो विदुषां भवेत् ।।१३।।

तया चेत् स्वीयदोषस्य गोपनार्थं निवेदितम् ।
स्वप्ने दृष्टमेवमेवं तेन किं सत्यता भवेत् ।।१४।।

स्वप्नस्य निर्णयो नास्ति ग्रन्थयोर्जानमार्कयोः ।
विचारयन्तु धीमन्तः किं स्यात् सत्यत्वधीरिह ।।१५।।

एवं स जारजातोऽपि याजकैरपि संस्तुतः ।
धर्मात्माहमिति ज्ञात्वा धर्म वक्तुं प्रचक्रमे ।।१६।।

कृत्वा तद्वाचि विश्वासमविचार्य कथञ्चन ।
अल्पबुद्धिजनास्तस्य जाताः सेवापरायणाः ।।१७।।

स्वीयदोषाच्छादनार्थमूचुरद्भुतचेष्टितम् ।
तथा तन्मायजा तेऽपि मोहिता हतबुद्धयः ।।१८।।

ईश्वरोऽयमिति ग्रन्थे वर्णनां चक्रुरद्भुताम् ।
एवं क्रमेण धर्मस्य प्रचारो जनितो भुवि ॥१९॥

भविष्यदुक्तिरपरं प्रमाणं विनिगद्यते ।
तत्र विज्ञा विस्मिताः स्युर्द्विपदाः पशवः किमु ॥२०॥

खृष्टिकाः केन विश्वासस्तैरेवं क्रियतेऽन्यथा ।
यदि भाविपदार्थानां वक्तारो देवमूर्तयः ॥२१॥

भवेयुरद्भुता वा र्ता शिष्यः सङ्गच्छते तदा ।
न जातु खृष्टिके शास्त्रे वर्ण्यन्ते तेऽपि देवताः ॥२२॥

कथं मानवलोकानां भाविनि स्यान्मनोगतिः ।
यदि मर्त्येषु पूर्वोक्ता शक्तिरीशेन दीयते ॥२३॥

कथं वा दृश्यते नैव कश्चिद्वक्ता तथादृशः ।
केवलं मूर्खलोकानां मोहाय वञ्चका नराः ॥२४॥

एवंविधप्रमाणानि चक्रुरीशाहितान्यपि ।
तथा भाव्युक्तिमध्येऽस्ति वर्णनं शिष्य दृश्यताम् ॥२५॥

वितल्हमाभिधे देशे यिहूदीनां भविष्यति ।
राज्यं परन्तु खृष्टस्य जन्मनः समनन्तरम् ॥२६॥

राज्यनाशोऽजनिष्टैषां कथं मिथ्या तथोक्तिषु
यद्ग्रन्थानां प्रमाणत्वात् खृष्टधर्मस्य मान्यता ॥२७॥

तेषां मिथो विरोधे स्यात् सर्वेषामेव हेयता ।
माथियोः प्रथमाध्याये वर्णना शिष्य दृश्यते ॥२८॥

खृष्टस्य जन्मतः पूर्वमाब्राहामादनन्तरम् ।
दाउदावधि यिष्वन्ताः अष्टविंशतिपूरुषाः ॥२९॥

किन्तु लिउकसंज्ञस्य तृतीयाध्यायवर्णने ।
तदादयस्तदन्ताः स्युश्चत्वारिंशत्त्रिभिर्युता ॥३०॥

एवं संख्याविरोधोऽस्ति तथा नाम्नां न तुल्यता ।
तन्मृत्युसमये चासीदन्धकारावृता मही ॥३१॥

विदीर्णा भूधराः सर्वे भूमिकम्पोऽभवद्भृशम् ।
देहाश्च मृतलोकानां निष्क्रमान्ताः कबरान्तरात् ॥३२॥

बभ्रमुर्बहिरित्येवं माथियुः प्राह विस्तरात् ।
तदानीन्तनवृत्तान्तजातं जानन्तु पण्डितः (ताः) ॥३३॥

विशिष्य व्यलिखत् सर्वं किन्तु किञ्चन नेदृशम् ।
गते तत्कबरं द्रष्टुं मेरिसंज्ञे स्त्रियौ परम् ।।३४।।

रात्रिशेषे दिने भानोरित्याह माथियुः कविः ।
मेरिजोनाप्रभूतयो योषितो बहुसंख्यकाः ।।३५।।

गातस्तद्दृष्टुमित्येवमुवाच लिउकः पुनः ।
जानो लिलेख तद्दृष्टुं मेरिमेक्डिलनाभिधा ।।३६।।

जगाम केवलं शिष्य नान्या कापि गता तदा ।
मार्कस्य तु मते दुष्टिर्न रात्रावुषसि स्मृता ।।३७।।

तद्विचारय शिष्य त्वं सत्यत्वं क्व प्रतिष्ठितम् ।
यदा दिवंगतः खृष्टो निष्क्रान्तः कबरान्तरात् ।।३८।।

तदा मेरिद्वयं प्राह स्वर्गीयो दूत आगतः ।
खृष्टो दिवमुपैतीति तद्वाक्यप्रतिबोधिते ।।३९।।

ते परं दृष्टवत्यौ तमित्याह माथियु : सुधीः ।
तस्य शिष्यगणाः सर्वे गोपनीयस्थले किल ।।४०।।

कस्यचिद्भूधरस्यासन् विद्रुता राजभीतितः ।
पुनर्जीवन् समस्तेभ्यस्तेभ्यः स्वं परिदर्शयन् ।।४१।।

आरुरोह दिवं खृष्ट-इत्याह लिउकः पुनः ।
दर्शयनृ पुनरात्मानं पर (परं) शिष्यद्वयाय सः ।।४२।।

आरुरोह दिवं खृष्ट एवं मार्कस्य सम्मतम् ।
एवं विरोधादेतेषां परस्परमनेकधा ।।४३।।

नैव प्रामाण्यमेतेषु शिष्य कस्यापि गम्यते ।
अतस्तात्कालिकैर्भव्यं (र्भाव्यं) विज्ञैर्वा लिखितं न तत् ।।४४।।

तथात्वे कथमन्योन्यं विरोधः परिदृश्यते ।
तस्माद्विजेयमेतद्यत्काले बहुतरे गते ।।४५।।

धर्मभ्रंशाय लोकानां लिखितं वंचकैः परम् ।
वर्ण्यते माथियोर्ग्रन्थे नक्षत्रोदयदर्शनात् ।।४६।।

खृष्टजन्म ज्ञायते स्म पूर्वदेशीयपण्डितैः ।
तथा पण्डितवर्गस्य खृष्टदर्शनचेतसः ।।४७।।

पन्थानं दर्शयामास तत्रक्षत्रं पुरोऽव्रजत् ।
यत्र स्थाने स्थितः खृष्टस्तदूर्ध्वे निश्चलं तथा ।।४८।।

जातं नक्षत्रमेतेन खृष्टस्थानं निरूपितम् ।
विज्ञैर्विवेच्यमेतस्मिन् कुत्रचित् किंचितदीदृशम् ।।४९।।

नक्षत्रं जायते दृश्यं कस्यचिज्जन्मसूचकम् ।
अचेतनं हि नक्षत्रमिंङ्ग्लण्डीयमते स्थिरम् ।।५०।।

कथं ज्ञात्वा खृष्टजन्म दर्शयामास पध्दतिम् ।
सर्वदा परिवर्तः स्यादस्य धर्मस्य रीतिषु ।।५१।।

कथं तत्तर्कयुक्तानां माननीयं मनीषिणाम् ।
केथालिकः प्रटेष्टान्टस्तथा डिसेष्टरः परः ।।५२।।

प्रेस्वेटेरीयानित्येते परिवर्ता यथाक्रमम् ।
सृष्टिकाले जगत्कर्ता धर्मरीतिविनिर्मितौ ।।५३।।

न शक्तः खृष्टरूपेण पश्चात् सा तेन निर्मिता ।
खृष्टे मृतेऽपि पोपादिरूपेणैते विनिर्मिताः ।।५४।।

परिवर्ताः परेशेन नैकदोद्बुद्धबुद्धिना ।
मियुरादिस्वरूपेण तेनाद्यापि विनिर्गितिः ।।५५।।

क्रियते धर्ममार्गस्येत्येवं यो मन्यते जनः ।
स एव धर्मतत्त्वज्ञो नास्मादृगतिदुर्मतिः ।।५६।।

एवं खृष्टीयधर्मस्य सत्यता शिष्य बुध्यताम् ।
अपरः संशयः शिष्य तद्देशीयमहाजनाः ।।५७।।

अत्युच्चपदसंयुक्ताः पक्षपातविवर्जिताः ।
दृश्यन्ते बहवो विज्ञा न मन्यन्ते यिषोर्मतम् ।।५८।।

न वा कदाचिद्गच्छन्ति चर्चे ते भजनार्थिनः ।
केवलं पूर्वपुरुषैरल्पबुध्दिभिराश्रितः (ताः) ।।५९।।

धर्मोऽयमिति मात्रेण मान्यास्ते खृष्टिका इति ।
राज्यशासनमध्ये यद् वर्तते धर्मशासनम् ।।६०।।

तेन खृष्टमुरीकृत्य ते जाताः कर्मकारकाः ।
सत्यत्वे धर्ममार्गस्य नैवं भवति कुत्रचित् ।।६१।।

ज्ञातायां सत्यतायां यत् सर्वे यत्नपरायणाः ।
भजेरन् पैतृकं धर्मं शासनस्याप्रयोजनम् ।।६२।।

आस्ते तुरुष्कदेशस्तु पारसीदेशपश्चिमे ।
कानष्टान्टीनोपलाख्यं नगरं तत्र वर्तते ।।६३।।

तुरुष्कराजधानी च तत्रैवास्ते चिरन्तनी ।
कानष्टनिति विख्याता तत्रैकोऽभूत्रृपः पुरा ।।६४।।

असौ मूर्खतया खृष्टधर्मं जग्राह मोहितः ।
प्रचारयितुमैच्छच्च धर्ममेतदकिञ्चनम् ।।६५।।

छलेन धनदानेन कौशलेन बलेन च ।
ग्राहयामास तद्धर्मं स्वराज्यस्थान् समन्ततः ।।६६।।

राजशासनमात्रेण ततः प्रभृति केवलम् ।
प्रचारो जायतेऽद्यापि नृणां स्वेच्छा न तद्ग्रहे ।।६७।।

यदि कश्चित् सप्रकाशं खृष्टधर्मं न मन्यते ।
तदैवास्य विशापेन क्रियते दण्डनिर्णयः ।।६८।।

न प्राप्तव्यं राजकर्म तेनेति घुष्यते मुहुः ।
एवं क्रमेण पूर्वस्मात् कालादद्यापि मान्यते ।।६९।।

यस्य धर्मस्य तत्कि स्यादन्यैर्ग्राह्यं कदाचन ।
हियूमश्चैव टाम्पेनो बलटायस्तथा परः ।।७०।।

पामर् पेनोगिवानद्या बहवो विज्ञमानवाः ।
तर्कयामासुरेतेभ्यः पृष्टेभ्यो निर्भया यतः ।।७१।।

तस्मात्तात्रास्तिकानाहुः पृष्टवर्गा निरुत्तराः ।
बाहुल्यशङ्कया नैव मतं तेषां विलिख्यते ।
तेषां ग्रन्थास्तु दृश्यन्तां विस्तारार्थबुभुत्सुभिः ।।७२।।

।। विज्ञापनम् ।।

एतद्देशीयलोकानां सहस्रात्र्यूनमानवाः ।
जानन्ति संस्कृतां भाषमतः प्रायेण निर्मलम् ।। ७३।।

एतादृग्लिखनं तस्मान्मियुरः प्रार्थ्यते मया ।
यदि तेन प्रकाश्यं स्याद्वारं वारमितीदृशम् ।।७४।।

तदेग्लंडीयभाषा वा बांगला वोभयाथवा ।
ग्राह्या मया तया देयमुत्तरं तस्य निश्चितम् ।।७५।।

यादृशं संस्कृतं तेन लिखितं तत्तु नोत्तमम् ।
निपुणाः पण्डिता यस्मात्र भावार्थविबोधने ।।७६।।

समर्थाः केवलं खृष्टगीतातुल्यं विनिर्मितम् ।
खृष्टगीता विनिर्मातू रचनैवेति बुध्यते ।।७७।।

अपरं विनिवेद्यं मे वयं नोऽपृष्टवत् सदा ।
पालिता राजवित्तेन न वा भूरिधनान्विताः ।।७८।।

तस्माद्विना वेतनेन न शुक्ताः क्रमिकोत्तरे ।
न वा मुद्रार्थमेतस्य व्ययं कर्तुं पुनः ।।७९।।

क्रियते यदि तेनैव श्रमव्ययविशोधनम् ।
तदाहं सर्वयत्नेन नियुक्तोऽस्म्यत्र कर्मणि ।।८०।।

किमर्थं तेन दातव्यं धनमेवंविधं वृथा ।
इति नैवास्ति वक्तव्यं यतः सर्वोद्यमेन सः ।।८१।।

खृष्टधर्मग्राहणार्थं प्रवृत्तो व्ययपूर्वकम् ।
खृष्टधर्मस्य सत्यत्वं मिथ्यात्वं वेदवर्त्मनः ।।८२।।

यदि बोधितमेव स्यात्तदाहं बन्धुभिः सह ।
खृष्टधर्मं ग्रहीष्यामि प्रतिज्ञेयं कृता मया ।।८३।।

Vyādibhaktitaranginị̄ and Gohārīvisaharī Pujābidhi: A Study

7

AMALENDU BHATTACHARJEE
JAHAR KANTI SEN

One method (Pujābidhi) of celebrating the Pujā of Manasā, when performed with great pomp and grandeur, is the Puthi Vyāḍibhaktitaranginị̄, which is preserved in the collection of Puthis in the University of Dhaka, Bangladesh. The Call No. of the Puthi is K-531.1; the Puthi which is about hundred and fifty years old has 15 folios. The first as well as last page is empty. The measure of the Puthi is 14" × 2¾" and it is written in hand made paper. In the initial pages there are only three lines in each page and in the last pages four lines. The Puthi is incomplete; the last part has not been written. There are two parts in the Puthi — Pramāṇataraṅga and Prayogataraṅga. In the Pramāṇ part supporting quotations have been given from different Puranas, Tantra and Smritiśāstras, for example Gauḍa-Mithilā Kṛtyasār, Suddhidīpikā, Gauḍa-Mithilā prācyādi kṛtyasār, Kṛityacintāmaṇi, Śāntidīpikā, etc. The Pramāṇ part has been written in imitation of Smriti, Agama, Puranas and Lokaprabād (Folk belief). About Lokaprabād it has been maintained:

> *te ca bhutaḍākinyādytiśāntyartham laukikauṣadhamantrādayo-viṣaharīmangalacaṇḍikāgītādayaśca.*

(The folk medicines and incantations which are used to put to rest ghosts and witches and the songs relating to Viṣahari Mañgalcaṇḍikā have become famous as Lokaprabād).

Only a small part of Prayoga has been written. First, the methods of Adhivās have been written. The copyist did not proceed after writing about Ghataśodhana. The Puṣpikā (colophon) part has been written after the completion of Pramāṇataraṅga: Vidyāpati composed Vyāḍibhaktitaranginị̄ in accordance with the orders of the brave conqueror of battles Sri Darpanarayana Deva.

The Puthi was kept in the house of Krishnadas Acharya Choudhury, the Zaminder of Muktagacha in the then district of Mymensingha. Krishnadas Acharya Choudhury was a scholar and patron of learning. But Krishnadas had never revealed to any one that he had in his collection a Puthi containing the Bhanitā of Vidyāpati. When he donated his collection to the University of Dhaka, this manuscript came to the notice of Subodh Chandra Bandopadhay, the custodian of the collection of Puthis. At his request Prof. Ganeshcharan Bose wrote an article on this Puthi in New Indian Antiquary (Vol. VII no. 3 & 4, June and July 1944), but he did not publish the whole Puthi. Later on Prof. Ahmad Shareef of the University of Dhaka wrote in the magazine 'Itihas' (1375) published from Dhaka, an article under the title 'Vyāḍibhaktitaranginī: Maithil Kavi Vidyāpati Viracita' and published in it the original version as well as the translation. The Bengali transliteration of the original Sanskrit Puthi was done by Prof. Santosh Chandra Bhattacharjee of the Department of History, Dhaka University.

So far as the title of the method, scholars are of the opinion that the Sanskrit word 'Vyāḍa' is masculine, meaning serpent; the feminine is 'Vyāḍi'. In the said method Manasā is called 'Vyāḍi'.

As already mentioned, the method of the grand and pompous worship of Manasā has been described in the Puthi. Clear instructions have been given as to which gods and goddesses are to be worshipped in the Pramāṇataraṅga:

lakṣmīdhareṇa naurdattā yasmānmadhukarābhidhā
tasmānmanoramāṃ nāvaṃ kṛtvā tatra prapūjayet
mṛnmayīṃ pratimāṃ kṛtvā devatādyaiḥ samāvṛtāṃ
ghattayitavā vicitrāñca pūjayed gītanartanaih /...
adhamā viṃśahastā nau cattāriṃścca madhyamā
uttamā ṣaṣṭihastā ca śatahastottamottamā /
caturdaśakarānyunā naukā parikīrtitā
sannidhau bhūtanāthasya vipulāyāśca nartane
ye samāgatāḥ draṣṭuṃ tāṃstu tatsthāna prapujayet
brahmāṇaṃ mādhavaṃ rudram vāṇīṃ laksmīñca pārvatim
kārtikeyam gaṇeśañca kāliyaṃ pannagāṣṭakaṃ /
jaratkārumastikañca martye candradharam tathā /
svarṇarekhāñca tatpatnīṃ putraṃ lakṣmīdharaṃ tathā /
tatpatnīṃ vipulāñcāpi śrīdharākhyaṃ dvijaṃ tathā /
yaśodharāñca daivajñaṃ karṇadhārañca durlabhaṃ /
agre gaṇeśaṃ naukāyāḥ pattīnaṣṭau manoharān /
bhāṇḍāriṃścāstradharān madhyeh'gre mulake tathā /
lekhyāṃ rajakīñcaiva sugandhāñca tathāparām /

sureśvarīṃ tathā durgāṃ devīṃ dikṣu samantataḥ /
indrādilokapālāmśca sāyudhāṃśca svavāhanān /

(As Lakṣmīḍhara gave a boat called Madhukara so a beautiful boat is to be built in which the Pujā is to be performed. A clay image of Manasā is to be built and then variously adorned, surrounded by all gods and goddesses and then worshipped in the accompaniment of dance and song... the boat 20 hands long is the inferior, 40 hands long is mediocre, 60 hands long is good and 100 hands long is very good. The boat must have a length of 14 hands at the least. Those who assembled before Bhutanath to see the dance performance of Behulā are also to be worshipped, among them are Brahmā, Mādhava, Rudra, Sarasvatī, Laksmī, Pārvatī, Kārtika, Ganeśa, Kāliya, Aṣṭ anāga, Jaratkāru, Āstika, Chandradhar and his wife Svarnarekhā, his son Lakṣmīdhara and son's wife Bipulā, Dwija Śridhar, fortune-teller Jaśodhara, Durlav steersman. At the beginning Ganeśa and eight beautiful boatmen are to be worshipped; Weapon-holding Bhāndāri is to be worshipped at the beginning, at the middle and the ending. Lekhyā, Rajaki, Sugandhā, Sureśvarī, Durgā, all the gods of all the sides and Indra with his weapons and carrier and the Lokapālas are to be worshipped).

Manasā and all the gods and goddesses assembled in the Devasabhā at the time of the dance of Behulā are to be placed in the boat minimum 14 hands long and then worshipped. The specific days of worship are Thursday and Sunday in the Pañchamī Tithi or the Daśamī or Troyodaśī Tithi of the Suklapaksya (bright half). The months are Vaiśākha, Aṣāḍa and Śrāvaṇa.

Scholars have expressed their opinions about 'Vyāḍibhaktitaranginī' and the method of worship described in it. Prof. Ahmad Shareef called it a 'rare wealth' and concluded that the Puthi of the Maithil poet describing the method of worship of Manasā may have become non-extant in Mithila, but there is the probability that the manuscript is still extant in East Bengal, for Manasā Pujā has attained the status of a national festival in East Bengal.[1]

Sukumar Sen wrote, "The method of worship of Manasā as prescribed by Vidyāpati is as huge an affair as the worship of Durgā... these images were also built of clay, also painted in 'Vicitrā.' Vrindavan Das has referred to the clay images. 'Vicitrā' means a huge fan, that is, a 'Pat' of the shape of a fan. The tradition of the worship of Manasā painted in the 'Pat' is still current in North Bengal, and especially in the district of Goalpara in Assam."[2]

Ashutosh Bhattacharjee has expressed doubt about whether 'Vyāḍibhaktitaranginī' was composed by the Maithil poet Vidyāpati, and wrote, "Although this is written in Sanskrit' and imposed upon Vidyāpati, the only copy of this Puthi has been discovered in the district of Mymensingh in East Bengal. So it cannot be doubtlessly accepted to have been really composed by Vidyāpati, the Vaisnava poet of the medieval period."[3]

About the non-existence of any copied version of this Puthi, his conclusion is, "The Puthi has been transported from Mithila to East Bengal by some means. The reason is, the worship of Manasā could not be widespread among the upper classes of the society in Mithila; so this Puthi was not copied there, and as it was written in Sanskrit, it was not copied in East Bengal even after taken there."[4]

Scholars have acknowledged 'Vyāḍibhaktitaranginī' as the only composition on the especial method of the worship of Manasā. So this Puthi was supposed to have been written in Mithila and the method of worship of Manasā described in it is accepted as the method followed in the Mithila region. It may be pointed out that in the Barak Valley at least two Puthis on the same subject have been discovered. But the two manuscripts bear the title 'Gohārīviṣaharī Pujābidhi'.[5] It is worth mentioning that in the Jatindra Mohan Sangrahashala in the Bangiya Jatiya Siksha Parishad also there are two Puthis on 'Gohārīviṣaharī Pujābidhi'.[6] The Puthi found in the Barak Valley, on the basis of which the present article is being written, does not contain the Stuti part; rather the Pramāṇa part begins directly :

om namo gaṇeśāya
atha gohārīviṣaharī pujāvidhiḥ / tat promāṇaṃ /
tatra garuda samhitāyām jaimini praśne kapila vākyam /
sarvve nidrānvita devāḥ kalaujāgartti pannagī /
tasmāttāṃ pūjayedbhaktyā pratyakṣa phaladāyinīṃ /
lakṣmīdhareṇa naurddhttā yasmānmadhukarābhidhā /
tasmānmadhukaraṃ nāvaṃ kṛtvā tatra prapūjayet /
mṛnmayīṃ pratimāṃ kṛtvā devatādaiḥ samāvṛtāṃ /
gaṭhitvā suvicitrāñca pūjayedbhakti narttanaiḥ /
adhamā viṃśahastā nauścattāriṃśacca madhyamā /
uttamā ṣaṣṭihastāca śatahastottamottamā /
caturddaśakarānyhnān naukā parīkīrttitā /...
sannidhaubhūtanāthasya vipulāyāśca narttane /
ye ye samāgatādraṣṭuṃ gaṭhitvātān prapūjayet /
brahmāṇaṃ mādhavaṃ rudraṃ vāṇīm lakṣmīñca pārvatīṃ /
kārtikeyaṃ gaṇeśañca nāgānaṣṭau ca kāliyam /
jaratkāru muniñcaiva marttye candradharattathā /
svarṇarekhāñca tatpatnīṃ putraṃ lakṣmīdharantathā /
tatpatnīṃ vipulāñcaiva śrīdharākhyam dvijantathā /
yaśodharāñca daivagyaṃ karṇadhārañca durllabham /
agre kuleśaṃ naukāyāḥ pattinaṣṭau tathaivaca /
bhāṇḍāriṇaṃ sandradharaṃ madhyeh'gremūlake tathā /
netañca rajakīṃ devyāḥ sugandhāñca tathā parāṃ /
someśvarīṃ tathā durgāṃ devyāḥ pārśe vinirmmitāṃ /
savāhanān sāyudhāṃśca sarvāndevān prapūjayet /
indrādayoh'ṣṭau lokeśāh pūjitavyāḥ savāhanāḥ /

(*Praṇām* to God Ganeśa. Now the method of worship of Gohārīviṣaharī is being told. Its Pramāṇa. The utterance of Kapila at the question of Jaimini in the Garuḍa Saṃhitā. During Kaliyoga, when all the gods and goddesses remain asleep, the goddess Viṣaharī, also called Pannagi, wakes up. So she should be worshipped with devotion. She is the giver of results. As Lakṣmīdhara uses the boat called Madhukar, so the worship of the goddess should be done by building a boat and giving it the name of Madhukar. The worship should be performed devotedly with dance and music by placing a beautiful clay image surrounded by gods and goddesses. 20 hands boat is inferior, 40 hands is mediocre, 60 hands good, 100 hands very good, and 14 hands boat is the said to be the least... . The images of those who assembled near Bhutanath to witness the dance of Bipulā should be worshipped. For example — the images of Brahmā, Viṣnu, Rudra, Sarasvatī, Lakṣmī, Pārvatī, Kārtika, Ganeśa, Aṣṭanāga, Kāliya, Sage Jaratkāru and earthly beings Chandradhar, his wife Svarṇarekhā, son Lakṣmīdhara, his wife Bipulā, a Brahmin called Śridhar, fortune-teller Yaśodhar, steersman Durlava, Kuleśa at the head of the boat, eight infantry men, in the middle, the store-keeper Sandradhar, at the tip of the boat Netā, the washer-woman of the goddess, after that Sugandhā, by the side of the goddess Someśvarī and Durgā must be placed and all the gods and goddesses with their carriers and weapons and the eight Lokapālas with their carriers should be worshipped).

From the unmistakable similarities of the methods of the Pujā given in 'Vyāḍibhaktitaranginī' and 'Gohārīviṣaharī Pujābidhi' it is clearly understood that in both the methods the same Pujā is referred to. The Puthi was also copied.

This method of worship has not yet become extinct. This Pujā was once performed in the Barak-Surma Valley very widely. But now the number has come down significantly. As the image of Manasā is placed on a boat and worshipped, so this special method of the Pujā is also known in this area as Naukā Pujā (Boat Worship). There is a description of Naukā Pujā in Cachar District Gazetteer : "A special form of religious ceremony is known as the *noaka* or boat puja and is performed by a wealthy man in satisfaction of a vow, who generally spends from Rs.300 to Rs.500 on the ceremony. A shed is built, at the end of which is a boat painted and gilt, from which rise tier upon tier, the images of various Gods, amongst whom Bishahari is generally the most prominent. For several days sacrifices are offered to the deities, and Brahmans, who are well-paid and feasted for their services, offer up their prayers. At the end of this time the house and its contents are abandoned and allowed to fall to pieces."[7] This ceremony was also called Gohārīviṣaharī Pujā. This is supported by the writings of the local writers. "Although Manasā is the bestower of the fear of serpents, she is also the giver of wealth. A rich man with a desire to amass greater wealth worshipped Manasā with pomp and grandeur in the past. The grandeur and paraphernalia of this puja was an object to be seen. So this Pujā is wide awake in the old memory. This Pujā is called Naukā or Gohāri Pujā."[8]

It was Sujit Choudhury who first brought to the notice that Manasā Pujā as described in 'Vyāḍibhaktitaranginī' is really Naukā Pujā of the Barak-Surma Valley.[9] But he did not make any reference to 'Gohārīviṣaharī Pujābidhi'.

In 'Vyāḍibhaktitaranginī' too there is reference to Gohāri :

darśanācca vicitrāyā vāgdṛṣṭiharaṇaṃ bhavet
nāganāmnāca gauhārī vikhyātāsā mahītale /

In the article of Prof. Ahmad Shareef this extract is translated thus, "A sight of this Vicitrā (?) seizes speech and sight. That Gauhārī is famous on the earth as nāga."

Ashutosh Bhattacharjee rendered these two lines thus : "That Gauhārī is famous in the world as nāga."[10] Pradyot Kumar Maiti holds that Gauhāri is the name of a boat: "... that after the return of Lakhindar to life the worship of Manasa was arranged on a boat named Gauhari, and not on land, as is said in all the Bengali versions."[11] In the Puthi collected by us the text of these two lines is given as follows:

dṛṣṭā citram pūrvvañca vāgḍṛṣṭi stambhito yataḥ
ato nāmnāca gohārīkhyātā naukā mahītale /
yato nūnaṃ kṛtā devyā vajratulyā mahāpadaḥ /
ato viṣaharī devī gohārīti prakīrttitā /
gohāriṃ manasāṃ kṛtvā yoarccayati mahītale /
sa iṣṭakāmānāpnoti brahmalokaṃ tathā mune /

(As the sight of this wonderful image seizes our speech and sight, so this boat is famous in the world as Gohārī. As the goddess destroys great dangers as powerful as the thunder, so Visahari is reputed as Gohārī. The person who worships Gohārī Manasā by building her image, achieves his desired objects and attains Brahmaloka).

Puthi No.1156 preserved in the Jatindra Mohan Sangrahashala also the text of this passage is almost the same :

dṛṣtā vikrama pūrvvañca vāgdṛṣṭi stambhitoyataḥ
etā nāmnāca gohārī khyātatā naukā mahītalem /
to devyārddhato nunam vajra mahāpadaḥ /
ato viṣaharī devī gohārīti prakirttitā /
sa istakāmānāpnoti brahmalokaṃ tatha muneḥ /

There is a reference to Gohārī Pujā in 'Manasā Pāñchāli' of Radhamadhav Dutta, a poet of the Barak-Surma Valley, in which this Pujā has been considered to be as great as Aśvamedha Yagña.

a) *kalite gohārī śeve/pañcajagña phal lābhe*
caturvarga ādi dhan jan
jay muni kapile vāṇī/garuḍ purāṇe suni
alpa kichu kari vivaraṇ //[12]

b) *kalikāle asvamed ādi yagña naye*
śei phal pāiva jei gohāri pujaye //[13]

It has been held in 'Gohārīviṣaharī Pujābidhi' that the worshipper achieves similar results :

yastāṃ viṣaharīṃ devīṃ pūjayedbhakti bhāvataḥ /
tatkule pannagabhayaṃ kadācinnaiva jāyate /
agniṣṭomañcāśvamedhaṃ rajasūyādikañca yat /
tattat samaphalam prāpya brahmasāsvatamāpnuyāt /

(He who worships Visahari Devi with devotion, his lineage never suffers from fear of snakes. He attains results equal to those achieved by the performance of Yagñas like Agniṣṭoma, Aśvamedha and Rajsūya and reaches the feet of eternal Brahma).

An inevitable question confronts us in this perspective — what is the meaning of the word 'Gohārī'. In the Amarkosa 'speech' and 'eye' are given as two among many meanings of the word 'Go'. In 'Raghuvansa' of Kalidas and 'Sisupalvadh' of Magha, the word 'Go' has been used in the meaning of 'speech'.[14] So the word 'Gohārī' may mean 'one who carries off speech'. This implies that the image the very sight of which makes one dumb with surprise is Gohārī. The image of Visaharī used in Gohārīviṣaharī Pujā is so huge that it makes the onlooker dumb with surprise.

Another problem is related to, 'Rayhāni'. There is no reference to 'Rayhāni' in 'Gohārīviṣaharī Pujābidhi'. About this 'Vyāḍibhaktitaranginī' holds —

darśanāpāyate yasyā rayahānistu akhilāṃ/
rayahāniriti prokta pratimā bhavyadāyinī/

(That from whose sight Rayhāni is attained, that image which showers happiness and prosperity is called 'Rayhāni')

The meaning of the word 'Ray' is flow, current, speed etc. In Kalidas's 'Meghadutam' the word 'Ray' has been used in this sense.[15] So the meaning may be construed as the sight of the image that paralyses speed or flow or current or makes motionless — that prosperity and happiness giving image is called 'Rayhāni'. It may be relevant to mention that in Barisal region Manasā is called 'Rayāni'. Ashutosh Bhattacharjee has correctly surmised that 'Rayāni' is related to 'Rayhāni'.[16] At one time in this region also this grand Puja was celebrated.

About the size of the boat and the image we have some suggestions from both the Puthis under our study in the part called 'Pramāṇa'. Only a small part of 'Prayoga' is found in 'Vyāḍibhaktitaranginī'. But in 'Gohārīviṣaharī Pujābidhi' the whole of 'Prayoga' is seen. In it we find the list of names of gods and goddesses who are also placed along with Manasā so that a huge structure is created. The list is awe striking — Ananta, Vāsuki, Takṣaka, Kulika, Karkotaka, Śankhapāla, Kambala, Padma, Kāliya, Jaratkāru, Āstik, Someśvarī, Durgā, Mahādeva, Gangā, Brahmā, Viṣnu, Lakṣmī, Sarasvatī, Bhuvaneśvarī, Matsya, Kurma, Barāha, Nrisṃiha, Vāmana, Paraśurām, Srirām, Balarām, Buddha, Kalki, Kṣetrapāl, Bhairava, Sri Kriṣna, Indra, Sri Rāmchandra, Lakṣmaṇa, Sitā, Kuber, Varuṇa, Kārtikeya, Harihar, Ardhanāriśvara, Yama, Nabagraha, deities of the Shrines, Sixteen Mātrikās including Gauri, Aśvini and other Stars, the Zodiacal signs, Yogas including Viṣkambha, Seven Seas, Aṣṭavasus, Seven Islands, Seven Days. Other than these, the images of different characters referred to in the Pramāṇa part of Manasamangal are also built. This accounts for why in the popular mind Naukā Pujā is considered to be the Pujā of Thirty three crore gods and goddesses.

With all these images are created the huge image of Gohārīviṣaharī. The hugeness of the image makes it essential to build the image in a high shed in the open field. The boat is constructed according to the set rules with materials like wood, bamboo and cloth. The boat is made seven, five or three storeyed according to the capability of the worshipper. In a plainer language there are three, five or seven shelves, one above the other and in each shelf are placed in rows the clay images of gods and goddesses. There may be images of deities not mentioned in the list. Chand Saudagar, Sanakā, Behulā, Lakṣmīdhara, the sailors, store-keeper (Bhāndari), fortune-teller and such earthly beings are placed on the deck. In some places the four figures of Chand Saudagar, Sanakā, Behulā and Lakṣmīdhara are placed not in the boat, but on the land. Manasā is placed at the centre of this assembly of gods and goddesses. Her size is twice or thrice as big as the other images, and sometimes even bigger. In 'Vyāḍibhaktitaranginī' there is clear reference to the specific month of her worship. But in 'Gohārīviṣaharī Pujābidhi' there is no specific reference to the month of her worship.

In the Barak Valley the Pujā starts on the Śukla Pañchami (fifth day of the bright half) in the month of Māgha or Fālguna. Principle has been laid for the worship of the goddess for seven or five or three consecutive days. Everyday from morning to night Manasāmangal Kāvya is sung with dance. There is no dearth of the groups of singers, for there is a tradition current among the singers of Manasāmangal — whenever the singers come to know that Naukā Pujā is being celebrated in any place, they go to the place of worship and sing Manasāmangal without any payment.

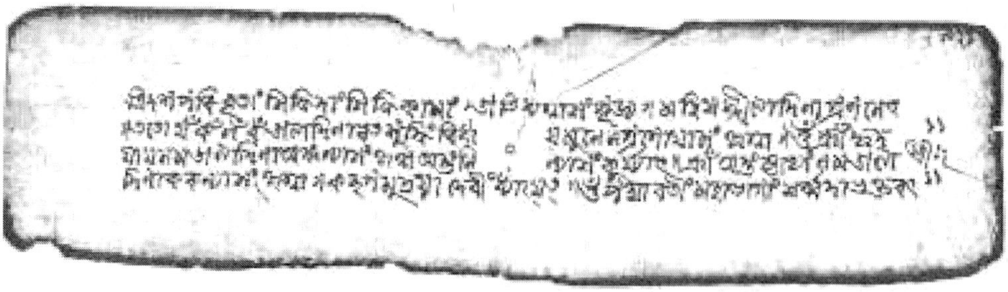

Plate 1: One Page of Gohari Visahari Pujabidhi.

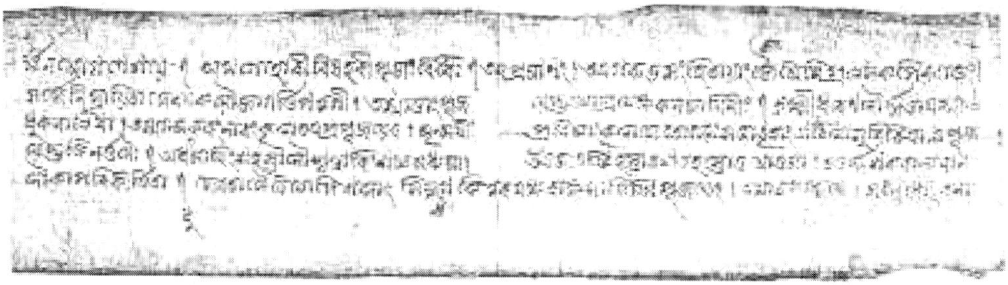

Plate 2: First Page of Gohari Visahari Pujabidhi.

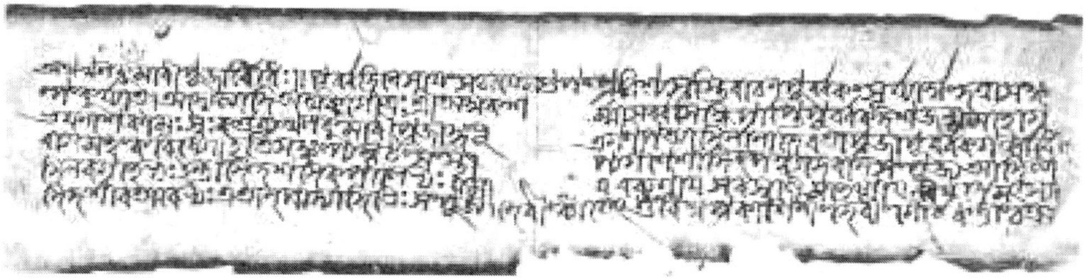

Plate 3: First Page of Khalkumari Pujabidhi.

Plate 4: The Image of Gohari Visahari.

There is the custom of buffalo sacrifice in the Pujā. There is the sacrificial Mantra:

om mahiṣavalirūpeṇa dāturbhāgñādupasthitaḥ /
praṇamāmi tataḥ sarvvaṃ rūpiṇaṃ vali rupiṇaṃ /
viṣaharī pritidānena dāturāpadvināṣanaṃ /

(For the satisfaction of Viṣahari and for vanquishing the misfortune of the giver the buffalo has appeared as the sacrifice, Praṇāma to this sacrifice).

Naukā Pujā is not the cultural tradition of only the Barak-Surma Valley. In Manasāmangal Kāvya there is the hint of worshipping other god and goddess placing their images along with that of Manasā in the boat. There is the description in Manasāmangal Kāvya of Ketakadas Ksemananda of the boat worship. When Behulā requested Chand Saudagar to worship Manasā after her return from Devaloka, he laid one condition —

cānd bene vale āmi tave pūji tāy. /
śuṣka dāñgāy caudda diñgā ghare yadi yāy //[17]

(Merchant Chand says I will worship her if fourteen ships reach my home across dry bank)

Manasā, with a view to proving her greatness accepted this condition. According to her instruction four hundred 'nāga' took the boats to the abode of Chand Saudagar.

yadi se jagātī dilen ārati
cale cāriśata ahi /
bahitra laiyā priṣṭhe vaisāiyā
cānder vatīte vahi //
cānd bhāgyavān diñgā cauddakhān
nāgete vahiyā dila /
ullasita haiyā putravadhu laiyā
nij ghare vasāila //
jvāli dhupdhunā viyālliś vājnā
vahitra arcanā kare /
mañgal śaṅkhadhvani ghana ghana śuni
devī suprasanna tāre //[18]

(When the goddess gave her orders four hundred nāgas started carrying the boats on their back for the abode of Chand. Fortunate is Chand for all his fourteen boats were carried by nāgas. He alongwith his daughter-in-law, being pleased, placed the boats in his house. He worshipped the boats with light and aromatics and different musical instruments. Fortune-giving conch is sounded again and again and the goddess is pleased with him).

The boat-worship in the Kāvya of Ketakadas, Manasā Pujā in 'Vyāḍibhaktitaranginị̄' and Naukā Pujā or Gohārīviṣaharī Pujā of the Barak-Surma Valley follow the same method of worship.

It has been said about Viṣahari Pujā in 'Chaitanya Bhāgavata' of Vrindavandas that :

dambha kari visaharī puje kona jan
puttali karaye keha diyā vahudhan (Adi Khanda, 2nd Chapter)

(Some people worship Viṣahari with pride. Some build the image spending huge amount of wealth)

To build the image by spending lots of money and to express one's pride through Manasā worship — these are hints towards the worship of Gohārīviṣaharī with great pomp and grandeur. Our hypothesis is that this worship was once spread over vast area in eastern India. But it is probably due to the involvement of huge sums of money and lack of patronage of the so-called nobility that this Pujā is on decline and approaching extinction. In the remote rural areas, however, this patronage is given by the mass-participation of people of all classes and so even now, after every 5 or 6 years, the festival of Naukā Pujā is celebrated, though there is noticeable an increasingly declining grandeur in the image.

About the beginning of this Pujā there is an explanation in the Kāvya of Ketakadas Ksemananda. We do not intend to enter into this question in the present article.

There is in 'Gohārīviṣaharī Pujābidhi' the name of an undiscussed goddess called Khal Kumari. Manasā has been called the Khal Kumari Mother.

mātā khalat kumarīsya bhaginītvañca vāsukeḥ
jaratkāru muneḥ patnī varadā bhava sarvadā

According to local folk-belief Darāi Viṣahari is the mother of Khal Kumari.[19] There is in the article of Sujit Choudhury a description of Darāi Visahari. "Darai is worshipped in image that depicts her as a stark-naked deity with red complexion. The four-armed deity holds a snake, a lotus, a conch-shell in her three hands whereas the fourth free hand covers her shame. A tortoise is her vehicle on whose arched back she rests her feet. Also, the tortoise is sacrificed on the occasion of her worship.

"There is no fixed date for her worship, but normally the fifth day of the bright half of the moon (Panchami) is preferred. She is worshipped at midnight for three consecutive days. Offering of eggs forms an essential part of her worship. At the end of each days puja, one egg is kept apart and others are hurled by the priest from a distance on the sharp of a cleaver. If all of them fall on the sharp edge, it is a good omen. The last one is besmeared with vermillion and the priest performs a vanishing trick with it. Darai is normally worshipped by a childless person for the purpose of having a child".[20]

In '*Khal Kumārī Pujābidhi*' the incantation for meditation of the goddess is as follows :

om viśvaprakāśinīṃ devīṃ gauravarṇāṃ caturbhujāṃ
viśveśvarīṃ bhayatrātāṃ vimātāñca kṛpālayāṃ /
sarvadevamayāṃ nitvā ghorarūpāṃ bhayañkariṃ /
kumbhīroparisaṃsthānāṃ nānāmālya suśobhanāṃ /
navayauvana sampannāṃ nānālañkārabhūṣitāṃ /
māyādharīṃ kāmarūpāṃ kuñkumāktāṃ manoharāṃ /
citrapaṭṭa paridhānāṃ devaganaiśca saṃstutāṃ /
khalarūpeṇa sammatāṃ trinetrāṃ abhayapradāṃ /

(The goddess the universe-influencing, white complexioned and four-armed. She is the owner of the universe, protector from fear and blessed by the step-mother. The goddess, who is eternally present in all gods and goddess, is deep-coloured and terrible. This goddess, well-decorated with various garlands is placed on the crocodile. This goddess coloured in saffron is illusion-creating and protean. She is attired in parti-coloured garment and is eulogised by gods and goddess. This three-eyed and safety-assuring goddess is acknowledged as Khal Devi).

Our conclusions from the foregoing discussion are :

a) 'Vyādibhaktitaranginī' and 'Gohārīviṣaharī Pujābidhi' are the methods of the same Pujā. There are a little difference in the texts of the two Puthis which are not unnatural in the cases of manuscripts.

b) The incomplete Puthi, discovered in Mymensingh district, has been given the title 'Vyādibhaktitaranginī' in imitation of 'Durgābhaktitaranginī'.

c) 'Vyādibhaktitaranginī' is not the work of the Maithil poet Vidyāpati, in support of which we would point out that in the Puspikā of 'Durgābhaktitaranginī' occurs the name of King Sridhar Singha Dev, the son of King Darpanarayan Dev.

iti samastaprakṛiyā virājamāna mahārājādhirājazzz
sivabhaktiparāyaṇa darpanārāyanadevātmaja samasta
prakriyālañkṛtanṛpativara vīra śrīdhīra siṃhadevānāṃ
samaravijayināṃ kṛtau śrīdurgābhaktitaraṅgiṇī paripurṇā /

On the other hand the name of king Darpanarayan occurs in 'Vyāḍibhaktitaranginī'—

iti samastaprakriyālaṅkṛta bhupativaravīra śrīdarpanārāyanadevena samaravijayināgñapta śrīvidyāpatikṛtau śrīvyāḍibhaktitarañgīṇyāṃ pradhāṇa tarañgaḥ prathamaḥ

This is a pointer to the time of the composition of the two Puthis.

According to the Puspikā, 'Vyāḍibhaktitaranginī' is earlier composition. But in the Pramāṇa part of 'Vyāḍibhaktitaranginī', there is reference to 'Durgābhaktitaranginī', for example,

pūjetyarthaḥ anuktaḥ yadanyaddurgābhaktitaraṅgiṇyām anusandheyam / granthagauravāsaṅkayātra punarnalikhitamiti

(Whatever is not written here may be seen in 'Durgābhaktitaranginī'. This is not repeated, for that would only increase the volume of the book)

This is a significant pointer — there cannot be any reference to a later composition in the earlier one.

d) According to Prof. Ahmad Shareef, the life-time of Vidyāpati is between 1360-65 and 1455 AD, that is, from the sixties of the fourteenth century to the middle of the fifteenth. The composition of songs of Mangalcandi had not yet been started. An interesting point is that in the Pramāṇa part in 'Vyāḍibhaktitaranginī' there is reference to the songs of Mangalcandi.

e) It may be surmised, that some priest, with a view to glorifying 'Gohārīviṣaharī Pujābidhi' associated the name of Vidyāpati to it and gave it the new title of 'Vyāḍibhaktitaranginī'. This rewritten but incomplete Puthi was preserved in the house of Krishnadas Acharya Choudhury.

f) Manasā Worship, as described in 'Vyāḍibhaktitaranginī' and 'Gohārīviṣaharī Pujābidhi' was used to be celebrated in a vast region in eastern India. But now Gohārīviṣaharī Pujā is only occasionally celebrated in the Barak Valley.

References

1. Ahmad Shareef : Vyāḍibhaktitaranginī : Maithil Kavi Vidyāpati Viracita, Itihas, Dhaka, 1375 BE, p. 155. (Trans. ours)

2. Sukumar Sen : Bangla Sahityer Itihas. First Ananda Publication, Kolkata, Ananda Publishers, 1991, p. 192-193. (Trans. ours)

3. Ashutosh Bhattacharjee : Bangla Mangalkavyer Itihas. Kolkata, A Mukherjee & Co., 1975, p. 297. (Trans. ours)

4. Ibid. p. 298.

5. Description of the Puthi 'Gohārīvisaharī Pujābidhi' :

Gohārīviṣaharī Pujābidhi. Hand-made paper. Complete. Language — Sanskrit. Archaic Bengali script. Name of the copyist not given. Measurement 36x7 cms. 22 folios. Written in both the sides. 6 lines in each page. No colophon. Date of copying not given.

6. Description of the Puthi 'Gohārīviṣaharī Pujābidhi' preserved in Jatindramohan Sangrahashala :

(a) No. 1156. Hand-made paper. Language - Sanskrit. Archaic Bengali script. Copyist — Sadananda Sharma. Measurement 38x8.5 cms. 25 folios. 6 lines in each page. No colophon. Date of copying not given. The last part of the Puthi contains Mahiṣotsargabidhi.

(b) No 2467. Machine-made paper. Incomplete. Language Sanskrit. Archaic Bengali script. Name of the copyist not given. Measurement 27x7.5 cms. 1 folio. 6 lines in the page. No colophon. Date of copying not given.

7. B. C. Allen : Cachar District Gazetteer. First ed., Shillong, 1905, p. 56.
8. Tarapada Bhattacharjee : Manasamangal 'Harano Bhavnar Punaruddhar' Ed. Tanmoy Bhattacharjee. First ed., Silchar, 1407 BE, p. 6.
9. Sujit Chowdhury : Vidyāpatir Vyāḍibhaktitaranginī, Sahitya Parishat Patrika, 47th yrs., 2nd Issue, Sravana-Aswin, Kolkata, Bangiya Sahitya Parishat, 1387 BE, p. 21-25.
10. Ashutosh Bhattacharjee : Bangla Mangalkavyer Itihas, p. 299.
11. Pradyot Kumar Maity : Historical Studies in the Cult of the Goddess Manasa, First ed., Reprint, Kolkata, Puthi Pustak, 2001, p. 309-310
12. Amalendu Bhattacharjee (Ed.) : Manasa Panchali (Radha Madhav Dutta), First ed., Shillong, 2004, p. 7.
13. Ibid. p. 176.
14. Raghuvansa : ityarghyapātrānumitavyayasya raghorudarāmpigāṃ niśamya | *(5|12)*

Sisupalvadh : vihagāḥ kadambasurabhāviha gāḥ kalayantyanukṣaṇamanekalayam | (4|36)

15. Meghadutam : jambūkuñjapratihatarayaṃ toyamādāya gaccheḥ | — (Purvamegha |20)
16. Ashutosh Bhattacharjee : Bangla Mangalkavyer Itihas. p. 297.
17. Bijan Behari Bhattacharjee (Ed.) : Manasamangal (Ketakadas Ksemananda). 2nd Reprint, New Delhi, Sahitya Akademi, 1977, p. 109.
18. Ibid. p. 110.
19. Suprava Datta : Gramya Pravachan Ba Meyeli Chada. Vijayini (Ed. Jyotsna Chanda). First Year, Issue 7, Silchar, Chaitra, 1347 BE, p. 15.
20. Sujit Choudhury : The Eunuch Priesthood and Deity Darai : A Case Study. Folklore in North East India (Ed. Soumen Sen), First ed., New Delhi, Omsons Publication, 1985, p. 137-138.
21. Isan Chandra Bhattacharjee, Vidyavinod (Ed.) Sri Sri Durgābhaktitaranginī. First ed., Srihatta, 1341 BE, p. 212.

The Manuscript of *Sabitri Brata Katha*: A Study of the 19th Century Prose Text of Barak Valley and its Context

8

DIPENDU DAS

The Story

Like the stories of Heer-Ranja, Laila-Majnu and Behula-Lakhinder, the Sabitri-Satyaban episode is a popular love story upholding constancy and sacrifice in love spread widely throughout India. Unlike the first two, depicting pre-marital unconsummated love, the Behula-Lakhinder and Sabitri-Satyaban stories relate the love of married couples, particularly the struggle, sacrifice and the ultimate success of the wives in bringing their respective husbands back from death to life.

The story of Sabitri-Satyaban begins as the childless king of the land of Madra, who used to worship the goddess Sabitri and pray to her for a son, was one day visited by the goddess who appeared before him. The goddess told the king that he would be blessed with a daughter who would be responsible for the continuation of the line of the descent of the king and thus for the expansion of his kingdom. A daughter was born to the king who grew up to be a beautiful maiden as she reached her youth. The king began the search for a suitable groom for his dear daughter. The daughter, who was named Sabitri after the goddess, told her father not to worry about her marriage. Taking permission from her parents Sabitri went out on a chariot in search of a suitable match for herself. She met Satyabanta or Satyaban, the son of Dyumatsen, and selected the young man as her would be husband. On her return she informed her parents about her choice. Lord Narada arrived there and divulged the secret that Satyaban would survive only for one year. Hearing this, the king tried to persuade his daughter to give up the idea of marrying Satyaban. Sabitri refused to do so as she had already selected Satyaban as her husband. The marriage took place, and after one year of happy married life Satyaban breathed his last on the lap of his dear wife. Sabitri refused to accept the death of her beloved and began to follow Lord Yama, the god of death, on his way back to hell with the life of Satyaban. Yama was moved by her prayer, restored life to her husband and blessed him with four hundred years of life. He also showered her with the blessings of one hundred sons each for Sabitri and her father and the restoration of the vision of her father-in-law and mother-in-law. Thus Sabitri succeeded not only in bringing back peace in her family but also accentuating happiness to a great extent.

The Genesis of the *Brata Katha* and the observance of the *Brata*

The origin of the story of Sabitri-Satyaban may be traced to the epic *The Mahabharata*, which has remained popular down the ages in various Indian societies and has gone through transformation acquiring local colour and variation in its tone and tenor. The story has been explored creatively in different art forms, ranging from painting to literary creations and even films, marking its appeal among the masses even today. One of the significant markers of its wide popularity among even common people is the observance of *Sabitri Brata*, a ritual particularly popular among the women of Bengali Hindu societies of Barak Valley in Assam and Surma Valley in Bangladesh.

The observance of the *brata* by women in the form of a ritual had even found a mention in the *Mahabharata*: 'brata triratrimuddishya dibaratra stitah bhabat' (250/3), which reveals that the *brata* had probably been widely observed in the past that, with the passage of time, gradually got restricted only to a few societies due to various reasons, one of which indeed is industrialisation and urbanisation. One of the few places where the *brata* still enjoys wide popularity is the eastern most part of erstwhile undivided Bengal, presently Barak Valley in Assam and Surma Valley in Bangladesh. It needs be mentioned here that even though the political boundary of these two valleys went through the process of reorientation several times before and in the wake of partition of undivided India, the regions in fact had inherited common cultural features and still share a lot of them.

Sabitri Brata is one such socio-cultural heritage shared by the peoples of the two valleys, which is still observed widely in these valleys from the day of the *Trayadashi* of Krishna *Pakhkha* of the month of *Baishakh* till the day of *Amabashya*. The *Brata* is observed for three days. Hindu women across caste barrier take part in the *Brata*. The woman performing the *Brata* prays for the long life of her husband and for having children, particularly male babies. The observance of the *Brata* is considered a must for a newly married woman who is supposed to observe this uninterrupted usually for first fourteen years, which sometimes is extended for the rest of the period of a woman's married life. The *Brata* is performed in the court yard or in the open veranda. A mound made of clay is prepared; then four small branches of banyan tree are inserted on the four sides of the mound and the branches are encircled seven times by a long red thread. Banyan leaves are tied to the thread, making it appear like a jungle in miniature. Sabitri and Satyaban are drawn on two leaves with pop made of flour. These two portraits are placed on the two sides of the mound and in between is drawn the image of Yama, the god of death, with a piece of coal. On the mound is kept tied in a piece of cloth some grains not cultivated through cattle-drawn ploughing. The other fruits offered to the deity should also not be the products of cattle-drawn plough cultivation. The fasting since the morning of each day of *Brata* is brought to an end with the consumption of fruits and milk. A union or sleeping with the husband is in these three days is forbidden. The ploughmen are supposed to avoid tilling land during the period of *Brata*. On the fourth day, after the *Brata* comes to an end with the devotional reception of the husbands, the wives take non-vegetarian food, particularly fish. The *Brata Katha* is narrated every day before the women engaged in the *Brata*.

The Manuscript/The Text: An Analysis

The manuscript of *Sabitri Brata Katha* that lies at the genesis of the present paper is a prose text originally written most probably in the early half of 19th century in Sylhet district. It is a *Katha* or a prose narrative to be told in front of the women engaged in the *Brata* or the ritualistic worship observed exclusively by married women and not a *Panchali* meant for recitation or singing. The manuscript of the *Brata Katha*, one of the texts written in prose or verse in that *Punthi*, narrates the story of *Sabitri-Satyaban* which used to be read before the the women devotees, who took part in the *Sabitri Brata*. The reading of the text was done either by one of the women worshippers or by the priest brought to perform certain specific functions in the *Brata*.

The number of *patras* or leaves of the present *Punthi* or the book is 13. Each leaf is of 21x4.5 centimetre. Every *patra* containing 7, 8, 9 or 10 *Panktis* (stanzas). It is a transmitted text, written by a scribe, where the paper used in copying the text was machine manufactured. The *Sabitri Brata Katha* is to be found between the page numbers 'M'of 1st *patra* (leaf) and the page number 'L' of *patra* (leaf) number 5. From the page number 'M' of patra number 5 begins the *Niyata Mangal Chandi Panchali*, another story concerning the *Brata* of goddess *Mangalchandi*, written in verse that continues up to the page number 'L'of *patra* (leaf) number 13 of the same *Punthi*.

There are two *pushpika* or colophons in the *Punthi*, one after *Sabitri Brata Katha* and the other after *Niyata Mangal Chandi Panchali*. The colophon after *Sabitri Brata Katha* reads:

Iti bhabiswata purane Sabitri Brata Katha samapta.
Pranamya girijakantan nattabachan punah punah bilikhya

pustikachai Jadinatha dwijanmana.
Sri Gurucharanebhyan Namah. Sri Durga Shivah.

As has been mentioned earlier, the *Brata Katha* is a transmitted text. The Dwijanath in the colophon is not the author but the scribe who has copied the text. The name of the author does not find a mention in the colophon or in the text. However, the *Bhanita* or the introduction and the colophon at the end of *Niyata Mangal Chandi Panchali*, which follows the *Sabitri Brata Katha* in the *Punthi*, provides a clue to the identification of the author. The colophon reads thus:

Iti Niyata Mangal Chandir Panchali samapta.
Karkatanka stita veda nakhatradirnibaschaya
Tadbinan lekhitan tatwan jatanam dwijanmanan.

The colophon above is a *heyanli* or a puzzle, the meaning of which can be unravelled through a close analysis of the intentional indirect manner of relating some important information related to the text and its author/ poet. A close study of the colophons reveals that the scribe, named Dwija Dinnath, had probably completed copying both the texts at the age of 44 years 27 days. The colophons do not provide any clue towards tracing the name of the author/ poet and ascertain the period of its composition. The *Bhumika* or the introduction to the *Niyata Mangal Chandi Panchali,* however, gives a clue to the author of both the texts in the *Punthi* and the time of composition. The *Bhumika* mentions the name of Krishnadev Dwija as the poet of *Niyata Mangal Chandi Panchali*. *Srihatter Itibritta*, (1910) a book on the history of Srihatta, mentions the name of Krishnadev Bhattacharya as the poet of the *Panchali* of *Niyata Mangal Chandi*. In the book called *Sahitye Eban Sanbadikatay Srihatter Abadan* (Bhattacharjee 1973) (The Contribution of Srihatta in Literature and Journalism), the approximate date of the composition the *Panchali* of Krishnadev has been mentioned as 1250 Bangabda, i.e., 1843 A.D. It would probably be not wrong if we consider the prose narrative *Sabitri Brata Katha*, which is found in the same *Punthi* along with *Niyata Mangal Chandi Panchali*, had been written by the same author, i.e., Krishnadev Dwija or Krishnadev Bhattacharjya in and around 1843 A. D.

As has already been mentioned, the text of *Sabitri Brata Katha* is a prose narrative of 19th century meant to be related to the women engaged in the *Brata*. The story element does not differ much from the *Sabitri-Satyaban* anecdote of *The Mahabharata*. The narration begins with a reference to an anecdote from *The Mahabharata* where Yudhistir asks the saint Markandya to tell him about a wife loyal and devoted to her husband. The *Brata Katha* is a narration of what had supposedly been told by the saint to Draupadi and the Pandavas in the period of their exile.

The difference lies in its focus and the folk elements added to the narration. The element of sublimity and elevation present in the narration and in the execution of the episode in the epic are naturally absent in this prose narrative aimed at addressing half literate or illiterate women-folk, the ordinary listeners of primarily rural areas. For example:

Barang tini onya onya bar grahan koribar bihita hoi/
Ei kotha sunia Sabitri uttara koria chilen/

And :

Sabitri swa mi eban sasru sbasurar seba kariten/
Eoimoto ek batsar kak seba kori achilen/

The folk elements in the narrative is evident in the portrayal of characters as the people belonging to higher rank, the kings, prince or princes, such as Sabitri, Satyaban and other characters in the story appear like ordinary folks, with no aura of grandeur attached to their description. Although some words used in the text are sanscritized, for example: *Markandya ubacha*; it is an instance of the practice prevalent in the usage of prose of 19th century.

The prose style adopted in the fictional narrative provides an indication towards the period in which the *Brata Katha* had been written. The characteristics of the 19th century prose are evident in the text. The only punctuation marks used are '|'or '||', which reveals that the text was written before the other punctuation marks came to be used in written Bengali under the influence of the writing methodology in English language and following the development of printing in the early 20th century. The hand written transmitted text is also an indication that the printing was not available at the time of the copying of the *Brata Katha*. Naturally the text does not bear any hyphen mark when any word in a sentence remains incomplete at the end of a line. The word is broken at random if it remains incomplete at the end of a line and the rest of the letters of the word is carried to the next line. This is done most arbitrarily according to the convenience of the writer or the scribe, revealing the absence of any set rule in this regard, which in turn helps us in ascertaining the period of the composition as well the writing of the present transcribed text.

The spelling used in the text also makes an interesting study. Before the introduction of printing technology in India and particularly in Bengal in a big way, Bengali spelling was quite arbitrary in absence of a standard and accepted spelling system. The writers or the scribes tended to spell according to the manner in which they pronounced a particular word.

The Transformation of the Text and the Context

The *Brata Katha* related by the priest or the woman worshipper before the gathering of the women devotees retained most of the parts of the anecdote found in *The Mahabharata* excepting one. The only extra information added to the oral narrative is that Sabitri on her way back home, after she had succeeded in bringing her dead husband back to life, untied all the bullocks from the ploughs. It is to be noted that while there is no mention of anything related to agro-based life in *The Mahabharata*, the Sabitri Brata, the rituals associated with it and the *Brata Katha* reflect an agro-based life that played as a context to the transformation of the text through the succeeding ages. The Sabitri and Satyaban portion in *The Mahabharata* portrays the immortal love of the prince and the saint like princes, who restores the life of her dead husband. The elements related to agricultural life was later addition to the story as the society with the passage of time went through transformation from pre-agricultural life style to the agricultural.

The story of a devoted wife restoring the life of her dead husband has been common to some of the myths prevalent in different parts of the world. The myths of Osiris and Isis of ancient Egypt, of Tammuz and Ishtar of ancient Babylonia, that of the pagan god Attis and goddess Cybele and the ancient Greek myth of Aphrodite and Adonis etc. bear testimony to that. The scholars agree to the fact that most of the distinctive and necessary elements of such myths regarding the restoring life of the dead have been incorporated from the world of nature. The god restored to life represents the vegetarian spirit or corn spirit. An analysis of the evolution of human societies through the ages in the different parts of the world makes it evident that what has been considered as vegetarian spirit, after the invention of agriculture gets transformed into corn god. As Fraser says, "Under the names of Osiris, Tammuz, Adonis and Attis, the people of Egypt and Western Asia represented the yearly decay and revival of life, especially of vegetable life, which they personified as a god who died and rose again." (Fraser 1963). It is to be noted that in the festival of Adonis women used to eat nothing which would be ground in a mill. The priestess engaged in the worship of goddess Cybele never took bread or similar food items. It was said that Osiris propounded the concept of ploughing in Egypt and Greek Dionysius said to have put plough on the cattle.

The similarities of the myths and the rituals mentioned above with the myth, the folk beliefs and the rituals associated with the *Sabitri Brata* are quite evident to be overlooked. In this context an observation made by Albert Reville seems pertinent, "All this shows once more how the same fundamental logic of the human mind asserts itself across a thousand diversities and reappears under every conceivable from every climate and every race."(Reville 1884) A study of such myths and rituals helps to understand the contexts from which those have emerged. As James Fraser rightly observes, "Myth and ritual mutually explain and confirm each other." (Fraser 1963) It is interesting to note that even though there was no element reflecting agro based life in *The Mahabharata* anecdote, the Sabitri Brata Katha and the rituals associated with the Brata are full of such elements. This transformation reflects the gradual changes in the context that took place with the passage of time. Like Cybele, Isis and Ishtar, Sabitri too was a symbol of earth goddess. "Under the names of Osiris, Tammuz, Adonis and Attis, the people of Egypt and Western Asia represented the yearly decay and revival of life, especially of vegetable life, which they personified as a god who died and rose again." (Fraser 1963) Likewise, Satyaban may also be interpreted as the Indian counter part of the corn spirit or vegetation spirit like Tammuz, Dionysus or Adonis.

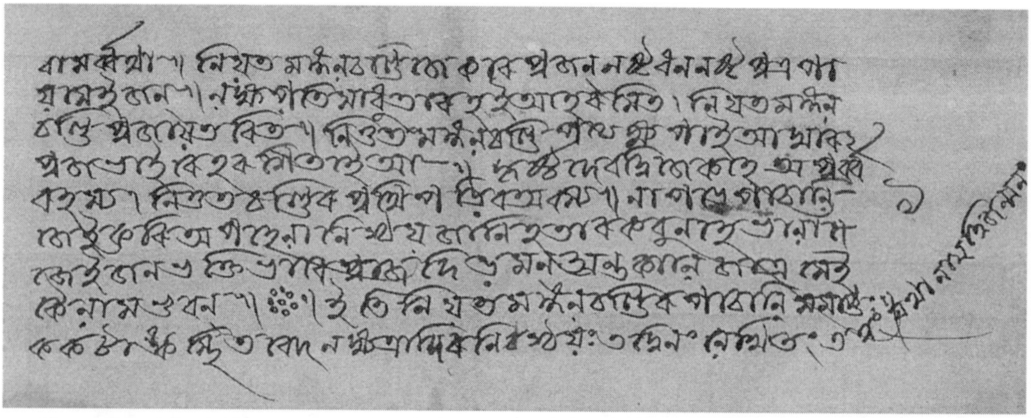

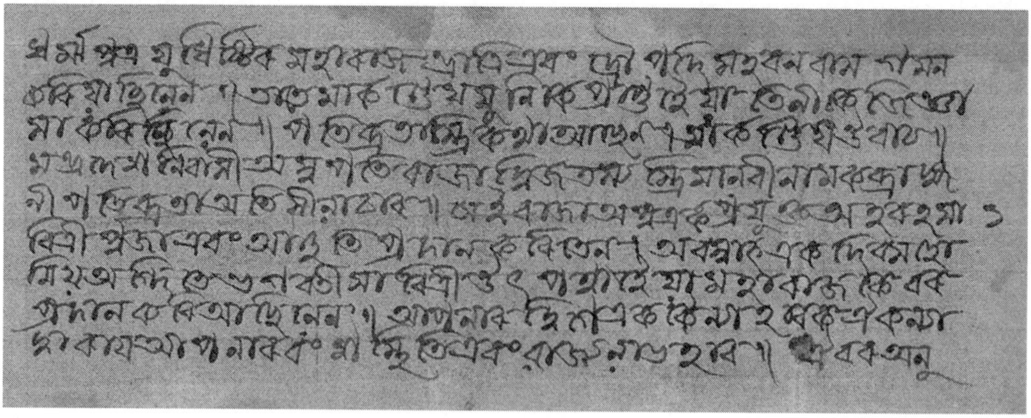

The text of *Sabitri Brata Katha* is open to feminist interpretation. The transformation of the text also reflects the transformation of the society from matriarchal to patriarchal set up. It is significant that Sabitri, a girl child and not a male baby, was considered the chosen one whose birth would lead to the continuation of the line of the descent of the king and thus for the expansion of his kingdom, whereas, the women, performing the Brata in a patriarchal society, observe the same praying for male babies. In this connection a mention may be made of S. Choudhury's 'Sabtri-Satyaban: Kinbadantir Punarbichar' a work on the Sabitri episode in *Prachin Bharatey Matripadhanya* (Choudhury 2000). Apparently a common place episode with some careworn rituals, the *Sabitri-Katha* contains elements from which social history of the early period of social formation may be deciphered.

The credit for discovering the art of cultivation goes to women. Naturally agriculture in the beginning used to be controlled by women. However, as "after the introduction of cattle-drawn plough, agriculture was transferred to man," (Thompson 1939) the role of women in the society gradually began to change and the societies began to transform more and more to a male dominated set up. The rituals such as the untying of the plough from the neck of the cattle by the woman performing the Brata may be interpreted as a protest of the womenfolk against the introduction of cattle-drawn plough that went a long way in changing the social set up, end the dominance of women in the economy and so in the society as cattle-drawn ploughing was found to be essentially a male activity; and thus the rise of patriarchal frame work and the gradual marginalization of women in a male dominated society.

References

Bhattacharjee, Kumud Ranjan. 1973. (1st ed.) *Sahitye Eban Sanbadikatay Srihatter Abadan*. Shillong: Bangio Shiksa Parishad.

Choudhury, Sujit. 2000. *Prachin Bharatey Matripadhanya: Kinbadantir Punar Bichar*. Kolkata: Papyrus.

Fraser, James. 1963. *The Golden Bough*. New York: MacMillan.

Reville, Albert. (Hibbert Lectures for 1884)."The Native Religions of Mexico and Peru". London.

Tatvanidhi, Achyut Charan. 1910. *Srihatter Itibritta*.(early part) Kolkata; (Later Part) 1927. Silchar.

Thompson, George. 1939. *Studies in Ancient Greek Society*. New York: Oxford University Press.

Padmapuran: A Case Study of a Manuscript of 1878 in Barak Valley of South Assam

9

SANJIB DEBLASKAR

Introduction

Barak Valley in South Assam is a land of *Manasha* cult. *Devi Manasa*, the snake deity is worshiped in the month of *Shravan* in the Hindu families of all social standing.

The most important part of the ritual is song recitals accompanied by loud reading. Prior to the emergence and availability of printing books, the practice of keeping a copy of *Padmapuran puthi* in the family was prevalent in the valley of Barak (erstwhile Surma Valley or Sylhet-Cachar region[1]). These hand-written copies were chiefly used by the womenfolk in the recitals with one of them giving lead by reading the *puthi* while others joined chorus. These semi-literate or illiterate women, however, did not have to depend much on the written text; they got the verses by heart through repeated renderings. But the book had to be kept open as a part of the sacred ritual of the whole affair.

The *puthi* is regarded as a sacred book. The book itself is revered as the symbol of the deity. At the time of reading, the book is opened with all solemnity, chanting *Padma stuti* in Sanskrit, placing incense- stick burning before it; it is closed with the same rituals performed.

This paper is about such a *Padmapuran puthi* in private possession dating back to 140 years i.e., 1878 A.D.The Ms., may be regarded as a heritage manuscript, as it represents as era with all its culture, belief and tradition. Attempts would be made in the paper to provide a detailed account of the *puthi* and a brief outline of the content; also, attempts would be made to touch upon the linguistic and literary merit of the text.

The Puthi

The Ms., contains 137 leaves i.e., 274 pages. The papers are hand-made; the size of the Ms., is 17x6 inches. In addition, there is an annexure of 5 pages. The Colophon i.e., *puspika* contains information about the date, and about the scribe(s) who prepared the copy. In the last page (137) the verse read thus:

Pustak sampurna hailo:sabe mile hari balo: pathak ar srutagan;suno ek Nibedan;lekhaker binaye sabar:kono kono sthane bhram haiyejadi thake Momo:sei dos khemiba amak:Samapta:
Lekhok Sri Jagamohon De. Eti shon 1285 Bong 31 Jaistha Brihaspatibar

That is, the text is dated 1285 B.S., 31 *Jaistha* (1878 A.D.). It is signed by Jagamohon de (deblaskar).Also there is another signature in a different page; it is by Jibankrisna, the brother of Jagamohon.There are four varieties of hand writing in the Ms.The ink used is the extraction of *pan* leaves mixed with extraction of *haritaki*; it is deep dark and fast, visible even today most clearly.

None of the scribes was professional, but they proved their skill in it. The letters, around 5cm. each, were arranged in neat symmetry forming lines of 12 inches with *payar*[2] division marked by punctuation as was current those days, i.e., I, II followed by one or two deep dots. All the gaps were filled up with designs resembling letters to carry the line unto the last. The scratches were all managed artistically by over-writing in most careful way.

Regarding the script, the pattern of the letters is just like the same as was current in medieval manuscripts in Bengali language. The spelling, the *a-kar, i-kar, u-kar* marks, the *juktakshar*, the punctuations were all in the medieval pattern. Regarding the names of the deities, there is no uniformity in spelling. The same name is spelt in different way even in the same page. Likewise, the same word, verb, adjective or other spelt differently depending on convention, also on convenience. Although, Bengali language had already gone through the process of a sort of standardization, still this was yet to be followed in Cachar in 1878, as, this district, earlier an independent kingdom under the Dimasa rulers[3], experienced the British administration only for four decades by then. (Cachar was annexed to the British territory in 1832).Of course, it needs be mentioned that prior to the British annexation, literary works of worth were produced in Cachar under royal patronage. There are records of a large number of Ms., mostly transmitted copies available in the kingdom, some of which were collected, edited and brought out in print at a later date.[4] About *Padmapuran puthi*, it was customary that every family of repute should have a transmitted copy of the book for use.

A Note on the Performative Aspect of the Padmapuran

Before coming to the theme and content of the *puthi*, we may take an overview of the performative aspect of *Padmapuran* or *Manasamongal* or *Bhasan gan* as it is called. Though *Padmapuran* is termed as *puthi*, yet it is not meant for silent reading. It is meant for reading in a musical tone before an audience with songs sung in between, while the listeners too join the chorus. This, of course, is about reading within the family, where a main performer sits with the book reading the text, offering lead in rendering of the songs; these songs are termed as *lachari,*[5] which, however, is conditioned by a *disha.*[5] This *disha* is the *sthayi* part of a song, which, however, does not occur in the written text but recurred in the rendering of the whole of a particular *lachari* under a particular *payar prabandha*, i.e., an anecdote in verse form. It needs be mentioned that, those who have collected the texts and brought out in print failed to collect the *dishas*, which were numerous and which represent the entire musical tradition of Bengal. It is probable that the collectors did not give due weightage to the performative part of the Padmapuran.

Besides the family performance, the songs and the rendering of the verse is performed by the professional singers too. There were and still are some singers in Barak Valley (also in other parts of Bengal), who dedicate their life to the veneration of the snake deity by singing the songs of *Padmapuran*. Their team consists of one or two accompanists in *pakhawaj* or *pakhaj,*[6] a folk variation of *mridanga*, a group of co-singers offering voice in chorus and playing *karatals* made of brass. The main singer, *Ozha*[7] and his main accompanist, the *Bayen*[7] render the recitals accompanied by dance. The singers or *Ozhas* have their own attair, a big gown and a chimney-potted cap on the head; they carry a pair of *chama*r (made of the tuff of the Himalayan cattle) in their hand. The singer may be male or female; there are some eunuch singers in Barak Valley to take this performance professionally; they are also known as *Gurma*[8] or Gurmi depending on the prominence of male or female contour in their body-structure.

A Textual Overview of the Padmapuran

The name of twenty-two poets is associated with the authorship of Padmapuran; but in the present *puthi* we have names of twelve poets, some of whom, however, found a mention in the list of twenty-two[9]. They are:

Narayan Deb
Jagnnath Deb
Shasthibar
Govinda Das
Banshi Badan or Dwija Banshi Das
Murari
Dutta Bardhaman
Bhanu Das
Dwija Krishna Das
Bani Kinkar or Bani Das
Chandrabati

Govinda Das, Banshi Badan, Dwija Krishna Das, Bani Kinkar and Chandrabati were not listed among the twenty-two poets, while there is a scope of taking Bhanupati as Bhanu Das listed here. Among the twelve, Narayan Deb is the most prominent in the *puthi*. Right from the invocation part to the concluding verse, Narayan Deb's composition dominated.

The text is divided into the following parts:

Vandana Kanda: It consists of the invocation to the deities of all land, and especially to the Goddess of learning, *Devi Saraswati,* to bless the poet with poetic gift to render the narrative in verse.

Deva Khanda: The Genesis, the *Garur-upakhyan*, birth of *Gauri* and her marriage to *Shiva*, the *Madan-bhasma,* birth of *Padma*, the escapade of *Shiva*, the *Samudramanthan*—these all form this part.

Bania Khanda: The *Manasa-Chandradhar* antagonism, the wrath of the Goddess, *Chandradhar*'s act of defiance of *Manasa*, his voyage towards Lanka, the conspiracy of *Manasa* and the fateful ship-wreck of *Chandradhar*, his return and the new beginning, the marriage of *Lakshinder* and *Behula*, the snake-bite on the wedding-bed at the behest of *Manasa* constitute this episode.

Bhasan: The journey of *Behula* with her dead-husband on the raft made of banana tree towards *Devapur*i and the way she persuaded the members in the pantheon to pressurize *Masasa* to bring her husband to life and arrange their return with all the lost ships along with the lost men who were drowned in the sea of *Kalidaha*.

Phira Bhasan: The successful attempt of *Behula* to make her father-in-law to agree to worship *Manasa*, and having their divine assignment completed the return of *Behula-Lakshinder* to their heavenly court of Indra wherefrom they were thrown to the earth by the supreme God—constitute this episode.

Plate 1 : Ozha, the professional singer of *Padmapuran* in their attire

Plate 2 : A view of the Manuscript

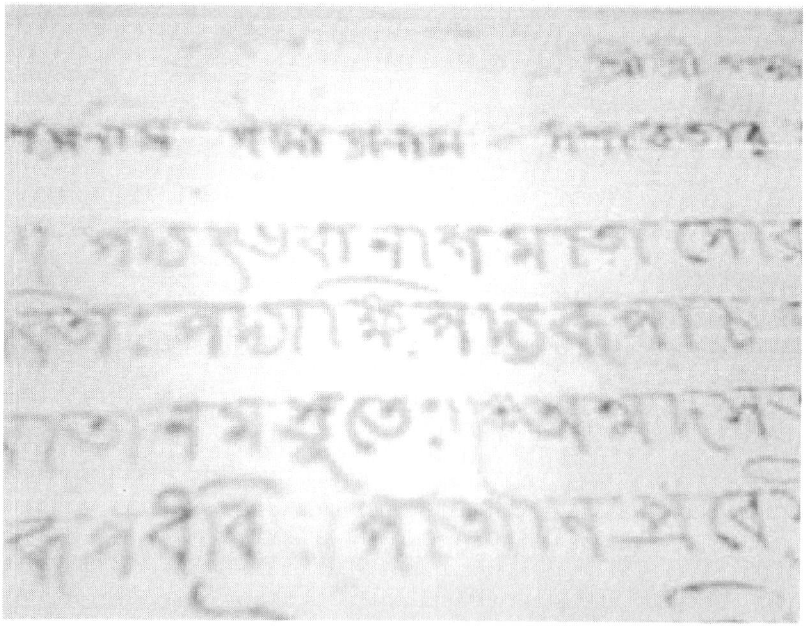

Plate 3: The First Page containing the *Padma-stuti*

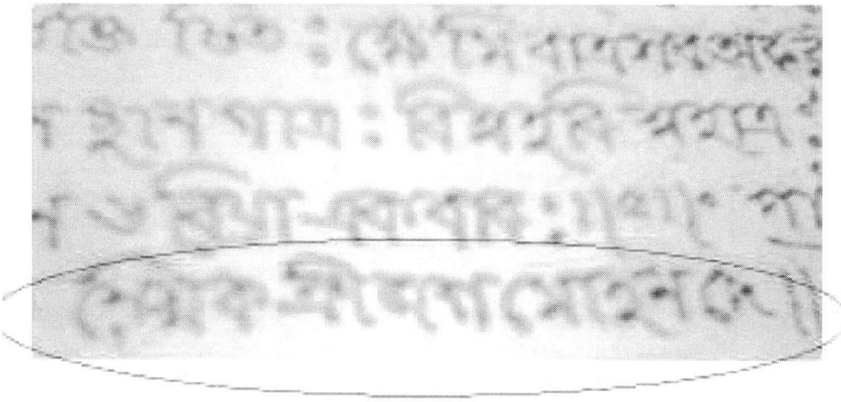

Plate 4: The scribe puts his signature in the last page

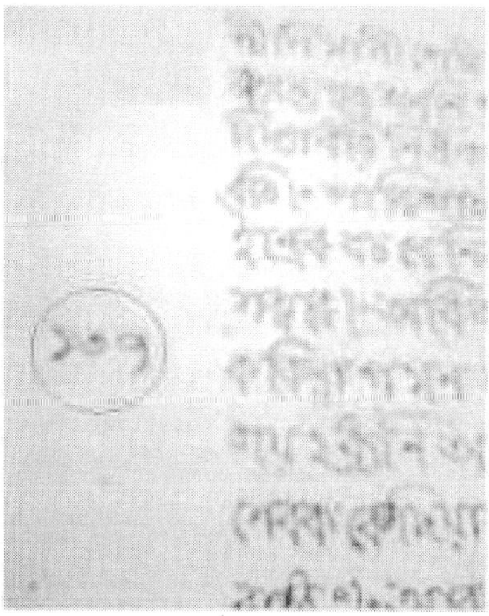

Plate 5: Page 137 of the Manuscript

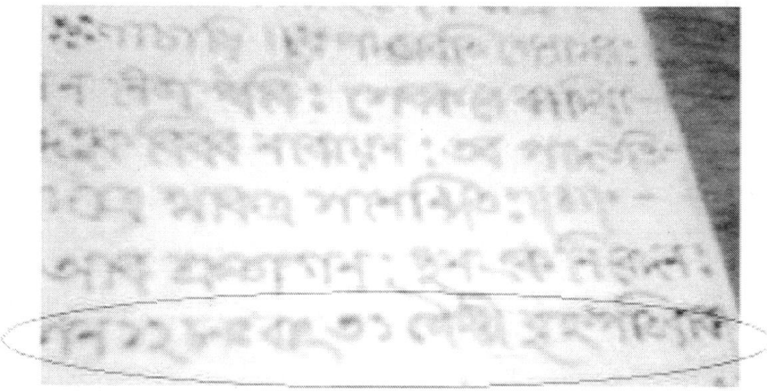

Plate 6: The Book ends with date 1385, 31 Jaistha written

Though compiled from different sources the structural unity of the theme was maintained strictly. It is clear that the scribes did not copy from a single book, but had collected from numerous copies, and also from the oral tradition; they might have also collected the verses from the performances given by the *Ozhas*. No printed version of *Padmapuran puthi* was available in 1878. But in any case, the *puthi* has a neat coherence, and the verses of numerous poets were so artistically compiled that the *puthi* in the final form gives the impression of totality.

Though a *puran*, yet the *Padmapuran*, as a matter of fact, has the characteristic of an epic, both in its theme and structure, especially as it has been organized in the present *puthi*. It represents the life of the people in the riverine Bengal, including the extended part of Gangetic-Bengal, i.e., Sylhet-Cachar region, with all their history, tradition, religious beliefs and practices. It is dated as well as dateless; it reflects the hopes and aspirations, visions and philosophy of the people whom it represents. There is no scope of going into the details of it here. We shall slightly touch upon the epical element evident in the in the *puthi*.In the epical tradition, this version of *Padmapuran* begins with an invocation to the deities in all direction, to all the holy shrines in the Indian sub-continent followed by humble submission to *Devi Saraswati*, the Goddess of learning in a befitting tone and tenor. As a unique part of narrative technique, the poet got the story told by *Lamancha* to *Shonok,* a dispassionate listener in an intimate tone placing the audience at a distance.

With innumerable anecdotes and characters the theme is laid on a vast span, and each and every part of the work is closely connected to the main and sub-plot of it. Along with the main plot of *Manasa-Chandradhar* conflict, there runs the sub-plot of *Lakhinder-Behula* sub-plot, who were actually *Aniruddha-Usha*, the divine entertainers in the court of *Indra*, thrown out of heaven by divine wrath, with an assurance to allow them regain the blissful seat through a long penitence. *Manasa* picked them up and put them to her service in the earth. After completion of their divine assignment, they had ascended the heaven in conformity with the epical tradition, especially of *The Mahabharata* (which begins with the genesis of the earth and life on it, and ended with the final culmination of the human representative of the God in their heavenly abode).

The Manuscript at present

Presently, the ms. is in the possession of the successors of the scribes, in the village, Barkhola, 15 km., off Silchar town in Cachar district in Assam. It is used by the family members in their yearly reading in the month of *Shravana* as a part of family *Manasa puja*. As the original copy is nearly brittle; they have a photocopy of it for their use.

References

1. The North-Eastern most part of the extension of the Gangetic-Bengal. N.R.Roy has observed that the valley of Barak-Surma is the eastern extension of the valley of Meghna (comprising Moymonsingh-Tripura-Dhaka); the valley presently termed as Barak valley is the truncated portion of that Barak-Surma valley, falls within Indian territory, but the culture, language and tradition prevailing in this portion of the undivided Bengal is the same as is prevailing in the other side of the border; see N.R. Roy, *Bangalir Itihas,* p.69, Calcutta, 1400 B.S.
2. This word in the medieval literature not only meant a particular rhyme, but also meant any poem or verse narrative. In Padmapuran there is frequent reference to *Payar-prabandha* meaning verse narrative.
3. Guhha, U.C. *Cacharer Itibritta,* c.1912, (ed., A.Bhattacharjee, S.Deblaskar), Agartala, 2006.
4. An important MS., of the Dimasa court, *Sri Naradi Rasamrita* by the Court-poet, Bhubaneswer Bachaspati (18th century) was brought out in print recently, edited by A.Bhattacharjee, Parul Prakashan, Agartala, 2007.
5. The words, lachari, disha frequent very often in the book; the former means a verse narrative, the later is the first line of a song which the singer repeats time again to sustain the audiences' attention at the time of reading the puthi.
6. An Indian earthen drum, used by the accompanist in the Bhasan gan; it is a typical accompanying instrument in Sylhet-Cachar region.
7. A professional singer of *Padmapuran*; their typical attire and the life long dedication to the Goddess Manasa make them a class by themselves; they do not have any pretence to magical power, but people seek their help in the event of snake-bite; to console people under the situation they say special prayer to Manasa, also sprinkle water on the victim with the holy *Chamar* they hold while singing the song; their accompanist is called *Bayen.*
8. They are the eunuch singers, who sometimes have a pretence to magical power; sometimes they administer medicine and perform black-art rituals to cure victims of snake-bite. For details see, S.Choudhury, '*The Eunuch Priesthood and Deity Darai: A case study',* Saumen Sen(ed.,), Folklore in North East India, p.137-145, New Delhi, 1985.
9. Choudhury, A.C. *Srihatter Itibritta,* vol.2, Annexure 1, p.1-12, 1324 B.S., Silchar.

Un-published Chishti Sufi Literature in India in the 17th Century

10

MUHAMMAD ISMAIL

An Introduction to Chishti Sufi Order in India

The Chishti Sufi Silsilah derives its name from Chisht, a village near Heart, Afghanistan, where the founder of the Order, Khwaja Abu-Is'haq resided for sometime in the twelfth century.[1]

Shaykh Mu'in-u'd-din Sijzi introduced the Chishti Sufi Silsilah in India. He was born in or about 536 A.H./C.E.1141 in Sijistan, a southern district of Afghanistan. His father was a pious man of some means. In a village called Harun near Mashhad, he stayed there for a long time of austerity and mortification under Khwajah Uthman Chishti[2] (d. 1220 C.E.) from whom he inherited Islamic spiritual education. He made independent journeys to Persia, Iraq, Makkah and Medinah and came into contact with eminent sufi saints and Islamic scholars of his times viz. 'Abdu'l-Qadir Jilani (1078-1166 C.E.). Shaikh Najibu'd-Din 'Abdu'l Qadir Suhrawardi, Shaikh Najmu u'd Kubra,[3] Shaykh Abu Yusuf Hamadani and many others.

It is reported that while he was at Medinah as a pilgrim he was spiritually instructed by the Holy Prophet to go to India. With this self-imposed duty in view he entered India at the beginning of the year 1193 C.E., reached Lahore where he lived for two months in the shrine of Data Ganj Bakhsh and then he had settled at Ajmer and preached Chishti Sufi doctrines. Muinu'd-Din Chishti was a great Sufi preacher and a poet. He died on the 18th March 1236 C.E. in Ajmer.

Two of Muinu'd-Din Chishti's disciples founded minor subdivisions in the Chishti Order in Bengal and Ceylon. One was Hazrat Shah 'Abdullah Kirmani (d. 1236) of Bengal, who founded the Kirmani order, [4] and the other was Hazrat pir Karim (d.1264 C.E.)[5] of Ceylon who founded the Karimi order.

Other important disciples and disciples of his disciples who propagated Chishti Sufi Order in India are as follows:-

Khwaja Qutb-d-Din Bakhtiyar Kaki (1142-1236 C.E.) of Aush[6] near Baghdad, was vicegerent of Khwajah Mu'inu'd-Din Chishit. He settled in Delhi and established a Chishti Khanqah there. Another eminent disciple of Khwaja Mu'inu'd-din Chishti was Shaikh Hamidu'd-Din Sufi[7] (ob. 693 A.H./1275 C.E.); Baba Faridu'd-Din Shakarganj, a spiritual successor of Qutbud'Din Bakhtyar Kaki.

Among innumerable disciples of Baba Farid Ganj Shakar the following seven are the most important ones :

1. Shaikh 'Ala ud'Din 'Ali Ahmad Sabiri
2. Shaikh Jamal u'd-Din Hansvi
3. Shaikh Najib'ud-Din Mutawakkil
4. Shaikh Badiu'd-Din Ishaq
5. Shaikh Arif
6. Mualana Fakhru'd-Din Safahani
7. Shaikh Nizamu'd-Din Auliya.

Sultanu'l-Mashaikh Nizamu'd Din Auliya (1236-1325 C.E.) lived and worked in Delhi for nearly half a century. His Khanqah in Delhi was visited by people of all creed and colour. It was under him that the Chishti order reached its culmination in India. His disciples were scattered throughout the country and through them this sufi order further reached as far as to Bengal by Akhi Siraj, to Malwa by Shaikh Kamalu'd-Din, to Daulatabad by Burhanu'd-Din Gharib and for Hansi by Qutbu'd-Din Munawwar, by Wajihu'd-Din Yusuf to Chandasi, by Hisamu'd-din Multani to Nahrawala and by Mugheesu'd-Din to Ujjain and Nasiruddin Chiragh i Dehli at Dehli. Two prominent Chishti sufi saints of late 14th and early 15th centuries were Mir Ashraf Jahangir Simnani (d. 1405) of Kachawcha in U.P. and Nur Qutb-i-Alam (1410) of Pandua in Bengal. Among other Chishti sufi saints of 15th century were Syed Muhammad Gesudaraz of Gulbarga and Shaykh Kamalu'd-Din of Gujrat and Ahad Abdul Haq of Radauli.

In the sixteenth century the important figures in this silsilah were Shaikh Abdul Quddus Gangohi (1537) the pir of Shaykh Jalalu'd-Din Thaneswari and Shaikh Abdul Ahad father of Mujaddid-i-Alf Thani. Shaikh Salim Chishti was also a prominent Chishti sufi saint of 16th century who was held in great esteem by the Mughal Emperor

Akbar. In the eighteenth century there was a rival of the Chishtiya in its Nizamiyya Suborder mainly through the efforts of Shah Karim Allah (d. 1729)[9].

The doctrine of this order was developed by the influence of Ibn al-Arabi's almost pantheistic ideas, e.g. Wahdat al-Wujud. The Chishti mystical practices were the same as those of other orders, and included dhikr-i-Jibr (Zikr by loud voices) regulation of the breath (Habsdam) which was probably an Indian influence, concentrated sceance (muraqiba) and an Indian practice, namely, secluded worship (chilla-i-makus), in which a sufi was suspended upside down in a well for forty days, an exercise of undoubted yogic origin. The Chishti sufi saint held assemblies devoted to spiritual music (majalis as sama), more coloured garments preferably light almond, tolerated non-Muslims in their midst and had a taste for literature.[10]

In the beginning the Chishti sufi saints remained aloof from the court and its politics and devoted most of their time in reforming the common people but in the later part of the history we find them attached or having close relation with the local rulers and accepting govt. employment otherwise they lived on the futah or Shughl i.e. ploughing the barren land.

At first we have given short biography of the author then we have discussed unpublished Chishti Sufi Literature in India in the 17th Century and locations have also been mentioned.

Ilahdiyah[11] or Allah Diyah, B. Shaykh Abdal Rahim B. Shaykh Bina Hakim Chishti Uthmani.

He was a disciple of Shah A'la Panipati[12] and a descendant of Shaykh Jalaluddin Panipati[13]. He lived at Kairanah[14] near Panipat.

His grand father, Shaykh Bina, or Bhina[15], was a noted Surgeon of Akbar's time, and his paternal uncle, Muqarrab Khan Jahangir's surgeon and friend, was Governor of Gujrat, Bihar and Agrah in Jahangir's reign and on his retirement in Shah Jahan's reign was given the parganah of Kairanah his birth place, as a jagir. Ilah-diyah and his two brothers, Shaikh Qasim and Shaikh Fudail, took part in Shah Jahan's march towards Kabul.[16]

Siyar Al-aqtab

This work consecrated to the lives of twenty-seven persons from Ali b Abi Talib to Shah A'la Panipati. The work began in 1035/1626-7 and completed in 1056/1646-7. I.O.D.P-669 (A.H. 1010/1610/1610 [1], perhaps a mistake for 1119/Rieu i 358 b (17th Cent.) 1889+.List of the sufi saints: Rieu i p. 359.

Shaykh Muhibb Allah (1058/1648)

Shaikh Muhibb Allah of Allahabad was a descendant of the celebrated Indian sufi saint Shaikh Faridu'd-Din Shakarganj. He was in 996 at Sarpur, a village at Oudh. He was an eminent pupil of Mulla Abd al Salam Lahori and class fellow of Sa'd Allah Khan, the celebrated minister to emperor Shah Jahan. He was a great Sufi scholar who closely followed the philosophy of Ibn Arabi and expounded his ideas so much so that in India he won the title of Ibn 'Arabi of India.'

(1.Hada'iq 412, 2. Tadkhirah, 175, 3. Mahbub 375, 4. Dhikr al-ma'arif (His bibliography by Shawkat Husayn, Allahabad 1928) 5. Qamus ii 176.)

Manazir-i-Akhassu'l Khawass

A systematic exposition of the principles of Tasawwuf, completed on the 13th Ram. 1050/the 27th Dec. 1640 by the 'old' (as he calls himself) Muhibbu'l-llah Mubariz, he is apparently identical with the well known divine, an associate of Prince Dara Shikoh, the author of a theological work 'Ibadatu'l Khwass (See IV ASB 1084) Camp. In 1053/1643, etc. Muhibbu'l-lah Mubariz Ilahabadi (d. ca. 1058/1648). The work is almost exclusively based on the Fatuhat of Ibn al-Arabi, from whom many passages are quoted, translated and completed upon, and Jami's Nafahatu'l-uns, in its first half dealing with the earlier Tasawwuf. References to other works are rare; almost no mention of the author's contemporaries of their compositions. The work is divided in 27 manzars of which the first two, as is explicitly stated on f.4. constitute a sort of introduction (muqaddims). MS — Ivanow Curzon Collection, Asiatic Society of Bengal, No — 1926 Rampur — 322.

Sharh-i-fususu'l- Hikam

A Persian paraphrase of and a commentary on Ibn al-'Arabi's famous Fususu'i-Hikam (See Prockelmann, I 442). The commentator does not mention his own name, or the date of composition in the usual places. The date of completion is added on the margin, against the colophon the name of the author is added by a different hand as Shah Muhibu'llah Ilahabadi. The same statement is repeated in a note on f.I. If this be correct, this writer may be identical with the author of the proceedings treatise, No. 439.

The commentary begins immediately, with explanations of Bismillah. The text begins on f. IV.

Al-hamdulillah and is continued on f. 2

Copied towards the end of the xii/xviii C.

MS — IV ASB — 1926

Sharh-i-taswiya

A persian paraphrase of and a commentary on a short Sufico theosophical treatise in Arabic, on the nature of the Deity, etc. The title is apparently given on f.16 as Al-Taswiya bayna'l ifadat wa'i-qabul'. The name of the author and of the commentator, the date of composition, etc., do not appear in this copy. There are only a few references of different persons, all being early celebrities, like Junayd Bagabadi, Imam Ghazali, etc. The work is almost based on Ibnu'l Arabi's Fususu'l hikam, which is referred to on every page. The treatise is apparently not mentioned in (Brockelman's Gesch.d. Ar. Lit. At the end (f 21V), the commentator refers to his other works, Anfasu'l Khwass and 'Aqa'idu'l- Khawass. If the latter be identical with 'Ibadatu'l Khwass (composed in 1053/1643, See IV ASB 1084), commentator may be the same Muhibbu'l Mubariz as Iiahabadi as referred to in two preceding notes. There is another copy of the same work in the library of Asiatic Society of Bengal, see No. 465 (I), dated 1122/1711, and this has so far to be regarded as the earliest fixed date before which the commentary must have been written. This copy does not contain the preface, give in No. 465(I), and open with the initial words of the original text.

Copied towards the end of the xii/xviii c.or beg of the xiii/xix c.

MS.Ivanow Curzon Collection, Asiatic Society of Bengal, No.1926.

B.iv) Anfasu'l Khawss: Rampur 322.

India Office 127 9: Rampur 883.

v) Maghalilu'l 'ammah: Rampur 366: India Office 1395.

vi) 'Aqa'idu'l- Khawass: Nadhir Ahmad 30: India Office 1392.

Abd Al-rahman B. Abd Al-rasul B. Qasim B. Shah Bud'h 'Abbasi Alawi (Chishti)

He was a descendent of the Sufi Saint Ahmad' Abd al- Haqq Rudaulawi[17]. He succeeded his brother in 1032/1622. He became the head of a local branch of the Chishti order at Rudauli[18]. According to the Mir'at 'alam, the author of which was a personal acquaintance, he lived at D'haniti, a village in the Sakar of Lucknow, and died there in 1094/1683 (See Rieu iii P. 973a). Among his works were B.i Mir'at al-makh tuqat, a translation and Islamising explanation, written in 1041/1631-2. Originally it was a Sanskrit verse treatise on Hindu cosmology in the form of dialogue between Mahadev and Prabate handed by the Muni Bashisht (Vasish'ha).

MSS: Rieu iii 1034a, Asafiyah ii. P. 1386, Bodleian 1823.

Mir'at Al Haqa'iq:

This work is a short translation of and Islamising explanation of the Bhagavadgita.

MSS. Rieu iii 1034 b,

Bombay Univ. P. 134.

Asafiya II P. 1356.

Nafs I Rahmani

(Edition: Place? 1307/1889-90.

See Asafiyah i. P. 494).

Aurad I Chishtiyah

MS: Asafiyah iii. P. 24)

Mir'at Al Asrar

The work begun in 1045/1635-6, completed in 1065/1654. It contains biographies of numerous sufi saints of Islam to Husain al-Din Manikpuri (d. 853/1449), divided into a preface (on Tasawwuf, the degrees of spiritual knowledge, the origin and contents of the work), a muqaddimah (on the Khirqah i Khilafat, the four pirs Hasan, Husain, Kumail, Hasan Basri, the fourteen Khanawadahs, and twelve of the forty derivative orders or Silsilahs (and twenty three tabaqat devoted to successive generations of Shaykhs.

Ivanow 261 (A.H. 1055/1677-8), Lindesiana P. 118 No. 196

(Circ.C.E. 1950).

Rieu I 359 b (A.H. 1189/1775), iii 973 b (extracts only. Circ. C.E. 1850).

Bankipur VIII 696 (A.H. 1220/1606), Suppt. 9 ii ii 2094 (Muqaddimah ony 19th cent.),

Buhar 89 (probably transcribed from Bankipur viii 676. B.S. 1301/1894)

Asafiyah iii P. 166 No. 167 (A.H. 1309/1891-2)

List and epitome of the biographies:

Bankipur viii PP. 55-63.

Mir'at I Madari

Mir'at I Madari, written in 1064/1654 at Makanpur and based on the imam I Mahmudi, a biography by the sufi saints Khalifah, Qadi Mahmud Kinturi, and the Lata'if i Ashraf i (see Rieu III ivanow 1214, etc) whose Author was a friend of Shah Madar. Mir'at l Madari contains a life of the Sufi Saint Badi' al —Din Surnamed Qutb al Madar and commonly called Shah Madar[19] who lived at Makanpur.[20]

Ivanow 263 (A.H. 1196/1733-4), Rieu i 361 a (18th cent)

Rieu i 361 a (18 cent) i.o.d.p 657 (C)

Buhar 88 (transcribed from the Bankipur Ms in 1304/ 1886) Urdu translation : Tawaqib al anwar li — mata li qutb al — Madar, by M, "abd al — Rashid Zuhur al — Islam, Farrukhabad 1325/1910.

Mir'at Mas'udi

Mir'at i Mas'udi, contains a life of the Sultan al-Shuhada' Salar Masud Ghazi,[21] who is a legendary hero and martyr. The work is said to have based on a contemporary history by Mulla Muhammad Ghaznavi, a servant of Sultan Mahmud. Ivanow Curzon 103 (A.H. 1233/1818),

Rieu iii 1029a (Circe. C.E. 1850),

Aligarh Subh. MSS P. 59 no.6

Abridged Urdu translation: Khulasah i- tawarikh Mas'udi, by Akbar Ali b. Muhammad Bakhsh, /Lucknow ? / 1288/1871.

Abridgement by the author himself: Qissah i Salar Mas'ud i Ghazi:

Rieu iii 1042 b. (Circ. C.E. 1550).

Autobiographical statements in Mir'at al-asrar (summarized by Rieu and 'Abd al-Muqtadir) and Mir'at i Madari; Sawati al-anwar no.29 (Ethe Col. 336).

Ala'uddin Muhammad Chishti Barnawi[22]

He wrote Chishtiyya i bihishtiyah or Firdausiyya[23] Qudsiyya. This work completed perhaps in 1066/1655-6, the date of Prof. Mahmud Sherwani's MS. (such dates as 1069/1658, 1071/1660-1 and 1076/1665-6, which occur in Ivanow Curzon 78, being presumably later insertions). The compilation of the work indicates that he was alive during the 2nd half of the seventeenth century.

Chisthiyya I Bihistiyya or Firdausiyya—I-Qudsiyya

This is a large and a detailed work on Chishti sufi saints. It is divided into a muqaddimah, twenty-eight dhikrs (of which the first twenty one are short notices of the early sufi saints, etc. from the Holy Prophet to Shaykh Nasiru'ddin Chiragh i Dihli, while the twenty second to twenty-eight are much longer notices of the local sufi saints of Barnawah and Rapri,[24] namely Badruddin b. Sharafu'ddin Ansari (d. 788/1386, Nasiru'ddin i Bazurg (d. 29 Sha'ban in an unspecified year), Badru'ddin i-Thani (d. 949/1543), Ala'u'ddin. Bayazid b. Pir Bud'han (d. 987/1579), Baha'uddin b. 'Ala'uddin (d. 1038/1628), whose biography occupies more than half the work), a

Khatimah (additional information concerning descendants of the foregoing Shaikhs, and was al-Khatimah (eulogies of the Chishti order). Lahore, Prof. Mahmud Sherawni's Private Library (A.H. 1066/1665-6, possibly autograph), Ivanow Curzon 78 (A.H. 1209/1795).

Asafiya i. P. 412 no. 562 (A.H. 1258/1842).

Abd Allah[25] Khweshgi[26] Qasuri[27]

He is known as Ghulam Mu'in uddin 'Abd Allah known as al Khalifah al-Khwesgi al-Chishti, Ross Brawne 56) Abdallah, known as Ubaid Allah, with the title Khalifah Hayy(read Khlifah ji[28] bin 'Abd-al Haq (known as 'Abd-al kadir al —Khwishi al Chishti) (Ethe' 1271), or Abdu'l-lah Khalifah-ji b.'Abdul Haqq' known as "Abdu'l Qadir Khwishigi" (Ivanow 273) or 'Abdu'l-lah Khwishagi Chishti' surnamed Khalifah of Qasur"(Ivanow 1294)' or'Ubaid Allah known as (al-ma'ruf bah)' AbdAllah al —khweshgi al—Chishti' who used the takhallus Ubaidi (OCM. III/4 p.21). He was born at Qasur (Ross Browne 56) and it was there that in Shah Jahan's reign after finishing his studies (tahsilul'ulum se faraghat pa-kar, OCM.III/4p.23) he completed the first volume of his first commentary on Hafiz the Bahr al firasah which he had begun while still a student. The second and final volume was completed long afterwards at Bijapur (OCM iii/4 p.23) form the preface to his second commentary, the Khulasat al-bahr also a productions of his early life, it appears that he was for a time attached to the Shaikh Maulana Abd al Rashid (known as Muhammad Rashid) Yuwanji and afterwards in the service of[29] Shaikh Pir Muhammad of Lakhnau" (Ethe' 1271). In 1077/1666-7 he was at Aurangabad, where he had gone in the service of Diler Khan,[30] and it was there that he wrote the Akbar al-auliya/ (Islamic Culture iii/3/ P.453). In 1133/ 1720-1, Muhammad Shah's Second regional Year, he was again at Qasur, and there he wrote, his Mathnawi at the instigation of two Khweshgi chiefs, Hasan (Husain ?) Khan and Sai'd Khan (Ross Browne 56). In the preface to his Asrar -i Mathnawi u anwar i manawi, a commentary on the first daftar of Rumi, completed in 1133/1721 (MSS: Ross Browne 56 (1133/1721, perhaps autography), Sprenger 373 (Moti Mahall) he gives a list of his earlier works which is quoted verbatim by Spenger. These are firstly three commentaries on the diwan of Hafiz, (1) Bahr al firasah (in the preface of which Shah Jahan (A.H.1067-68/1628-58) is praised. MSS: Kapurt'halah 123 (See OCM. iii/4 P.21), Peshawar 10281, (2) Khulasat al-bahr fi' Itiqat al- durar, a larger commentary (MSS: Asafiya (transcribed by Dara Shikoh, "who was disciple of Sayyid Adam Rasul[31] of Mawara' al-Nahr as would appear from the edophon". See Nadhir Ahmad 129), Ethe' 1271), (3) Jami al-bahrain (no MSS recorded), then (4) Rahat al-ashbah, a comment on the Nuzhat al arwah, of Husain b. 'Alim al-Husaini (no MSS recorded, (5) Makzam al-jaqa'iq, (6) Shahr i Hrf iatiyat, and (7) Ma'arij al-wilayat "Kihdar bayan in mashyakhi Hindustan — ast." In this list he mentions neither the

Akbar al-auliya' nor the two sufi works Tahqiq al-muhaqqiqin al mudaqqin (Ivanow 1294) (1) and Fawa'id al 'ashiqin (Ivanow 1294) (2).

Akbar Al-auliya' Min Lisan Al Asfiya'

An account of Kheshgi and other sufi saints written in 1077/1666-7 at Aurangabad and divided into six babs (1) dar bayan -i-ahwal-i- Khweshgiyan, (2) dar bayan i mashyaikh i sa'ir i Afghanan, (3) dar bayan i ahwal i misa i arifat (4) dar nasab i Afghanan u sahab i amadan az Bait al-Maqdis bakuhistan (5) dar ahwal i mashayikh i Qasur a nawahi i an, (6) dar ahwal i in ahqar i 'ibad Allah ('Abd Allah Khweshgi Chishti).

Ivanow 273 (A.H. 1294/1877, transcribed at Qasur for H. Blochmann).

This is one of the sources of M. Shafi's article An Afghan colony at Qasur I, in Islamic culture iii/3 July 1929)

(2) Ma'arij Al-Wazayat (dar bayan I mashayikh I Hindustan), mentioned by the author in the above mentioned list of his own works and often quoted in the Khazinat al asfiya' but not yet recorded in any published catalogue.

(Autobiography (without exact dates according to Ivanow P.620) in Bab 6 of the Akbar al-auliya' (a biography based on this chapter was to be included above, but no such second part seems to be traceable in Islamic culture from 1929 to 1937).

Muhammad Buzaq B. Shaykh Abu Muhammad Khalidi Dihlawi B. Shaykh 'Ali Akbar

He was a descendant of the great Chishti Sufi Saint Shaykh Nizam al-Din Auliya.

Matlub Al Talibin

In A.H. 1111/C.E.1699-1700, the author completed the work. It contains a detailed biography of Nizamuddin Auliya, his disciples and spiritual descendants. The work also gives short accounts of the other Chishti pirs and the different branches of the Chishti order, divided into seventeen matlabs.

Ethe' 653 (A.H. 1137/1724-5).

Urdu translation: Shawahid i Nizami (a Chronogram 1317/1899-1900), by M. Damin 'Ali, Delhi 1900.

Probably identical with the above mentioned Muhammad Balaq[32] (spelt without waw), who wrote the Raudah i aqtab.

List of Abbreviations

IODP - India Office Delhi Publications

Rieu	-	Supplement to the catalogue of the Arabic MSS in the British Museum, compiled by Rieu.
ASB	-	Catalogue of the Arabic and Persian books and Manuscripts in the Library of the Asiatic Society of Bengal, Compiled by Ashraf Ali.'
IVANOW	-	Catalogue of the Persian MSS in the Curzon Collection of the Asiatic Society of Bengal by Ivanow.
INDIA OFFICE	-	The Second volume of the catalogue of the Arabic MSS in the India Office Library by Catalogue of the Rampur State Library.
RAMPUR	-	Catalogue of the Rampur State Library.
ASAFIYA	-	Fihrist-i- Kutubkhana-i-Asafiyah, Hyderabad.
BODLEIAN	-	Cataglouge of the Persian Manuscripts in the Bodleian Library, begun by Ed. Sachu, Completed by H.Ethe.
BOMBAY UNIV	-	Catalogue of the Arabic and Persian books and MSS in the Bombay Univ. Library.
BANKIPUR	-	Catalogues of the Arabic MSS at Bankipur.
BUHAR	-	Catalogue raisonne of the Buhar Library, Vol.ii. Arabic
ALIGARH	-	Fihrist-i- nusuki qalani of Subhan Allah's Oriental Library, Muslim University, Aligarh.
OCM	-	Oriental College Magazine (in urdu edited successively by Prof. M.Shafi and Prof. M.Iqbal), Vols. I-xxii((Lahore, 1925-46).
NADHIR AHMAD	-	Notes an important Arabic and Persian Mss foundations various libraries in India by Hafiz Nadir Ahmad in the Asiatic Society Bengal, Vol. Xiii (pp-xxvii, (xxxix, and vol.xiv, pp. excix-cccix-cccivi).
ETHE	-	Catalogue of the Persina MSS in the library of the India Office.
DELHI	-	Hand written catalogue of Arabic, Delhi, MSS in the India Office.

References

1. Sarwar, Muhammad. Panjabi Adab, p. 222 Karachi, n.d.
2. For brief account, see, Amir Khurd, Siyaru-'l-Auliya. fi Muhabbat u'l Haqq Jall wa'ala, 1885, pp. 44-45.

3. Shaikh Najmu'd-Din Kubra (1145-1223 C.E.) was one of the most striking personalities among the Persian Sufis of 12th-13th century C.E. He was prolific writer and left a number of valuable treatises on various aspects. For his life, see Nafahat u'l Uns, pp. 375-379; Tarikh-i- Guzidah p.789, Raverty Taqbaqat-i- Nasiri, p.1100. Also E. Berthel's article in the Ency. of Ency. of Islam, Vol. III, pp. 822-823.
4. Mirza Muhammad Akhtar, Dihlawi, Tadhkirah Awliya-i-Hind (Urdu), Part, 1, p.103.
5. Ibid.
6. Ibid. pp. 103-104.
7. Aziz Ahmad, An Intellectual History of Islam in India Edinburgh p.38; Aziz Ahmad, Studies in Islamic Culture in the Indian Environment, Oxford.
8. Mirza Muhammad Akhtar Dihlawai. Tadhkirah Awliya-i-Hind. Aziz Ahmad, op.cit., p.38.
9. Ibid.
10. Ibid.
11. Diyah (or diya, as it is usually written) is a Hindi word-meaning "given".
12. D.765/1363.See Siyar al-aqtab; Mir'at al-asrar, tabaqah; Sawali'al anwar no.26; Khzinat al-asfiya' i, pp. 361-5.
13. D. 1033/1624. See Siyar al-aqtab (last biography: summarized by Rieu, i. P. 359a); Khazinat al-asfiya'a i, pp. 459-61.
14. Kairanah, now in the Muzaffarnagar district of the Uttar Pradesh, is about twenty miles East of Panipat, which "built many edifices" in Kairanah" and laid out a beautiful garden with an immense tank" (A'in-i- Akbari, tr. Blochmann p. 544). He also constructed a mausoleum near the tomb of the renowned sufi saint Sharfuddin of Panipat.
15. See Badauni, Muntakhab al-tawarikh iii, p. 169; A'in-i- Akbari p. 234 "(merely his name in the list of Physicians), Blochmanns tran's, p. 543.
16. Hakim Shaykh Hasan, d. al-Kairanah in 1056/1645, aged ninety. See Memories of Jahangir 10 Roger and Beveridge, p.27 and elsewhere (See Index); Ma'athir al-umara' iii pp.399-81; A'in-i- Akbari tr. Blochmann pp. 543-4; Rieu iii P. 1086.
17. See Persian Literature by R.A. Storey p. 968.
18. Thirty eight miles from Bara in Oudh, Uttar Pradesh.
19. Shaykh Madar, "One of the most popular sufi saint of India and subject of the most fabulous legend's (Rieu) is said in the Mir'at i Madari to have been a jew born at Aleppo in 715/ 1315, who visited Mekka embraced Islam at al Madinah, migrated to India and settled at Makanpur, where he died in 840/1436, after spending thirty five years of his life in Syria, forty at Mekka, al-Medinah and al Najaf and Fifty in India. He was treated with great respect by Ibrahim Shah Sharqi, who built his tomb. According to a pedigree quoted in the Khazinat al asfiya' he was descended on his father's side from Abu Hurairah and his mother's from 'Abd al-Rahman b. 'Auf (1) See Akbar al-Akhyar p. 164; Safinat al-auliya' pp. 187-8 (no. 358); Dabistan; madharib, trans., New York 1937, p. 279; Khazin at al-asfiya' ii pp. 310-12; Ain-i-Akbari, tr. Jarret, iii P. 370 Siyar al-Madar (in Urdu), by Zahir Ahmad Zhiri " Pt. i Lucknow 1800 Pt. ii Badyun 1920 Jafar Sharif, Islam in India or (Qanuni-Islam, tr. G.K. Herk 1015, revised W. Crooke, Oxford 1921, pp.195-6; Bankipur Gt. Viii pp 69-96 (where the Mir'at-i- Madari is summarized).

20. A village 8 miles N.W. or Bilhaur and 40 miles from Cownpore.
21. An alleged nephew of Sultan Mahmud Ghaznawi, born at Ajmer in 405/1014 and killed in battle against the idolaters in 424/1033 at Bahra'ich, where his tomb is a celebrated place of pilgrimage. See Safinat al-Auliya, P.160 (no290); Mir'at al asrar, tabaqah xii, Khazinat al asfiyah' ii PP. 217-24; Ghazi namah i Mas'ud (in Urdu), by 'Inayat Husain Bilgrami, Cownpore 1293/1875; Riue iii 1015; Beale Oriental biographical dictionary under Masu'd Ghazi, Ivanow 322; Ency. Isl.under Ghazi Miyan Hidayat Husain), where some further references will be found.
22. At the beginning of Professor Mahmud Sherwani's article mentioned below the name of this author is followed by the dates 1007 and 1088, presumably as those of his birth and death, but the authority for them is not specified.
23. In Risalah-i-musamma bi'sm Firdausiyah i qudsiyah? Yani (!) nami I in nushkah Chishtiyah i bihishityah etc. Ivanow Curzon 78 fo.2). In the Asafiyah catalogue it is called Chishtiyah-i- bihishtiyah musamma bah Firdausiyah-i-qudsiyah.
24. Rapri is a village, once a large town, in the Shikohabad tahsil of the Mainpuri District of the Uttar Pradesh. Barnawah is not mentioned either in Mainpuri District Gazetteer of India.
25. It will be seem that his proper name was 'Abd Allah but that he was known as 'Ubaid Allah (or vice versa, since there is some disagreement in the MSS.) Similarly his father was properly called 'Abd al-Haqq but was known as 'Abd al-Qadır.
26. The name of an Afghan clan (cf. Persian Literature by R.A. Storey, p. 661).
27. Qasur is 34 miles S.E. of Lahore. The Afghans of Qasur belong mostly to the Khweshgi clan, whose eponym appears to have flourished in the eleventh century (C.E.) (M.Shafi in the article entitled Shafi Qasur Ke muta'alliq iqtibasat by M. Shafi OCM. Xiii/2 (Feb 1937) pp. 92-98.
28. The Ji appended to the word Khalifah is the Hindi affix indicate of respect that occurs, for example, in Miyan-i, (cf.P.448 n.2).
29. Or rather visited Shaikh Pir Muhammad, Lucknowi died at Lucknow in 1080/1669-70 or 1082/1671-2. See Khazinat al-asfiya' i, pp. 482-3 (where there is a quotation from the Ma'arij al Wilayat telling how 'Abd Allah Khweshgi on his way to Bengal ba safar i Bagalah, possibly with Diler Khan, who took part in the campaign of Mu'azzam Khan Mir Jumlah against Shah Shuja' at Lucknow, showed him the Bahrat fihasah and was invested by him with the Chishti Khirqah); Tajalli-i nur — pp.81-2.
30. (i.e.) Jalal Khan Dawud Za'i, for whom see Ma'athir al-umara' ii pp. 42-56, Beveridge's translation, pp. 495-505.
31. Not identified. It is not clear why Dara Shikoh (Presumably, the well known son of Shah Jahan and disciple of Mulla Shah) should describe himself as a disciple of this person, who seems not to be mentioned in the Safinat al-Auliya' or the Sakinat al-auliya.
32. Edwards prefixes the title Sayyid to Muhammad Bulaq's names doubtless on the authority of a title page but the text of the work itself (to judge from Rieu and Bwmhardt) seems to give no warrant for this. Rieu writes Muhammad Yataq, but this is presumably a corruption.

Manuscripts of North-East India
A Case Study of Tripura

11

PROJIT KUMAR PALIT

North-East India, land of seven sisters: Assam, Arunachal Pradesh, Nagaland, Manipur, Mizoram, and Tripuar; was known as *'Pragjyotisha'* or *'Kamrupa'* in Ancient-India. The region got this name because of the earlier sunrise here as compared to the other regions of India. *'Prag'* means 'before' or earlier where as *'Jyotisha'* refers to the most important astronomical phenomenon, viz., sun[1].

Alternatively, *'Prag'* may be taken in the sense of 'East' and the name may be to denote 'the land of eastern sunrise' or 'the eastern land of sunrise.' The geographical proximity of this North Eastern region with Bhutan and Tibet on the north, Burma and China on the east and Bangladesh on the west has provided a special position and importance to it. Naturally, a region with such heterogeneous characteristic features will definitely give rise in course of time the sense of diversities in racial, linguistic, customary, social, religious and political aspects.[2]

Further, compared to the other parts of the India, this region has also the good collection of manuscripts in the different museums, libraries, academic institutions, temples, monasteries and in private collections. Manuscripts of this region are in different languages, such as, Bengali, Manipuri, Sanskrit, Pali, Tibetan, Arabic and Persian. But in Tripura, most of the manuscripts are found in two languages: Bengali and Sanskrit.

The present state of Tripura was named after the hill 'Tripperah' by the British and it was ruled by a dynasty called the 'Manikya Dynasty' since the beginning of the 15th century A.D.[3] In Tripura, Manikya kings were extensive and unparallel supporters to the creation of good literature. Majority of the important literary works of Tripura were written under the royal patronage, especially, during the period of Manikya dynasty.

The Manikya Kings were supported them only Dharmamanikya, Govindamanikya, Krishnamanikya, Rajdharmankya, Ishanchandramanikya and Birchandramanikya were patrons of creative activities and they provided ample opportunities to the manuscripts writer and even took initiatives to the compilations of numerous manuscripts to store their views for next generation. Subjects of manuscripts of Tripura are divided in various aspects like history, *'Bhokti Gatha'*, '*Dharma Shashtra*', '*Vaishnava Shashtra, Tantra Shashtra*', '*Kama Shashtra*', '*Puranas*' and '*Kabyas*'. Most of the manuscripts of Tripura were written in poem forms. The old manuscripts in Assam and in other parts of North East region were written on Sanchi Bark or bark of 'Agaru' tree which were and are still are plentifully available in forest of Assam, Tripura and others parts of the region. But most of manuscripts of Tripura were made by Tulatpatra, Palm leaves and Hand papers. The ink also was the most important writing medium which was used in old manuscripts and it was made with very peculiar ingredients. The ink was the product the distillation of 'Silikha', Terminalia, Citrina and the urine of bulls. The durability is proved by the fact that the writing of five hundred years old is still vivid to the bare eyes. *Rajmala* office was established by *Manikya* kings for collection of manuscripts but with the abolition of this special arrangement of the kings all manuscripts have been shifted to Maharaj Birchandra College library and later on to the museum managed by the Government of Tripura. However, plenty of manuscripts are yet to get adequate importance as they are under individual possessions and who are ignorant of their values. In case of the religious manuscripts they were wrapped up in a piece of red cloth or enclosed in a wooden box. The commencement of manuscripts is denoted by the insertion of a benedictory symbol and by the invariable – phrase *"Ganesaya Namah"* or *"Srikrishnaya Namah"*. In time of Manikya dynasty some rare and important manuscripts were written, translated and collected and even though they may not be vary much in quantity but certainly it is a treasure house of Bengali culture and literature. It is interesting that 'Kokborok' language was the mother tongue of Manikya kings but they heartily worked to develop Bengali language in Tripura during their time[4].

The *Rajmala*[5] is one of the oldest and most valuable manuscripts available in Tripura. It accounted the chronological feature of the Manikya Kings of Tripura. Apart from this, other important manuscripts are: *Shrenimala, Krishnamala, Chapakvijay, Ghazinama, Raj Ratnakar, Bhaktirasamitra Sindhu, Bidagdha Madhava, Lalit Madhave, Sastabali, Govinda Lila Mitra, Geeta Charanodaya, Prem-bhakti Chandrika, Geeta-Gobinda, Geeta Kalpataru, Krishna- Ashtanama, Hari Bhakti Rasamitra Sindhu, Kalika Purana, Skandha Purana, Kumara Purana, Padma Purana, Gadud Purarna, Brihannaradiyo Purana*, etc.

The manuscripts of *Rajmala* (also termed as *Rajamala*), or verse-chronicle of the kings of Manikya is one of the most important contribution to Bengali Literature. The six volumes of *Rajmala* were not compiled all at a time but was a continuous process spanning more than four hundred years. The first volume of *Rajmala* was compiled under a royal patronage of King Dharma Manikya at the beginning of the 15th Century A.D. The chronicles of the Manikya Dynasty was narrated by *Sukreswar* and *Vaneswar* with the presence of Uazir Durlavendra Narayan. It covered the period from King Daitya to King Maha Manikya.

The second volume of the *Rajmala* was compiled in the later part of the 16th century A.D. during the reign of King Amar Manikya. It covered the reign of nine kings of Manikya dynasty – Dharma Manikya to Jay Manikya. Rana Chatur Narayan was the narrator of this volume which recounts, at length, the description of the rule of all Manikya Kings.

The third volume of *Rajmala* was composed during the reign of king Ram Manikya in the later part of the seventeenth century A.D. It also covered the reign of four Kings from Amar Manikya to Kalyan Manikya. The court-narrator of this volume was the Royal Minister himself.

The fourth volume of *Rajmala* relates to the historical period beginning from Govinda Manikya to Maharaja Krishna Manikya. Here, in this volume, the anecdotes of the Queen of Govinda Manikya, Jahnabi Devi are pleasantly narrated. It was compiled in the reign of Ram Manikya at the end of the 18th century. The narrator was Uazir Jaydeb.

The fifth volume of *Rajmala* accounts the rule of Rajdhar Manikya and Maharaja Ramganga Manikya. It has entered into a chronicle hardly few decades after the compilation of the fourth volume of *Rajmala* in the first part of the 19th century A.D.

Under the Royal decree of Maharaja Krishna Kishore Manikya the sixth volume of *Rajmala* appeared depicting the reigns of Ram Ganga Manikya to Kashi Chandra Manikya. It dates back to the middle of the 18th century A.D[6]. The court narrator was Durga Mani Uazir himself who narrated the events, earlier, covering the periods of Rajdhar to Ramganga Manikya.

Another *Rajmala* of four volumes has been collected from *Bangiya Sahitya Parishad Library* (collection No. 2259). It was written on papers made of cotton pulp and the size of the manuscript is 17/2″ x 6″.[7] There is no mention of the author's name and surprisingly it has no title. It was published by the Directorate of Education, Govt. of Tripura, without correcting the syntactical and orthographical errors. Ram Narayan Deb was the transcriber of the manuscript and it was donated to *Bangiya Sahitya Parishad* by Manindra Mohan Ganguly.

Krishnamala

The *Krishnamala,* another notable work of history was composed by Pandit Ram Ganga Sarmah as told to him by Chantai Jayanta in the Royal presence of Maharaja Rajdhar Manikya who ruled from A.D. 1785-1803. It was the narration of King Krishna Manikya's vicissitudes in life.

This is the main theme of the story narrates like this:

Samser Gazi defeated Maharaja Indra and captured the throne with the help of the Nawab of Bengal. Indra being vanquished in the battle is taken as a prisoner to Mursidabad. But the Nawab sets him free. Instead of returning to his kingdom he, ashamed of disgrace, decides to live at a holy place where he passed away after sometime. Meanwhile Yubraj Krishna Manikya fled his capital and lived in penury and great hardship for twelve years. By dint of his valor and generalship he recovered his country back and shifted his capital from Udaipur to Agartala.[8]

Champak Vijaya

This book was composed by Shekh Mohaddin in the last decade of the 16th century as desired by Mir Khan who was serving in the Tripura Army. '*The Champak Vijaya*' as the very name suggests pertains to story of Prince Champak who was the grandson of Maharaja Kalyan Manikya and would have succeeded king Ratan Manikya II[9].

He was obliged to Mir Khan for his patronage and therefore he was placed as the principal character of the book. It was true that Mir Khan greatly helped Champak Rai in conquering Tripura again.

Sreni Mala

Durgamani Uazir was the writer of this historical book which is mere a descriptive genealogy composed in verse than history of the kingdom. It describes in details the kings and members of the Royal family and their matrimonial connections and gives a genealogical table.

Raj Ratnakar

This Sanskrit book in Devnagari scripts was compiled by Durlavendra Chantai, Baneswar and Sukreswar in the reign of King Dharma Manikya. It was later on translated into Bengali (*Rajmala*, Bengali version).

Some other rare and important manuscripts are also found in Tripura. These are either in written form or translated form. Tripura is certainly a treasure house of manuscripts comprising of jewels like manuscripts of '*Krittibasi Ramayana*' and *Mahabharata*.

Sri Ganga Gobinda Das Bardhan copied the *Krittibasi Ramayana* (MSS-67) under the direction of Maharaj Rajdhar Manikya in 1796 A.D. (1206 Tripura Era). Puspika or Colophone of the manuscript is:

> "*Bhinnasapi Rane Bhanga (Muninancha) Motibhramam*
> *Jatha Dristang Tatha Likhitang Likhaknasti (Duskarang)*
> *..................Ramakrishnanarayana Shiba Hog(?) Hari*
> *Laiya Shri Ramer Nam Anta Kale Mori.*" [10]

Two other manuscripts are also related to *Ramayana* which are *Lanka Kanda* and *Ramchandravisheka*, *Laxmaner Digvijay* (MSS-21 and 22), *Lankakanda* which was copied by Haragovinda Das of Narasinghapur during the reign of Maharaj Durga Manikya in 1812 A.D. The latter one written in 1818 A.D. is heavily damaged. Puspika or Colophone of the manuscripts is:

> "*Ramah Ramah Ramah*
> *Ramah Ramah Bala Bhai Sabe Badhan Bhori*" [11]

Another epic manuscript is Sanjoy's *Mahabharata* (MSS-21) which was copied by Ganga Govinda Das Bardhan in 1787 A.D. It is the largest manuscript comprising 595 pages which was copied due to the interest of Maharaja Rajdhar Manikya during his time. The manuscript of same text (MSS-17) was copied by Kritichandra Sharma in 1750 A.D. Puspika or Colophone of the manuscripts is:

> "*Om Namah Vyashdebaya Ha..............*" [12]

During the reign of Ramganga Manikya, *Addhantma Ramayana* was copied by Shibesh Dwijha in 1740 Shaka. It is mentioned that Maharaj name:

> "*Manikyan Bibhushitashya Nripateh Sri Ram Gangashaya*
> *Swarthe Pustak Malilekh Subodhang Shantra*
> *Shibesh Dwija*" [13]

The text of the Brihannaradiyopurana was translated by Siddhanata Saraswati in 1669 A.D. during the reign of Giovinda Manikya (1660-61 A.D. and 1667-76 A.D.) which is preserved at the Government Museum (MSS-91).

Virchanda Manikya (1862-96) was also too much interested about the text and ordered to Bharat Chandra, a Brahmin to make its copy.

Another Text '*Kriyayogosar*' was translated by Mukunda Brahmin in Bengali language as per the order of Jagat Manikya in 1648 Saka or 1726 A.D.

> "*Basu veda Ras Arka Shaka Pariman/*
> *Vaishaka Maser Dashdin Abasan//*
> *Sombar Amabasya Punya Tithi jani/*
> *Karila Dhharmer Chinta Bipragan Ani*"// [14]

According to Mukunda Brahmin, we can calculate the time of the manuscript, e.g. Basu-8, veda -4, rasa – 6, Arka – 1 = 1648 Saka (1726 A.D.)

Vaisnavism was the most widely prevalent and popular religion in Tripura region from the 6th century A.D. The development of Vaishnavism was unchecked during the next couple of centuries as a large number of Vishnu images of Pala - Sena Periods and various manuscripts of Manikya periods have been discovered in different parts of Tripura. The two important Vaishnava manuscripts of *"Chaitanya Mangal"* by Lochan Das had copied the *Chaitanya Mangal* (MSS-34) in 1805 A.D., Two manuscripts of *'Geet Givinda'* of Jayadeva was copied by Jagannath Dass Bairagi which are preserved (MSS-70 & MSS- 88) at Government Museum of Agartala, Tripura. "Lalit Madhava" is an important drama of Vaishnava literature which was copied by Swarup Goswami in 1760 Saka or A.D. Two copied manuscripts of *"Lalit Madhava"* (MSS – 4 & MSS – 6) are also stored at the same place. *"Bhati Yoga"* (MSS-21c) and *"Upasana"* (MSS-21D) are available at the museum of Agartala. *"Geetachanrodaya"* manuscript of Narahari Chakraborty which has been published into four parts:

(a) *Gourikrishna Rasamrita*

(b) *Gaurikrishna Bhabanamrita*

(c) *Gaurikrishna Charitamrita*

(d) *Gaurikrishna Lilamrita.*[15]

Radhamohan Dass copied three other important manuscripts which are *Geeta Sangraha* (MSS-22) and *Mathur Milan* (MSS-6) during the period of 1757 to 1761 saka Raghuinath Goswami wrote two another Vaishnava manuscripts in 1762 Saka (MSS- 4 and MSS – 8) which text are described of Radhakrishna's *"Padachinha", "Keshobasatak"* and *"Tulsi Bandana."* Jadhunandan wrote a drama Govinda Lilamitra (MSS-13) and he also translated another drama *"Vidagdha Madhaba"* (MSS-7). Durga Charan Sharma compiled the *"Vrindabana Lilamitra"* (MSS-89) during the period of Maharaj Ishan Chandra Manikya. There are a lot of praises for the religious and benevolent king in the post colophone statement.

Another significance of the period was discovery of the works of a lady copyist in Tripura *"Premabhakti Chandrika"* manuscript of Narottam Dass which was copied by Subhadra Vaishnabi (MSS- 58) in 1244 Tripura era or 1756 Saka or 1834 A.D., during the reign of Krishna Kishore Manikya. It is true that the women had a great position and respect in Tripura during that time. Megha Vaidya wrote an Ayurvedic text *"Vasaka"* to *Soudha Pustika*" (MSS-18) ion 1818 A.D. The manuscript of *"Gorkhavijoy"* was copied in 1249 Tripura era or 1761 A.D.

Plate 1: Painting of Alam Karigar in Manuscript "Gitakalpataru (Padakalpataru)"

The manuscripts of Tripura are the existing examples of rich culture and religious tradition of the region. These manuscripts provide us adequate evidences of our past heritage, development of language and also significance of literary works. Not only these, they also provide us detailed information about the socio-political, cultural and economic conditions of Manikya rulers. However, in spite of being an invaluable source, the accounts cited in these manuscripts invite a considerable degree of doubts relating to their authenticity, especially, during the early historical phase of Tripura. Hence, the facts and incidents as cited in these texts need to be verified by other means like archeological evidences. Unfortunately, no such comprehensive and systematic attempt to study the political, economic, religious and social conditions of Tripura from the early times of Manikya dynasty has so far been made. As a result, there is no sufficient convincing data to reconstruct an extensive history of the life and society of the people of Tripura in early period.

References

1. Shastri, Ajay Mitra, 2002, Ancient North East India, Pragjyotisha, New Delhi, p. 7.
2. Acharyya, N.N., 1982, Source Materials for the Early History and Cultura of North Eastern States of India, Bulletine of the Assam State Museum No.IV, Guwahati, p-1-2.
3. Palit, K. Projit (2004): History of Religion in Tripura, New Delhi, p-1.
4. Basu Juthika (1977): 'Tripurar Pnuthipatrer Barnanatmak Talika' (in Bengali), Vol.I, Shiksha Bibhag, Government of Tripura, Agartala, p-2: 'Nabadip Chandra Debbarma, sons of Maharaj Ishanchandra Manikya (1850-1862 A.D.) mentioned his unpublished Dairy, "*Abarjanar Jhuri*" (Dirty Basket) how to work manuscript writers in royal house and their position in the royal place of Tripura.'
5. Long James considered the first part of Rajmala as literary works of the early part of 15th Century A.D. According to him "we may consider this as the most ancient work in Bengali that has come down to us, as the Chaitanya Charitamrita was not written before 1557 and Krittyibas subsequently translated the *Ramayana*. The *Rajmala* of the Tipperah family which bears all the marks of antiquity is kept with greatest care. I have every reason to believe it to be a genuine record of Tipperah family." Analysis of Rajmala, J.A.S.B. Vol. X, IX, 1850, Calcutta, pp533-57. But the *Rajmala* is not as old as believed by Long. According to Prof. S.K. Chatterjee, "The historical value of these chronicles (*Rajmala*) is not much for the period prior to the 15th century A.D.". Kirata Janakirti, p-131, 1974 Calcutta. Rajmala was not composed before the 18th century A.D.
6. Deb Barman, Sahadev Vikram, 1995: Historical Literature of Tripura, Rajendrakrittishala, Commemorative Volume Agartala, p. 54.
7. Basu Juthika (2002): "Tripurar Pnuthi", Korak Sahitya Patrika, Kolkata, p-305.
8. Basu Juthika: 1977, Tripurar Puthipatrer Barnatmak Talika , Vol. I, Govt. of Tripura, Agartala, P-2.
9. According to Kaliprasanna Sen ('Rabi' – Vol. I, 1315 Bangabda, Agartala.), "The Krishnamala for its poetic excellence deserves a place of honour in the literary society. This book was composed during the time of Iswar Gupta and other mediaeval poets."
10. Das Shastri Rabindranath (1995*): "Tripurar Prachin Pnuthite Atmaparichitir Swarup sandhan", Rajendrakrittishala, Silver Jubillee Commemorative Volume,* Agartala, p-62.
11. *Ibid,* p-67.
12. *Ibid,* p-64.
13. *Ibid,* p-64.
14. Basu Juthika (2002): *op. cit,* p-306.
15. Basu Juthika (1995): A manuscript of Tripura: A Brief Introduction, Rajendrakrittishala, Silver Jubillee Commemorative Volume, Agartala, p-51.

Āngirasa Kalpa : A Study

12

PRANATI MOHAPATRA
HAREKRUSHNA MISHRA

In India it is traditionally believed that the Vedas are the eternal source of knowledge for both mundane and super mundane; and it is generally believed that the Athrvaveda is the lumber room of the source materials for diverse studies. As we know the Atharvaveda is known to having an exclusive group of adherent forming the aim Atharvana schools known as Paippāllda, Tauda, Mauda, Śaunaka, Jājala, Jālada, Brahmaveda, Devadarpa and Caraṇavidyā. Out of these texts only Śaunaka and Paipallāda have come down to us.

From the study of Atharvaveda, generally it is believed that this Veda principally contains formulas intended to protect against the baneful influences of the divine powers, against diseases and noxious animals; cursing of enemies invocations of healing herbs, together with formulas for all manner of occurrences in everyday life, prayers for protection on journeys, luck in going and etc. This Veda is known, in Indian literature as Atharvāngirasaḥ that is "the Ātharvaṇs and the Āngirasas. The two expressions Āthavaṇa and Angiras, however designated two different species of magic formulas. Ātharvana is holy magic, bringing happiness' while Angiras means "hostile magic, black magic." The old name Ātharvāngirasaḥ means these two kinds of magic formulae, which form the chief contents of the Atharvaveda. Another name available in the Parisiṣṭa is "Brahmaveda." This is explained by the circumstance that it claims to be the Veda for the chief sacrificial priest, the Brahmā. Regarding the availability of this Veda some later Vedic literature spells out same information. The earliest mention of the Ātharvana songs occur under the two names "Ātharvaṇa" and "Āngirasa", which belong to the two most ancient Ṛṣi-families, or to the common ancestors. They are also often specially connected with the ancient family of Bhṛgus. Further mention of Atharvaveda or more precisely the Ātharvaṇikas only available in the Nidāna sūtra of Sāmaveda. Regarding the historicity of Atharvaveda though there is no such concrete evidences available, from certain lingual studies; we can get some ideas only. The language of Atharvaveda both (Śaunaka and Paippalāda) is of later forms and some more populate forms; also the metre is not so strictly handed as in the Ṛgveda Saṃhitā.

Though Paipallāda Samhitā is being published but it is unfortunate that no initiatives have been taken so far for the publication of all other minor Atharvanic texts available in Orissa State Museum, Utkal University and in the remote villages of this state. Texts on Tantra, Kalpa and Karmakāṇda which are available under this tradition are not yet been studied by the scholars.

Orissa being a mine house of palm leaf manuscripts had deposits of thousands of palm leaf manuscripts and available Paippalāda tradition, sufficient initiatives should taken in this cause. Besides the Samhitā texts of all other Vedas, there are some unique manuscripts under the title of Kalpa.

Utkal the state of fine arts was not only known for its artistic characters but also it has a long tradition of cultural heritage. Though Orissa dominated by different tribes, yet Vedic tradition was very much prevalent. Notices of huge number of Paipallāda manuscripts, priests and traditional reciting Pandits who were still able to recite their own Samhitā, which transmitted to them orally by their teachers, gives us the proud that this land had a very rich tradition. We are fortunate enough that persons interested on Ancient India will remain ever grateful to the unassuming Atharvavedins of Orissa for preservation of the priceless treasure of Paipallāda texts from total destruction.

From study of the Ātharvanic contents one can find the following important texts. Gopatha Brāhmaṇa is the Brāhmaṇic text associated with the Śaunaka tradition of Atharvaveda. This has been divided into two parts. Second part of this Brāhmaṇa is based on the Vaitāna sūtra. An Anukramaṇi to the Atharvaveda is also extent, however, specifies for the most part only divine beings and seldom actual Ṛṣis, as authors. The *Kauśika sūtra* is the sole existing ritual sūtra literature. To this sutra belong further five so called Kalpas, the Nakṣatra-Kalpa, the *Śāti-Kalpa*, the Vitāna-Kalpa, the Samhitā-Kalpa and the *Abhicāra-Kalpa*. Instead of Abhicāra Kalpa the Viṣṇupurāṇa and *Caraṇavyuaha* mentioned the name Āngirasa Kalpa, which is not yet published in any form. It is well established that this Āngirasa Kalpa is belong to the Paippalāda tradition as it is well mentioned in different texts of Atharvaveda.

The Mss of Āngirasa Kalpa are available in the State Museum of Orissa, Parija Pāthāgāra of Utkala University and Saraswati Bhavana Library of Sampurnananda Sanskrit University, Varanasi. Here in this paper noble attempt has been taken only on the MSS of Orissa State Museum, (OSM) Bhubaneswar and the MS at Utkal University. These Kalpa manuscripts studied here are in Oriya character, and inscribed on palm leaves with iron styles. Out of these four mss the largest and the only systomatic ms vide. OSM catalogue No. V/124 has been presented here for a firsthand idea on the text of Āngirasakalpa. This may be treated as Phase-I.

EPITOME OF THE MANUSCRIPTS

MSS- 01
OSM. Catalogue No. - V/124
Name of the MS - Āngirasa-kalpa
Purchased from—Sri Krushnachandra Kar
Condition - Good, Nos. of Folios- 210, Size - 17.5" x 2.5", Nature - Complete
Script - Oriya
Beginning -

om gaṇeśāya namaḥ /
om lakṣmīnṛsimhāya namaḥ /
om kadācannaimiṣāraṇye gomatī-tīra-vāsinaḥ /
sutaṃ dṛṣṭvā-mahābhāgaṃ+prachuste maharṣayaḥ /
ṛṣayaḥ uccu /
nirvighnena tu kāryāṇi kathaṃ siddha+ suvrata /
arthasiddhiḥ kathaṃ pumṣāṃ dhana-saubhāgya-sampadaḥ //

Colophone -
Likhitaṃ Mārakaṇdadeva Śarmaṇā...../ /
Content -
Skandapurāṇe Siddhivināyaka-vrata-stotra
Narasimha-purāṇe-ikṣāku-suta-samvāde-Gaṇapati-stotra
Āngirasakalpe Gopālapūjā
Atharvaveda-mahātmya
Vakratuṇda-mahātmya
Dhanakāmaḥ
Vidyākāmaḥ
Śatrujaya-kāmaḥ
Aśva-kāmaḥ
Rāja-kāmaḥ/Rājya-kāmaḥ
Āyu-kāmaḥ
Bhūmi-kāmaḥ
Kanyā-kāmaḥ
Dharma-kāmaḥ
Brahmavarcasa-kāmaḥ
Punarukta-gaja-kāmaḥ

Rājaputra-kāmaḥ
Brahmaṇārthi-putra-kāmaḥ
Strīvaśa-kāmaḥ
Śrī-kāma-vidhiḥ
Rāja-rakṣā-kāma-vidhiḥ
Rājya-rakśā-kāma-vidhiḥ
Ārogya-kāmaḥ
Śānti-kāma-vidhiḥ
Vṛṣṭi-kāmaḥ
Dhānya-kāmaḥ
Go-kāmaḥ
aṣya-kāmaḥ
+ + + +kāmaḥ
Ratna-kāma-vidhiḥ
Vastra-kāma-vidhiḥ
Anna-kāma-vidhiḥ
Homābhāve-japa-lakṣaṇaṃ
Gaṇeśābhiṣeka-vidhiḥ
Sarva-kāma-sidhiḥ
Mānasa-japa-vidhiḥ
Stamvana-vidhiḥ
Vidravaṇa-vidhiḥ
Punarukta-vidravaṇa-vidhiḥ
Vidveṣaṇa-vidhiḥ
Mohana-vidhiḥ
Ākarṣaṇa-vidhiḥ
Uccāṭana-vidhiḥ
+ +kalpa-prayoga-vidhiḥ
Dhanakāmaḥ
Dhana-siddhi-kāmaḥ
Prayoga-siddhilakṣaṇaṃ
Mahānidhiprāpti-kāmaḥ
Akṣayadhana-kāmaḥ
Punarukta-mahānidhi-kmaḥ
Punarukta-strivasa-kāmaḥ
Kanyāprāpti-kāma-vidhiḥ

Mṛtyunjaya-āyuṣkāma-vidhiḥ
Śatru-jaya-kāma-vidhiḥ
Śatru-kula-samagra-nāśana-vidhiḥ
Śatru-māraṇa-vidhiḥ
Śatru-dveseccāṭana-vidhiḥ (?)
Abhicāra-vidhiḥ
Samasta-pāpa-nāśana-vidhiḥ
Aśva-sparśanavidhiḥ
Vṛṣṭi-kāma-vidhiḥ
Āsurī-mantraḥ
Anāgata-kathana-vidhiḥ
Vakratuṇda-pūjā-vidhiḥ
Bhutaśuddhi-mātṛkā
Vakratuṇda-pūjā-vidhiḥ
Stambhana-vidhiḥ
Homa-samvāra-vidhiḥ
Vidravaṇa-vidhiḥ
Mantra-pratisthā-vidhiḥ
Punarukta-vidravaṇa-vidhiḥ
Nakṣtra-kalpokta-homavidhiḥ
Vidvesaṇa-vidhiḥ
Kuṇde-agni-sthāpana-vidhiḥ
Mohana-vidhiḥ
Svasākhā-karma-vidhiḥ
Agni-prajvalana-vidhiḥ
Samkalpa-vidhiḥ
Brāhmaṇavaraṇa-vidhiḥ
Kmapralopa(?)
Vāratithinakṣatra ṣubhābhāsubha-vidhiḥ
Ṣaṭkarma-vidhiḥ
Ṣaṭkarma-māsanirṇaya-vidhiḥ
Homa-kālanirṇaya-vidhiḥ
Punarukta-ṣaṭkarma-nakṣatra-vidhiḥ
Homa-dina-nirṇaya-vidhiḥ
Homa-brāhmaṇa-lakṣaṇa-vidhiḥ
Kāmasiddhi-lakṣaṇa-vidhiḥ

Homa-diga-nirṇaya-vidhiḥ
Āśana-lakṣaṇa-vidhiḥ
Vedi-lakṣaṇa-vidhiḥ
Śami-lakṣaṇa-vidhiḥ
Homa-dravya-parimāṇa-vidhiḥ
Hasta-homa-lakṣaṇa-vidhiḥ
Karma-bhede agni-nāmāni
Agni-svarupakathana
Agni-jihva+ +lakṣaṇaṃ
Āgni-deva-kathana (?)
Agni-svarupa-kathana (?)
Agni-diga-nirṇaya
Agni-phalāphala-doṣa
Agni-jihvā-lakṣaṇaṃ
Agni-jihvā-varṇāni
Agni-jihvā-varṇa-phala
Agni-dhyāna
Kuṇda-lakṣaṇa
Yoni-lakṣaṇa
Nakṣatra-kalpokta-pūrva-tantra
Pradhāna-karma-nakṣatra-kalpa
Tantra-yajamānaḥ
Snāna-vidhiḥ
Gaṇapati+ +(homa)-vidhiḥ
Gaṇeśābhiṣeka-vidhiḥ
Gaṇeśābhiṣeka-phala
Siddhodaka-phala-vyavasthā
Ṣaṭkarma-cinhāni
Vaśa-cinhaāni
Stambhana-cinhāni
Mohana-cinhāni
Vidveṣana-cinhāni
Vidravaṇ-cinhāni
Uccāṭana-cinhāni
Māraṇa-cinhāni
Atha-Mantrarāja-vidhiḥ

Rājā Rājya-Jaya-Kāma-Vidhiḥ
Homa-dina-samkhyā-nirṇaya
Para-dūrga-krya-vidhiḥ
Śatru-jaya-kāma-vidhiḥ
Homa-saktau(asaktau) japavidhiḥ
Vṛṣṭikāma-vidhiḥ
Pujā-homa-japa-nirṇaya-vidhiḥ
Śrīkāma-vidhiḥ
Āyuṣkāma-vidhiḥ
Śrī-homa-vidhiḥ
Śānti-kāma-vidhiḥ
Dhānya-kāma-vidhiḥ
Anna-kāma-vidhiḥ
Go-kāma-vidhiḥ
Anādeśa-homa-vidhiḥ
Upaśliṣṭa-śānti-vidhiḥ
Roga-nāśana-vidhiḥ
Gṛha-śānti-vidhiḥ
Su-prasava-vidhiḥ
Sarva-roga-śānti-vidhiḥ
Tatkāla-japa-dravya vā Śānti-vidhiḥ
Galagraha-roganāśana-vidhiḥ
Abhicāra-śānti-vidhiḥ
Kṛtyākṛtya-nāśana-vidhiḥ
Medhā-kāma-vidhiḥ
Putra-kāma-vidhiḥ
Mṛtyu-vasta(?)-putra-kāmavidhiḥ
Vandhya-putra-kāma-vidhiḥ
+ +putra-kāma-vidhiḥ
Dhana-kāma-vidhiḥ
Śatru-jayakāma-vidhiḥ
Bhūmi-kāma-vidhiḥ
Dhānya-kāma-vidhiḥ
Āyuṣkāma-vidhiḥ
Uttama-strī-kāma-vidhiḥ
+ +śānti-vidhiḥ

Rājāvaśakāma-vidhiḥ
Strī-vaśakāma-vidhiḥ
Bhartṛ-vaśa-kāma-vidhiḥ
+ + + vaśa-kāma-vidhiḥ
Rāja-śatru-vaśa-kāma-vidhiḥ
Mānya-vaśa-kāma-vidhiḥ(?)
Sāmānya-vaśa-kāma-vidhiḥ
Savisa-divasa-kāma-vidhiḥ(?)
Annāyatta-vaśa-kāma-vidhiḥ
Mahā-śatru-vaśa-kāmaḥ
Śatru-mohana-kāma-vidhiḥ
Śatru-vidveśana-kāma-vidhiḥ
Śatru-uccāṭna-kāma-vidhiḥ
Śatru-māraṇa-kāma-vidhiḥ
Homa-nirṇaya-vidhiḥ
Māraṇa-ni + (si)ddha-vidhiḥ
Māraṇa-ukta-vidhiḥ
Āyuṣkāma-vidhiḥ(?)
+ + + + +
+ + + + + +
Mṛtyunjaya-homa-vidhiḥ
Mahāmṛtyunjaya-kāma-vidhiḥ
Maha-roga-nāśana-vidhiḥ
+ + + + + +
+ + + + raṇa-japa-vidhiḥ
Āyuṣkāma-vidhiḥ
Ārogya-kāma-vidhiḥ
Aisvarya-kāma-vidhiḥ
Śatru-kṣaya-kāmaḥ
Saubhagya-kāmaḥ
Śatru-kṣaya-kāmaḥ
+ + kāma-vidhiḥ
Viṣṇu-loka-prāpti
Kāmavidhi-rāja + + + +
Jayannābhimantrita-vidhiḥ(?)
Śrī-kāma-vidhiḥ

+++(A) bhiṣeka-vidhiḥ
Samumudragā-nadī(a)bhiṣeka-vidhiḥ
Urddhva-vāhu-japa-vidhiḥ
Rājā-rājya-lābha-vidhiḥ
Anna-homa-vidhiḥ
Ādityabhimukha-japa-vidhiḥ
Vighna-śraṣṭā-apa-vidhiḥ(?)
Adhi-rātre-japavidhiḥ(?)
Śrī-kāma-vidhiḥ
Rajā-rājya-lābha-vidhiḥ
Urddhva-vahu-japa-vidhiḥ
Anna-homa-vidhiḥ
Tejaśrī-arogya-śatru-kṣaya-kāma-japa-vidhiḥ (?)
Aṇīmādi-śrī-kāma-vidhiḥ
Padma-vane-japa-vidhiḥ
Śasya-kāma-mahatī-dhana-kāma-vidhiḥ yāvajjiva-lakṣmīkāma (?)
Avasya-bhūmi-kāma-vidhiḥ
Vaśya-kāma-vidhiḥ
Dhāny-kāma-vidhiḥ
Dhana-dhāny-kāma-vidhiḥ
Sarva-roga-nāśana-vidhiḥ
Śrīman-Garuḍa(o)tpāta-śānti-vidhiḥ
Sarva-vyadhi-nāśana-mṛtyunjaya-vidhiḥ
Ārogy-kāma-vidhiḥ
Roga-śānti-vidhiḥ
Upasarga-śāsana-roga-nāśana-kṛtyā-śānti-apasṛtya-nāśana-graha-śānti-āyuṣkāma-vidhiḥ
Apa-mṛtyu-jvara-cāpasmāra-vidhiḥ
Rajā-rāiya-lābha-vidhiḥ
Vidyā-kāma-vidhiḥ
Candra-sūrya-parāge-japa-vidhiḥ
Vṛṣti-kāma-vidhiḥ
Varṣākāle-vṛṣṭikāma-vidhiḥ
Kanyāprāpti-kāma-vidhiḥ
Putra-kāma-vidhiḥ
Kumāra-roga-śānti-vidhiḥ

Vastara-kāma-vidhiḥ
Dusvapna-susvapna-vidhiḥ
Go-samṛddhi-kāma
Samasta-viṣanāḥśasna-vidhiḥ
Śūla-gulma-viṣanāśana-vidhiḥ
Japa-dravya-śānti-kāma-vidhiḥ
Parama-prāptya-nity-japa-vidhiḥ (?)
Nitya-grha-vidhi-japa
Nṛsimha-anugraha-japa-apasṛtya-nāśana-graha-śānti-vidhiḥ
Vimukta-sarvdgatyo (?)
Vimuktasya-sukha-akṣaya
Sarva-siddhi-kāma-vidhiḥ
Sarvatāgre-japa-vidhiḥ
Rājā-vijaya-kāmaḥ
Rājā-rājya-kāma-dehe-abhimantrita-bhasma-vidhiḥ
Catuḥ-samaṃ-nitika-vidhiḥ (?)
Duṣṭo(a)-bhavati-sujana-vidhiḥ (?)
Rāja-vaśa-kāma
Strī-vaśa-vidhiḥ
Vaśīkaraṇa-vidhiḥ
Vaśa-vidhiḥ
Rājā-vaśīkaraṇa-vidhiḥ
Punaḥ-vaśīkaraṇa-vidhiḥ
Caura-vaśīkaraṇa
+ +dravya-śānti
Sarpa-byāghrādi-śānti
Japa-sarva-kāma-vidhiḥ (?)
Sarva-vaśa-kāma-vidhiḥ
Jalāgni-dhana-vastra-stamvana-śatru-svadesa-palāiti (?)
bhraṣṭa-vidhih
Śatru-uccāṭana-vidhiḥ
+ +śatru-āśana-vidhiḥ
Sarva-kāma-vidhiḥ
Āyuṣkāma-vidhiḥ
Kṛtyā-kṛtya-nāśana-vidhiḥ
Kṛtyā-vidhiḥ

Atharvaṇa-praśamsā
Nigaḍa-bhanjana-vidhiḥ
Para-vidyā-nivāraṇa-vidhiḥ
Para-karma-nivāraṇa-vidhiḥ
Nṛsimha-sāma-gāna-vidhiḥ
Atha-puraścrṇa-vidhiḥ
Śrī-Nṛsimha-pūjā-vidhiḥ
Śrī-Nṛsimha-dhyāna-stotra
Śrī-Nṛsimha-pūjā-vidhiḥ
Samkṣyepa-Nṛsimha-abhiṣeke-vidhiḥ
Sāmāny-Nṛsimha-pūjā-vidhiḥ
Iti-mantroddhāre (?)
Nṛsimha-ṣaḍangi-pūjā-vidhiḥ
Nṛsimha-snāna-vidhiḥ
Nṛsimha-snānādi-tarpaṇa-vidhiḥ
Nṛsimha-sandhyā-vidhiḥ
Nṛsimha-devatā-snāna-vidhiḥ
Nṛsimha-nitya+ +(karma) (?) vidhiḥ
Nṛsimha-vibhuti-snāna-vidhiḥ
Hṛdaye-Nṛsimha-cakra-nyāsa-vidhiḥ
Nṛsimhābhiṣeka-vidhiḥ
Nṛsimhābhiṣeka-samvāra-vidhiḥ
Mṛt-kumbha-Nṛsimhābhiṣeka-vidhiḥ
Samkṣyepa-Nṛsimhābhiṣeka-vidhiḥ
Nṛsimhābhiṣeka-phala-vidhiḥ
Pratimā-abhiṣeka-vidhiḥ
Bhārgava-sambitāyām-prayoga-vicāra-vidhiḥ
Samkṣyepa-devatā-pūjā-vidhiḥ
Mantra-rāja-vijñāna-praśna-vidhiḥ
Aṣtakarma-vicāra-vidhiḥ
Kāryākārya-vicāra-vidhiḥ
Karma-virodha-vidhiḥ
Karma-vighna-pratikāra-vidhiḥ
Karma-siddhi-pratimā-mantra-vidhiḥ
Parākrama-nirarthaka-vidhiḥ
Abhaya-nṛsimha-vidhiḥ

Aindra-bhaya-mantra-vidhiḥ
Dakṣiṇa-kālī-mantra
Punaśca-nṛsimha-mantreṇa-sāma-gāyana-vidhih
Āngirasa-kalpe-gaṇeśa-mantra-vidhiḥ
Saubhāgya-kāṇde-dakṣiṇa-kālī-yantra-vidhiḥ
Punaśca-kālī-yantra-vidhiḥ
Punaḥ-dakṣiṇa-kālī-yantra-vidhiḥ
Āngirasa-kalpe-mahācakra-yantra-vidhiḥ
Ākrama-cakra-vidhiḥ
Dakṣiṇa-kālī-yantra-vidhiḥ
Dakṣiṇa-kālī-yantra-devatā-vidhiḥ
Vakra-tuṇda-yantra-vidhiḥ
Para-vidyā-nivāraṇa-yantra-vidhiḥ
Gopāla-aṣṭādaśākṣara-vidhi
Punaḥ-vṛṣṭi-kāma-vidhi
Pātāla-nṛsimha-vidhi
Mūṣala-nṛsimha-mantra-vidhi
Homa-vidhi
Sahaśrākṣa-nṛsimha-mantra-vidhi
Vaivāhe-kuśa-rajvādi-vandhana vidhi
Punaḥ-vṛṣṭi-kāma-vidhi
Atha-divya-bhaumāntarikṣābhūtā + dṛṣṭādṛṭa-phalamābha-vidhi
Ityāngirase-bhūta-śānti-vidhi-prathama-addhyāya
Vāra-tithi-dośa-vidhi-kathana
Ityāngirasakalpe-bhaumādinā-pippalikādi-śāntistṛtīyodyāyaḥ
Atha-antarikṣotpāta-śānti-vidhi
Ityāngirase + + dyantarikṣa-śānti-prathama-patala-vidhiḥ
Punaśca-bhaumā + da-bhutā + (di) (?) ityāngirasa-kalpe + + +
Antarikṣa-bhūta-śānti

Basic Findings

1. Mss no. V/124 is only completed one.
2. Mss no. V/219; V/220; V/277 are incomplete in nature.
3. Every Mss studied here have beginning stanzas.
4. Mss no. V/219; V/220; V/277 have no colophons.

5. There are references regarding Paippalāda origin i.e atha Āngirasa prājña Pippalāda kātṛnjali..(mentioned in the Ms. available in Parija Pāthāgāra, Utkala University)
6. The term used for the broader division is known as Patala.
7. From this macro study of first hand source materials we could not get much similarities in the texts of different Mss.
8. Though there are same titles available in these Mss. it is hardly textual similarity.
9. All these Mss. may be considered as corrupt assets for a critical study.
10. Mantras have similarities with the other Tantra texts available.
11. Most of the copies have completed illustrations of Jantras.
12. There are also some vacant places for the Jantras discussed in the concerned chapters.

Role of Manuscript in the Development of Chinese Writing System

13

AVIJIT BANERJEE

Humankind began writing long before paper appeared. In ancient times, people used whatever suitable material that was easily accessible and relatively durable. Generally the term manuscript is referred to any document written by hand. But, besides this, manuscript is also applied for information that is recorded in any other ways than writing, for example inscriptions on stone tablets or on any other things. In China, manuscripts of various forms were discovered. These were Oracle —Bone Inscription or Jiaguwen, Inscriptions on Bronze Objects, Bamboo and Wood Slips, Inscriptions on Drum-shaped Stone Blocks, Inscriptions on Stone Tablets, Silk, Rubbings, paper and scrolls.

Chinese script is one of the oldest and most widely used writing systems in the world, boasting a history of five or six thousand years. About one-fourth of population on earth uses it. The creation and evolution of Chinese characters are closely interwoven with the development of Chinese culture. Chinese characters are the basic carriers of traditional Chinese culture, and, as an important tool for extending, spreading and exchanging ideas have played a critical role in the long history of the Chinese nation. One may well argue that without Chinese characters Chinese culture would not have achieved the splendors it did. It is difficult to determine the specific time when Chinese characters emerged.

There have been various stories about the origin of the Chinese script, with nearly all ancient writers attributing it to a man named Cangjie. Cangjie, according to one legend, saw a divine being whose face had unusual features that looked like a picture of writings. In replication of his image, Cangjie created the earliest written characters. After that, certain ancient accounts go on to say, millet rained from heaven and the spirits howled every night to lament the leakage of the divine secret of writing. Another story says that Cangjie saw the footprints of birds and beasts, which inspired him to create written characters. Evidently these stories cannot be accepted as the truth, for any script can only be a creation developed by the masses of the people to meet the needs of social life over a long period of trial and experiment. Cangjie, if there ever was such a man, must have been a prehistoric wise man who sorted out and standardized the characters that had already been in use. A group of ancient tombs have been discovered in recent years at Yanghe in Luxian County, Shandong Province. They date back 4,500 years and belong to a late period of the Dawenkou Culture. Among the large numbers of relics unearthed are about a dozen pottery wine vessels (called zun), which bear a character each. These characters are found to be stylized pictures of some physical objects. They are therefore called pictographs and, in style and structure, are already quite close to the inscriptions on the oracle bones and shells, though they antedate the latter by more than a thousand years. The pictographs, the earliest forms of Chinese written characters, already possessed the characteristics of a script.

The development of Chinese Writing System can be divided into the following stages:

Oracle—Bone Inscription (Jiaguwen)

The earliest Chinese written language appeared in the Shang Dynasty (1600-1100 BC). At that time, people believed in ghosts and practiced divination on important occasions. They inscribed the divination words on tortoise shells or animal bones, and painted them red to symbolize good luck or black to symbolize potential disaster. The words were inscribed with knives. Some of them are big, some are small, some are complicated, some are simple, but they are all well defined.

Examples of shell and bone writing were not found until Emperor Guangxu's reign during the Qing Dynasty (1644 -1911), thousands of years after they were made. The discovery occurred in Anyang, Henan Province, which was the capital city of the Shang Dynasty. In 1899, the banks of the Huanshui River in Henan Province collapsed, and many tortoise shells with carved patterns on them were revealed. At first, people regarded the shells as dragon bones and used them as medicine. The oracle bone inscriptions received their name after their content that is invariably related to divination. The ancient Chinese diviners used these bones as records of their activity, providing us with a detailed description of the topics that interested the Shang kings. Most of these divinations refer to hunting, warfare, weather, selection of auspicious days for ceremonies, etc.

Inscriptions on Bronze Objects — (Jinwen or Zhongdingwen)

A different type of early Chinese script in its long history of development is represented by the inscriptions cast or carved on ancient bronze objects of the Shang and Zhou dynasties. It is called Jinwen (literally, script on metal) and, as ancient bronzes are generally referred to as zhongding (bells and tripods) it is also called zhongdingmen. The ding, originally a big cooking pot with three (rarely four) legs, became a ritual object and a sign of power, and the owning of such tripods, as 41 as their sizes and numbers, was a status symbol of the Shang slave-owning aristocrats. At the beginning only the names of the owners were cast or engraved on the tripods. Later the tripods (and other bronzes) began to carry longer inscriptions stating the uses they were put to and the dates they were cast. Towards the end of the Warring States Period (475 221 B. C.) - the states of Zheng and Jin had their statutes promulgated and cast on tripods. Thus the inscriptions on the bronzes grew longer, from a few characters to a few hundred, from simple phrases to detailed accounts.

Many bronze objects bearing inscriptions have been unearthed in China and can be seen in a large number of museums. A priceless tripod is the Daynding (Large Tripod Bestowed upon Yu) dating from the early Zhou Dynasty (c. 11th century to 771 B. C.), now kept at the Museum of Chinese History in Beijing. About one meter high and weighing 153.5 kilograms, it has on its interior wall an inscription of 291 characters in 19 lines, by which Emperor Kang summed up the experience in founding a new nation and drew lessons from the failure of the preceding Shang Dynasty. The inscription also mentions that the King awarded his aristocrat follower Yu 1, 722 slaves of various grades and large numbers of carriages and horses. Another important bronze called Maogongding, now kept in Taiwan Province, belongs to the late Western Zhou. It bears an inscription of 497 characters, the longest ever discovered on any bronze hitherto unearthed. It is an account of how King Xuan admonished, commended and awarded Maogong Yin; it also reveals the instability of the Western Zhou regime at the time. Both tripods furnish rare and valuable information to throw light on the slave society under the Western Zhou. The ancient bronzes reflect not only the high level that Chinese metallurgy attained in their time. The inscriptions they bear may well be regarded as "books in bronze" which fill important gaps left by the scanty written history of that remote age.

Scrolls

Scrolls constitute an important part of Chinese manuscript. Paper was invented in China around the 1st Century BC. Different fibers were used to make paper including hemp and bark from the paper mulberry. Several panels were glued together to form a scroll. Almost all of the Dunhuang manuscripts are in the form of scrolls.

Bamboo and Wood Slips - Zhujian yu Mujian

In museums of ancient history one often sees bamboo or wood strips written with characters by the writing brush. These slips are called Jian, the earliest form of books in China. The practice of writing on slips began probably during the Shang Dynasty (c. 16th-11th century B. C.) and lasted till the Eastern Han (AI) (25-220), extending over a period of 1,600 - 1,700 years. The historical Records, the first monumental general history written by the great historian Sima Qian (c. 110 B.C.-?), consisting of 520,000 characters in 130 chapters and covering a period of 3,000 years from the legendary Yellow Emperor to Emperor Wudi of the Han, was written on slips. So were other well known works of ancient China, including the Book of Songs (the earliest Chinese anthology of poems and songs from 11th century to about 600 B. C.) and Jiazhang Suanshu (Mathematics in Nine Chapters completed in the 1st century AD, the earliest book on mathematics in the country). Excavations in 1972 in an ancient tomb of the Western Han Dynasty (206 B. C.-A. D. 24) at Yinque Mountain, Linyi, Shandong Province brought to light 4,924 bamboo slips. They turned out to be hand-written, though incomplete, copies of two of China's earliest books on military strategy and tactics "The Art of War" by Sun Zi and "The Art of War" by Sun Bin. The latter had been missing for at least 1,400 years. The bamboo slips run from 20 to 70 cm in length. Judging from those unearthed from ancient tombs, royal decrees and statutes were written on slips 68 cm long, texts of the classics on 56-cm-long slips, and private letters on 23 cm ones. The brush was used in writing and, in case of mistakes, the wrong characters would be scraped off by means of a small knife to allow the correct ones to be filled in. The knife played the same role as the eraser today. Writing on bamboo or wood slips was done from top to bottom, with each line comprising from 10 to at most 40 characters. To write a work of some length, one would need thousands of slips. The written slips would then be bound together with strips into a book. Some books were so heavy that they had to be carried in carts. In some cases the blank slips were first bound into books before they were written on. Ancient books of bamboo and wood played an important part in the dissemination of knowledge in various fields. Besides the historical and administrative writings, the bamboo strips contain the famous Chinese philosophical texts, such as Laozi, Liji and Lunyu. They were in circulation over a long period until gradually replaced by paper which was invented in the Eastern Han Dynasty (AD 23-220).

Inscriptions on Drum-shaped Stone Blocks - Shiguwen

Shiguwen, the earliest Chinese script cut on stone, is in the form of inscriptions, on 10 drum-shaped stone blocks, of 10 poems of 4 character lines, depicting the ruler of a state on a big hunt. The characters are written in a style called dazhuan (big seal character) and have been taken as the "earliest model of zhuan-style writing", important to the development and studies of Chinese calligraphy. The "stone drums" were discovered in the Tang Dynasty (Al) 618-907) at Tianxing (present-day Baoji in Shaanxi Province) and caused a uproar among men of letters and calligraphers. Celebrated poets like Du Fu, Han Yu and Su Dongpo sang of the discovery in verse. Before the invention of paper and printing, the best way in China to keep outstanding writings and calligraphic works was to carve them on stone. Those cut on drum shaped blocks are called shiguwen (stone drum inscriptions); and those cut on steles and tablets are called beiwen. The former, being much earlier and rarer, are greatly treasured. Shiguwen (stone drum inscriptions) were engraved in the state of Qin during the Warring States Period (475-221 B. C.) and are therefore well over 2,000 years old.

Inscriptions on Stone Tablets - Beiwen

Before the invention of the art of printing, ancient Chinese relied to a great extent upon inscriptions on stone tablets to preserve and disseminate their culture and art. These inscriptions are known as beiwen (writings on stelae) or, less common, shishu (stone books). The earliest examples so far discovered are a set of 46 stelae engraved with the Confucian classics after the handwriting of the great Eastern Han calligrapher Cai Yong, carved in (Al) 175 or the fourth year in the reign of Xiping. They are called "Xiping Shijing" (Xiping Classics on Stone). The stelae stand side by side like walls of stone, a veritable library of stone books. The Forest of Stelae at Xi'an is not only a treasure house of Chinese literature and history but represents, a galaxy of the best calligraphers of different ages and schools, including all the different scripts-zhuan seal character, li (official script), cao (cursive) and kai (regular) -each with its representative works.

Writings on Silk

From sometime in the Warring States Period (475-221 B.C.) and over a long period of time in ancient China, plain silk of various descriptions joined bamboo and wood slips as the material for writing or painting on. Silk had advantages over the slips in that it was much lighter and could be cut in desired shapes and sizes and folded, the better to be kept and carried. But owing to its much greater cost, silk was never so popularly used as the slips. The most valuable find of ancient silk writings was made in 1973 from an ancient tomb known as the No. 3 Han Tomb at Mawangdui, Changsha, Hunan Province. It is in the form of 30-odd pieces of silk, bearing more than 120,000 characters. They consist largely of ancient works that had long been lost. For instance, Wuxingzhan describes the orbits of five planets (Venus, Jupiter, Mercury, Mars and Saturn) and gives the cycles of their alignment, all with a precision far more remarkable than similar works that appeared later. Also found were three maps drawn on silk, showing the topography, the stationing of troops and the cities and towns of certain regions of China. They are the earliest maps in China, and in the world as well, that have been made on the basis of field surveys. Silk was considered in old China an exquisite material for writing on; some were pre-marked with lines in vermilion. During the Tang Dynasty (618-907), it was the fashion to weave the lines into plain white silk to be used exclusively for writing. Many artists of today have carried on the ancient practice of painting and writing on silk.

Rubbings—Taben

To make rubbings from carved inscriptions was the earliest method of making copies in China before printing was invented. In ancient times, engravings were often made on stone of important imperial decrees, texts of Confucian classics, Buddhist scriptures, proved medical recipes as well as poems, pictures and calligraphic works by noted men of letters so that they may be appreciated and preserved for posterity. To make rubbings is to make copies from these cut inscriptions or pictures. The method followed is rather simple in principle. First a wetted piece of soft but firm paper was pasted (xuan paper is normally used) closely over the stone tablet or bronze and it was lightly beaten all over with the cushioned end of a stick so that the parts of paper over the cut hollows will sink in. The paper is then left on to dry. Then ink is applied by dabbing it on until the paper is turned into a copy with white characters or drawings on a black ground. Removed and dried, it becomes the rubbing. Rubbings vary and are called by different names according to the ink used. Wujinta (black gold rubbings) are made with very black ink; chanyita (cicada wing rubbings) are made with very light ink; zhuta (vermilion rubbings) with vermilion ink. With the bound book form, the rubbings become beitie (stele rubbings), which may be used either as models for calligraphy or kept in a collection for appreciation or research. As inscriptions on bronze, stone or wood wear out with time, early rubbings made from famous pieces of work are more valued and cherished than the ones made later.

This demonstrates that, with the development of Chinese writing system at various period of history, many important documents and texts were inscribed on bones and bronzes and some earliest manuscript of some famous Chinese philosophical and historical texts were written on bamboo strips, silk etc which played an important part in preserving and disseminating the culture and art of the Chinese people.

References

1. "The Cambridge Encyclopaedia of Chinas" ed. Brian Hook, Cambridge University Press, Cambridge, new York, 1982.
2. "Information China-Vol.1" ed. C.V.James, Pergamon Press, Oxford, England, 1989.
3. "A Study of Chinese Characters", ed.Li Dasui, Beijing University Publishing House, Beijing, 2003.pp.18-33.
4. "Zhongguo Wenhua Yaulue", "An outline of Chinese Culture" ed. Cheng Fuzhen, Foreign Language Training and Research Publishing House, Beijing, 2007. pp.61-65.

The Development of Script for Nagamese

14

Ajit Kumar Baishya

Nagaland is one of the smallest states in India having an area of 16,579 sq. km. Nagaland became the 16th full-fledged Indian state on the 1st of December 1963. Up to 1961, this area was known as the Naga Hills and Tuensang Area (NHTA). The total population of Nagaland is 19,90,036 as per census 2001. Nagaland has a total number of 1112 inhabited villages where people from different linguistic background reside.

Nagaland is the abode of 23 officially recognized indigenous ethnic groups beside many other tribes. They are the speakers of Tibeto-Burman languages which are mutually unintelligible. According to Lasuh (2002), 66 Naga tribes are found in India and Myanmar. Apart from their home state Nagaland, Nagas arc also found in the Indian states of Arunachal Pradesh, Assam, and Manipur. Though the language profile in 1991 census mentioned that Ao, Sema, Konyak, Angami, Lotha, Phom, Chokri, Sangtam, Yimchungre, Zeliang, Rengma, Chang, Kuki, Assamese, Pochury, Bodo, and Dimasa speakers are found in Nagaland but in reality, it will be more as no detailed study has been done to ascertain the actual number of languages spoken in the state of Nagaland. Similarly, it is also very difficult to say the actual number of Naga tribes found in Nagaland as new tribes are 'discovered' every now and then.

Nagaland is probably the first state in India which was created on the ethnic lines, not on linguistic lines. It is said that in Nagaland language changes abruptly from village to village barely a few kilometers away from each other. As a large number of languages are spoken in Nagaland which is mutually unintelligible, "...in earlier days men and women in the same household sometimes had to use different forms of speech" (Elwin, 1961). The direct consequence of this is the creation of a kind of linguistic islet among the different Naga villages, which may consists of only a few families. Another outcome of this kind of isolation is the breaking down of the communicative channel as far as the usage of an indigenous Naga language for this purpose is concerned. It is interesting as well as baffling to comprehend the fact that none of the Naga tribes want to learn the language of the other tribe as a means of inter-lingual communication. This refusal to learn the language of the other tribe seems to have certain socio-political reasons. But in order to survive, all the human beings need a language to communicate with each other. The Nagas also had to communicate sometimes with other tribes. Since the Nagas did not want to learn the language of the other tribes even for the sake of minimum level of communication as they are having a kind of antagonistic attitude towards each other which goes back to the primitive days of head-hunting, the Nagas developed a lingua franca, Nagamese, which is based on Assamese, the state language of Assam. Since Nagamese is not the mother tongue of any of the Naga tribe, there is no apparent antagonism towards the use of Nagamese on the part of any of the Nagas though they do not like to acknowledge the knowledge or even the existence of Nagamese in Nagaland. Above all, "Naga-Assamese (read Nagamese), though a somewhat clumsy vehicle of conversation, is very easy to pick up and with a little application can be spoken perfectly provided the learner has no previous knowledge of real Assamese. It is, moreover, an excellent vehicle for the expression of Naga turns of speech and thought, and therefore infinitely better as a medium for conversing to Nagas than Hindustani, or even English, would be, being capable, as it is, of representing almost the precise shade of meaning required" (Hutton, 1921). Nagamese is the de facto lingua franca of Nagaland, which is spoken and understood in almost every nook and corner of the state.

Nagamese is the medium of expression among the various Naga tribes as well as non-Nagas who are living in Nagaland. Nagamese evolved as the Nagas were maintaining a regular contact with the Assamese speakers over a very long period of time. In fact, the evolution and development of Nagamese goes back to the time of invasion of Assam by the powerful Shan ethnic group from South East Asia (popularly known as Ahom in Assam) in 1228. The Ahoms (including the Assamese) and the Nagas were maintaining some kind of social, political and economic contact with each other from 1228 onwards which was marked by both aggression and camaraderie. It is assumed that this socio-political contact and trade between the Nagas and Assamese helped the formation of Nagamese. Apart from that, Assamese was also taught to the Naga children for some time in the government schools of Nagaland just after India's independence. But after the formation of Nagaland state, Assamese was abandoned in favour of the indigenous Naga languages and English became the only official language of Nagaland. But Nagamese in Nagaland is so omnipresent that "... for a long time past Nagas of different groups have talked to one another ... in Assamese, and the Nagas themselves observed with some amusement that at a conference at which they demanded separation from Assam, many of the speakers made their speeches in the Assamese language" (Elwin, 1961).

Nagamese is the unendorsed lingua franca of Nagaland. Therefore, it can not be used in the government offices in Nagaland. But in reality, almost everywhere one can find the usage of Nagamese including the primary education system. The primary school teachers use both mother tongue and Nagamese in the classroom because English is still a foreign language to the students. The usage of Nagamese is more common in those classes where students belong to different linguistic groups. We have observed that the primary level students understand the lesson better in Nagamese than English. Nagamese is used throughout Nagaland for day today oral communication. There is an easy code switching from English/Hindi or a Naga language to Nagamese. Nagamese is abundantly used in all sorts of communication, except for some specific, restricted, formal functions. It might be a variety with restricted structures and vocabulary but it is not a restricted code. It carries the maximum functional load amongst the Nagas, especially the uneducated Nagas.

Though one has to use Nagamese in order to survive in Nagaland, it is not written down. In other words, it is an oral language, not a written one. It does not have a writing system of its own. Though a number of Nagamese programmes are broadcasted at different points of time by the All India Radio Centre, Kohima, different scripts were used by different individuals. A lot of short films, video films, music videos, audio cassettes in Nagamese are also being produced and different scripts having diverse styles, conventions are used according to the convenience of the individuals. Hence, there is no consistency in the present writing system, if we can call it a system at all. Apart from it, thc Nagaland government also does not recognize this language as we mentioned above. But nobody can deny its importance, at least, in Nagaland. Therefore, if we can devise or prepare a uniform writing system for this language, it will be immensely helpful not only to the people of Nagaland but also to all the language lovers of the world.

In order to develop a writing system of an unwritten language, one must remember that the proposed system should be scientifically adequate, easy to type in the computer or type writer and at the same time it should be acceptable to the concerned speech community. Keeping the above points in mind, the phonemic based orthography in Roman script can be used for writing the Nagamese language. The phonemic based orthography has the advantage of having one to one correspondence between the letter and sound. There is no variation of any sorts. Roman script is advocated for Nagamese because of the simple reason that the few Naga languages that have a writing system use the Roman script. Hence, the Naga speakers will not face much difficulty in reading and writing Nagamese if the Roman alphabets are used as they are already conversant with the alphabets.

The proposed phonemic based orthography for Nagamese will try to wipe out as much inconsistencies and inadequacies as possible so that we can have a uniform pronunciation system of Nagamese. This will not only help the Naga speakers but also any learners who want to learn the Nagamese. It will also help the language to get standardized.

Based on our fieldwork conducted in different parts of Nagaland over the last couple of years, we have found out that Nagamese has the below mentioned six vowel phonemes without having any kind of contrast as far as length is concerned.

i **u**

e **o**

∂

a:

These six vowels may be represented orthographically by the following Roman alphabets with some minor modifications here and there.

Phoneme	**Grapheme**		
/**i**/	<**i**> as in English pronunciation		'kill', 'deal', 'sheep' etc.
/**u**/	<**u**>	do	'cook', 'shoe', 'put' etc.
/**e**/	<**e**>	do	'cake', 'break', 'bad' etc.
/**o**/	<**o**>	do	'ox', 'cot', 'dog' etc.
/ /	<**a**>	do	'caught', 'sir', 'birth' etc.
/**a:**/	<**a:** >	do	'calm', 'arm', 'cut' etc.

So if the above mentioned Roman graphemes for the six Nagamese vowels are followed, we believe that all the Nagamese words can be conveniently written down. Consider the following cases.

<**i**> as in /itu/ 'this', /ita:/ 'brick', /iki/ 'same' etc; <**u**> as in /ukil/ 'lawyer', /ut/ 'camel', /ulu/ 'owl' etc.; <**e**> as in /ek/ 'one', /tep/ 'tap', /a:ste/ 'slow' etc; <**o**> as in /okra:/ 'simpleton', /bosti/ 'village', /ka:so/ 'tortoise'; <**a**> as in /anda:/ 'egg', /nakli/ 'artificial', /pandra/ 'fifteen' etc; <**a:**> as in /a:ko/ 'again', /gha:s/ 'grass', /nila:/ 'blue' etc.

Nagamese has the following twenty six consonantal phonemes having identical allophones.

Stops

p	**b**	**t**	**d**	**k**	**g**
ph	**bh**	**th**	**dh**	**kh**	**gh**

Continuants

m		**n**		**η**
	s		**š**	**h**
	č	**ĵ**		
	čh	**ĵh**		
		r		
		l		
w				**y**

All the Stop phonemes with the exception of /**gh**/ occur initially, medially and finally in Nagamese words. We have not found the occurrence of /**gh**/ in word final position. According to the phonemic principle, one should never mark the allophones of phonemes orthographically. Since Nagamese consonants have no separate allophones, we do not face any problem here. Therefore, /**p**/, /**b**/, /**t**/, /**d**/, /**k**/, /**g**/, /**ph**/, /**bh**/, /**th**/, /**dh**/, /**kh**/ and /**gh**/ phonemes may be represented by the existing Roman alphabets <**p, b, t, d, k, g, ph, bh, th, dh, kh, gh**>. Consider the following examples.

<**p**> /puk/ 'ant', /ka:pur/ 'cloth', /pa:p/ 'sin'.

<**b**> /billi/ 'cat', /kubudur/ 'pigeon', /jib/ 'tongue'.

<**t**> /ta:ra:/ 'star/s', /guti/ 'pox, pimples', /da:t/ 'tooth'.

<**d**> /da:m/ 'cost', /ba:ndor/ 'monkey', /dud/ 'milk'.

<**k**> /ka:n/ 'ear', /iki/ 'same', /na:k/ 'nose'.

<**g**> /gola:/ 'neck', /ba:ga:n/ 'garden', /mag/ 'mug'.

<**ph**> /phul/ 'flower', /sa:pha:/ 'clean', /ma:ph/ 'pardon'.

<**bh**> /bha:k/ 'tiger', /bha:bha:/ 'to think', /la:bh/ 'profit'.

<**th**> /thu/ 'spit', /matha:/ 'head', /a:th/ 'eight'.

<**dh**> /dhup/ 'sunshine', /a:dha:/ 'half', /gondh/ 'smell'.

<**kh**> /khun/ 'blood', /na:khun/ 'nails', /dukh/ 'sorrow'.

<**gh**> /ghora:/ 'horse', /egharo/ 'eleven'.

As far as the continuants are concerned, there is not much problem. Out of the three nasal sounds, /**m**/, /**n**/ can be orthographically represented by the existing Roman alphabets **<m>**, and **<n>.** As there is no available Roman symbol for /η/, this phoneme can be easily represented in Nagamese by the Roman digraph **<ng>.** Similarly, for /š / sound in Nagamese, Roman digraph <**sh**> can conveniently be used.

For the purpose of writing down the four affricate sounds, viz. /c̆ /, /ĵ /, /c̆**h**/, /**jh**/, in Roman system for Nagamese language, it will be logical to use digraphs <**ch**> for /c̆ /, <**jh**> for / ĵ /, <**chh**> for /c̆h/, and <**jhh**> for /ĵh/. Regarding the fricative /**h**/, trill /**r**/, lateral /**l**/, and semi-vowels /**w, y**/, the Roman alphabets <**h, r, l, w** and **y**> can be used without any problem.

The above discussion on the usage of Roman script for an unwritten language like Nagamese makes it clear that the Roman alphabets can be easily used for writing the lingua franca Nagamese and we do not see any major problem in this. Whatever minor problems one faces in this regard, can easily be worked out by slightly amending the existing Roman alphabet system. Therefore, we are proposing this phonemic based orthography for writing Nagamese in Roman script.

The usage of Nagamese is found ubiquitously all over Nagaland. It is profusely utilized in almost all types of communication not only between Nagas belonging to different tribes but also between Nagas and non Nagas as well as between non Nagas. Nagamese is developing and expanding lexically day by day as its domains of usage are increasing gradually in the state of Nagaland. It can be said that Nagamese is the only tongue in Nagaland, which is understood and operated in every part of Naga speaking precincts. So, Nagamese is escalating and adapting itself to new socio-cultural environment, though the Nagas, particularly the educated Nagas, do not like to admit this reality. Nagamese holds the utmost practical weight in Nagaland, though unofficially, and it offers a strong base for the harmony in multiplicity in a state like Nagaland where multilingualism and multiculturalism are the orders of the day. Therefore, we must try our level best to transform this unwritten lingua franca into a written one so that Nagamese can flourish more and keep on serving the people of Nagaland altruistically. This can only be done by accepting a script unanimously. Roman script seems to be the only feasible answer. This will not only help the further growth of Nagamese but it will also revitalize this language and as a result of it, there can not be any possibility of language death or attrition as far as status of Nagamese in Nagaland is concerned. The development and the usage of script will also make it easy for the Ethno linguists to preserve the varied culture and oral literature of the Nagas in Nagamese language for the future Naga and non-Naga generation.

References

Baishya, A. K. (2006). "The making of Nagamese: A Historical Perspective", in *Assam University Journal,* Vol. I, No. 1, Silchar. Pp 105-108.

—— (2007). "Relexification in Nagamese: An Observation", in *International Journal of Dravidian Linguistics,* Vol. XXXVI, No. 2, Thiruvananthapuram. Pp 197-206.

Dhongde, R. V. & A. K. Baishya. (1998). "Nagamese: An Orphan Language", in *Indian Linguistics*, Vol. 59, No. 1-4, Pune. Pp 81-94.

Elwin, V. (1961). *Nagaland.* The Research Dept. Shillong.

Florian, C. (2003). *Writing Systems: An Introduction to their Linguistic Analysis*. CUP, Cambridge.

Gai, G. S. (1986). *Introduction to Indian Epigraphy*. Central Institute of Indian Languages, Mysore.

Hutton, J. H. (1921). *The Angami Nagas*. Macmillan. London.

Lasuh, W. (Ed). (2002). *The Naga Chronicle*. Regency Publications, New Delhi.

Sinha, A. J. (1990). *Script for Tribal Languages*. Amar Prakashan, New Delhi.

Dimasa Writing System: A Linguistic Approach

15

KH. DHIREN SINGHA

It is a common phenomenon that a large number of languages in the present world which do not have their own script or writing system, are used only in spoken or oral form. One of the prime instances is that the tribal languages of North Eastern India lack their own script except Khamti. They used to adopt a script or a writing system which may be either Indian or foreign origin. Dimasa, also a tribal language which belongs to Tibeto-Burman language family, is widely spoken in N.C.Hills, Karbi Anglong, Cachar, Nagaon, and Hailakandi districts of Assam, and Dimapur Sub-division of Nagaland by over 90,000 speakers according to 1991 Census of India. Like many other tribal languages of North East India, Dimasas do not have their own script or writing system for writing their language. For the fact, they used to write Bengali, Assamese, Devanagiri and Roman scripts according to the convenience of the individual. As a result, there is no consistency in the current writing system but in order to make consistency in their writing system, the Dimasa Literary Organisation (Dimasa Lairidim Mel) have adopted the Roman script for writing Dimasa language in the last meeting of DLM held on 20th to 21st December, 2003 at the Cultural Hall, Haflong.

Devising or preparing a writing system for the unwritten languages or languages which do not have their own script, is not only an important but also a difficult task. In true sense, while attempting to devise the same for the development of a particular language; one generally needs to follow the following points, that is, the proposed device should be:

- scientifically adequate.
- as easy as possible to learn.
- easy to type in the computer or type writer.
- acceptable to the community concerned.

On the basis of the above points, it is proposed to suggest a phonemic based orthography for writing Dimasa language in Roman script. The objective of the phonemic based orthography is that there is one to one correspondence between the letters and the sounds that correspond. In other words, the correspondence of sounds and letters should not be variable in character. For instance, the present writing system of English is highly variable in character i.e., there is quite arbitrary between the letters and sounds that correspond. Here, the same letters or combinations of letters do not always have the same sounds. The following letters have different sounds in different words:

e.g. *'a'* as in f*a*ther, t*a*ke, *a*ss, *a*bove, etc.

'i' b*i*t, b*i*nd, b*i*rd, d*i*rt, etc.

Again, the same sound is often represented by different letters, for example,

f' as in *f*ather, gra*ph* and tou*gh* etc.

The phonemic based orthography for Dimasa language has been devised for representing the actual pronunciation of language. However, the case of tone in the language, other than phonemic, the conventional recourse should be taken for representing the same orthographically, because diacritics like acute (') and grave (‘) for **high** and **low** tones cannot be typed conveniently in the computer or typewriter. Similarly, in the use of central mid vowel /∂/, the modern typewriter or computer generally do not have the letter corresponding to it. Hence, the phonemic based orthography is required not only for having greater word recognition skills but also for having proficiency in reading and writing from the learners' point of view. Along with the phonemic based orthographic lines, some modifications or additions are suggested below in the Roman script in use for writing Dimasa.

Phonemic inventory:

Vowels:

	Front		Central		Back	
	UR	R	UR	R	UR	R
High	i					u
Mid	e		∂			o
Low			a			

Fig. 1

Consonants:

		Bilabial	Alveolar	Post. Alv.	Palatal	Velar	Glottal
	vl.	p		t		k	
Stops							
	vd.	b		d		g	
Nasals		m	n			ṇ	
	vl.		s			h	
Fricatives							
	vd.		z				
Lateral			l				
Trill			r				
Semi-Vowels		w			y		

Fig. 2

Tones:

high	low
/	\

Level tone is unmarked.

Fig. 3

In order to devise Dimasa writing system according to their phonemic inventory, Roman alphabets are no exception to represent the number of phonemes available in the language. However, Dimasa do not have the corresponding sounds available in Roman alphabets like c, f, j, q and x.

As I have shown earlier, Dimasa has six vocalic phonemes /a, i, e, o, u and ∂/ without having length contrast. These may be represented orthographically by the following graphemes of Roman alphabets with some modifications.

phonemes	**graphemes**	
/a/	<a:>	as in English father, heart, bucket etc.
/i/	<i>	as in English seat, hit, kid, etc.
/e/	<e>	as in English sat, dead, get, etc.
/o/	<o>	as in English dog, pot, box, etc.
/u/	<u>	as in English book, shoe, do, etc.
/∂/	<a>	as in English bird, alone, author, etc.

It is to be noted that other than the above, the alternative device which is more preferable by the community regarding the orthographic representation of vocalic phonemes of Dimasa is that the vowel phonemes / a, i, e, o & u/ will be represented by Roman letters < a, i, e, o & u >. However, the central mid vowel /∂/ will not be represented orthographically for the convenience of typing, it will be used to write with consonants inherently, that does in the Devanagiri writing system. So it is not applicable in the case of Dimasa language not only for identifying consonant clusters (CC), but also for representing the /∂/ vowel in the language, that is, there are number of syllable initial CCs in Dimasa like/ pl-, kl-, pr-, kr-, br-, gr-, bl, gl- / etc. as in / ***pluŋ//*** 'no fixing' /***kl***ai/ 'do', /***pr***ik/ 'silent', /***kr***asi/ 'century', /***br***ai/ 'buy', /***gl***ai/ 'fall' etc. and we have many more lexical items with /∂/ vowel like //b∂dam 'many', / gôdain/ 'new', /gônaŋ/ 'rich', /gôsain/ 'cold', etc. Here it should be mentioned clearly that if we write /bôdam/, /gôdain/, /gônaŋ/ and /gôsain/ as *bdam, gdain, gna?,* and *gsai?*, there must be confused that / bd-, gd-, gn-, gs- / are consonant clusters or not? Therefore, these kinds of problems arise if we follow the above convention.

Dimasa has three voiceless unaspirated stops / p, t, k /. Each of them has two allophones, (i) the voiceless unaspirated stops [p], [t], & [k], which occur in syllable final positions, while (ii) the voiceless aspirated stops [ph], [th] & [kh] which occur in syllable initial position as shown below:

/p/	[rep]	'write'	[phai]	'come'
	[bedep]	'brance'	[phlao]	'fertile'
/t/	[buzut]	'inconvenience'	[than]	'go'
	[matla]	'maid'	[thao]	'oil'
/k/	[thailik]	'banana'	[khlai]	'do'
	[grik]	'intelligent'	[khuzer]	'lip'

According to the phonemic principles, the members (allophones) of phonemes should not mark orthographically. So, it is proposed to use only < p, t, k > for the sake of the principle of economy as in the following examples.

rep, pai, bedep, plao, buzut, tang, matla, tao, tailik, klai, grik, kuzer etc.

It is also important to note that Dimasa does not have labio-dental fricative sounds /f/ and /v/. Sometimes, the native speakers used to write ***f*ang** for ***p*ang** (the suggested one) or ***ph*ang** 'plant'.

Dimasa also has three voiced unaspirated stops /b, d, g/ which occur only in syllable initial position as in the following examples.

/bai/	'dance'	/subuη /	'person'	*re*b*
/gupu/	'white'	/lugu/	'friend'	*zi*g*
/dao/	'bird'	/bedep/	'brance'	*buzu*d*

In the case of above phonemes / b, d, g / which can be represented by the existing Roman alphabets < b, d, and g> respectively.

In Dimasa, we have three nasal sounds viz. m (bilabial), n (alveolar) and ? (velar). Orthographically, they can be represented by the existing Roman alphabets <m> and <n> except the velar nasal / η /. Since, there is no symbol in the Roman alphabets for the velar nasal, it can be represented by the digraph <ng>. So it is applicable in the case of Dimasa tha no consonant clusters comprised of a sequence of /n/ and /g/ phonemes in Dimasa. Thus, we can use the digraph <ng> for the velar nasal / η.

Regarding the lateral /l/, trill /r/, semi-vowels /w, y/ and the voiceless glottal fricative /h/ phonemes, the Roman symbols < l, r, w, y and h> can be used without any problem.

Dimasa has two alveolar fricative sounds /s/ and /z/. Each of them have two allophones, the phoneme /s/ has (i) the voiceless alveolar fricative [s], and (ii) the voiceless alveo-palatal affricate [ts]. The former [s] occurs elsewhere while the latter [ts] occurs only when it is followed by the high vowels /i, & u/. Similarly, the phoneme

/z/ has two allophones (i) the voiced alveolar fricative [z], and (ii) the voiced alveo-palatal affricate [dz]. The former [z] occurs elsewhere while the latter [dz] occurs when it is followed by high vowels / i & u /. However, it is not necessary to mark the allophones of phonemes /s & z/ for the sake of economy. So these two phonemes can be represented by the Roman alphabets <s> and <z> respectively.

Dimasa has two tones which are phonemic. It is important to represent tones orthographically for the better semantic interpretation of the language. So, we can make different orthographic representation for tonal distinctions in Dimasa in the following principles.

(i) The words which carrying high pitch can be represented by marking <***h***> after the vowels or diphthongs e.g. **su*h*** 'wash', **dao*h*** ' bird', **tu*h*** 'sleep', **so*h*ng** 'stand' **ka*h*** 'bind'etc.

(ii) The low tone is proposed to be left unmarked, e.g., **su** 'measure', **dao** 'weave', **tu** 'wear', **song** 'cook', **ka** 'bitter' etc.

In marking tones, the low tone is left unmarked while the high tone is marked by <h>. Here, it should be made clear that there is no phonetic value of the voiceless glottal fricative /h/ in syllable or word final position in the sound system of Dimasa.

In addition to the above discussion, the phonemes with their allophones and their corresponding graphic representations particularly in Roman alphabets in the current writing system of Dimasa are given in the following chart.

Phonemes	Allophones	Present Graphemes	Suggested Graphemes et al
Vowels:			
/i/	**[i]** **[I]**	**<i>**	**<i>**
/e/	**[e]** **[E]**	**<e>**	**<e>**
/a/	**[a]**	**<a>**	**<a:>**
/ə/	**[ə]**	**Not othog- -raphically marked**	**<a>**

Consonants:

/p/	**[p]** **[ph]**	**<p/ph/f>**	**<p>**
/b/	**[b]**	**<b>**	**<b>**
/t/	**[t]** **[th]**	**<t/th>**	**<t>**
/d/	**[d]**	**<d>**	**<d>**
/k/	**[k]** **[kh]**	**<k/kh>**	**<k>**
/g/	**[g]**	**<g>**	**<g>**
/m/	**[m]**	**<m>**	**<m>**
/n/	**[n]**	**<n>**	**<n>**
/η/	**[η]**	**ng>**	**<ng>**
/s/	**[s]** **[ts]**	**<s/sh>**	**<s>**
/z/	**[z]** **[dz]**	**<j/z>**	**<z>**
/h/	**[h]**	**<h>**	**<h>**
/w/	**[w]**	**<w>**	**<w>**
/y/	**[y]**	**<y>**	**<y>**

Tones:

H /	**/**	**not ortho- -graphically marked**	**<h> after vowel or diphthong.**
**L **	****	**do**	**left unmarked**

Abbreviations and symbols used:

H=high, L=low, Alv.=alveolar, vl.=voiceless, vd.=voiced, UR=unrounded, R=rounded, / /=phonemic, [ ]=phonetic, I=the lower high front unrounded vowel, E= the lower mid front unrounded vowel, U= the lower high back rounded vowel, Ū = the lower mid back unrounded vowel.

References

1. Barua, N. 1985. Anglo-Assamese-Dimasa Dictionary. Publication Board, Assam, Guwahti.
2. Florian, Coulmas. 2003. Writing Systems: An Introduction to their Linguistic Analysis, Cambridge University Press, Cambridge.
3. Gai, G.S. 1986. Introduction of Indian Epigraphy, CIIL, Mysore.
4. George, L. Campbel. 1977. Handbook of Scripts and Alphabets. Routledge : London and New York.
5. Hagjer, Nirupoma. 1972. Dimasa, Guwahati.
6. I. J. Gelb. 1974 (4th ed.) A Study of Writing. University of Chicago Press: Chicago & London.
7. Jeba Singha, Ananthi. 1990. Script for Tribal Languages. Amar Prakashan, New Delhi.
8. Krishna, Sumi. 1991. India's Living Languages. Allied Publishers, New Delhi.
9. Miri, Mrinal (ed.) 1982. Linguistic Situation in North-East India. NEICSSR, Shillong.
10. Pike, Kenneth L. 1947. Phonemics: A Technique for Reducing Languages to writing. University of Michigan: Ann Abor.
11. P. Daniels et.al (eds) 1996. The World's Writing System. United Bible Society. North - Holland Publishing Co., Amsterdam.
12. Singha, Dhiren kh. 2001. The Phonology and Morphology of Dimasa. Unpublished M. Phil dissertation, Assam University, Silchar.
13. Singha, Dhiren kh. 2004. The Structure of Dimasa: A Typological Study. Unpublished Ph. D. dissertation. Assam University, Silchar.
14. Singha, Dhiren kh. 2007. An Introduction to Dimasa Phonology. DVS Publishers, Guwahati.
15. Smalley, W. A. (ed.) 1964). Orthography Studies: Articles on new Writing Systems. United Bible Society. North-Holland Publishing Co., Amsterdam.

Problems in Editing the Sanskrit and the Tibetan Texts of the Kāmadhenu

16

LATA MAHESH DEOKAR

Kāmadhenu

Kāmadhenu, one of the earliest commentaries on the Amarakośa (A.Ko.), was known to Sanskritists from the citations scattered in the Amara commentaries such as Rāyamukuṭa's Padacandrikā (PC), Mallinātha's Amarapadapārijāta (AP) etc. and other works such as Śaraṇadeva's Durghaṭavṛtti, Ujjvaladatta's Uṇādisūtravṛtti etc. T. R. Cintamani was the first to locate a fragmentary manuscript of this commentary that is preserved in the Government Oriental Manuscripts Library, Chennai. In 1935 and 1937, Rahul Sankrityayan discovered three more incomplete Sanskrit MSS of the Kāmadhenu from the Ngor and the Sa-skya monasteries in Tibet.[1] He also informed us about one more incomplete MS of the Kāmadhenu preserved in the Lalchand Research Library (Lahore). Thus, we come to know about the existence of as many as five incomplete MSS of the Kāmadhenu.

From the colophon to the first *kāṇḍa,* we come to know that the author of this commentary on the Amarakośa is Subhūticandra (Subhūti). Most of the classical Indian authors refer to him by a shorter name Subhūti[2]. The Tibetan tradition refers to him as Subhūticandra [Rab-'byor-zla-ba].[3] He is supposed to be a Buddhist, which is clear from the mention of Lord Samantabhadra who is invoked in the benedictory verses of his commentary, which, though missing in Sanskrit, are preserved in the Tibetan translations. Though his commentary was translated into Tibetan, we do not find any reference to Subhūticandra in the Tibetan histories by Bu-ston Rin-chen-grub and Lāmā Tāranātha.

Subhūti's Kāmadhenu was written in the second quarter of the twelfth century A.D. just before Sarvānanda's Ṭīkāsarvasva (TS). He is considered to have hailed from Bengal as he is cited mainly by Puruṣottama, Śaraṇadeva, Ujjvaladatta,

Rāyamukuṭa and many other Bengali writers.[4] His reference to certain dialectical words such as *bhava* (= *bhrama* "whirlpool, swirl") and *pāhnī* (= *vāriparṃī)* as prevalent in Magadha and Varendrī respectively, points to the same conclusion.

Importance of the Kāmadhenu

Subhūti is cited by many subsequent Amara commentators such as Rāyamukuṭa, Mallinātha and Bommagaṇṭi Appayārya, which shows his considerable influence on later writers. Subhūti's Kāmadhenu is the only commentary on the A.Ko. that crossed the boundaries of India and reached Tibet and Mongolia. Kāmadhenu, being one of the earlier commentaries on the A.Ko., can prove very helpful in deciding the original text of the A.Ko. and discovering changes which took place since then.

This is an exhaustive, word-to-word commentary and if restored in Sanskrit, it would be the biggest commentary on the A.Ko.. Though both the MSS. of the Kāmadhenu are incomplete, one can get a fair idea of its exhaustive nature from whatever is available to us at present. It is more elaborate than Jātarūpa's commentary (Jā) and Kṣīrasvāmin's Kṣīrodghāṭana (KS), the two earlier commentaries of the A.Ko. Fullness of treatment supplying a wealth of details is a characteristic of Subhūti's commentary. It provides derivations with the help of grammatical rules.[5]

Though P. K. Gode had expressed a need for the publication of this commentary,[6] this dream could not materialize due to several possible reasons. First reason is that both the Sanskrit MSS of this commentary are fragmentary in nature. Secondly, the Tibetan canonical translations are also incomplete and they are not word-to-word translations. Many times, the Sanskrit text and its Tibetan counterpart do not match with each other. Third and the most important reason is that, though scholars are aware of Si-tu's translation of the Kāmadhenu, probably nobody had an access to his translation.

In my doctoral dissertation I have ventured to prepare a critical edition of the Kāmadhenu, both in Sanskrit and in Tibetan. Though the biggest fragment available extends upto the commentary on the A.Ko. II.2.5, the scope of that critical edition was restricted up to the commentary on the A.Ko. I.4.8, i.e. till the extent of the oldest Māgadhī MS. The main reason for curtailing the scope of the critical edition was that the Grantha MS and its Devanāgarī transcript, which are available up to the commentary on the A.Ko. II.2.5, contain certain interpolated passages. At this stage, it is difficult to identify them in the absence of the Māgadhī MS.

In this article, I have tried to shed some light on the problems faced while editing this text in Sanskrit and Tibetan.

Sanskrit MSS of the Kāmadhenu

Out of the three incomplete MSS that R. Sankrityayan discovered in Tibet, he could bring the photo plates of only one MS with him. This is the first MS (henceforth R) which was used for the critical edition. This is a palm-leaf MS written in the *Māgadhī* script. The commentary available is from A.Ko. I.1.1 up to I.4.8.

Another palm-leaf MS of the Kāmadhenu written in the Grantha script was previously preserved in the Lalchand Research Library (Lahore). After the partition of India, the entire collection was taken to the Vishweshwarananda Vedic Research Institute, Hoshiarpur. Afterwards, it was shifted to the D. A. V. College, Chandigarh. This MS (henceforth C) contains the commentary on the A.Ko. I.1.51 up to II.2.5.

R is supposed to be closer to the original text. The first and the foremost reason is that, R is written in the Māgadhī script prevalent in Eastern region from where Subhūti is supposed to have hailed. Secondly, the Māgadhī script belongs to a period 10th - 12th century A.D., which matches with the floruit of Subhūti. In order to transcribe the text into the South Indian Grantha script, there should have been at least one MS as an exemplar in some Eastern script, as Subhūti belongs to the Eastern part of India. These facts point to the fact that the Grantha MS is not the oldest one. Another fact, which strengthens this assumption, is that many a times readings in C are of elaborate nature and some portion appears to have been interpolated.

The fragment of the MS, which T. R. Cintamani examined, extended from the commentary on A.Ko. I.1.51 up to the commentary on II.2.5. This is a paper MS (henceforth M), written in the Devanāgarī script. It is mentioned on the last page, i.e. on p. no. 205, that this MS was transcribed in 1919-20, from a MS of M. R. Ry. Narayana Nambudripad, Kutalurmara, Narei, Malabar district. When this MS was compared with C, it became clear that the extent and the contents of both these MSS are exactly the same. D. D. Kosambi (1954:69, n. 1) informs us that "The Subhūticandra (between 1062 & 1172) fragment was copied out for my use from a Malabār palm-leaf at the D.A.V. College library, Hoshiarpur, Madras Govt. R. 2933 being a recent paper transcript". Thus, it is clear that M is a direct copy of the MS C.

Tibetan translation of the Kāmadhenu

In the thirteenth century, grags-pa rgyal-mtshan (1283-1359 A.D.), the translator (lo-tsā-ba) of Yar-kluṅs and Kīrticandra translated both, the A.Ko. and its commentary, the Kāmadhenu, into Tibetan. The translations were done at Yambu (= Svayambhū), the ancient capital of Nepal. Both these translations are found in the *mDo* [*Sūtra*] section in the Narthang (N) and the Peking (P) editions of the Tibetan Tripiṭaka. This is an abridged translation of only the first part, extending from the beginning up to the commentary on the A.Ko. I.3.15. Though the text of the Kāmadhenu as preserved in P is exactly the same, unlike N, it extends up to the commentary on the A.Ko. II.8.82. It seems probable that originally the extent of P was also the same as that of N and that from I.3.15 onwards the translation was borrowed from some other source, most probably from the Derge edition as it also extends up to II.8.82 and from I.3.16 onwards P and D are exactly the same, leaving aside some spelling variations. N omits references to authorities and quotations from the literature. At some places, it gives mere synonyms.

Revisions of the Tibetan Translation of the Kāmadhenu

In the 15th century A.D. *Chos-skyoṅs-bzaṅ-po* [Dharmapālabhadra] (1441 - 1528 A.D.), the translator of the Zha-lu monastery, revised the Tibetan translations of both these texts. These are included in the *mDo* [*Sūtra*] section of the Derge (D) and the Cone (Cn) editions of the Tibetan Tripiṭaka. The translation of the Kāmadhenu extends up to the commentary on the A.Ko. II.8.82. In general, this translation is literal, but there are occasions where the translator has made blunders by giving improper translations.[7] On a number of occasions this translation provides mythological accounts that are not found in any other commentary on the A.Ko.[8] While translating such portions where Sanskrit might have been unintelligible to the translator, he seems to have split the original Sanskrit expression into parts that could make some sense to him and then translated those bits and pieces to give a complete translation. Since such translations are based on the phonetic similarity, their meaning does not agree with the original Sanskrit.[9]

In the 18th century A.D., Si-tu Paṇ-cen, an outstanding grammarian of Tibet, again took up the revision of the Tibetan translations of both these texts. These appear in the Vol.s NGA and CA of his collected works. Unlike all the canonical translations, Si-tu's translation is almost complete. It begins with the commentary on A.Ko. I.1.1 up to III.5.12. The translation of the commentary on the A.Ko. III.5.12 up to the end i.e. III.5.46 is not available. That is, the commentary on only thirty-four verses is missing in Si-tu's translation (S).

Si-tu's translation shows large improvement over that of D. Si-tu takes note of the variant readings found in other MSS of the Kāmadhenu or those found in the Rāmāśramī commentary by Bhānujī Dīkṣita. On numerous occasions, S has corrected the blunders found in D.[10] In comparison to D, the number of such words, which are left untranslated, is very low in S.[11]

Recensions of the Kāmadhenu

As mentioned before, two MSS of the Kāmadhenu have come down to us. R belongs to the Eastern region whereas C belongs to the South India. As M is a transcript of either C or of some MS belonging to the same group, it is not considered as a separate MS. The commentary on the A.Ko. I.1.70 cd up to I.4.8 c is available in both these MSS. Leaving aside the scribal errors found in R and C, at many places we come across some major differences in both these MSS. For instance, at the gloss on *himāṁśu* (I.3.12), R reads:

himāḥ śubhratvāc chaityād vā'ṁśavo'sya /

On the other hand, C reads:

himāś ca śītāś ca aṁśuḥ kalā aṁśavo'sya /

Such differences in the reading of the Kāmadhenu undoubtedly point to the two different recensions of that text that have come down to us.

Interpolations in the Sanskrit text of the Kāmadhenu

The first known / identified source of interpolations in C is KS (second half of the 11th century A.D.). These interpolations are missing in R as well as in S. Following are some of the main causes of these additions:

1. To supply the derivation of those words that are not commented upon by Subhūti
2. To provide an alternative derivation
3. To provide an alternative explanation ascribing it to *anye, pare, eke* 'others'
4. To justify a particular reading
5. To supply the text with *Deśī* words belonging to some regional dialect or with synonyms that are not listed by Amara.

Other sources of interpolations in C are TS (1159 A.D.) and PC (1431 A.D.). However, in comparison with KS, they are fewer in number.

Mallinātha (14th century A.D.), who hailed from Āndhra, cites Subhūti forty-one times, out of which only nine occurrences fall within I.1.1 up to II.2.5. Among these nine, in the first reference, Subhūti is referred to by name only whereas the rest are quotations from his commentary. Interestingly, three out of these eight references are found in the so-called 'addition' part of the commentary, i.e. citations that are taken over from KS in C, are attributed to Subhūti by Mallinātha.

Mallinātha refers to Subhāti's commentary on the word *aśvinīty ādayaḥ* (I.3.20), where the constellations beginning with the *Aśvinī* are taught. Mallinātha's text reads:

Kāmadhenu as found in the AP	*The constituted text (as found in R)*	*Reading found in C and M*
aśvinī … kṛttikāḥ ṣaḍ bahuṣu, … mṛgaśirāḥ strīklībayoḥ, … punarvasū dvau, āśleṣamaghāḥ striyāṁ bahutve ca, pūrvottaraphalgunyau, … viśākhe dve, mūlaṁ napuṁsakam, … śravaṇaḥ pumān /	*aśvinī … kṛttikāḥ striyām bahuṣu ca / … mṛgaśirāḥ striyāṁ klībe ca / … punarvasū / aśleṣā / maghā / pūrvaphālgunī uttaraphālgunī / … viśākhā / mūlaṁ / … śravaṇaḥ /*	*aśvinī … kṛttikāḥ ṣaḍ striyām bahuṣu ca / … mṛgaśirāḥ strīklībayoḥ / … punarvasū dvau / āśleṣaḥ/ maghā striyām bahutve ca / pūrvaphalgunyau uttaraphalgunyau dve / … viśākhe dve / mūlaṁ / … śravaṇaḥ /*

As can be seen, there are eight differences in the text of the Kāmadhenu found in AP and that of the constituted text. Out of these, six are recorded in C and M. At five places, S's reading matches with C and M. Here Mallinātha's text matches with C and M and not with that of R. This is the only example from AP where both the MSS are available.

Another example is found at I.II.17 on the word *matsya*. Mallinātha says:

maccho'py atreti subhūtivacanān maccho'py asti / (I.167)

The constituted text reads as below:

> *madeḥ syan* (C.U. 2.112) */ striyāṁ gaurāditvāt ṅīṣi matsyasya yaḥ* (C 5.3.51) *iti yalopaḥ, matsī /*

Here there are two additions in C. The first is found immediately after the Cāndra rule. It reads:

mādyatīti matsyaḥ /

Second addition takes place at the end of the discussion on this word:

maccho'py atra /

Both these additions can be traced back to Kṣīrasvāmin. Cp. KS (42):

mādyati matsyaḥ, maccho'pi /

R is not available for the portion found in both these citations.

Rāyamukuṭa (Mukuṭa) (1431 A.D.) cites Subhūti one hundred and thirty seven times out of which only sixteen occurrences are found up to II.2.5. Not a single citation quoted by Mukuṭa is either attested in the constituted text or in the 'addition' part. It is possible that these are from some version of the Kāmadhenu that is different than C. R is not available for all these citations.

Ujjvaladatta (12th-14th century A.D.) in his Uṇādisūtravṛtti cites Subhūti eleven times. Out of these, only two fall between I.1.1 - II.2.5. Between these two instances, one agrees with the constituted text and another one comes closer to the one found in S. The first one occurs on the commentary on Uṇādi 2.111 (p. 97). The citation reads:

... jyotiṣāṁ gaṇitaśāstram iti subhūtiḥ /

While explaining *jyotiṣāṁ śrutiḥ,* one of the six *Vedāṅga*s, the constituted text reads:

jyotiṣāṁ śrutiḥ grahanakṣatrāṇām udayāstasamayapratipādakaṁ śāstram /

This reading is different from the one found in Si-tu's translation. It reads:

dzyo ti ṣāṁ śru tiḥ ni skar rtsis thos pa ste / gza' rtsi ba'i bstan bcos so /
[jyotiṣāṁ śrutiḥ grahagaṇanāśāstram /]

Ujjvaladatta's reading is closer to S. Also cp. TS and PC:

grahaṇādīnāṁ gaṇanaśāstraṁ jyotiḥśrutiḥ / (TS I.117)
grahādigaṇanaśāstraṁ jyotiḥśrutiḥ / (PC I.195)

When we turn to the Tibetan translation as preserved in D, we find that D in general, agrees with C. Sometimes the 'additions' in C are also translated in D.[12] Again, there are some portions in D, which are neither found in any of the Sanskrit MSS of the Kāmadhenu nor in Si-tu's translation.

These examples, though few in number, point to the fact that

1. as early as 14th century, the 'additions' found in C were considered to be a genuine part of the Kāmadhenu as prevalent in South India
2. either C or some copy of it was available to Dharmapālabhadra
3. there might have been yet another version of the Kāmadhenu to which the East Indian writers such as Mukuṭa and Ujjvaladatta had an access.

Problems related to the Canonical Translations

1. All the four canonical editions are incomplete.
2. As N is an abridged translation, it was not possible to compare it with the Sanskrit MSS.
3. From the *Digvarga* (I.3) onwards, the difference between the Sanskrit MSS and the D starts increasing. While commenting on the word *glau* (I.3.14), Subhīti says:

pratimāsaṁ glāyati / glānudibhyāṁ ḍauḥ /

D reads:

zla ba shar ba na chags pa 'phel lo zhes zer ro / /yang dag par 'grib pas na 'grib byed de / /glā nu di dag las ḍauh'o / glauh / [*udite candre rāgo vardhate iti vadanti / samyak chādayatīti glauḥ / glānudibhyāṁ ḍauḥ / glauḥ /*].

From I.3.16 onwards, D becomes abridged and at some places, it merely gives the Tibetan equivalents, omitting the derivational and mythological part. Hence, it was not possible to compare the Sanskrit MSS with D.

Role of Si-tu's translation in preparing a Critical Edition of the Kāmadhenu

On this background, Si-tu's translation proved very much helpful in editing the Sanskrit text of the Kāmadhenu. He has taken pains in translating each and every word of the original Sanskrit text. The omissions and commissions in C can be confirmed with the help of S. When we compare the C with S, the gaps in the former become clear, which would not have been so with D. Cf. for instance, the discussion on the word *bhadrapadā* (I.3.21). C reads:

... phalgunīproṣṭhapadayoś ca iti promīpyāt tu yadā candre'pi tācchabdyaṁ tadā ...

Here the word *promīpyāt* is confusing. The topic under discussion is the use of plural in Pāṇini's rule that reads: *phalgunīproṣṭhapadānāṁ ca nakṣatre* (P 1.2.60). Both N and D omit this discussion. In this case, S agrees with R and confirms the omission in C. R reads:

phalgunīproṣṭhapadayoś ca iti pro{ṣṭhapadayor dvayoḥ pākṣikabahuvacanātideśavacanaṁ Pāṇiner vyarthaṁ, yataḥ 'kadā pūrve proṣṭhapade' iti tārakayor dvitvāt dvivacanam / tatsā}mīpyāt tu yadā candre'pi tācchabdyaṁ tadā ...[13]

If S were not available, it would have been difficult to confirm the omission.[14] Thus, S would help to fill up the lacuna in C from A. Ko. I.4.8 onwards where R is not available.

Again, there are many readings in C, which are not intelligible due to wrong readings, wrong punctuation etc. For instance, while deriving the optional form *urvasī* (I.1.52), C reads:

dantyasāvivaṃadeśenoyandarśitā /

The reading is corrected on the basis of S, which reads:

so can sa yig kyang ste yig gi ston pa las mthong ngo / [*dantyaso'pi varṇadeśanāyāṁ darśitaḥ /*][15]

However, even Si-tu's translation does not match fully with any of the MSS available to us. A comparison of the Sanskrit text of the Digvarga (I.3) with that of S reveals following facts:

a. At twenty-seven places, S differs from R, out of which at three places, S's reading matches with both TS and PC and once with TS only.

b. A commentary on eight words is missing in R, but found in S. Out of these, a commentary on three words matches verbatim with PC and Rāmāśramī (Ra), one with Ra only, one with Amarapadavivṛti (AV), PC and Ra. A commentary on three words does not have parallel in any of the commentaries.

c. There are nine important additions in S. These do not have parallel else where. Thirty-seven additions are minor in nature.

After comparing S with R and C, we find that:

a. S differs from R, C for 27 times.

b. At 34 places, C differs from R and S's reading matches with C.

From this analysis, we may say that neither R nor C was at the basis of S's translation. It might be yet another version of the Kāmadhenu, conflated with the readings from the TS and the PC. It is also possible that the MS, which Si-tu used for his translation, had some lacuna, which he filled up with TS and PC's readings as will be clear from the following examples:

At II.1.4, while explaining the word *urvarā,* Subhūti comments:

sarvasasyotpattibhūr iti samorvarā /

S translates it as:

lo tog thams cad 'khrungs shing shin tu brtan pa'i sa gzhi ni / u rva rā / sagshin pa ste / [*sarvasasyotpattibhūmiḥ atisārā bhūḥ urvarā /*].

This agrees verbatim with TS (II.4):

sarvasasyotpattibhūmiḥ atisārā bhūḥ urvarā /

There are two instances in S where the reading found in S differs from Sanskrit and matches with one MS of PC. One example is discussed here. It is found at I.1.10. Subhūti quotes a verse listing the *Viśvedeva*s. The verse reads:

indro dhātā'tha parjanyaḥ ...

S reads *yongs gzhan* [*paryaṇyaḥ*] in the place of *parjanyaḥ*. It is noteworthy that PC (I.19, fn. 83) records *paryanya* as a variant reading for *parjanya.*

An interesting example is found at I.1.36. While explaining the eight powers of Śiva, Subhūti says:

anekārthatvāt dhātānāṁ syatis tiṣṭhatyarthe /

Here S reads

śiṇ zhes pa 'dir gnas pa'i don te / [*śīn itīha tiṣṭhaty arthe* /].

This agrees verbatim with the corresponding line in TS (I.28):

śīn iha tiṣṭhaty arthe /

About the MS that was available to Si-tu there are two possibilities: the MS, which Si-tu used, was actually another recension of the Kāmadhenu or that the lacuna in his MS were filled by using some other commentaries such as TS, PC and Ra, which Si-tu himself acknowledges in the colophon to his translation of the Kāmadhenu.

Critical principles followed in the constitution of the text

The main problems in deciding one single MS. as a base are as follows:

I. Neither R nor C records the date of the MS. There is no clue to know it either.

II. R is available from the commentary on the A.Ko. I.1.1 up to I.4.8. C is available from the commentary on the A.Ko. I.1.51 up to II.2.5. As R is a shorter MS it cannot be made as the base for the entire commentary available to us.

III. Even if C is larger than R, it cannot be made as the base, firstly because it is not available right from the beginning. Secondly, there are some additions in C that are not found either in R or in S. Most of these additions can be traced back to KS. This makes it clear that C is not faithful to the original text of the Kāmadhenu.

Considering all these facts, since from the commentary on I.1.1 up to I.1.40, R is the only MS available, it is accepted as the base. It is compared with S and the different readings found in S were noted down and discussed in end-notes.

For the portion, which is missing in R, (i.e. from the commentary on I.1.51 up to I.1.70c), that portion, which is common to both C and S, constitutes the main body of the Sanskrit text. However, at places, even that portion in C, which is not found in S but is apparent and necessary to maintain consistency in the content and style of the text was retained in the main body of the text.

The commentary on the A.Ko. I.1.70d up to I.4.8 is available in R as well as in C. There were many passages in C, which were different in reading. Most of the times, these different readings were found in S as well. In case of this portion, R was accepted as the base and C's readings were recorded in foot-notes. In cases where S matched with the variant readings in C, that reading was given in footnote with the remark 'S agrees' or 'So does S'. If S agreed with R and the same portion was omitted in C, then it was noted in the end-notes as 'C omits'. When S's reading differed from both R and C, it was recorded in end-notes. An attempt was made to trace S's reading in all the commentaries of the Amarakoṣa that were consulted for the critical edition.

After I.4.8, that portion of the text, which is common to C and S, would constitute the main body of the Sanskrit text.[16] All the additions, omissions and deviations would be placed in the foot-notes.

Most of the quotations from the Kāmadhenu as quoted by the subsequent commentators are from II.2.5 onwards, i.e. the part of the commentary which is not available to us now. Bhānujī, one of the latest commentators on the Amarakoṣa, who flourished in the 17th century, quotes Subhūti. The latest commentary by some anonymous commentator from Orissa quotes Subhūti almost 250 times! Si-tu Paṇ-chen who flourished in the eighteenth century A.D. has translated the entire commentary leaving last 34 verses of the A.Ko. This leads to the conclusion that the Kāmadhenu was available in entirety till 18th century. A fresh search for the MSS of the Kāmadhenu is necessary in the Eastern part of India, as well as in Nepal, where Si-tu discovered the MSS of this commentary. Here it should be noted that the Catalogue of the National Archives, Kathmandu, lists not a single MS ascribed to Subhūti. Nothing can be said with certainty unless one goes through all the MSS of the commentaries on the Amarakośa preserved there. Secondly, as Mallinātha and Bommagaṇṭi Appayārya who heavily quote Subhūti, flourished in Āndhra, a fresh search is necessary in that area also.

Bibliography

Primary Sources

1. *Amarakośa in Tibet*. Ed. by Lokesh Candra, New Delhi : International Academy of Indian Culture, 1965.

2. *Amarakośa with the Unpublished South Indian Commentaries*. Ed. by Prof. A. A. Ramanathan, Chennai : The Adyar Library and Research Centre, 1971.

3. *Amarakośodghāṭana of Kṣīrasvāmī*. Ed. by K. G. Oka, Poona : 1913.

4. *Collected Works of The Great Ta'i Si Tu Pa Kun mKhyen Chos kyi Byuṅ gNas bsTan Pa'i Nyin byed Vol. 5*. Published by Sherab Gyaltsen for Palpung Sungrab Nyamso Khang, Sherab-ling Institute of Buddhist Studies, P. O. Sansal, Kangra, Himachal Pradesh, 1990.

5. Jātarūpa's Commentary on the Amarakośa (Parts I and II), Ed. by M. R. Pant, Motiḷal Banarsidass, New Delhi, 2000.

6. Kalpadrukośa Vol. I (With an Introduction), Sharma Ramavatara, Oriental Institute, Baroda, 1928.
7. *Kṛṣṇamitra's Commentary on Amarakośa*. University of Malaya, Kuala Lumpur, 1972.
8. *The collected works of Bu-ston*. Ed. by Lokesh Chandra, Shatapitaka series, International Academy of Indian Culture.
9. *The Nāmaliṅgānuśāsana of Amarasimha With The Commentary Ṭīkāsarvasva of Vandyaghaṭīya - Sarvānanda*. Ed. by T. Ganapati Sāstrī, The Travancore Government Press, Trivandrum, 1914.
10. *Padacandrikā of Rāyamukuṭa*. Ed. by K. K. Dutta, Sanskrit College, Calcutta, 1966.
11. *Rāmāśramī of Bhānujī Dīkṣita*. Chaukhambha, Varanasi, 1970.
12. *Ujjvaladatta's Commentary on the Uṇādisūtras*. Ed. by Pandit Jibananda Vidyasagara, Calcutta, 1873.

References to the commentaries are by Volume no. followed by the page no.

1. Apte, V. S. (1979). *The Practical Sanskrit-English Dictionary*, Poona : Prasad Prakashan. (Revised Edition 1957).
2. Bagchi, Jhunu (1993). *The History and Culture of the Pals of Bengal and Bihar (Cir. 750 A.D. - Cir. 1200 A.D.)*, New Delhi : Abhinav Publications.
3. Banerji, Sures Chandra (1973). *Contribution of Bihar to Sanskrit Literature*, Patna : K. P. Jayaswal Research Institute.
4. Banerji, Sures Chandra (2004). *Sanskrit Culture of Bengal*, Delhi : Sharada Publishing House.
5. Barua, Dipak Kumar (1969). *Viharas in Ancient India*, Calcutta: Indian Publications.
6. Bose, Phanindra Nath (1923). *Indian Teachers of Buddhist Universities,* Madras : Theosophical Publishing House, Adyar.
7. Bühler, G. (1959). *Indian Palaeography*, Calcutta : Indian Studies Past and Present.
8. Cintamani T. R. (1934). '*Subhūticandra's Commentary on The Amarakośa*', Madras : Journal of Oriental Research, Vol. VIII, pp. 372-380.
9. Dani, Ahmad Hasan (1963). *Indian Palaeography*, Oxford : Oxford University Press.
10. Das, S. C. (1965). *Indian Pandits in the Land of Snow*, Calcutta : Firma K. L. Mukhopadhyay.
11. Dasgupta, N. N. (IC, II, No. ii, pp. 157-266)
12. Dutta, Kali Kumar (1974). *Bengal's Contributions to Sanskrit Literature*, Calcutta : Sanskrit College.
13. Dutta, Sukumar (1962). *Buddhist Monks and Monasteries of India*, London : George Allen and Unwin Ltd..
14. Dwivedi, J. P. (1987). *Buddhist Sanskrit Grammarians* (in Hindi), Sarnath, Varanasi : Central Institute of Higher Tibetan Studies.

15. Gairolla, Vacaspati (1991). *Sanskrit Sāhitya kā Itihās*, Varanasi : Chaukhamba Vidyabhavan.
16. Gode, P. K. (1953). *Rare Mss of Subhūticandra's Commentary on the Amarakośa*, and *Date of Subhūticandra's Commentary on the Amarakośa-Between A.D. 1062 and 1172*, Studies in Indian Literary History, Vol. I, Bombay : Singhi Jain Sastra Sikshapith, Bharatiya Vidya Bhavan, p. 215-221.
17. Hinuber, Oskar V. (1980). *Remarks on the Problems of Textual Criticism in Editing Anonymous Sanskrit Literature,* Kathmandu : Proceedings of the First Symposium of Nepali and German Sanskritists, Institute of Sanskrit Studies, Tribhuvan University, and Nepal Research Centre, 1978.
18. Katre, S. M. (1954). *Introduction to Indian Textual Criticism,* Poona : Deccan College Post-graduate and Research Institute.
19. Lozang, Jamspal (1992). *Zhalu lo-tsa-ba Chos Skyong bZang Po and His Literary Works*, Narita : Tibetan Studies, pp. 175-179.
20. Macdonell, Arthur A. (Third Indian Edition, 1972). *A History of Sanskrit Literature*, New Delhi : Munshiram Manoharlal. (First Edition 1899).
21. Majumdar, R. C. (1971). *History of Ancient Bengal*, Calcutta : G. Bharadwaj & Co..
22. Majumdar, R. C. (1985). *Lāmā Tāranātha's Account of Bengal,* The Indian Historical Quarterly, Ed. by N. N. Law, Vol. XVI 1 - 4 (June 1940).
23. Niyogi, Pushpa (1980). *Buddhism in Ancient Bengal*, Calcutta : Jijnasa.
24. Omalley, L. S. S. (2005). *History of Magadh*, Revised Edition by J.F.W. James, Delhi : Veena Publications.
25. Patkar, M. M. (1981). *History of Sanskrit Lexicography*, Delhi : Munshiram Manoharlal Publishers Pvt. Ltd..
26. Paul, Pramode Lal (1940). *The Early History of Bengal (From the Earliest Times to the Muslim Conquest)*, Vol. II, Calcutta : Indian Research Institute.
27. Samaddar, J. N. (1927). *The Glories of Magadha*, Patna : Published by the Author, Pataliputra. (First edition by the Patna University, 1924).
28. Sankrityayana, Rahul (1935). *Sanskrit Palm Leaf Mss in Tibet*, Journal of Bihar and Orissa Research Society, Vol. XXI.
29. Sankrityayana, Rahul (1937). *Second Search of Sanskrit Palm Leaf Mss in Tibet*, Journal of Bihar and Orissa Research Society, Vol. XXIII, Part I.
30. Sankrityayana, Rahul (1938). *Search for Sanskrit Mss in Tibet*, Journal of Bihar and Orissa Research Society, Vol. XXIV, Part IV.
31. Shastri, Kali Charan, (1972). *Bengal's Contribution to Sanskrit Grammar, In the Pāṇinian and Cāndra Systems, Part I - General Introduction*, Calcutta : Sanskrit College.
32. Shyuki, Yoshimura (October 1955). *Tibetan Translators of the Tri-Pitaka in the Derge Edition,* Kyoto : Ryūkoku Daigaku Ronshū, No. 350, pp. 1-36.
33. Sinha, Bindeshwari Prasad (1977). *Dynastic History of Magadha*, New Delhi : Abhinav Publications.

34. Sinha, Nirmal C. (1977). *Sanskrit Across the Himalayas*, Bulletin of Tibetology, New Series, 2, pp. 18-24.

35. Smith, Gene E. (Winter 2000). *The Autobiography and Diaries of Si-tu Panchen,* Dharamshala: Lungta 13, Si tu Paṇ chen : His contribution and legacy, Amnye Machen Institute, McLeod Ganj.

36. Srivastava, Kamal Shankar (1995). *History of Magadha (From the 6th Century B.C. to 12th Century A.D.)*, Varanasi : Sangeeta Prakashan.

37. Sukthankar, V. S. (1933). *Prolegomena to the Ādiparvan*, Pune : Bhandarkar Oriental Research Institute.

38. Suzuki, D. T. (1924). *A Complete Catalogue of the Tibetan Buddhist Canons*, Sendai, Japan : Tohoku Imperial University.

39. Theodor, Aufrecht (1989). *Catalogus Catalogorum*, Indological Book House.

40. Upadhyay, Baladev (1970). *Sanskrit Śāstron kā Itihās*, Varanasi : Sharada Mandir.

41. Verhagen, Peter C. (2004). *Notes apropos to the Oeuvre of Si-tu Paṇ-chen Chos-kyi-'byuṅ-gnas* (1699?-1774) (2): *Dkar-chag Materials,* Tokyo : H.W. Bodewitz & M. Hara (eds.), Gedenkschrift J.W. de Jong: International Institute for Buddhist Studies (= Studia Philologica Buddhica, Monograph Series XVII), pp. 207-238.

42. Vogel, C. (1979). *Indian Lexicography*, History of Indian Literature, Vol. V, No. 4, Ed. by Jan Gonda, Otto Harrassowitz, Wiesbaden.

43. Williams, Monier (1979). *Sanskrit English Dictionary*, Motilal Banarsidass.

44. Tāranātha's History of Buddhism in India, Translated from Tibetan by Lama Chimpa, Alaka Chattopadhyaya, Edited by S. Rinpoche, First Edition - Indian Institute of Advanced Study, Simla, 1970, Reprinted Motilal Banarasidass, Delhi, 1990.

45. The History of Buddhism in India and Tibet by Bu-ston, Companion Volume to *The Jewellary of Scripture*, Translated from Tibetan by Dr. E. Obermiller, Sri Satguru Publications, Delhi, First Published : Heidelberg 1932, Second Edition : Delhi, 1986, 1996.

46. The Nyingma Edition of the sDe-dGe bKa'-'gyur / bsTan-'gyur, Research Catalogue and Bibliography, Volume 7, Dharma Publishing.

Footnotes

1. R. Sankrityayan (1935:21-43); (1937:21).
2. Rāmāśramī (154, 176).
3. Cf. the colophons of Kāmadhenu to the sDe dGe edition (fol. 317 a) and to Si-tu's translation.
4. Kali Kumar Dutta (1974:65).
5. *abdhiḥ* (I.11.1): *āpo dhīyante'sminn iti / vyāpyād ādhāre ca* (C 1.3.72) *iti kih, abdhiḥ /*
6. P. K. Gode (1953:220).
7. For instance, at *bahavaś ca samāsikatāvarṣā'psumano-jalaukaso'psarasaḥ* (I.1.52), D understands *āp* and *sumanas*, as one word, a genitive compound, and translates it accordingly as *chu'i me tog*.

8. The commentary on the word *caturānana* (I.1.16), though missing in Sanskrit, is found in Si-tu's translation. Si-tu briefly says:

   /'di la gdong pa bzhi yod pas/ ca tu rā na naḥ ste gdong bzhi pa'o / [catvāri ānanāny asya, caturānanaḥ /].

   Chos-skyong-bzang-po narrates the entire story: gdong bzhi ni tshangs pas thig le mchog ma zhes pa'i bu mo zhig sbrul pas de la rang nyid chags te / bu mo de g.yas g.yon la sogs pa'i phyogs bzhir song ba la bltas pas gdong pa bzhi byung ngo / /steng gi phyogs su song ba la bltas pas steng gi gdong pa dang lnga byung ste / dbang phyug gis nam mkha' nas mthong nas der ngo tsha ba'i chad las la steng gi gdong pa bcad do / /de nas gdong bzhir grags te/ 'di la gdong bzhi yod pas so/ [brahmaṇā tilottamā nāma ekā kanyā nirmitā / tasyāṁ svayam eva āsaktaḥ / *...]. (257b-258a)

9. For instance, the proper name Aruṇadatta is translated as: *ar dang uṇ dang at mtha' rnams* / [ar-uṇ-at-antāh].

10. For instance, Si-tu has correctly transliterated the word Aruṇadattah, mentioned before, as: *a ru ṇa da ttas* / Si-tu correctly understands the words *āp* and *sumanas* mentioned before, as two independent words. Though he does not translate the sentence, he transcribes the words accordingly as: *āp dang / su ma nas dang / ...*

11. For example, the above-mentioned hemistich occurring at *danujāḥ* is translated by Si-tu as:

    gser can zhes pa'i da nu'i bu bzhing du / /thang ngu mche bas gcod cing za bar byed / [hiraṇyākhyadānavam iva daṃṣṭrāvibhinnabhakṣaḥsthalam /].

12. For instance, in C, we come across a sentence introducing the words for 'fire': *ślokacatuṣṭayaṁ vahnau* / Cp. D: 'khyog 'gro zhes pa la sogs pa tshigs su bcad pa bzhin me'i ming ngo / [*vahnyādiślokacatuṣṭayaṁ agnau /*].

13. pha lgu nī dang pro ṣṭha pa dā dag gi'ang ngo / /zhes pas pro ṣṭha pa da'i phyogs gnyis ni mang tshig gi yul las 'das par pā ṇi ni las khyad par gyi don du bshad pa gang gi phyir / pū rve pro ṣṭha pa de zhes pa gang gi tshe skar ma gnyis nyid brjod pa'i phyir gnyis tshig go / /de dang nye ba las ni gang du zla ba la'ang de'i sgra nyid de / ...

14. At I.3.16, under the word *lakṣaṇa*, C and M read: *pakṣe lakṣmaṇaḥ puṁsi saumitrau śrāmati triṣu iti / ...* S reads: 'dis mtshon par byed pas la kṣma mtshon byed de ma nin'o zhes pas ma nin'o / /la kṣa ṇaṁ ni mtshan nyid de lyuṭ'o / /la kṣa ṇaṁ ni ming dang rtags / /zhes drag pos so / /ra bha sas ni ma yig dbus ma can du bshad de / chu skyes 'od ldan ma la mo / /ma ning ming dang mtshan ma la / phyogs la pho ste la kṣa ṇah / bshes bzang dpal ldan la ni gsum / ... On the basis of S, the suggested reading is: [*lakṣyate sūcyate'nena iti lakṣma / manin iti manin / lyuṭi lakṣaṇam / lakṣaṇaṁ nāmaliṅgayor iti rudraḥ / rabhasas tu makāramadhyaṁ paṭhati - jyotiṣmatyāṁ sārasyāṁ strī klābaṁ tu nāmacihnayoḥ / syāt*] *pakṣ e lakṣmaṇaḥ puṁsi saumitrau śrīmati triṣu iti // ...*

15. Another example is provided at the gloss on the word *sphuliṅga* (I.1.57). C and M read: *khaṇḍati khat* / S correctly reads: khaḍ'o zhes pas khaḍ rkyen te / [*khaḍ iti khaḍ /*].

16. Cf. V.S. Sukthankar (1933:109): "The principle I have tried to follow religiously - and I hope never deviated from it - is to accept as original a reading or feature which is documented uniformly by all manuscripts alike".

A Glimpse of Scientific Knowledge in Ancient India: Evidence of Manuscript

17

ANITA BAGCHI

The Latin word '*manus'* means hand.[1] Manuscript generally means a hand written or type written version of a book, article or other work prepared by an author. But in the context of the present article the word 'manuscript' should be taken to mean any material written by hand before the invention of printing technology. ''Hand written manuscripts were the chief records of man's history for about 4,500 years until printing came into general use during the 1400's''[2] *Papyrus* manuscript was mainly used for writing in ancient times as early as 3000 B.C. in Egypt, Greece, Rome and other areas surrounding the Mediterranean sea.[3] The main problem for *papyrus* manuscript is that it decays in damp climate as it is made of plant material.

Parchment was also used as writing material in ancient period. Parchment is made of the skin of goats, sheep and other animals. High quality parchment is called '*vellum*'. Besides, wax tablets and clay tablets were also used for writing purpose. The Chinese were the first to invent paper about 100 A.D. The art of paper making was introduced into India by about 11th century A.D. probably from Nepal which in turn might have imported the technique of paper production from China.[4] There is no doubt that the Arabs learnt the technique of paper-making earlier than the Indians and it would appear that some parts at India especially the western part obtained the knowledge from the Arabs.

Before the introduction of paper in India, the vast mass of ancient literature on all sorts of subjects had to be preserved either on palm leaves (*tāla patra*) or birch bark (*bhurja patra*). Besided leather, silk or wood could be used for writing purpose.

The practice of using *tāla patra* was popular in south India and that of the bhurjapatra was in *Kāśmīr* and northern region of the country.[5]

It is said that the earliest vedic manuscripts are not older than the 10th century A.D.[6] Before that, oral preservation as well as verbal transmission practically was the only means to protect the store house of knowledge from being obliterated.

The people of India in the past made books of strips cut from palm leaves which were about three inches wide and two feet or more in length. They made holes in the strips and then strung them together in order to give it a form of book[7]. Most of the manuscripts can be identified with the particular period by the materials on which they are written, and also by the language and form of scripts used for writing as languages and scripts bear a changing character.

Investigation into the Indian past began with the work of the Indologists. They were mostly the European scholars and their main area of study was language. The study of Sanskrit language rendered practically the main source material for the reconstruction of ancient Indian society.[8] At the outset, the scholars paid much attention to the study of general history of the past, which covered political, economic as well as social life of the people. Religious, cultural and artistic activities also came under the purview of their discussion. But the achievements of the ancient Indian people in the branch of science and technology remained ignored and untouched for a long time by the eminent scholars of the early period. The reason might be that the Indological study was then in its formative stage. The study of ancient and medieval Indian science and technology which involved the method of the linguists, the philologists and simultaneously the knowledge of scientific disciplines could not make much advance. The discovery of manuscripts, extraction of accurate knowledge from the manuscripts by patient study and attempts at co-relation with relic of antiquity by the great scholars like Anquetil du Perron and Sir William Jones and others, prepared the way for opening up of new areas of study in the days to come.

The first attempt in the direction of developing a branch of study of science and technology in historical outline was made jointly by the UNESCO and the *Indian National Science Academy* (at that time called as National Institute of Sciences in India). Under the joint initiatives of the two organizations a symposium on the *History of Sciences in South East Asia* was held in Delhi in 1950. Such an initiative was highly needed to understand the history and culture of the people of the ancient civilization. The recommendations of the 1950 symposium got its practical shape in the form of the book '*A Concise History of Science in India*' containing exhaustive researches on different disciplines of science in India through out the ages. In the preface of the book the editors have made a remark which is very significant. 'Despite vicissitudes in intellectual and scientific endeavors and period of stagnation, e.g. about the time of the Renaissance in Europe, the Indian sub-continent is one of the few areas where a fairly continuous tradition in science and technology is clearly seen'.

Such an assertion in favour of the presence of a continued and unbroken chain of cultural practices in the branch of science and technology in India makes it clear that the editors could find out the source materials which are not insufficient to reconstruct a consecutive account of the development of science and technology in India in the past. A picture of attainments of our ancestors in the field of science and technology may reliably be drawn with the help of textual evidences (mostly retained in the form of manuscripts) accompanied by archaeological corroborations wherever possible for the pre-printing days. Thus it can be argued that manuscripts actually constitute the principal sources of history of the development of science and technology in the past. Nevertheless, there are certain limitations involved with the manuscripts. Errors are often made while making a new copy from an existing ones. Variations, discrepancies and inconsistencies are frequently visible in copies of the manuscripts and sometimes these appear as hurdles on the way to getting at the essence of the texts of the manuscripts.

Besides, materials used for manuscripts such as *papyrus,* parchment, palm leaves, birch-bark, silk, leather, wood and cloth—all are vulnerable to damage and are of temporary nature. Plant materials turn fragile in course of time. Furthermore, all the materials are subject to damage due to weathering and the attack of fungi, bacteria, insects and rodents.

With all these sorts of problems were associated natural calamites and occasional cases of fire. Incident of fire was frequent and it was nearly impossible to protect the manuscripts from incineration in those days as the materials for writing manuscripts were mostly inflammable. That the occurrence of firing was frequent in the ancient period is clearly evident from the elaborate precautions which *Kauṭilya* lays down for extinguishing of fire. To avoid large-scale destruction, *Kauṭilya* suggests some preventive as well as protective measures which highlight a considerable level of consciousness of the state authority for the danger of fire-accidents and its efforts for keeping the people alert and ready in combating such calamitous situations.

It is said in Book-II *of Kauṭilya's Arthaśāstra* — (If a house owner is not found to have ready with him) five water pots, a *kumbha*, a *droṇa*, a ladder, an axe, a winnowing basket, a hook, pincers and a leather bag, he shall be fined one-fourth of a *paṇa*[10].

The accessories mentioned, give an impression that the people of the time developed a primordial system of technology to protect human life and wealth from fire.

Besides accidental cases of fire, deliberate attempts to incinerate towns, cities, monasteries and libraries are witnessed in History. About the middle of the eleventh century, the Somapurī *Mahāvihāra* was set on fire by the armies of *Vaṅgala* or South-

East Bengal. Though, a whole-sale renovation was done by *Vipulaśrīmitra*, a monk of the *Vihāra*, yet it could not be restored to its former glory.[11]

The invasion of the Muslims and the ruthless destruction of the Buddhist monasteries by them also dealt a great blow to the traditional method of preservation of knowledge in manuscripts. Vivid description of wanton destruction of the famous monastery at Uddandapur is given by Minhājuddin Sirāj. It helps us to get an impression of the exact disaster the monasteries had to face during foreign invasion. The *Vihāras* of *Nālandā, Vikramaśilā* which were the great centers of learning in different branches of knowledge including science and technology met their tragic ends and the world lost the store-house of knowledge accrued through the ages in the rows of writings of manuscripts at the hands of some insane destroyers.

But all the inherent inconvenience lying with manuscript can not minify its importance as source of history and manuscripts still provide the most dependable tool for study of the achievements of our ancestors in the discipline of science and technology. In the present article an endeavour will be made to high-light a few manuscripts containing important information regarding the achievements of the ancient Indians in the field of Science and Technology.

First of all mention may be made of *Kauṭilya's Arthaśāstra,* the encyclopedic work from which scientific knowledge of the past may be sieved out. *Arthaśāstra* is a wide term which, as Winternitz has recognized, embraces technology, science and all knowledge of practical arts besides politics.[12] The text has become an indispensable source-book for any kind of historical information including even scientific studies based on empirical observation in the field of agriculture, forestry, methods of elephant lore, horse training, mining and so on. This invaluable text in the form of manuscript was first handed over by a pundit of the Tanjore District to the Mysore Government Oriental Library. The manuscript was accompanied by a commentary on a small part of the main text, ascribed to one *Bhaṭṭasvāmin.* Fortunate enough are the students and scholars of ancient Indian history and culture that Dr. R. Shamasastry was then the Librarian of the Mysore Government Oriental Library and he missed no time to publish a tentative English translation in the *Indian Antiquary* (1905). Active encouragement of the Mysore Durbar inspired him further to publish the text itself in 1909 as Vol. 37 of the *Bibliotheca Sanskrit* of Mysore. Later two or three other manuscripts were traced and that helped further to come out of obscurities in later works on the text. J.F. Fleet in his Introductory Note to Shamasastry's monumental work on the *Arthaśāstra* unequivocally gives his expression of gratitude to the great scholar in the following words: 'we are, and shall always remain, under a great obligation to him for a most important additions to our means of studying the general history of ancient India'.

It is already mentioned that at the outset, the study of ancient and medieval history of science and technology was not given much importance. It was looked at as a component unit of general history and studies in antiquities of ancient India. Still the genesis of history of science and technology may be traced in the efforts of Sir William Jones and Anquetil du Perron and others since the initiatives for collection and reading of manuscripts for Indological study, were taken by them.

The chapters in the *Arthaśāstra* dealing with the duties and responsibilities of different *Adhyakṣhas* e.g. the Superintendent of agriculture, Superintendent of cows or horses or elephants make it evident that the people of ancient India had developed a scientific knowledge system through observation and empirical study. This has been established scientifically that the genesis of agricultural practice in India can be traced back to a period around 7000 B.C.[13] By the time of *Kauṭilya* who is assumably to assigned to C. 3rd century B.C., Indian agricultural knowledge reached a level of development and agricultural science took a definite shape. That agriculture had become a specific subject of study is proved by the use of the word '*Kṛṣitantragul-mavṛkṣāyurvedajñaḥ* in the *Arthaśāstra*. The relevant statement is quoted below: *Śitadhyakṣaḥ kṛṣitantragulama vṛkṣāyurvedajñastajjña sakho bā sarbba dhānyapuṣpa-phalaśāka-kanda-mūla pāllīkya-kṣauma kārpasavījani yathakalaṃ gṛṇhıyat* || (*Arthaśāstra*, II.XXIV.I.p.127).

The English translation is — possessed of the knowledge of the science of agriculture dealing with the plantation of bushes and trees, or assisted by those who are trained in such sciences, the superintendent of agriculture shall in time collect seeds of all kinds of grains, flowers, fruits, vegetables, bulbous roots, fruits of creepers, fibre-producing plants and cotton.[14]

So we find that the required qualification of the Superintendent of agriculture was specified in the *Arthaśāstra*. He had to be a person who was highly experienced and knowledgeable in the disciplines of agronomy and horticulture.

There is also hint at the rainfall study and soil classification. The relevant *sūtra* runs thus 'the quantity of rain that falls in the country *of jāngala* is 16 *droṇas*; half as much more in moist countries i.e. *Anūpa* region; as the countries which are fit for agriculture (*deśavāpānām*) 13½ *droṇas* in the country of *Aśmakas*, 23 *droṇas in Avantī* and an immense quantity in western countries (*aparāntānām*), the boarders of the Himalayas, and the countries where water channels are made for use in agriculture (*Kulyavāpānām*) (Ibid, II.XXIV.IV.p.127). Thus it seems that the tradition of making keen observations on various aspects of crop cultivation must have continued since long before *Kauṭilya*. By the time of *Kauṭilya*, forecasting on rainfall based on planetary movements and related phenomena was in good practice. India has had a rich tradition in mathematics and astronomy and there were definite attempts on the part of the early Indian researchers to correlate rainfall with astronomical phenomena which in the opinion of Y.L. Nene may be described as "astrology-based-rain-forecast" model for predicting rainfall in a season.[15]

The book *Kṛśi-parāśara* is also a profound treatise on agriculture and relates to meteorological problems. Composed in Sanskrit by a sage named *Parāśara*, the text is one of the oldest texts on Indian agriculture. The *Kṛśi-parāśara* also known as *Kṛśi-saṃraha, Kṛṣi-paddhati* and *Kṛṣitantra* was written between A.D. 950 and 1100. The original Sanskrit text was published by the Asiatic Society, Calcutta in 1960. The book was edited by Dr. G.P. Majumdar a renowned botanist and S.C. Banerjee. Majumdar fixes its date not later than the 5th century A.D.[16] Nalini Sadhale made a further translation of the book *Kṛṣiparāśara* and prefers to date it back to the first century B.C.[17] A number of maxims in different languages like Maithili, Tamil, Bengali, Hindi has been in vogue in India for ages. Many a popular saying has been found in one-of the manuscripts on *Vṛkṣayurveda* and in the *Kṛṣiparāśara* enshrined in the Adyar Library, Chennai. N.R. Ray in the context of the *Vacanas* of *Khanā* and *Dāk* commented that these sayings bear the tradition of a very early period and cover a wide range of knowledge about soil, ploughing, sowing, planting, reaping, harvesting and meteorological observations as well[18]. Majumdar's observation in this regard is also to be alluded here, 'the striking resemblance between some of the aphorisms of *Khanā* relating to agriculture and some of the verses in the *Kṛśi-parāśara* on the same subject may warrant us in the supposition that the authentic treatise in Sanskrit might have a good deal to do with the mythical author of the aphorisms of *Khanā,* who carried the lessons contained in the *Kṛśiparāśara* to particular applications in minute details.[19] Along with the treatise on agricultural science we have in our possession a separate text on botany. Plant science as it is called *Vṛkṣāyurveda* in Sanskrit is discussed in the *Agnipurāṇa* and *Bṛhatsamhitā* in separate chapters. But *Vṛkṣāyurveda* of *Parāśara*, which is available in manuscript form in different libraries makes it evident that a separate branch of study was developed for plant science.

Such a manuscript of the *Vṛkṣāyurveda* of *Parāśara* was discovered by Vaidyasastri Jogendranath Visagratna. An article under the title 'An Introduction to the *Vṛkṣāyurveda* of *Parāśara*' of N.N. Sircar, son of Jogendranath was communicated to the Asiatic Society of Bengal by Dr. G.P. Majumdar and it was published in the Journal of the Society in Vol.XVI.No.1., 1950. In this article a preliminary account of the manuscript and of the contents with a list of technical terms and their English equivalents were furnished[20]. N.N. Sircar informs us that Vaidyasastri Jogendranth Visagratna who lived in Navadwip became a great scholar in *Parāśarian* Botany by its application in actual nature study. He also made a Bengali translation of a portion of the manuscript.

A more curious information is given by D.K. Kanjilal in the foreword of the book *Vṛkṣāyurveda* of *Parāśara* (edited and translated by N.N. Sircar and Roma Sarkar) that the said manuscript was probably traced from Coochbehar where Jogendranath spent long span of his life. Coochbehar under the rule of the Maharajas from the late 13th Century onwards had experienced a prosperous cultural life and grew up as a centre of study where number of scholars assembled.

Roma Sarkar informs us that Vaidyasastri J.N. Sircar was an Ayurvedic physician in the erstwhile princely State of Coochbehar in Bengal. The manuscript was discovered sometimes before 1928. The manuscript is written in the *Sṃtra* style. The style became so dominant a feature that this was adopted by the writers of different philosophical schools, the grammarians, phoneticians, writers of the *Arthaśāstra*, the *Kāmasūtra*, the *Nātya Śāstra*, the *Caraka-Saṃitā, Śusruta-Saṃhitā* and others. The main purpose was to facilitate easy memorization of a vast body of ritualistic and other materials. The language used is classical Sanskrit. The manuscript even with its simple linguistic structure contains words and expressions which suggest its basic antique character.[21] *Vṛkṣāyurveda* literally means 'the science of plant life' and is known to have existed in ancient India from a very early period. N.N. Sircar held that *Paraśara* of the *Vṛkṣāyurveda* is identical with that *Parāśara* cited in the *Caraka Saṃitā*. There is enough evidence to show that branch of the knowledge on plants and plant life was intricately related to the art of healing since the most ancient days. In the hymn of the *Rgveda* the poet makes mention of 107 applications of plants to make people free from diseases. A same tone is apparent indicating the importance of knowledge on plants and their use in the *Caraka Saṃitā*. *Caraka* comments 'it is only a person well acquainted with the names and external features of plants and able to use them properly according to their properties is to be called an expert physician (*Caraka Saṃitā,* Ch.1, 56). The treatise *Vṛkṣāyurveda* evidently made the basis of botanical teaching preparatory to medical studies in ancient days.[22] As an illustration, may be cited the story of *Jivaka* given in the Buddhist canonical texts about *Jivaka*'s final test after completion of his study at the university of Taxila. Jivaka studied medicine at Taxila for the prescribed period of 7 years[23]. But before he was given the license to start his career as medical practitioner he had to undergo a unique test of his knowledge. He was given a spade by his celebrated teacher, *Bhiksu Ātreya* and was asked to collect from the adjacent area, a *yojana* round the city of *Taxila*, any plant which was devoid of medicinal properties. But *Jivaka* could not discover any such plant and came back empty-handed. The teacher was satisfied with the perfection of knowledge of his student and allowed him to leave for his home town. *Jivaka*'s episode confirms the view that ancient Indian medical science was intricately related to the study of plant life.

The text of the *Vṛkṣāyurveda* of *Parāśara* is divided into six parts.[24]:

Bījotpattikāṇda
Vanaspati kāṇda
Vānaspatya kāṇda
Gulmakṣupa kāṇda
Vīrudha vallikāṇda
Cikitsita kāṇda

The last portion of the said work dealing with the treatment of plant diseases is found missing. The *Vīrudha vallikāṇda* which seems to be incomplete, enumerates only twenty three different creepers. The manuscript here ends abruptly. The first part i.e. the Bījotpattikāṇda is again subdivided into eight chapters and the information presented in the various chapters bear upon the following topics: origin of life, ecology, description and distribution of forests in India, morphology of plants, classification and nomenclature, histology and physiology. The nomenclature of the eight chapters is as follows: *Bījotpattisūtrīyādhyāya, Bhūmivargādhyāya, Vanavargādhyāya, Vṛkṣangasūtrīyādhyaya, puṣpāṅgasūtrīyādhyāya, phalāṅgasūtrīyādhyāya, Aṣṭāṅgasūtrīyādhyāya, Dviganīyādhyāya.*

In the *Bījotpattisūtrīyādhyāya* there is a reference to a conference of the sages which was held in the *Caitraratha* forest. The sages under the leadership of *Bharadvāja* assembled in the conference and asked *Maharṣi Parāśara* to give an account of the herbs and plants that were beneficial to the mankind.[25]

The concerned *sūtra* may be cited here:

Ete kṣitiruhāḥ sarve jagato hitākarakāḥ /
Vane caitrarathe ramye sametāḥ puṇyakarmanaḥ //

Bharadwājādayaḥ sarve ye cānye, munisaptamāḥ /
Jñātumicchantāḥ papracchuḥ parāśaraṃ maharṣayaḥ //

Pṛṣtena munibhiḥ sarvaiḥ parāśaroabrabittataḥ/
Atharvāṅgam pravakṣyāmi Brahmoktaṃ Vṛkṣa Vaidyakam //

(Eng. Trans: In order to acquire knowledge about the plants beneficial to the world, performers of holy rites like *Bharadwāja* and other foremost of the sages assembled in the beautiful *Caitraratha* forest (in the Himalayas) and questioned *Parāśara* (to enlighten them).

From the above reference, it is evident that the wise and knowledgeable personalities in that remote ancient age were aware enough to exchange their knowledge and thereby could develop their status of wisdom. Such type of scholastic assemblages would have certainly helped them to carry on with their studies and research.

The Arbori-Horticulture attained a great perfection in ancient India. There is no full treatises on the subject but a small chapter the '*Upavana-vinoda*' as a branch of *Vṛkṣāyurveda* is found in the *Śāraṇgadhara-paddhatia*, a 13th century work. The text has been edited, translated and published by G.P. Majumdar with a 'Foreword' by B.N. Seal.

Thus we observe that botanical studies and medicinal science went hand in hand in the ancient period. Medicine, it appears, had taken already a momentous step from magico-religious therapeutics to rational therapeutics. D.P. Chattopadhyaya comments, 'In ancient India, the only discipline that promises to be fully secular and contains clear potentials of the modern understanding of natural science is medicine'[26]. The Indian medical science is known as the '*Āyurveda*'. The common English translation of the '*Āyurveda*' is the 'Science of Life[27]. Our knowledge of this medical science in the ancient period comes mainly from the surviving written treatises, the oldest of which are the *Saṃhitās* of *Bhela, Caraka* and *Suśruta*. The *Bhela Saṃhitā* has survived till now through a single and incomplete manuscript. The manuscript is in a mutilated form.

The *Caraka* and *Suśruta Samhitās* are available as later redactions.

Mention may be made in this context of the famous Bower Manuscript which was unearthed from Kashgar in course of an archaeological exploration carried out in Central Asia. The manuscript was named after Major General L.H. Bower who obtained it from a man in Kucha. The Bower Manuscript is also called *Nāvanītaka*. The manuscript is written in a kind of barbarous Sanskrit and abounds in *Prākṛt* words. Hoernle dated the Bower MS. to between A.D. 350 and 370[28]. The text follows the practice of ancient medical *Saṃhitās* and claims its authority from *Ātreya*, *Kṣarapāṇi, Jatukarṃa, parāśara, Hārita*, *Bhela* and *Suśruta*. There is no uncertainties regarding the spread of Indian Ayurvedic concepts and texts in Central Asia in view of the discovery of datable manuscripts from the depths of sand.

Another manuscript containing a few pages only was unearthed from Kucha in Central Asia. This bilingual MS. Known as *Yogaśataka* is ascribed to *Nāgārjuna* or *Vararuci*[29]. The *Yogaśataka* belonging to the seventh century A.D. possibly is a copy of the similar text attributed to *Nāgārjuna* dated three centuries earlier and it was once popular in Tibet, Nepal and some parts of India[30].

The history of the origin and development of mathematics in ancient India is related to rudiments of metrology and computations. A manuscript exclusively dealing with mathematics in this period is the *Bakhśāli Manuscript*. The manuscript was discovered in 1881 in a small village called *Bakhśāli* near *Peshwar* now in Pakistan[31]. The work was published by Hoernle in Indian Antiquary XVII and was later edited in the Archaeological Survey Report (New Imperial Series)., XLII. The manuscript is written on birch bark in *Śārada* script. It survives in about seventy folios some of them in fragmentary form. Hoernle assigns it to the 3rd or 4th century A.D.

The manuscript is exclusively a mathematical work containing rules with examples. The work deals mostly with arithmetic. Algebra and problems of mensuration also have been dealt with in the manuscript. *Bhāskara* 11 represents the culminating point in the discipline of mathematics. His entire mathematical and astronomical work *Siddhānta śiromaṇi* is divided into four parts of which two chapters entitled the *Līlāvatī* and the *Bījagaṇita* are the most important[32]. Arithmatic, geometry and algebra have been dealt with in these two chapters. The form of the *Līlāvatī* is unique in the sense that a beautiful maiden is addressed by the author. An opinion though not accepted is held by some people that the authoress of the *Līlāvatī* chapter was *Bhāskarācārya's* daughter. But this is not true[33]. However, the work obtained much popularity and is still available in a large number of manuscripts. As regards contents, it is based on earlier works of *Brahmagupta* and *Śrīdhara*[34].

In the eighth century a number of Indian scholars went to Baghdad and they took with them books on different subjects including mathematics and astronomy. Nehru's comments to this aspect may be quoted here, 'probably even earlier than this, Indian numerals had reached Baghdad but this was the first systematic approach and *Āryabhatta*'s and other books were translated into Arabic[35].

In course of this discussion on mathematics a few words may be said on the existence of a kind of a simple system of mathematical calculation which in the words of Maity should be called as 'Folk Mathematics'[36]. Maity has drawn a comparison between the *Subhankari Arya* and the *Rhymes* in the *Paṭan* Manuscript[37]. 'The *Paṭan* Manuscript is written in *Nāgari* script and is kept preserved in Sri Hemachandracharya Jaina Gyan Mandir of Paṭan in Gunjrat. This is an anonymous manuscript reflecting the problems related to classical and folk mathematics as well. It was either a copy of the *Gaṇitasāra* (C.1315 A.D.) or was written on the basis of this book. That the village women even were conversant with simple method of calculation is known from a verse of *śaraṇa* in *Suduktikarṃāmṛta*[38]. The verse runs thus

Etāstā dibasānta bhāskara sadṛśo dhābanti paurāṅganāh /
skandha praskhaladaṃśukāñcala dhṛti vyāsaṅgabaddhā dārāḥ //

prātaryāta kṛṣibalāgamabhiyā protplutyā bartmacchido/
haṭṭa krayya padārtha mulya kalana vyāgrāṅguli gṛanthayaḥ //

It is said that the peasants have gone to work in the field in the morning and their women are returning quickly to their home after finishing their marketing in the evening by galloping steps. The hanging ends of their cloths being slipped from their shoulders but still they are reckoning their expenditure in nimble fingers.

It is a unique picture giving a glimpse of working knowledge of the village women folk in numerical calculation.

The ancient Indians had good deal of knowledge on animal husbandry. As comprehensive medical science for all creatures, Indian Āyurvedic science shows concern simultaneously for animals, trees and human beings as well. A treatise dealing with medical knowledge concerning bovine animals attributed to *Gotama* must have been current up to the middle age but at present no authentic version is available.

Aśva Śāstra or Equestrian science is another branch of Animal science in ancient India. The *Aśva-śāstra* of *Nakula* is based on a manuscript which contains twenty one coloured illustrations of horses and knowledge of equine anatomy. There are many manuscripts in the Sarasvati Mahal Library, Tanjore, dealing with horse lore.

The classic treatise on Fish culture, believed to have been written around 500 B.C. by Fan Lei, a Chinese politician turned fish culturist, makes it evident that commercial fish culture existed in China even during that time. An interesting information for the oriental world is that the British biologist Charles Darwin made an effort to collect information from the Far-east and China and cited extensive examples from these sources as evidence for his theories of evolution and variation of species. Recent scholarship has shown that Darwin read some Chinese originals (in translation) as well as English, French, German and even Japanese (also in translation) works[39]. Darwin pointed out that the Chinese were the first to domesticate gold fish and wrote on the silkworm 'believed to have been domesticated in China as long ago as 2700 B.C.[40].

In any case it is easily conceivable that the translations which Darwin consulted were originally stored in Chinese manuscripts as it is known that one of Darwin's major sources was French translations of Chinese original works made by French Jesuits and Sinologists. Thus it is evident that Darwin studied and utilized the Chinese scientific heritage.[41]

However coming to the Indian context, we find that *Kauṭilya's Arthaśāstra* talks about fish culture in reservoirs. A very interesting description of fishing for royal recreation is available in the *Matsyavinoda* section of *Mānasollāsa* which was compiled by the Chalukya king *Someśvara* in the 12th century A.D.

It is clear from the *Matsyavinoda* section of the *Mānasollāsa* of *Someśvara* that a systematic body of knowledge had accumulated in India by 12th century A.D. S.L. Hora expressed his wonder at the range of knowledge revealed in the *Matsyavinoda* in the following words. 'In the absence of records of any observational data, which must have formed the basis of the knowledge embodied in *Matsyavinoda,* one must wonder as to the length of time that our ancients must have taken to accumulate so much factual and deductive knowledge. In some respects, it has not been surpassed even now.'[42]

Lastly some light may be thrown on elephant lore of Assam bearing the name *Hastividyārṇava*. The author of this monumental treatise is Sukumar Barkath. The text was composed by the author under the direct patronage of the Ahom King Siva Sinha and his queen Ambika Devi in 1734 A.D. The manuscript was also painted by two painters Dilbar and Dosai under the order of the King and the Queen.

The manuscript copy of the treatise was in the custody of Mohidhar Burhagohain who was a grandson of Purnananda Buragohain, the famous Prime minister of Assam (A.D. 1783-1817). Pandit H.C. Goswami recovered the manuscript and it ultimately came to the possession of the Department of Historical and Antiquarian studies, Gauhati[43]. It was edited and translated by Dr. P.C. Choudhury, an eminent scholar of Assam. *Hastividyārṇava* is a comprehensive treatise on elephants incorporating all aspects like behaviour, classification, types, training, elephant's diseases and their treatment. According to Niko Tinbergen, the famous ethologist, the first tasks of the study of behaviour are observation and description.[44]

The manuscripts practically reflect a similar content. According to Choudhury, the lore probably was originally compiled in Tai-Ahom language and was recomposed by Sukumar Barkath with materials drawn from Gajendra Cintamani. The most important part of the treatise is its paintings. The materials used for the paintings also reveal that the artists Dilbar and Dosai had good knowledge in chemical properties of natural products.

In this context the illustrated *Gajaśāstra bhāsāprabandha* of King Serfoji of the Bhosle dynasty may be mentioned. This work was composed by the King in 1820 with coloured illustrations and preserved in Thanjavour Saraswathi Mahal Library[45]. A copy of *Hastiāyurvedasaṃhitā* (A manual of the Science of elephant life) of *Palakappya* is also in the possession of this library.[46])

So we find that manuscripts practically were the most dependable sources for transmission of scientific knowledge to the future people of the world. A survey of some of the manuscripts mentioned above warrants us believe that the ancient Indian people had excelled in many branches of science and technology. Further discoveries may unveil some hidden truth regarding India's contributions to the development of scientific knowledge in the past.

References

1. *Compton's Pictured Encyclopedia and Fact Index,* Vol.9, F.E. Compton and Company, Chicago, 1956, p.81.

2. *The World Book Encyclopedia.* M. Volume 13, Field Enterprises Educational Corporation, Chicago, 1976, p.130.

3. *Ibid.*

4. Subbarayappa, B.V., Chemical Practices and Alchemy in Bose, D.M., Sen, S.N., and Subbarayappa (ed) *A Concise History of Science in India.* (CHSI) Indian National Science Academy (INSA), New Delhi, 1989, p.341.

5. *Ibid.,* p.342.

6. Sharma, R.S., *Aspects of Political Ideas and Institutions in Ancient India.* Motilal Banarsidass, Delhi, 2001, p.15.

7. *Op. cit.,* The World Book Encyclopedia, p.131.

8. Thapar, R., *Interpreting Early India,* Oxford University Press, Delhi, 1995, p.2.

9. Bose, D.M. *et al.*(ed) CHSI, INSA, Delhi, 1989, p.v.

10. Shamasastry, R., *Kauāilya's Arthaśāstra,* Mysore Printing and Publishing House, Mysore, 1961, p.162.

11. Majumdar, R.C. (ed), *The Struggle for Empire,* Bharatiya Vidya Bhavan, Bombay, 1989, p.416.

12. Sastri, K. A. N. K. (ed) *Age of the Nandas and the Mauryas,* Motilal Banarsidass, Delhi, 1996, p.192.

13. Balkundi, H.V., Placing the period of Krishi Parashara in Y.L. Nene (ed) *Glimpses of the Agricultural Heritage of India,* Asian Agri-History Foundation, Secunderabad, 2007, p.76.

14. Shamasastry, R., *Op. cit.,* p.127.

15. Nene, Y.L., Modern Agronomic concepts and practices, Evident in Kautilya's Arthasastra (c.300B.C.) in *Op. cit.,* Y.L. Nene (ed), p.114.

16. Majumdar G.P., *Vanaspati: Plants and Plant Life as in Indian Treatises* and Traditions, Calcutta University, 1927, p.207.

17. Sadhale, N., Krishi-parashara (agriculture by Parashara), *Agri-History Bulletin No.2* Asian Agri-History Foundation Secunderabad, 1999.

18. Ray, N.R., *Bangalir Itihas : Adiparva I,* Saksharata Prakashan, Kolkata, 1980, p.158.

19. Majumdar, G.P., *Op. cit.,* 1927, p.211.

20. Sircar, N.N., An Introduction to the *Vṛkśāyaurveda* of *Parāśara* in the *Journal of the Royal Asiatic Society of Bengal,* Vol. XVI No.1 1950, pp.123-139.

21. Kanjilal, D.K., Foreword to N.N. Sircar and Roma Sarkar (ed. and Tran.) *Vṛkṣāyurveda of Parāśara* (A Treatise on Plant Science), Sri Satguru Publications, Delhi, 1996, p.iii.

22. Majumdar, G.P., History of Botany and Allied Sciences (Agriculture, Medicine, Arbori-Horticulture) in Ancient India (c.2000 B.C. to 100 A.D.) in D.P. Chattopadhyaya (ed), *The History of Science and Technology in Ancient India: The Beginning,* Firma KLM Pvt. Ltd., Calcutta, 1986, p.375.

23. Mookerji, R.K., *Education* in R.C. Majumdar (ed) *The Age of Imperial Unity*, Bharatiya Vidya Bhavan, 1990, p.588.

24. Sircar, N.N. and Sarkar, R. (ed. and Trans.), *Vṛkṣāyurveda of Parāśara* (A Treatise of Plant Science) Sri Satguru Publicatinos, Delhi, 1996, p. XVII.

25. Sircar, N.N., *Op. cit.,* p.125-126.

26. Chattopadhyaya, D.P., *Science and Society in Ancient India,* Research India Publication, Calcutta, 1979, pp.3-4.

27. Majumdar, R.C., Medicine in D.M. Bose *et al.* (ed) *CHSI* p. 213.

28. *Op. cit.,* Bose, D.M. *et al.*; p.53.

29. Roy, M., Aurveda in P. Ray (ed), *The Cultural Heritage of India*, Vol. VI, The Ramkrishna Mission Institute of Culture, Calcutta, 2000, p.176.

30. *Op. cit.,* Bose, D.M. *et al.,* p. 53.

31. Sen, S.N., Mathematics in CHSI, p.164.

32. *Ibid,* p.168.

33. Patra, S., *Vigyancharchay Prachin Bharat O Samakalin Anyanya Desh,* Banisilpa, Kolkata, 1983, pp.144-145.

34. Majumdar, R.C. (ed), *The Struggle For Empire,* Bharatiya Vidya Bhavan, 1989, pp.328-329.

35. Nehru, J.L., *The Discovery of India,* The Signet Press, Calcutta, 1946, p.252.

36. Maity, N.L., Lokaganit: Ganiter Bikash O Samriddhite ek Phalgu Dhara in A. Basu (ed), *Bharater Itihase Vigyan O Prajukti,* Bangiya Vigyan Parishad, Kolikata, 1997, p.49.

37. *Ibid.,* pp.56-57.

38. *Op. cit.,* Ray N.R. p. 374.

39. Pan, Jixing, Charles Darwin's Chinese sources, *Isis*. Vol. 75, No.3 (Sep., 1984).pp.530-534, http/www/jstor.org.

40. *Ibid.*

41. *Ibid.*

42. Hora, S.L., Knowledge of the ancient Hindus concerning Fish and Fisheries of India. *Matsyavinoda* or a chapter of Angling in the *Mānasollāsa* by King *Someśvara* (AD.1127), *Journal of the Asiatic Society of Bengal,* Lett. 17, 1951, pp.145-169.

43. Choudhury, P.C., *Introduction to Hastividyāṃava,* Publication Board Assam, 1976.

44. Dewsbury, Donald, A., *Comparative Animal Behaviour,* McGraw-Hill Book Company, New York, 1978, p.3.

45. Sadhale, N., and Nene, Y.L., On Elephants in Manasollasa-I. Characteristics, Habitat, Methods of Capturing and Training in Nene, Y.L. (ed), *Glimpses of the Agricultural Heritage of India,* Asian Agri-History Foundation, Secunderabad 2007, pp.215-216.

46. *Ibid.*

Styles of Islamic Calligraphy in Manuscripts

18

G. S. Khwaja

The *Hindustan* of medieval period which is broadly constituted by the present subcontinent of India, Pakistan and Bangladesh has contributed to the Islamic calligraphy to such an extent that any study in the field of manuscriptology specially in the field of calligraphy on paper, will be considered incomplete if we do not refer to the different styles of Islamic calligraphy, its evolution and arrival to medieval India. The valuable contribution of Indian calligraphers who created master pieces in this art, is a glorious chapter in the history of art.

Islamic calligraphy on medieval monuments as well as on paper developed simultaneously in Indian subcontinent. A critical glance on its evolution here will show us how their application went hand in hand with each other. Though monumental Islamic calligraphy is not the main area of study but to draw the evolution and application of this art we will have to note few points because epigraphs are the only imperishable source- material recording the history of evolution of different arts.

The Origin of the Arabic Script

The history of evolution of signs from phonic expressions to the present developed form of script is a journey spread over nearly 4500 years.

When ancient man started adopting symbols and signs for his phonic syllables, pictograph came to existence and through the stages of hieroglyphs, cuneiforms and semitic alphabet it has gone a long way to reach a distinct form of alphabet representing nearly all consonant letters, needed for a successful communication.

It was 3rd and 4th century A.D. when the Arabic script started taking a definite shape. Its basic letters of alphabet were like some of their other semitic counterparts, consist of consonants. Its script was derived from the Nabataean script which itself had been derived from Aramaic script. As every body knows that Arabic script is written from right to left.

The Art of Calligrapy

اَلّذِی عَلَّمَ بالقلم عَلَّمَ الانسان ما لم یعلم القرآن

Translation: " *He, who taught the use of pen. Taught man, that he knew not.*"

(Quran, Chapter XCVI, verses 4 and 5).

These are the two of the five verses from the first revelation of Allah on Prophet Muhammad (pbuh).

Plato says : "*Writing is the geometry of soul.*"

In his famous work '*Ain-i-Akbari*' Abul Fazl writes : "*Pictures are much inferior to the written letters, (which is) spiritual geometry, emanating from the pen of invention.*"

The writing achieved an unprecedented religious as well as cultural importance in Islam. As pictures, icons and figurative images were prohibited in Islamic tenets, the skills of calligraphers, scribes and graphic artists got manifestation in the form of the art of calligraphy which has a rainbow of seven well-known styles namely Kufi, Naskh, Thulth, Riqa, Diwan, Nastaliq & Tughra and various different varieties.

In Arabia, calligraphy got such an important place in the cultural arena that nearly every quarter of public life was influenced by it.

The Styles

There are seven principle styles of Islamic calligraphy but there can be numerous off shoots and varieties of these styles. There are regional variations also.

Kufi

In the 7th century, after the advent of Islam, Kufa, the then capital of a province, became important centre of art and Arabic literature. The linguists, scholars, poets and calligraphers started efforts for the development of the Arabic script. After meticulous experiments they devised a specific script with short vertical strokes, extended horizontal lines, square and some-what angular alphabet to be called *Khat-e-Kufi* named after its place of origin. This was the first ever Arabic script. In the coming years innovations and ornamentation resulted into plaited and foliated varieties of Kufic. Inscription in the Dome of Rock at Jerusalem and letters of Prophet Muhammad, calligraphed by Hadrat Ali the IV Caliph, are also written in Kufic only. The early copies of holy Quran executed on parchment or papyrus, which we inherited and still preserved at various museums and private collections, are written in Kufi only which was also called Mashq.

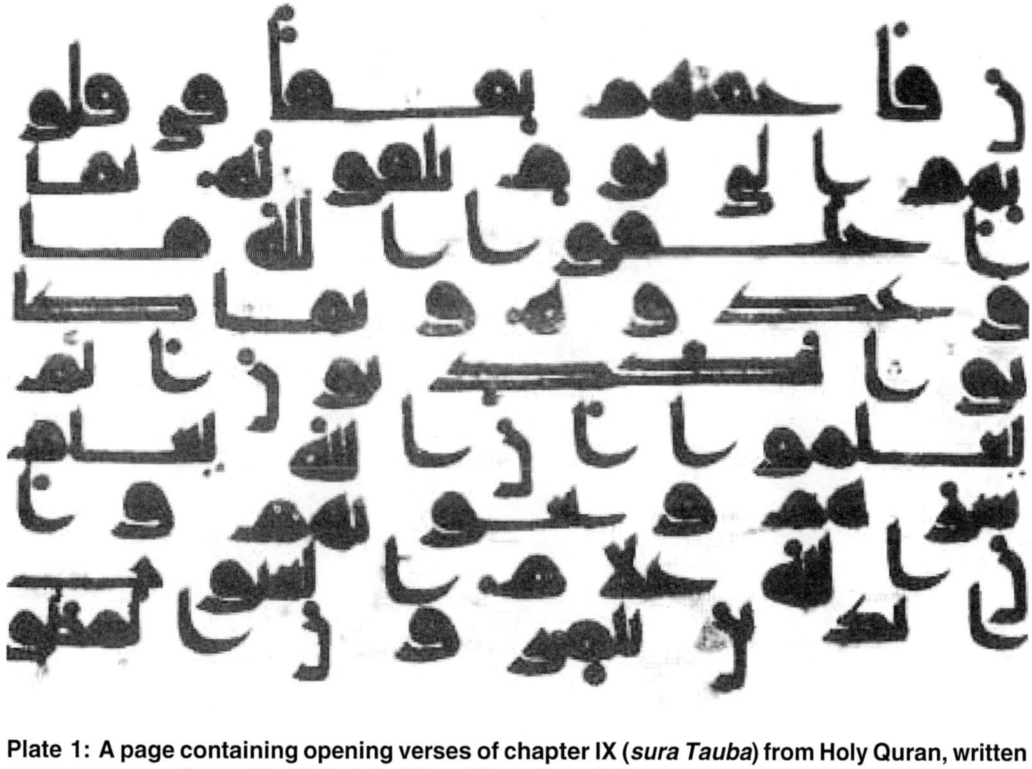

Plate 1: A page containing opening verses of chapter IX (*sura Tauba*) from Holy Quran, written on parchment in Kufi style Circa 9th century A.D.

Cursive Styles

By the end of 9th century Ibn-i-Muqlah, a genius calligrapher from Baghdad, added new dimensions to the Arabic script by simplifying the strokes and adding more cursive characters to it. His mastery over science of geometry facilitated him to frame specific rules and ratio among the alphabet. Thus came into existence cursive styles of calligraphy such as Naskh, Thulth, Riqa Taliq etc.

Naskh

Naskh style, as its name suggests, was script for copying Quran, books etc. It was a developed from of Kufic with cursive characters. Letters were given more curves and roundness with equal height and width with a consistency. The easiness involved in its execution made it popular in a short time and this style became the multipurpose script for epigraphs, coins, copying holy Quran and books. Even now world over the holy Quran is being printed in Naskh script only.

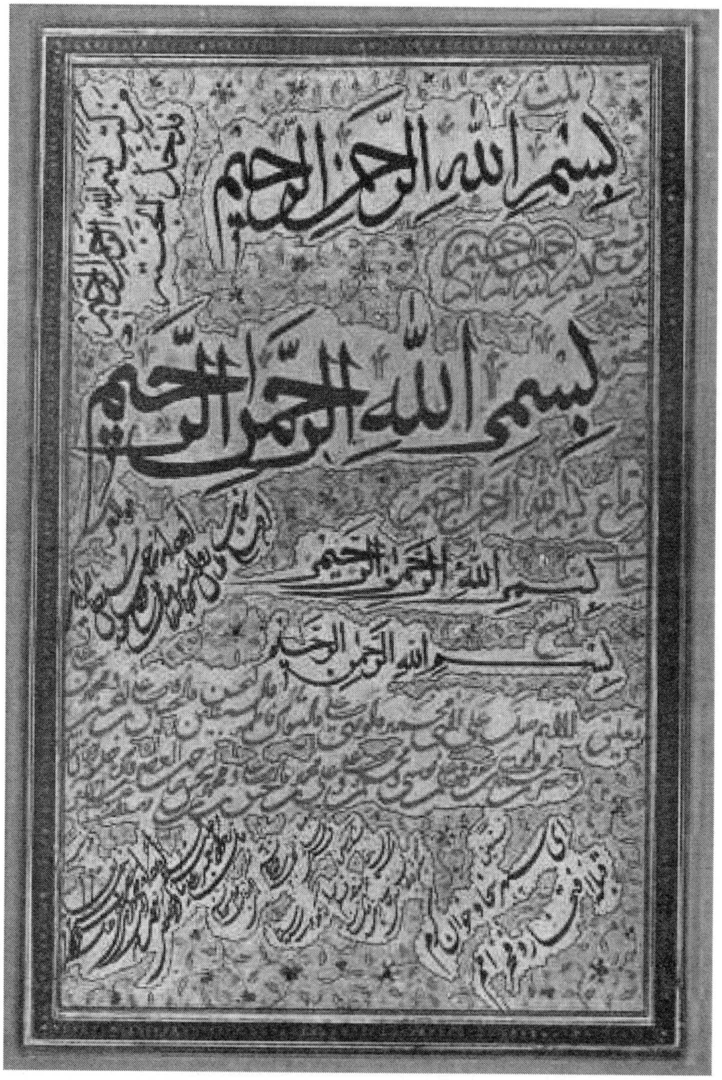

Plate 2: Naskh, Thulth and other cursive styles masterfully calligraphed on a manuscript page.

Thulth

Then entered the Thulth, the most elegant and decorative form of Arabic script. Thulth in Arabic means 'one-third' which in terms of geometric interpretations is defined as the rule of ratio between vertical and lateral strokes. As per its principles the rounded letters (*dairas* or circles) were 1/3 of vertical *alif*. The measurements were to be made with the unit of rhombic dot i.e. *qat* (width of the pen's tip).

The accommodative and overlapping quality of Thulth made it the most popular script for aesthetical writings, such as title of book, first page of Quran, headings, inscriptional bands on monuments, medallions etc.

Kiswah (the golden band woven in the black velvet cover of holy *Kaba,* at Mecca) is the best example of its being accepted by royality as well as masses.

Nastaliq

When, after the conquest, Islamic arts reached Iran, an another phase of variation in the prevailing scripts took place and after masterfully blending of Naskh and Taliq (here the latter literary means 'hanged') a new style Nastaliq was invented in the 15th century which was more delicate and fine in its terminal strokes and was proportionately thick and regular-circular for rounded parts of letters. Its was much suited to Iranian temperaments of artistic pursuits and subtleties of Persian poetry. Khwaja Mir Ali Tabrizi, the master calligrapher is considered as the founder of this style in 15th century who after great efforts fixed specific rules for this style. Ever since Nastaliq became the national script of Iran and even now Persian and Urdu languages are written in this style only.

Islamic Calligraphy in India

After the advent of Islam this art of calligraphy has gone a long way from west Asian & Central Asian countries to Indian sub-continent, to achieve the status of such an art that without its mention the cultural history of medieval India will be considered as incomplete.

Indo-Islamic architecture, royal stationary, royal orders (*farmāns*), coins, seals, wall hangings (*waslīs*), fabrics, books (in manuscript form) etc. were evidently influenced by this art.

When muslim rule was established in India in 12th century A.D., the building activities, alongwith socio-cultural institutions started taking its origin and shape on Indian soil and thus started a process of innovation and blending experiments in respect of art of calligraphy. And thus India of the period of Muslim rule could claim possession of some of the marvels of calligraphy in the world.

Indian Kufic

After the establishment of first Muslim Sultanate in India at the end of 12th century, the tradition of adorning monuments with large scale calligraphy was set. We get good specimen of Kufic on monuments of Sultanate period, which were generally comprised Bismillah, Quranic verses, names of Allah etc.

Facade of Quwwatul Islam mosque near Qutb Minar (New Delhi) and Facade of Adhai-din-ka-Jhonpda mosque, Ajmer are good examples of plaited Kufic style.

There are number of varieties in Kufic itself where square and angular letters are ornamented with foliated lateral and vertical strokes. Some varieties are strict square arranged in a geometric form. Some of the Golconda inscriptions contain this type of Kufic.

By the end of 14th century this style disappeared from Indian monuments. But in the manuscripts the titles of the books & headings of the chapters were being calligraphed in Kufi style, even upto 16th -17th century A.D.

Indian Naskh

Another popular style which was flourishing side by side, was Naskh which totally ousted Kufic and had a sway over the inscriptions till 16th century. Naskh was the most popular style for executing inscriptions for the quality of its consistency and facility of easy writing and reading. Most of the inscriptions of the period of Turk Sultans, Khaljis, Tughluqs, Lodis and early Mughals are executed in this style. All pre-Mughal coins carry legends in Naskh style only. Manuscripts on Islamic sciences in the pre-Mughal period and their *farmans* & documents used to be written in Naskh style only.

Indian Thulth

Thulth was though introduced in India right from the 14th century but it never ousted Naskh completely. Area of both the styles was different.

Thulth was more dignified and much more artistic. It had a great ornamental value for decorational bands on central *mihrabs* of mosques, medallions etc. Qutb Shahi and Mughal calligraphers used this style generously. Jami Masjid Golconda, Taj Mahal, Agra, among others, are the best example of this styles. The greatest quality of this style is its visual value which adds elegance and beauty to the monument on which it appears. In the manuscripts the headings were to be written consistently in Thulth only.

Bahar

India can very well boast of contributing a new style of calligraphy to the world of Islamic arts. Infact calligraphers in India were equally talented to add dimensions to the already well developed art of calligraphy. In the 14th century the world of graphic art saw a new style of calligraphy in the form of Bahar style. This purely indigenous style was a bold variety in which round strokes left without sharp ending. This characteristic added new attractiveness to it. We get very few epigraphs in this style but copies of Holy Quran were generously calligraphed in it.

ومن يقنت منكن لله ورسوله
وتعمل صالحا نؤتها اجرها
مرتين واعتدنا لها رزقا كريما
يا نساء النبي لستن كاحد
من النساء ان اتقيتن فلا
تخضعن بالقول فيطمع الذي
في قلبه مرض وقلن قولا
معروفا وقرن في بيوتكن
ولا تبرجن تبرج الجاهلية الاولى
واقمن الصلوة واتين الزكوة
واطعن الله ورسوله انما يريد الله
ليذهب عنكم الرجس اهل
البيت ويطهركم تطهيرا
واذكرن ما يتلى في بيوتكن
من ايات الله والحكمة ان

Plate 3: A Page of Quran written in Bahar style Circa 14th century A.D.

Indian Nastaliq

The start of the 16th century, saw a very delicate cursive style called Nastaliq. Leaving one or two examples, Nastaliq was introduced and popularized by Great Mughals. Mughals preferred Nastaliq for writing any thing, except Quranic verses. The *Farmans*, epigraphs, coins, seals, potteries, arms, books etc. were inscribed in Nastaliq.

Inscriptions on the Black Throne of Agra Fort, epitaphs of Khusrau Bagh, Allahabad (Jahangir's period) Sarai Azam Khan, Ahmedabad (Shah Jahan's period) and Safdar Jung's tomb (later Mughal's period) are the excellent specimen of Nastaliq style. The well-laid out coins, royal insignia and seals are the best example of masterful use of Nastaliq style by Mughal rulers. There *farmans*, royal history chronicles and other books were written in this style only.

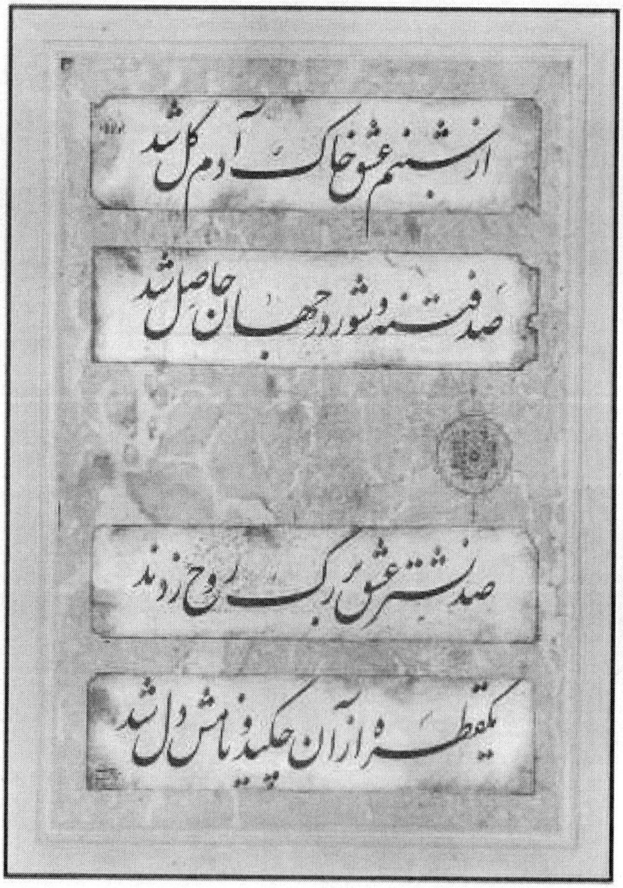

Plate 4 : A Quatrain *(rubai)* of sufi poet Maulana Rumi in elegant Nastaliq style.

Shikasta

When Nastaliq written in a running hand without much precision is called Shikasta which literary means broken. For the sake of fast and informal writing, strokes were

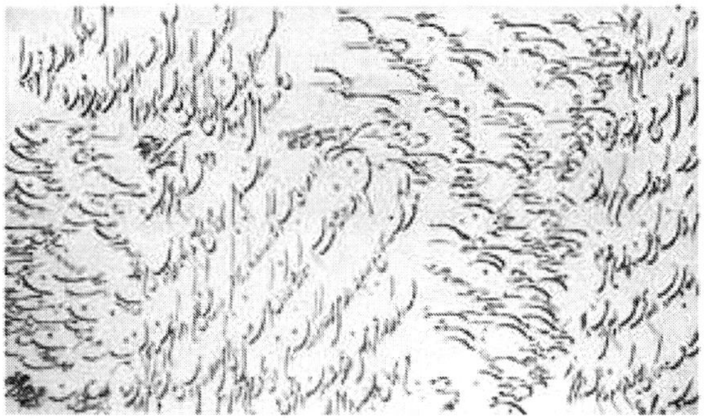

Plate 5: A Page of Shikasta style (left) and dedallion executed in Tughra style.

cut short and left broken or say incomplete. Shikasta cannot be designated as a separate style but it is a corrupt form of Nastaliq introduced by one Murtada Quli of Herat in early 17th century. This from was mostly used for informal letter writing, maintaining official diaries etc. The *dimn* (i.e. endorsement at the back of *farmans* is written in this style only. We rarely find inscriptions in this style.

Tughra

Tughra is a form of Calligraphy in which the names of Allah, Quranic verses, king's name, emblem of government are written in bird or animal form or beautiful geometric arrangement. The Ottoman Sultans of Turkey used this form to write their names and titles on the royal orders, documents, stationery etc. In India also this tradition was adopted by nearly all muslim rulers.

Tughra is not a separate style as such. Kufic, Naskh, Thulth, Nastaliq etc. can be arranged in geometric designs, bird/zoomorphic or floral forms to be called Tughra. It is generally found in medallions, arms, flags, guns, coins, seals and *farmans*. Some time a mirror effect is also created with the true and retrograde image written face-to-face to be called *Tughra-i-Makus*. The *waslis* (wall hangings) are also executed in Tughra style.

Manuscript Use and Manuscript Preservation with Special Reference to Palm-Leave Manuscripts

19

SUBODH GOPAL NANDI

Introduction

Manuscripts are rare in nature. The origin of manuscript restricts for a single copy only. This particular copy has been copied, translated, edited, and adapted by several scholars and copyists. In recent past manuscripts were a great interest of Kings, Priests, scholars, etc. and that were kept under their custody. Organizations like museums, archaeologies, libraries and other similar repository institutes have always showing their interest after having the information of a particular manuscript. These organizations have always taking care to add manuscripts into their collection.

This is only because manuscripts are of great important knowledge source of humankind. Georges Cartier[1] has pointed out this fact in his study thus: "Manuscripts are the lifeblood of history. In them it is possible to trace the development of writers and their work, the lives of statesmen, the manifold activities of peoples. Their value is impossible to calculate, and even if it is perceived as relatively slight in the world context, within each culture and each country it is absolute."

Manuscripts are the primary sources of information on folk literature, native medicinal formulae, religious writings, astrological texts, astronomical facts, records of cultural practices, traditional systems of medicine, veterinary, agricultural science, crafts and skills, etc. These primary sources of human civilization stored on a variety of mediums viz. clay tablets, stone, metals, tree barks, palm leaves, animal skins, cloth, paper, etc.

According to Grace Morley,[2] "Manuscripts in India have a long tradition. They were produced in all parts of the country: they are in many languages and scripts and on wide of religious, philosophical, historical, literary and scientific subjects. Frequently, they have reach illuminations and illustrations of outstanding quality, in a great variety of schools and styles of miniature painting. In some periods and places in India their importance to the history of the development of painting is great. Everywhere they are a reflection of profound and wide ranging learning, and of the richness, variety and long history of Indian culture".

1. Manuscripts and Role of Library

Some of the original manuscripts available in libraries or archives, which were collected earlier or just now, may have, getting old and become brittle day by day. Scholars involved in research have been using the library or archive materials and such facilities are to be extended for future also, which leads to preserve the original manuscripts for future use. In case of preservation care should be taken for two reasons: a) to save the original document and b) to keep ready the document to serve the researchers' interest.

An ideal library or manuscripts centre in respect of storage, preservation and rendering services to the serious researchers of local, national and global; some guidelines have to be followed. This is principally needed for the fair use of the treasure of knowledge as well as save the same for any decaying. It is well-known fact now-a-days that library has a pervasive role regarding the collection, storage, preservation of manuscripts and provides services to the learned scholars with these treasures of knowledge. Readers have three general will in their mind before to come to the library or manuscript centre which are: a) their admission always would be open to the Reading Room, b) every ordering or requisition from manuscripts collection should be attended by the library, and c) every request for copies from manuscripts collection should be provided by the library. General will also expecting that librarian should always be careful on these three points for providing services to any serious reader for the use of manuscripts from library's manuscript collection.

2. Need for Guidelines for Manuscript Use

Researchers are always fond of using the original, primary or rare sources of information by their personal touch with fully knowing that the document may damage due to his / her handling. Manuscripts are the primary sources of human thought and knowledge in various fields of human endevour. These are primary sources of human civilization stored on a variety of medias viz. clay tablets, stone, metals, tree barks, palm leaves, animal skins, cloth, paper, etc. In historical research, researchers are engaged to dig up facts of pasts and verification of these events stimulates the findings to establish as legitimate when primary sources would be available. These primary sources are particularly indispensable because only they are entirely reliable, since secondary sources may have chances of errors as these are repetitive in nature and generally multiplied from one edition to the next. The French political philosopher Montesquieu wrote in his Lettres persanes (Persian Letters, 1722) : "I have a little room full of very precious and very dear manuscripts; although I ruin my eyesight reading them, I much prefer to use these rather than printed works, which are less reliable..."[3].

The manuscript library or the manuscript section of a library should have to follow some procedure or guidelines. If the librarian maintains all these procedures in his / her library that would definitely be regarded as 'guidelines for using the manuscript' and which will not only help the library to maintain safety for its manuscript collection, but also to help researchers to have proper services. The Bodleian Library, University of Oxford[4] has maintained some procedure for its Manuscript Division, which are much relevant in context of Indian Libraries. The guidelines, with some modifications, may be stated as under:

2.1 Guidelines for Admission to the Manuscripts Reading Room

Admission to the Manuscripts Reading Room is not open to all. Access will be provided to those who can demonstrate a legitimate need of using manuscript items on production of reader cards issued by the Library. Any researcher / academician/ member of a professional association will be required to show a letter of recommendation from their organization, confirming the surname and forenames of the applicant, the applicant's position, academic degree, etc. The letter should contain status of the researcher, the research topic or academic purposes and must be in writing on letter headed paper of the head of the organization, duly signed with date. Students of final years may provide access, if they can present a letter of recommendation from their institution or Head of Department of studies about the reasons for using manuscript material.

Readers who have no such identity would be asked to write an application to the Librarian by explaining the purposes of using the Manuscripts in the Reading Room, for this purpose one prescribed application form may be maintained by the library.

The permission to use the manuscript collection will be issued by the Librarian or Head of the Manuscripts Department of a library for a specific period only. The researcher will be required to produce a new or fresh written recommendation from their organization, if the permission period over or research topic is changed. However, the complete list of regulations covering the use of the Manuscripts Reading Room should be available in the Manuscripts Reading Room.

2.2 Guidelines for Requisition of Material from the Manuscripts Collection

Readers, who are allowed to enter the library, place their requisition or order for required manuscript to the librarian or the manuscript-in-charge. The library should maintain one 'requisition slip' which is to be available easily in the manuscript reading room. Each and every reader can place demand or request for the specific manuscript to filled-up all the columns of requisition slip. The library personnel may take reasonable time for searching the requisite manuscript, before to supply that in the Reading Room. The librarian should always take care that this searching time may not exceed 24 hours. Readers may request for items at least one hour before closing time. The requisitioned items will be issued at least one hour before closing time of the library. One particular reader may request for two / three manuscripts at a time which are to be served for the same reader for one week in the reading room. This reserve time period may be extended by the librarian, if the concerned reader submit application and express his / her desire for further using the same.

3. Guidelines for Copying from Manuscripts Collection

Researchers may request for copies of required manuscripts and need to apply to the Librarian or Head of the Manuscripts Section for permission. Copying facility of Manuscripts are made available strictly in accordance with the subject of the research, indicated in the written recommendation which a researcher presented or submitted on the first visit in the Manuscripts Reading Room. Readers can also order for copies or reproductions (scanning and photography) to be used as illustrations in their research works. All orders must be paid for in advance and for a limited reproduction numbers up to some limit, say twenty in number, excepting fragile manuscripts. Copies of items of Manuscripts are to be collected by a researcher in person. Foreign researchers, who are unable to collect their order in person, can be obtained from archival institutions of the concern countries or through the recommending Institutes of researchers. Again, in exceptional cases, negatives may be loaned to institutions where the researcher belongs. But this type of loan has some risks and readers should not insist the library.

Researchers can copy illustrated material from manuscripts by hand in the Manuscripts Reading Room only with prior consent of the library authority. Readers may engage a draftsman or a painter to make a copy or to engage a professional copyist with prior consent of the library authority or the Head of the Manuscripts Division. Manuscripts may be copied by using of researcher's own equipment, if the same is not available in the Library. Manuscripts collection can only be copied under the supervision of a Manuscripts Reading Room staff. However, in this case, negatives of photocopies and microfilms remain with the Manuscripts Department without compensation.

From the above discussion it may be clear that manuscripts always have the heritage value and should be protected as property of the Nation. The National Government and State Governments should take care for its proper preservation. It is a great pleasure to observe that the National Government has already formulated National Manuscript Mission (NMM). This national body should have policies for conducting seminars and workshops to involve and motivate the librarians where these heritage items have been housed though not in scientific way. Scientific conservation techniques should be adopted to conserve these items as have already been followed in different modern famous archives of the World. There should be arrangement of microfilms and digitization, which secure the long life of these materials.

4. Why Preservation and Conservation?

History of preservation relates to cultural history of humankind. There is a scientific history of production of manuscripts, which is directly linked to the entire cultural legacy and innovations of methods of a locality that were introduced and transmitted for its manufacture. There were scientific approaches of using inks, pigments and dyes for making of these manuscripts. As the lacquers and organic dyes are the most fragile and they are also the most susceptible to changes in climate, light, storage and handling. It is essential to develop our knowledge in such a way that we can select the most appropriate method or approaches — to avoid or minimize damage of manuscripts. Correct usage of colour and chemical elements and sound critical selection of materials will help to minimize deterioration and guarantee conservation.

In India, a huge number of manuscripts have been collected and stored in several libraries, museums, manuscript centers or other repositories. Manuscripts that are available throughout India have written in stone, bhurjapatra, talpatra (palm leaves), animal skin, paper, etc. A large number of palm leave manuscripts have been found in Orissa, West Bengal and some other states and those are kept in several libraries. So it is the duty of a librarian to have the details idea about palm leave manuscript and its preservation and conservation methods. The following discussion may provide some basic ideas, which are to be kept in mind for the effective management of palm leaves collection of manuscripts.

5. Palm-leaf as Manuscript Writing Material:

When the manuscript is written in palm leaves is called palm leave manuscript. Palm-leaves are collected for writing purpose from palm tree (Borassus Flabellus).

All leaves are not used for writing purposes. To select leaves for writing purposes four things were considered: a) leaves are not too old, b) leaves are not too young, c) leaves are not too curve and d) leaves are not torn. After selecting the leaves some processes were normally taken for making them durable in nature, as writing material. These methods of treatment were: a) according to required length and breadth leaves would be selected, b) leaves then needed seasoning for which kept buried under the sand with little watering over the sand for at least 24 hours and this method named as 'Bali-kasa', c) another process of seasoning of leaves required to darkening the colour of leaves for using them as manuscript writing material and in this process leaves further put into a solution of turmeric and sour boiled-rice water at least for half an hour, which was called ' haldi-kasa', d) the fourth step of processing was fully drying of leaves either by taking direct heat treatment of sun or with the flow of air.[5]

After completion of the above process palm leaves now ready and to be for used as writing materials for manuscripts. As the manuscripts need bundle of leaves for its completion, two holes have been made in the middle of each leave with sharpen boring instrument, and one string passes through the wholes of leaves. Finally the string passes through two pieces of wooden covers having same type of holes as already done into palm leaves and thus manuscripts have its binding. The edges of palm leaves now need to cut according to the size of its wooden binding cover. The two sides of the string has a naught in such a way that the pages can be opened one by one putting one wooden cover on the ground and the other front to front. Now the reader or user can easily read the manuscript placing in front of him/her and open the pages one after another through string. After the use manuscript is to be kept tight over the wooden binding by using another peace of thread.

6. How to Preserve and Conserve Palm Leave Manuscripts?

Palm leaves are flexible in initial stage but after a certain period became dry. Palm leaves have some natural oil and this oil acts as preservatives itself and remains leaves flexible. Basically, palm leaves are most fragile in nature and do not last long, so the special care should be taken to preserve these manuscripts.[6]

In case of using paper as manuscript writing material, different preservatives have been used in paper manufacturing processes to make durable the paper for long. Hand made paper has the natural durability for more than 400 hundred years if stored and handled in good manner and some minimum preservation methods has been maintained. When Palm leaf is used as manuscript writing material then some methods have been used to make it durable. The manuscripts are normally preserved by casing and boxing, with an insect repellant inserted in the box. Now-a-days some scientific methods have been used which has extended the life of palm leaves and these methods have now been followed by the museums and libraries.

6.1 Fumigation

For fumigation each group of manuscripts is to be removed from their boxes and placed in an airtight container for fumigation. The container may be made of plastic with a lid or it may be the fumigation chamber made of steel almirah. It is necessary to remove set of manuscripts from its box and place the same opening pages in loose form on the shelves of the fumigation container with the appropriate quantity of para-dichlorobenzene kept in the base. Now the lid of the plastic container or the almirah should be sealed, and the manuscripts left on the closed cover for not less than one week. By employing more than one fumigation chamber, it is possible to complete the job within short period. After removing the fumigated palm leaf manuscripts from the fumigation chamber it should be ensured that each cased manuscript is returned to the correct box and to ensure it the cases and first leave of each manuscript should be marked in soft pencil with the box number.

6.2 Cleaning

After removing the manuscripts from the fumigator the leaves should be cleaned before to put the same into boxes. Some care should be taken for this process. Firstly, each leave should be numbered impalpably in the lower right corner with a soft pencil. Secondly, the covers and strings should be removed carefully. Thirdly, all the leaves should be cleaned from dust and insect parts by using a soft dry brush. Fourthly, if any manuscript folio becomes fragment it should be set-aside in a polyester envelope bearing the leaf number for future attachment. Fifthly, after the cleaning of the surface of leaves with the brush, the leaves are to be carefully cleaned on both sides with a lint-free cloth and little warm water (preferably distilled). But before starting this process, it should be checked to ensure that the writing of the manuscript is incised and not surface-written and a small area to be tested to ascertain the stability of the image. Sixthly, if water cleaning is possible then leaves should be placed between sheets of blotting paper to dry them fully.

6.3 Repair and Support

The manuscripts have the chances to be damaged by insects or due to tearing by use of rough handling. It is most essential to repair these damages at this point without any time loss; otherwise it will damage the manuscript more and more.

The palm leaves may be repaired in the following ways. The leaves can be fixed to the surface with 5% solution of polyvinyl acetate in toluene. Then a piece of tissue (Tengujo or any other best quality) is to be covered the damaged area along with a small square of polyester film. The tissue is to be carefully pasted; the tissue laid into place on the palm leaf, and gently rubbed down through the film with a bone folder and after sometime the film is to be removed to allow the repair to dry.

Another repair technique is the use of tissue coated with a dry fish gelatin solution. This technique stresses that the tissue is to be laid dry over the dampened surface of the damaged palm leaf, and pressed into place with damp clothe until firmly set. The advantage of this method is that repaired portion dry very quickly, adhesive does not have to be prepared, and adhesion is very strong.

If a significant portion of the palm leaf is missing, a piece of Kitakata paper is to be carefully covered due matching the missing area, and tipped into place. It is then supported on both sides by the tissue in the manner noted above. Loose fragments of palm leaves are similarly secured in place in this fashion.

To prepare the stable adhesive it is required to follow some procedures. Firstly, to place one cup (225 ml.) of water, preferably distilled, in a sealable container. Next to add one and half teaspoonful (7.5 ml.) of methylcellulose and to stir to blend it completely with the water. It will attain a jelly-like consistency after preserving the solution for one hour approximately, and now it will be ready for use.

6.4 Oiling

The oiling of the palm leaf imparts a smooth surface, which also increases the flexibility of leaves. In case of oiling it is suggested to use the insect-repellant oil, like cedarwood oil and thus the leaves have added protection. A thin coat of cedarwood oil is to be applied to the entire surface of leaves on both sides of the leaf. Another suggested method of oiling by introducing the camphor, oil and citronella oil and the same could be introduced in the palm leaves with a mixture of alcholon in a ratio of 3:2.

It is true that the oil does not release tissue repairs, but they blend further into the leaf surface. Each leaf should be air-dried in a constant air blow to avoid molding. The useful drying method is to secure the leaves to a line by a peg or spring clip. When the leaves dry completely, the surface should be lightly polished with a soft dry cloth. And finally the manuscript folios are re-strung, re-cased, re-boxed and re-shelved.

7. Rabindranath and Manuscript Preservation

Gurudev Rabindranath Tagore has shown his eagerness and great interest to procure manuscripts scattered throughout Bengal.[7] The Poet has collected several manuscripts in different times and donated in different institutions like Bangiya Sahitya Parishad, etc. before to establish the manuscript centre at his Visva-Bharati. He has collected the manuscripts of 'Yogir Gan', 'Kumarkhalir Lalan Sampradayer Baulder Ganer Khata', 'Bhaktamal', etc. Tagore has taken a noble drive to collect invaluable manuscripts scattered in different places all over the country, which is unique in nature. To draw the attention of the then learned people one advertisement, in appeal form, has been published in two newspapers "Hindu" and "Bihar Herald" on December 19, 1923. In this advertisement Poet appealed to the people thus: "It is needless to say that any old manuscripts sent to us having a literary or historical importance, will be gratefully received by our institution and preserved in Visva-Bharati Library in Santiniketan with care."[8] The effort of Gurudev has been very successful and manuscripts have been collected from different parts of the country since then and stored at the Manuscript Section at Visva-Bharati regularly. The Manuscript Section at Visva-Bharati has been established in the year 1922 under the guidance of Gurudev Rabindranath Tagore, the founder of Visva-Bharati.

8. Manuscript Collection at Visva-Bharati

Presently Visva-Bharati has 18011 valuable manuscripts in different languages. Out of these good numbers of manuscripts collection language break-up is thus: Bengali - 7741, Sanskrit - 6574, Oriya - 1918, Indo-Tibetan - 1620, Persian - 116, Arabic - 32 and Urdu - 10. The earliest manuscript in Visva-Bharati is in Bengali, entitled Sanjaya Mahabharata of 15th — 16th Century. There are 50 palm leaf manuscripts in Sanskrit and the earliest is of 18th Century. In Oriya, 557 manuscripts are in palm leaf and the earliest one is of 18th Century. Among these invaluable manuscripts holdings on seven different languages at Visva-Bharati, 1978 has already been processed. Descriptive catalogue has been prepared for the manuscripts of Bengali - 829, Sanskrit - 672, Oriya - 181 and Indo-Tibetan — 138. All Manuscripts of Urdu (10), Arabic (32) and Parsian (116), which are housed in Central Library, have completed the processing work i.e. cataloguing, classification, etc.

The Oriya Department, Visva-Bharati has 557 volumes of palm-leaf manuscripts in its collection containing 70764 folia of different length. All manuscripts are in Oriya script and the texts are of three languages, Oriya, Sanskrit and Bengali. Some volumes contain more than one text and as a result this palm-leaf manuscript collection contains 401 texts in Sanskrit, 342 texts in Oriya and 12 texts in Bengali.[9]

8.1 Planning for Manuscript Preservation at Visva-Bharati

There are three ways of preservation of manuscripts; a) Copy the original by hand, b) Microfilm and c) Digitization. The third one is most currently added in case of manuscript preservation. This approach has come out as the 'digitization of Manuscript', which will help to protect the original document, against again and again direct handling by the reader and will provide better access facilities to the researchers on their required materials. But it is most essential to preserve the original manuscripts, which may be used by the researchers or serious readers in case where the digitized copy has some poor impression or has some portion damage due to insect or tearing out. So we may consider preserving and conserving the manuscripts as well as framing some guideline for our Manuscript Centre, Lipika as noted earlier.

For the best preservation of these invaluable documents all manuscript collections of Visva-Bharati are to be housed under one roof. Visva-Bharati has built one centralized Auditorium cum Manuscript Center "LIPIKA". It has a reading space to provide the scope for use of this treasure of knowledge to the learned scholars of the locality, country and abroad. Thus Visva-Bharati Manuscript Centre: Lipika will come out as one of the modern manuscript library in our country.

Presently Digitization Unit of Visva-Bharati Library has started digitization of books and has already been digitized more than sixteen lakh pages of old books and journals along with writings of Tagore. Soon after the completion of digitization work of old and rare collection of library documents, the digitization of library manuscript would be started.

The Digitization Unit of Visva-Bharati Library has two scanners, five PCs, one centralized UPS, one modem for building 'Unit-LAN', software (Abbyy Find Reader 7.0 and Scan Fix) and some other IT equipments for digitization and storage processes, which can be used to initiate the programme of digitization of library manuscript at Visva-Bharati. The specification details of equipments are as under:

Two Scanners (Model Zeulshel OS 500) having four parts: a) base panel which can accommodate 24"x18" inches documents, b) tower panel which has the provision of movement of camera, c) one camera and d) provision of focusing sufficient light arrangement over the scanned item.

One camera (Model Kodak) which can be moved towards tower panel for taking scanned image of different size documents ranging 2 x A4 pages to 2 x A2 pages. The resolution of this camera is 600 DPI.

Five PCs (Pentium - 4).

Star LAN.

9. Conclusion

In case of the preservation and protection of these invaluable human knowledge items, importance and priority should be given by the Government like other heritage items monuments, museums, national parks, etc. through out the country.

One of the important areas of concern for the National Manuscript Mission (NMM) is to protect the existing manuscripts of India from decay, damage and destruction. It is felt that there is a need to re-focus on the programme of conservation, to make it more widespread, befitting a national mission for the preservation of manuscripts. To fill the gaps in terms of geographic spread and number of manuscripts in need of

Plate 1: Chitra Kavya Bandhyodaya Oriya Palm leaf Manuscript

Plate 2: Geeta Govinda Oriya Palm leaf Manuscript

conservation, the Mission plans to strengthen conservation activities through the following strategies:

— Giving preventive conservation treatment to all the deserving manuscripts in India

— Setting target for curative conservation of the most endangered manuscripts in consultation with the Manuscript Resource Centres (MRC) and Manuscript Resource Centres (MCC). In the current year the Mission should set a target of one lakh manuscripts to be conserved across the country

— Setting up 200 Manuscripts Conservation Centres with all basic conservation facilities and at least two trained conservators

— Arranging Training programme for making a pool of conservation specialists across the country on preventive conservation

— Preparing a panel of trained personnel on curative conservation through training programmes.[10]

Actually, our country has rich and diverse cultural heritage, which are embodied in the form of manuscript. Some of them are very old, preserved knowledge on various subjects, which are historically worthy of being, and price of such documents cannot be measured. They are frequently used or may be used by serious scholar and researchers as per their needs. In the process of handling many of them suffer irreparable damage and in some cases they are preserved in such a way that they are totally unavailable for use at all.

Lastly, for preservation and conservation Librarians have to know or study the details of manuscript. Knowledge of the structure of manuscripts and of the various elements involved will help us to date, identify and understand the techniques used by calligraphers, scribes and binders. For this comprehensive study, it requires an interdisciplinary team of professionals like archivists, subject specialists, chemists and conservators. This will enable Librarians to establish the common criteria for the safekeeping and conservation of such manuscripts, as well as establishing guidelines for creating appropriate protocols for preservation, conservation.

References

1. Cartier, Georges: Libraries to the rescue - manuscript preservation. UNESCO Courier, May, 1989.

2. Grace, Morley: National Museums of India. [As referred by Abbasi, N.A. and Saini, M.L.: Manuscript wealth of India. *In* Gupta, B.M. (eds.): Handbook of libraries, archieves & information centers in India, vol.2: libraries and archives. New Delhi: Information industry Publications, 1986. p. 490-515].

3. Abbasi, N.A. and Saini, M.L.: Manuscript wealth of India. *In* Gupta, B.M. (eds.): Handbook of libraries, archieves & information centers in India, vol.2: libraries and archives. New Delhi: Information industry Publications, 1986. p. 490-515.
4. University of Oxford Website.
5. Chakravarti, MM: Language and Literature of Orissa. *Journal of the Asiatic Society of Bengal*, 1897. p.328-330
6. Mahapatra, Manmohan: Why and how to preserve Palm-lief Manuscripts. *Orissa Historical Research Journal*, Vol.24-26.
7. Nandi, SG: Manuscripts: its Preservation and Management in Visva-Bharati Library. In XXVI All India Conference of IASLIC papers on Digital media and library information services, Jamia Millia Islamia, New Delhi, 2007. p.227-233.
8. Biswas, Achintya. Bangala Punthir katha. Kolkata: Ratnavali, 2003. p. 159.
9. Mahapatra, K (ed.): A Descriptive Catalogue of Oriya Manuscripts. Santiniketan: Visva-Bharati, 1983.
10. National Manuscript Mission: Kriti Rakshana.

Tagore, Visva-Bharati and Manuscriptology

20

BUDDHADEV ACHARYA
SAILEN KUMAR DE

The Brahmacharya Vidyalaya (The Upanisadic School) was transformed into Visva-Bharati Society in 1921 and the Indological studies gained ground at Santiniketan. Gurudev Rabindranath Tagore visualized its great importance. He made arrangement for the collection and preservation of the ancient Manuscripts (MSS), under Vidya-Bhavana (the Institute of Humanities and Social Sciences); from then on the scholars got the opportunity for research work in this field. Immediately an advertisement was released in the Behar Herald in 1923 seeking public cooperation and help.[1] It was for the first time that a special emphasis was given to the importance of various ancient mss. Sri Anantakrishna Sastri, a learned scholar from Trivandram, joined the project, lived for some time at Santiniketan, and helped in collecting many Bengali and Sanskrit mss from the surrounding localities. Various other mss were also collected from different parts of the country.[2]

During the life time of Tagore from November 1940 to March 1941 the following eminent scholars of Visva-Bharati, Santiniketan like Prof. Ramesh Chandra Chakravorti, Prof. Harazari Prasad Dwivedi, Prof. Sujit Kumar Mukherjee, Prof. Sukhomaya Bhattacharya, Prof. Upendra Kumar Das and Prof. Nagendranath Chakravorti made a comprehensive list of scripts on Moksha dharma from Śānti Parva of the Mahābhārata. Those valuable docoments are carefully preserved in historic collection of Sanskrit Manuscripts at the Visva-Bharati MSS. Section (Lipika), Santiniketan.

Poet Rabindranath had also a deep love for the ancient literature and culture. He was struck with shame when he came to know of the indifferent attitude of the Indian scholars towards the mss. What a shame it was that the foreign scholars first came forward to explore the Indological sources while the Indians remained sitting idle; what an useful it would have been if they could organize exhibitions on various

Indological findings like regional language, literature and history, prakrit language and literature, folk lore, ancient architecture, temples, buildings, ponds, historical places with illustrations, old mss, inscriptions and coins of archaeological value etc.

With the coming of the printing press the Bengali types were put to use for the first time in Hooghly. The Bengali letters were transliterated in English by Hallhead and a book was printed in 1778. The elite personalities, both foreign and Indian, like Thomas Kwery, Words, Marshman, Iswarchandra Gupta, Iswarchandra Vidyasagar and others took special interest and initiated the printing of the Bengali edition of the Rāmāyana (Kṛttivāsa) and the Mahābhārata (Kashirām Dās) and like other publications from the Sreerampore Press and the Battala Press. At that time Sri Ramkṛishna Datta became very famous for his bulk collections of thousands of original mss.

In 1946 Professor Probodh Chandra Bagchi, the then Principal of Vidya-Bhavana, approached Rathindranath Tagore for the permission of formal collection of Bengali mss by Visva-Bharati. The permission was granted. Adhyapak Panchanan Mondal, an able student of Linguist Suniti Kumar Chattopadhyay and Acharya Sukumar Sen, build up a valuable mss repository at Santiniketan. He made a special drive for the bulk collection of the mss. Tapanmohan Chattopadhyay, an eminent Barrister, joined the drive and donated some 218 mss from his own collections. In course of time some thousands of mss were collected from Sibratan Mitra, who had his Ratan Library at Suri. Many other famous people from different parts of Bengal came forward to enrich this repository. Other than Visva-Bharati, the institutions like the Asiatic Society, Bangiya Sahitya Parishad, the Kolkata University, the Dacca University, Varendra Research Society, Bardhaman Sahitya Sabha etc. also became the pioneers in this field. Thus Bengal became the core centre for the study and research of the mss.[3]

The mss are not only the literary composition and prosody but also the important documents for socio-cultural history of the country. Had there been no mss we might have lost the context of the Vedas, the Upanisadas, the Purānas, the Rāmāyana and the Mahābhārata. Nor do we become able to discover the creativity of the great ancient poets like Kālidāsa, Bhāsa, Bhāravi, Bānabhatta, Bhavabhuti, and many others. It would have been the same with the charyāpada (the lyrics composed by the religious sects) and the Śrīkṛisṇa Kīrtana (the songs of the cycle of the god Srīkrisṇa) and with the Bengali poets like Chandidāsa, Vidyāpati, Krittivāsa, Kāśhirāma Dāsa, Mukundarāma Chakravorty, Bharatchandra Roy and others. How do our generations come to know of the biography of the great lord Srīchaitanyadeva and Nityānanda if we did not find the relevant mss.

In these days of technological advancement very few people show interest for the old mss. But the hand written antiquated cotton-pulps and palm leaves etc, the so called documents for the India's past glory, still survive and will survive for centuries to come even against many environmental odds. To-day these documents are preserved in the library as books and papers. Till to-day many of these documents are found in the families of Bengal. We can better pay respect to our past glory and heritage if we can collect those documents, edit those properly and make those easily available to the readers. No specific knowledge is necessary to understand the fact that without a past glory and heritage no society and no civilization exist. Only for this reason famous Indians came forward to save the golden treasury to inspire the future generation.

What do we mean by the old mss ? Generally we mean the saved copies of the hand written documents of our ancestors, which were kept in the cover of a red coloured small piece of cloth.

These sacramental documents contain full details of the ritualistic ideas and practices, and record the sacred hymns and incantations. But that is not all. The mss are the true documents relating to education, literature and philosophy.

Making of Mss Paper

In those days there was no paper in the modern sense. The ingredients were collected from nature and put to use as paper. It served as an essential requirement for education and literature. The kings had engraved inscriptions on stone and copper. But the common mass of people wrote on palm-leaves, terata-leaves, leather, bark, cotton-pulp or tulot-paper. The mss were written on those papers. A system of the nature was followed in making those papers to be of the full proof longivity. Those were first collected, processed and then cut into size of the mss paper. After the invention of the cotton-pulp (Tulot-paper) extensive mss writing started. There arose the paper making class who produced papers. The poets and the copy writer bought from them. Generally the palm-leaves and the terata-leaves were large in length. The shortage in breadth had to make up by length. The tulot-paper made of cotton-pulp was short in length but big in breadth. A slight round slot was left in the middle of the finished paper to pass a sting through it to tie the set of the mss with a sizable piece of wood and with a small piece of red coloured cloth.

After the making process was complete, the paper was first washed by the mulberry compounded water and then dried up. It was done to counter the attack of the insects. Sometime the coating of the mirobalan, sulphur and red sandal was applied for the same purpose. The complete sets of mss were bound with a casked made of hard tick wood. In its scarcity leather-band and intertwined queue shaped palm-leaves with fine artistic designed cane were used. Some time for full-proof longivity the wood and leather were combinedly used. Again the slough was put inside the pages so that the insects could not seize the papers with the teeth. The margosa-leaves were in wide use as insecticide.[4]

Ink making

Usually in those days the ink was made by available ingredients. The contemporary poets some times mentioned the items. The sesame, three kinds of myrobalan, bark of the silk cotton plant compounded with goat milk had to be grinded by lac in an iron pot. This would produce the best quality ink superior in comparison to the paper and pen. The ink was made instantly at the time of each writing. It was very sticky and could smear with the inkpot or with the paper. On the other the metal Nibs were in use. The feathers of the peacock or the feathers of the vulture or branches of the bamboo tree were in use as pen. It was necessary to hard press the nibs for writing.[5]

The system of writing

Beautiful hand writing, clear conception of spelling, clear ideas of the subjects, the endless patience for work, etc. were the essential qualities for a good writer. Any auspicious day was considered suitable for the beginning of writing ceremonially, obviously by worshiping the Lord Ganesha or by pronouncing one hundred eight times the names of gods and goddesses. This is called Ānji or the beginning of creation or the preamble. Ānji is a symbol of the Lord Ganesha and also the symbol of the affluent supreme god and goddess like Durgā, Kāli, Kṛishṇa, etc. whose names were written at the top of the front page.

Ānji

Ānji is also symbolically a mathematical term denoting the number 108. It means 108 times pronouncing the names of the god and goddess. There is an old formula with this number 108. It is sacramental root over 7 (seven). It is 1 pana and 7 gandas. By old arithmetical enumeration 1 pana = 20 gandas, 1 Ganda = Multiple 4. 1 pana = 20 x 4 = 80, 7 ganda = 7x4=28. It does mean number 108 (80 + 28 =108).

Secondly, it means the glorification of Lord Ganeśa, the god of wisdom. By this glorification, the writer achieves success.

According to Ṣaṭcakra Nirūpaṇa by Kālicarana (Commentator). Ānji is Ānjikalā, means Bodhinī Śakti, the power of knowledge, one of the seven powers beginning from Āgñā cakra the power of command to the power of determination. Ānjikalā also means (Byapikā Śakti) spreading power placed above the Mahānāda. It is due to this power of knowledge that the writer can create.[6]

Vyāsadeva could create the Mahābhārata only due to the grace of Lord Ganeśa, an identity of wisdom. A lay man cannot do it.

In those days the children got to the first base literacy by ceremonially observing the Ānjikalā on the auspicious day of the Saraswati Puzā festival.

Collection of the Mss

Usually the Sanskrit mss were available in the Toll (the Sanskrit grammar-school) and in learned Brahmin families. Many Bengali mss were also available there. In a Toll the Amarakośa (Sanskrit word book), the Māgh (condensed Sanskrit grammer by Jumara) and Naiṣādha, Raghuvaṅśa, the Rāmāyaṇa, the Mahābhārata and like other Sanskrit texts were kept in the desk of the students. In the Mosque, in the Maktāb (Muslim primary school), in the Mādrassā and in the well-to-do Muslim families various hand written documents were available like the Korān, the Kālām, the episode and the couplet in Arabic, Persian and Urdu. (Naskh, Nastālik, Kissā, Sikastaā etc.).

The people lower to the Brahmin by caste had to go to the teachers of the primary school, where they learnt mentally the critical arithmetic. Mathematical sums, octuple, octosyllable, Amarakośa etc.

In the Mongal Kāvya (the poetic sayings of the goddess Mongal Chaṇḍī), the educational system of the mediaeval Bengal has been described at length. One part of this poetic saying has been devoted to the rich merchant class. A list of the subject of studies has been incorporated. Śrīmanta, the son of the rich merchant Dhanapati, in his boyhood first learnt the voice (consonant and vowel) then mathametics, poetry, word spelling, blending, conduct, grammar, version, number, (singular and plural), word compounds, sanskrit word book (Amarakoṣa), the prosody of Jumara Nandi, and also the Sanskrit text books like Bhaṭṭikāvya, Māgha, Meghadūta, Kumār-Sambhava, Kāmasūtra, Āyurveda etc. This was the vast course curriculum of mediaeval Bengal.[7]

After the emergence of Lord Śrīchaitanya, the mss containing his biography was available in almost all the families of Bengal. Some thousands of Vaiṣṇava lyrics, Vaiṣṇava methodology, various Sāhajiyā traditional writings were also found there in the Vaiṣṇava assemblies, as also the Sāhajiyā lyrics and the satires by Gorakha Gopichandra was not unknown.

The families, those were traditionally keeping the collections like the Rāmāyaṇa, the Mahābhārata, the digestive of the prayer methods of the god Satyanārāyaṇa, the biography of Śrīchaitanyadev, the Mongal Kāvya etc., were regarded as the noble families. The practice of keeping of such collections and listening occasional recitations was a part and parcel of the then Bengal culture. Be the educated or uneducated everyone believed that by this practice one could get a thorough fare to the eternal world or a clear conception of the utmost moral sense; a righteous life was highly esteemed. In the words of Kāśirāma Dāsa the poetical sayings of the Mahābhārata is just like the nectar for which pious people hear its recitals or by hearing its recitals people become pious. Again in, the words of Kṛttivās the duty of the people is to do good to others and the Rāmāyaṇa is written to produce a firm belief in it by evidence, arguments etc. The influence of the Rāmāyaṇa is so deep rooted that the lifelong enjoyment from its poetical singing still survive in the society of modern Bengal. As also the virtuous songs on Mother Goddesses (mainly on Kāli and Durgā) by Rāmprasāda and Kamalākānta still echo in the houses of Bengal. Apart from those creative imaginations and in need of the practical purposes of life, the people had to bring the collections of the copies of the Āyurveda, the Muslim Pharmacology, exorcism, the hocus-pocus, the amazing magic, the sexology, the astrology etc.

An artistic get up

Writing or copying of the mss was a herculian task. During the keeping of the collections the mss were treated divinely. For bringing to an artistic get up the papers of the mss were designed by using red colour polish, yellow colour and ink. Sometimes those were beautified by drawing the picture of flowers, animals, and birds. Again the mythological stories, the stories of Lord Kriṣṇa and Gourānga (Chaitanya), the epic stories of the Rāmāyaṇa and the Mahābhārata, the mythological stories of killing the demon Mahisāṣura, the image of the goddess Kāli, the picture of the holy chariots etc. were the subjects of picture writing.

Thus inside the manuscripts the works of interesting calligraphies are found. Such picture writings were also found in the wooden casked made of shal or tick. It is very astonishing how do they get rid of the monotony of continuous writing by their recreation providing artistic skill. It was possible for they were solely absorbed in the art of beautifying the mss writing.

Date

According to Adhyāpaka Panchanan Mondal the poets' minds are as transparent as mirrors. The contemporary society and its ethical and spiritual standards are all reflected in their poems. To that extent the poets may be called the historian of their times.[8] In this sense the Chandimongal Kavya (the poetical saying of the Goddess Chaṇḍī) by Mukundarām is a historical source of the $16^{th}-17^{th}$ century Rādha Bengal (a part of Bengal on the western bank of the Ganges).

In those days the poets mentioned the year, date, day and lunar day using words of different symbols. In the same way the names of the king and the emperor were also noted. The era identification was symbolically made by using synonyms of the sun, the moon, the sky, the ocean, the poetical taste, five weapons, the eyes, the omnipotent, the seasons, the fire etc. Multiple meanings led the scholars to great controversy. Non mention of the date sometime led the scholars to equate the historical co-incidents for an anticipatory conclusion. Careless and unintelligent editing turns the text to major controversy.

Puspika or the Colophon

The Puspika or the colophon is a tailpiece at the end of the mss. In it the information of the authority of the writing is given. Here the poet introduced himself eclectically and showed his generosity. The copy writers also followed the same pattern. Admittedly their short coming is that they submit to the will of the readers by saying that "This is a copy and nothing but a copy. There is no fault of my own. Please forgive me. See that the strong iron man like Bhīma had left the battle field by mistake. Sometimes the sages are out of their wit leading by their passions. So a faithful copy writer like me cannot be the exception." In this way the text ended. The copy writer recorded the year, month, day, date, count of meridian, lunar day, star, hour, minutes, seconds, the address of his residence, Taluk, Pargana, Tangi etc. He also recorded the place of work, direction of sitting arrangement, names of the person present, name of the writer whom he followed, the amount of payment he received either in cash or in kind, the name of the owner, the name of the readers, etc. Be it a sorrow or joy the coincided facts were also recorded. It was immaterial whether the writer was a Hindu or Muslim, but certainly mattered if the work was not done properly. The owner was raised to the position of morally perfect and pure as his dues.[9]

The classes of wise and educated writers were very conscious of the spelling and were very attentive in scrutinizing the text line by line. They corrected the errors by noting upward sign at the top and downward sign at the bottom as the case ought to be. They also marked with distinction the missing words and lines, which were not at all traceable. It was also mentioned whether the mistakes were done by the previous writer for any defective method of writing. As such, the readers were always cautioned not to be misguided by any misconceived notion. On the other, careless writing of the copies in a large scale corrupted the original text by major insertion. So it is said that repeated imitation makes the original lose its identity.

None the less, the description of the historical incidents those which are known from the copies of the conscious writer are most valuable in history. The colophon part of a copy of the Chaṇḍīmongal Kāvya (the poetical saying of the goddess Chaṇḍī) by Mukundarām Chakravarty preserved in the Visva-Bharati Manuscript Section is worth mentioning. It bears the accession no. 1540.[10] The colophon reads as follows: "Here ends the copy of the text of the poetical saying of the goddess Śrī Śrī Mongal Chaṇḍī. It is a copy and nothing but a copy. Therefore, I have no fault of my own. Everyone does mistakes, even the strong man like Bhīma had withdrawn from the battle field untimely, the great sages went out of their wit driven by passion, so please do not be merciless to deprive me of your favours. The wise men should only read the text but not the foolish one, because a foolish does not know the a b c of the mss. I Śrī Nandalāl Roy Debsharmana end this copy on Thursday the 27th day of Jaiṣṭha, 1177 B.S. The omnipotent goddess Chandikā, god Siva, goddess Durgā, and my teacher please take my regards. I live in the village of Khaṇḍaghosh. In 1177 B.S. there was a great devastating famine, there was no monsoon and none could rest in peace. In South Bengal and in some adjoining moor land area the situation was slightly better where 12 seers of rice was sold by 1 rupee. But in other places, one seer of rice was sold by 1 rupee 2 annas and 6 paise, one seer of oil by 2 rupees 8 annas, one seer of salt by 1 rupee, one seer of pulses by 11 rupees. There were no vegetables and nothing else. The old men belonging to later life never saw such a devastation. Many men died by starvation. Even the rich one did not have the food for cooking. Such disastrous situation continues up to the month of Bhādra, 1177 B.S. Things go on this year also. I do not find any way out. I am helpless. The copy ends with 182 pages and 430 sub-chapters. Then in the month of Śrāvana four seer of rice was sold by one rupee and many people were affected by the great famine."

Even during the disaster by the great famine in Bengal, energy for writing was not lacking completely. In the colophon Nandalal Roy Sharmana willingly said that the illiterate, layman must not be allowed to touch the text. Because they are not like the learned and they are unable to decipher an obscure piece of writing.

In the colophon we get the direct evidence of the devastating great historical famine of the eighteenth century Bengal, which is also familiar as the great famine of 76 B.S.

We also know from it how did the rich families suffer from high price rise of the food grains, how did the agricultural production suffer from no monsoon, and how did the great calamity devastated the people's life in 1177 B.S. or 1770 A. D the very next year. To that extent the colophon is not simply a literary narrative, but a direct evidence of history.

The Recital Class

In those days the people earned the spiritual merits by employing the copy writer, and the copy writer earned their living by writing the copy of the mss. As also the recital class made their earnings by reciting poetical sayings woundering from place to place. This recurring system continued to survive in the then society.

In those days the system of education created a tradition in which the four principal aims of human life, Piety, wealth, love or fulfilment of desire and salvation of the soul could be achieved. Those recital classes used the religious places as platform for the propagation and spread of the ideas. Sometime they took more than a month to complete the recitals on the sayings of the Rāmāyaṇa, the Mahābhārata and the Bhāgavata and thus raised the ethical sense of the general mass and spiritually entertained them. On listening those recitals the common people got rid of three kinds of affliction spiritual, material and supernatural. The singer class those who sang on Rādhā Kriṣṇa and Chaitanya made use of the beautiful letters with refrains of songs in the poetical sayings and performed before the audience. This served the double purpose and obtained piety and wealth. The singers obtained the hightest good by singing while the audiences were deeply absorbed by the devotional sensation. In to-day's Bengal this singer class has largely popularized the poetical sayings on Rādhā, Krişņa and Chaitanya. So, by reading the mss the learned men used to enjoy the poetical taste of the literature but the entire common mass educated themselves by listening to the songs sang by the singers. The continuity of this prime education still survives, and for this the sense of moral value in the society of Bengal exists unhurt.

At the end this may be concluded that those professional class of people applied their mind to rearrange the plot of stories as they thought it to be necessary for an appropriate sequence of a lyrical drama. It requires such a major insertion that it becomes very difficult to identify the reading of which of those text is original. They deserve appreciation for their useful services they render to satisfy the urdent spiritual need of the common people. In major disagreement with the so called intellectuals who hesitate to rely on their achievement, the general people whole-heartedly acknowledge their activities as very sacred. It seems that they have largely contributed to the unending flow of invaluable tradition of Ancient Indian Culture.

References

1. Punthi Parichaya, vol-4-1980, (Des. Cat. Of Bengali MSS. Vol-4,) Visva-Bharati Research Publication, Dr. Panchanan Mandal (Letter to the editor in quest of rare manuscripts — Santiniketan Feb. 2 Rabindranath Tagore, Behar Herald, 19.2.1923).
2. Punthi Parichaya, Vol.I / Dr. Panchanan Mandal, Visva-Bharati, 1358 B.S.Asardha, 1951 Jun-July P-I (Preface Prof. P.C. Bagchi, Principal, Vidya-Bhavana).
3. Punthi Parichaya, Vol.I Dr. Panchanan Mandal, Visva-Bharati, 1358 B.S. Asardha, 1951 Jun-July introduction P-3-29.
4. Punthi Parichaya, Vol.I Dr. Panchanan Mandal, Visva-Bharati, 1358 B.S. Asardha, 1951 Jun-July introduction P-3-29.
5. Punthi Parichaya, Vol.I Dr. Panchanan Mandal, Visva-Bharati, 1358 B.S. Asardha, 1951 Jun-July introduction P-3-29.
6. Sastra Mulaka Bharatia Sakti Sadhanā, Vol-II, Dr. Upendra Kr. Das, Visva-Bharati Research Publication, (1395 B.S., 1988) Page - 1042.
7. Chandi Mangal (Banik Khanda) – Mukundarama Chakraborty, Edited by Acharya Sukumar Sen.
8. Punthi Parichaya Vol-I, Dr. Panchanan Mandal, Visva-Bharati Research Publication 1951, introduction — 3-29.
9. Punthi Parichaya Vol-I, Dr. Panchanan Mandal, Visva-Bharati Research Publication 1951, introduction — 3-29.
10. Punthi Parichaya, Vol-4, Dr. Panchanan Mandal Visva-Bharati Research Publication, 1980 - MS - 540.

The Study of Manuscripts and Modern Critical Scholarship

21

JAGATPATI SARKAR

"One of our major misfortunes is that we have lost so much of world's ancient literature in Greece, in India and elsewhere... probably an organized search for old manuscripts in the literary of religious institutions, monasteries and private persons would yield rich results. That, and the critical examination of these manuscripts and, where considered desirable, their publication, and translation, are among the many things we have to do in India when we succeed in breaking through our shackles and can function for ourselves. Such a study is bound to throw light on many phases of Indian history and especially on the social background behind historic events and changing ideas."[1]

Manuscripts and holographs are invaluable sources for the creation and preservation of art, history, culture, tradition of any land. The term manuscript has its origin in two Latin words, namely 'manus' meaning hand and 'scribo' or scripture denoting the written character, script etc. Thus, the term literally denotes a book or rather a written document, prepared by hand either by author himself or copied by a competent scribe. There are many self-denotative terms in various Indian languages that represent manuscripts. They are: hastalekha, Pandulipi, matrka, pustaka, pustika, pusta, potha, pothi, pothaka, mulakosa, adarsa and so on. Terms like potha, pothi, pothaka etc. are derived from one of the following Sanskrit words, Pusta, pustika or pustaka. In Amarakosa pustaka is defined as pustam lepyadhikarman[2].

Traditions cannot be dissociated from the modern. The study of Manuscripts is extremely necessary to introduce a vast wealth of knowledge of human civilization. My knowledge on the subject is poor, to say the least. But I have the opportunity to say something in this regard. Stella Kramrisch was one of the first scholars who identifies the intrinsic relationship of the ritual texts specially the Śatapatha Brāhamana and the architectural plan of the temple. This was a finest contribution of a fundamental nature. I like to say that they were not subscribers to the theory of decline and decay propounded by their predecessor. They developed the new perceptions. Naturally fresh evidence called for fresh assessment and modification of some conclusions. Ancient wisdom can reflect the state of being (bhāva) and modern critical scholarship is always the state of Karma (action). This joint effort can evoke the spirit of any creation on innovation. Without anything nothing can be done. The master (guru) stands in relation to his pupils and pupillary succession (guru-parampara) grows accordingly. At the sametime the possibility of a direct access to the higher source of knowledge is realized. The invention (anuvritti) is to be found in the Rgveda. The Paippalada Samhita of the Atharva veda, Vol . II edited by Professor Dipak Bhattacharya has been published by the Asiatic Society. The Paippalada Samhita of the Atharva veda is next only to the Rgveda in importance and Antiquity in Indo European Literature. A mutilated and hopelessly corrupt sarada Manuscript of the text was known from the Seventies of the 19th century through the efforts of Rudolph Von Roth. But with its lacuna and undetermined readings edited by L.C. Barret, 1905 — 1940 it hardly generated any decisive philological research into the Atharva veda. The situation changed with the discovery of Late Durgamohan Bhattacharya. After his erudite scholarship and research many things came into light. The present edition is based on complete and much better manuscripts in Oriya Script. Durgamohan Bhattacharya edited the first four kandas from Sanskrit College in 1964 and 1970 respectively. But Sri Bhattacharya did not have the opportunity to complete the work.

The Sulvasutras deal with geometrical constructions, a large majority of them for the purpose of carrying out the vedic rituals. Baudhayana's Sulya sutra is believed to date to the 18th century B.C. Other authors are Apastamba, Manava, Katyayana, Satyasadha, Hiranyakesin, Vadhula, Varaha and Kathaka. The first five of the Sulya sutras is found available in text form while the manuscripts of the others are known to exist. In more recent times there have been commentaries written by Thibault and Val Geldner in the 2nd half of the 19th century A.D. This was followed by Professor Samarendranath Sen and the last by A.K. Bag in 1983[3].

The standard of moral and social justice in our two Epics, Puranas, smriti literature, Buddhist Jatakas have added a special significance to our cultural heritage. Ancient wisdom is there but with the help of our modern critical knowledge this has been evolved a new look. A synthetic approach was very much needed. Both the old and the new, the past and present have got harmoniously blended, people always feel the new of the hour and their persistent zeal and enquery open a new chapter in the history. Iswar Chandra Vidyasagar loved his country with her rich and glorious traditions. His legs were firmly rooted in the soul of the country. His hatred against those who tried to break away from the tradition of the Country was no less genuine. He himself studied the ancient texts with deep interest and felt an impelling necessity to reform the system of education and Society. Vidyasagar was above all, a man of the world and was not a dreamer or an idle visionary; he was rather out and out a realist. Number of Smriti texts have been critically examined line by line by him and presented in a new vision. The possession of good MSS of important texts offered social prestige and those were displayed on important occassion. The Asiatic Society received a picture from Lord Bentinck as presentation. This picture contains the Durbar of the King of Kota in Rajasthan held in honour of the Government General. Beautiful and well preserved manuscripts occupy the central position in the picture. MSS were considered the poor scholars riches. Men of culture decorated their houses with Mss and a glimpse of the same is found in the Mrcchakatikam of Sudraka (Act. III) where MSS were visible in the houses of Carudatta and Vasantasena.[4]

Sri Madhusudana Gupta, being a traditionally nurtured Sanskrit scholar and being a broad minded person enlightened with western ideas, had translated earlier the Ayurvedic medical text of Susruta Samhita into English. The 1st volume of Sri Gupta was published in 1835 and 2nd volume was published in 1836. Another ayurvedic medical text, 'Asvavaidyakah' on horse treatment was duly edited and published by Umesh Chandra Gupta Kaviratna in 1836. The English translation of Susruta Samhita was printed by the well known English Scholar A.F.R. Hornele in 1887.

The contribution of classification of Animal in Ancient India authorized by Vincent Ghildal Sharma and Ramesh Ch. Sharma (Published in the Journal of the Asiatic Society Vol. XXXI, Nos. 3-4, in 1989, pp. 45-55) embodies the account of knowledge of ancient texts concerning classification of animals. Four major works on classification of Panini's classification, Manu's classification, Umasvati's classification and Carak and Susruta's classification have been taken into account for discussion. These works were based on the study of the manuscripts on the subjects. But incorporated modern critical knowledge opened a new avenue no doubt.

Rasarnavam another text on Alchemy on treatment with various preparations of mercury was edited by Sir Prafulla Chandra Roy and Harish Chandra Kaviratna. This text was published in the Bibliotheca Indica Series of the Asiatic Society from 1908 to 1910 A.D.

Rasarnava and Rasa Kalpa are associated with Rudrayamala. The Suvarnatantra and Svarnatantra describe the synthetic preparation of valuable metals like silver and gold. The above two MSS have been taken into consideration for critical editing. The text of Vastusastras, Silpasastras, Citrasastras and many technical sciences are still in the store house of ancient wisdom. But the value of the work is enhanced when it is done with modern critical outlook and systematic study. The credit goes to open an altogether new vista of vision in explaining the depth of the subject. Matsya Purana: A Study (Varanasi; All India Kasiraj Trust, 1963, pp. 333-335 of V.S. Agrawala) contains the allegorical significance of the famous relief of Nalanda Site No.-2. The Agni Purana is a very pertinent text of Art and Archaeology. India owes its cultural heritage to various ancient sources and to understand the Indian character. This is necessary to shake off all sorts of Euro centrist ideas. This process had started from last half of Eighteenth century with the development of scientific approaches to understand the philosophy of change. Today it is a strong and general trend in the West as well as in the East to shake off logocentric understanding. Large number of scholars has already begun to take steps in this direction.

The organizing for survey manuscripts is not mere matter of safeguarding one class of Indian antiquities. The systematic survey of manuscripts will throw up several outstanding Sanskrit classics of early creative periods of Sanskrit literature in all branches of knowledge. They have gone into oblivion and whose discovery would re-orient and enrich our knowledge of the different systems of ancient Indian thought, branches of literature and criticism, and arts and sciences. One need mention only the example of how the discovery of the manuscript of Kautilya's Authasastra revolutioned the ideas about ancient Indian culture or of the fragments of Asvaghosa's dramas in central Asia put back the antiquity of Sanskrit Drama. The slow recovery of the Sanskrit Philosophical works from the Chinese and Tibetan renderings enable us today to understand better the earlier phases of Indian systems of thought like Samkhya, Vedanta and Nyaya. The days of discoveries in Sanskrit Manuscripts and Texts are not yet over.

The legal thought of Kautilya on a whole range of themes, has been distilled with a touch a many contemporarity. Thus we hear, perhaps for the first time, concerning Kautilyan thought on labour law, constitutional and administrative law, the law of commercial transactions, family law, international law, civil law and many others. Accordingly the text of the mss. has been restructured which permit and indeed enable the reader to develop her own understandings of its relevance. Then for a close study of Kautilyan thought with modern critical knowledge on law, power and justice in view to continuities in statecraft in Indian history till the present day is noteworthy. The contemporary reconstruction and critical aspects of Kautilyas justic thought and in the process interrogate those views. Those views have proved tenacious in our own times from the time of ancient period. Kautilya was imbued with a high social conscience.[5]

The Manuscripts form as precious part of our cultural heritage as stone monuments or other artistic antiquities or historical documents for understanding the history and culture of the country. The literary treasures enshrined in the manuscripts cannot be ignored. Today nothing is more common than to think that he who possesses books is a learned man, but for a longtime after the development of the power of speech and expression, man communicated and preserved knowledge only personally, voice and ear acted as the prevailing media, this was all the more so in India when knowledge was called in Sanskrit 'Sruta' that which has been heard or listened to.

The Subhankari by Dr. Santanu Chakraborty published by the Asiatic Society gives a comprehensive account of an indigenous tradition of elementary mathematical instruction in thirteen chapters. This is indubitably an original and interesting work which reveals the historical fact that the common people of our great country had an admirable arithmetical knowledge. The Subhankari method of computation was imported to young students in the so-called pathsalas by teachers who were known as gurumahasayas. At least seven MSS have been consulted in this work in which the traditional verses were written for remembrance. The arithmetical verses of Subhankari deal with carpentry, agriculture, currency, commerce and other subjects. The work sheds light on pre-modern productive methods and their marketing.[6]

Contemporary significance of the theory of ancient wisdom states the relations of modern conception. This develops the critical outlook and survives the balance of relevance. Man's circumstances and his living and the term goes back to the beginning of any record of doing of the far-off times are carefully reconstructed human existence.

Therefore the idea of studying MSS is a result of (a) inquisitive mind of the heritage and (b) an attempt at understanding the foundations of the culture and civilization. When the French scholars were studying Chinese, they thought that Buddhism ia a Chinese religion. They referred to it as Fo-ism. The word Fo stands for Buddhism in Chinese. But when H.A. Giles translated the travels of Fa-hien to India and for the first time it was realized that Buddhism went from India to China. So India became even more important in order to understand the Chinese socio-political context. Whenever Europeans wanted to understand the Chinese history or Chinese people, they had to go back to the Sanskrit original texts. They had to at least understand what the ideas were in Sanskrit. Sanskrit was clear than Chinese, since Chinese is an un-conjugated language and therefore more difficult.

Dr. Benoytosh Bhattacharyya was appointed as the first Director and the General Editor of the Gaekwad's Oriental Series, Baroda. The publication of the Kavyamimansa paved the way for the perennial publication activity of GOS. So far 187 works have seen the light of the day. This list can be multiplied. This may be a revaluation to many that a large number of GOS works are out of print and are still in great demand from the scholarly world. This has universally been accepted that manuscripts constitute one of the most important basic source materials for knowledge. We often hear that the early part of the twenty first century constitute a new era of knowledge. This is also argued that all sections of the society should equip themselves adequately to become partners in the Global knowledge society. But this is not the first when mankind has had the opportunity of stepping into the realm of a knowledge society. The Bhagvadgita pronounces 'na hi jnanena sadrisam pavitramiha hi vidyate' (There is nothing as sacred as knowledge in this world). Another verse says 'Sarvam Karmakhilam Partha Jnane na Parisamapyate.' (Oh, Partha, all activities have acquisition of knowledge as their ultimate goal). Now this is very important to recognize that the scope and content of the notion of knowledge have also undergone significant changes from time to time. Our assessment of human capabilities will not be complete if we do not consider the knowledge revolutions occurred in the past. There was knowledge revolution when Panini introduced a fundamental theory and practice in the fields of linguistics, phonetics and grammar in 7th century B.C. A century later there was another moment when Kanada made pioneering contributions in the field of physical sciences. Similarly there were knowledge revolutions when Aryabhata of the 5th century A.D., Varaharmihara of 6th century A.D., and Bhaskaracharya of 13th century A.D. made their valuable contributions to the field of mathematics and Astronomy. The pride in our knowledge heritage is an essential pre-requisite for capacity building required to face the challenges of the new knowledge societies that are evolving at present.[7] The recent IT revolution should be considered in the perspective of Navya Nyaya system of Philosophy of India. This is only in the Indian knowledge that such a perfectly integrated approach to the process of acquiring knowledge is recognized. Here dimensions of the knowledge system are (i) the physical aspect (ii) the spiritual aspect and (iii) the attributes of the knower. The study of MSS. meant to look at the culture through broad window.

Finally, I can conclude with the verse of the Ramayana. 'The Ramayana says that Religious persons are called parama dharma as practicing truth. Dharma is not religion here; I can easily amend this verse. Here dharma is the ancient wisdom and those who practice dharma, they are the modern critical scholarship, because they are practicing truth only. Thus says-

ahu satyam hi paramam dharma dharmavido janah /
satyamasritya ci maya tvam dharmam praticoditah //

samsruta saivyah sonaya svam tanum jagatipatih /
Pradaya pakshine raja jagama gatimuttamam //

And we the persons will be productive with the assimilation of both.

References

1. Nehru, Jawaharlal, The *Discovery of India*.
2. Kriti Rakshana, vol. 1, no. 1, Aug.-2005.
3. Kriti Rakshana, vol. 2, no. 6, June-2007

4. Basu, Ratna and Das, Karunasindhu, Aspects of Manuscriptology, The Asiatic Society, Kolkata, 2005.

5. Gupta, V.K., Kautilya Arthasastra, Bharatiya Kala Prakashan, Delhi, 2004.

6. Monthly Bulletin, Vol. XXXVI, No. 5 May 2007, The Asiatic Society, Kolkata.

7. Kriti Rakshana, Vol. I, No: 4, February, 2006.

Anatomy of Manuscripts

22

NABA GOPAL ROY

Manuscripts are the existing example of the humanistic and imaginative activities of the earlier period of human-civilization. Manuscripts are unique and fragile things, which are still far from being protected as art of the national heritage, despite that they are the focus of widespread interest. Although their importance may be acknowledged, the resources allocated to safeguard them are in many cases slender. And yet collections of manuscripts are surely just as much a part of any national heritage as the monuments which states pay large sums of money to preserve, as the works of art amassed by museums, and the areas of outstanding natural beauty which are protected by their status as national parks. "A manuscript speaks of the past, reveals history, unfolds perspectives and reflects the socio-cultural, even socio-political scenes of its time. Its contents are significant literarily, scientifically, historically; its form fascinating palaeographically, calligraphically, and technically."[1]

The literary, scientific, social or political history of a people can only be written objectively if it is based on the original sources, and those sources are manuscripts or archival documents. Indeed, one meaning of the word "source" is precisely that of "original document". Manuscripts are the lifeblood of history. In them it is possible to trace the development of writers and their work, the lives of statesmen, the manifold activities of peoples. Their value is impossible to calculate, and even if it is perceived as relatively slight in the world context, within each culture and each country it is absolute. But on a large scale ancient literature has been preserved on palm leaves (the short and stiff variety which is more common and the broader are more flexible called *Sritala*) and on birch-bark in the south and some other parts of India.

The principal materials employed in the making of manuscripts have been papyrus, parchment, and paper. In exceptional cases other materials have been used (e.g. the linen books of Etruria and Rome, a specimen of which was found on an Egyptian mummy in the museum of Agram; the silken books of China, etc.). Besides, in ancient time and during the Middle Ages tablets dipped in wax on which characters were traced with a stylus were made us of for fugitive writings, accounts, etc.; these might be folding in two (diptychs), or in three (triptychs), etc. Papyrus (*charta aegyptica*) was obtained from a long-stemmed plant terminating in a large and elegant umbrella; this was the Cyperus Papyrus, which grew in the marshes of Egypt and Abyssinia. The stem was cut in long strips which were placed one beside the other. On the vertical strips others were placed horizontally; then after they had been wet with the water of the Nile they were submitted to strong pressure, dried in the sun, and rubbed with shells to render them solid. To make a book the separate pages (*selides*, *paginae*) were first written on, then they were put end to end, the left margin of each page being made to adhere to the right margin of the preceding page. A roll (*volumen*) was thus secured, of which the dimensions were sometimes considerable. Some Egyptian rolls are forty-six feet long by nine or ten inches wide, and the great Harris papyrus (British Museum) is one hundred and forty-one feet long. The end of the last page was fastened to a cylinder of wood or bone (*omphalos*, *umbilicus*), which gave more consistency to the roll. The page having been ruled, the writing was done with a sharpened reed on the horizontal portion of the fibres. From being almost exclusively used in Egypt, the use of papyrus spread to Greece about the fifth century, then to Rome and throughout the West. Its price remained very high; in 407 B.C. a roll of twenty leaves was worth twenty-six drachmas, or about five dollars (Corp. Insc. Attic. I, 324). Pliny the Elder (Hist. Nat., XIII, 11-13) gives a list of its various grades (*charta Augusta, Liviana*, etc.). Egypt retained the monopoly of the manufacture, which furthermore belonged to the State. Alexandria was the principal market. In the first centuries of the middle Ages it was exported to the West by the "Syrians", but the conquest of Egypt by the Arabs (640) stopped the trade. However it still continued to be used for diplomas (at Ravenna until the tenth century; in the papal chancery until 1057). The Arabs had attempted to cultivate the plant in Sicily.

Parchment (*charta pergamena*), made of the skin of sheep, goats, calves (*vellum*), asses, etc., was used by the Ionians and the Asiatics as early as the sixth century B.C. (Herodotus, V, 58); the anecdote related by Pliny (Hist. Nat., XIII, 11), according to which it was invented at Pergamus, seems legendary; it would seem that its manufacture was simply perfected there. Imported to Rome in ancient times, parchment supplanted papyrus but slowly. It was only at the end of the third century A.D. that it was preferred to papyrus for the making of books. Once prepared, the parchment (*membrana*) was cut into leaves which were folded in two; four leaves together formed a book of eight folios (*quaternio*); all the books formed a *codex*. There was no paging before the fifteenth century; writers merely numbered first the books (signature), then the folios. The dimensions of the leaves varied; the most in use for literary texts was the large quarto. An Urbino catalogue (fifteenth century) mentions a manuscript so large that it required three men to carry it (Reusens, "Paléographie", 457); and there is preserved at Stockholm a gigantic Bible written on ass-skin, the dimensions of which have won for it the name of "Gigas librorum". The page was ruled in dry point so deeply that the mark was visible on the other side. Parchments were written on both sides (opistographs). As parchment became very rare and costly during the Middle Ages, it became the custom in some monasteries to scratch or wash out the old text in order to replace it with new writing. These erased manuscripts are called palimpsests. With the aid of reacting chemicals the old writing has been made to reappear and lost texts have been thus discovered (the Codex Vaticanus 5757 contains under a text of St. Augustine the "De Republica" of Cicero; recovered by Cardinal Mai). Manuscripts thus treated have been nearly always incomplete or mutilated; a complete work has never been recovered on a palimpsest. Finally, by sewing strips of parchment together, rolls (*rotuli*) were made similar to those formed of papyrus (e.g. Hebrew Pentateuch of Brussels, ninth century, on fifty-seven sewn skins, forty yards in length; "rolls of the dead", used by the associations of prayer for the dead in the abbeys; administrative and financial rolls used especially in England to transcribe the decrees of Parliament, etc.)

Paper is said to have been invented in China in A.D. 105 by a certain Tsai-Louen (Chavannes, "Journ. Asiatique", 1905, 1). Specimens of paper of the fourth century A.D. have been found in Eastern Turkestan (expeditions of Stein and Sven Hedin). It was after the taking of Samarkand that the Arabs learned to make paper, and introduced it to Bagdad, and to Damascus (*charta damascena*). It was known in Europe as early as the end of the eleventh century, and at this early date it was used in the Norman chancery of Sicily; in the twelfth century it began to be used for manuscripts. It was sold even then in quires and reams (Arabic, *razmah*) and in the thirteenth century appeared the filigranes or watermarks. According to chemical analyses, the paper of the middle Ages was made of hempen or linen rags. The expression "charta Bombycina" comes from the Arab manufactory of Bombyce, between Antioch and Aleppo. The copyist of the middle Ages used chiefly black ink, *incaustum*, composed of a mixture of gall nuts and vitrol. Red ink was reserved from ancients times for titles. Gold and silver inks were used for manuscripts de luxe (see Evangeliaria). The method of binding codices has varied little since ancient times. The books were sewn on ox sinews placed in rows of five or six on the back. These sinews (*chordae*) served to attach to the volume wooden covers, which were covered with parchment or dyed skin. Covers of the manuscripts de luxe were made of ivory or brass, ornamented with carvings, precious stones, and cut and uncut.[2]

Manuscript culture refers to the development and use of the manuscript as a means of storing and disseminating information until the age of printing. The Early Age of manuscript culture consisted of monks copying mostly religious text in monasteries. Medieval manuscript culture deals with the transition of the manuscript from the monasteries to the market in the cities, and the rise of universities. Manuscript culture in the cities created new jobs built around the making, copying and trade of manuscripts, and typically was regulated by universities. The Late Age of manuscript culture existed immediately before and during the rise of the printing press. Late manuscript culture was characterized by a desire for uniformity, well ordered and convenient access to the text contained in the manuscript, and ease of reading the text aloud. The material used to be specially processed leather, leaves or barks from trees; during the latter times i.e. the medieval period, paper made from cotton-pulps, hemp, and linseed showed up. This facilitated the making of large sheets, which were then cut to the required size and tied together with strings to give it the appearance of a book, with two firm boards sufficing for covers. A manuscript is any document that is written by hand, as opposed to being printed or reproduced in some other way. The term may also be used for information that is hand-recorded in other ways than writing, for example inscriptions that are chiseled upon a hard material or scratched (the original meaning of graffiti) as with a knife point in plaster or with a stylus on a waxed tablet, (the way Romans made notes), or are in cuneiform writing, impressed with a pointed stylus in a flat tablet of unbaked clay.

India's manuscripts spread all over the country and abroad, are composed in different Indian languages such as Sanskrit, Pali, Prakrit, Urdu, Persian and the different regional Indian languages. They are written in different scripts such as Brahmi, Sarada, Modi, Newari, Grantha, Kutila, and Bengali among others. Given India's immense linguistic diversity and sophistication, many documents are inaccessible because there is little knowledge of the languages and scripts used. One of the major challenges is that there are a dwindling number of scholars who can read, decipher, read, translate, take up research and interpret India's manuscripts. Being treasures of immense value, nowadays, many of the educational institutions are preserving the original ones and making microfilms out of them; though the act shall preserve these great works of art for many more days to come, nothing can be done now regarding bringing back the scribes, who have now become extinct due to the industrial advancements.

Manuscripts are of various sizes, the smallest one having a dimension of 6 inches x 3 inches and the biggest one measuring 3 and half feet in length and 1 feet or 18 inches in breath. The most significant thing to note that is the outer covers of these MSS. were in general made of wood belonging to different parts of India. The covers were made of Kashmir birch trees. Northern Indian teak, sal, palm trees and of other endurable wood. These covers chiseled smoothly and painted with oil or grasy substance.[3] The traditional abbreviations are MS for manuscript and MSS for manuscripts. The second S is not simply the plural; by an old convention, it doubles the last letter of the abbreviation to express the plural, just as pp. means "pages".[4] And the contents of the manuscripts are proposed by *Folio* not by the pages. The faced position is called *Recto* and the backside of the folio is called by *Verso.*[5]

In Bengali the handwritten scripts are called *pandulipi*; the material on which they were inscribed was either grey or pale yellow in color. This is one of the reasons behind the name pandulipi, since *pandu* stands for yellow in Bangla and *lipi*, for writing. Ancient periods depended more on the manual works rather than upon machinery and it reflected on the ancient literatures as well; prints, being more recent a phenomenon, like many other ancient texts, Bengali books also used to be handwritten. Sharp contrasts to the run-of-the-mill trend, these copies were made on demand and required special skills. The Punthis so far discovered in Bengal have Sanskrit or Bangla as the language; those written in Bangla used the old Bangla Script. Inscribed by the professional scribes of yore, they also used to add their personal details at the end of the pnuthi as a kind of an acknowledgement or disclaimer, from which, it was discovered that a lot of Muslims also earn their livelihood through the profession.

A good handwriting was the primary criteria and so was accuracy, but without a good knowledge on the language, the first two qualities were considered to be vain. However, a shortcoming on the latter part proved beneficial in terms of interpolations and textual variants. But a lot of people hold counter-opinions regarding the limited knowledge of the language of certain scribes for denoting the date of the creation in verse riddles instead of numerical figures required a lot of talent and depth.

A puthi has a certain anatomy; while the chief portion comprised the main body text, the part where the scribe used to flaunt his own wordsmith comprise of the following parts:

Bhonita or pre-amble: Describes the name of the book and the writer; a variant of *Pushpika*.

Pushpika or colophon: Generally found on the first leaf, at the end of the chapter or act, and on the last folio, the Pushpika is a short, composite work made of a brief autobiography of the writer, the name of the puthi, the date of writing/copying and the name of the person who is the provider of the task. When it is on the first folio or at the end of a chapter or an act, the Pushpika contains the names of the scribe and the book whereas in last folio, the former content is placed along with the dates of writing or copying.[6]

Manuscripts are not defined by their contents, which may combine writing with mathematical calculations, maps, explanatory figures or illustrations. Manuscripts may be in the form of scrolls or in book form, or codex format. Illuminated manuscripts are enriched with pictures, border decorations, elaborately engrossed initial letters or full-page illustrations.

In the west Manuscript books began to supplant papyrus scrolls in Antiquity. Rare surviving books of the Fourth Century are surprisingly similar in general appearance to works written a millennium later. Until the late middle Ages, the great majority of western books were written in monasteries by scribes, who enjoyed the highest social status in their communities. As civilization progressed and the demand for books became greater, later works were executed by pupils of the Renaissance "writing master", who taught the craft to apprentices. Some early students' copybooks survive as witnesses to the difficulties of mastering this exacting skill. These early books were mostly written on vellum.[7] Pens used by the copyists were generally natural quills, plucked from geese, crows, or turkeys, or later, iron pens.[8]

Being treasures of immense value, nowadays, many of the educational institutions are preserving the original ones and making microfilms out of them; though the act shall preserve these great works of art for many more days to come, nothing can be done now regarding bringing back the scribes, who have now become extinct due to the industrial advancements.

Conservation has two aspects, preservation and restoration; both of them are complementary to each other. Preservation is wider perspective and includes such activities as storage, handling, disinfecting etc. In a nutshell preservation is any action taken to prevent or retard deterioration.[9] Like most old things, the ancient books and leaves that have survived the attrition of the centuries have done so because they were purposely cared for. Thus they tend to be found in surprisingly fine condition. Old paper is made of a durable mixture of natural plant fibers that were not exposed to harsh Industrial Age chemical finishes. Thus they are not found embrittled or badly discolored. Ancient vellum is also extremely durable and survives in fine condition, though all old skins exhibit natural variations in tone and color.

Briefly, the enemies of all old documents are heat, humidity, and sunlight. To maintain their fine condition, they should be kept in a stable storage environment free of excess fluctuation in temperature and humidity. There should be limited contact with circulating air and strong light. To accomplish these goals, select a dry, cool place in your home to store your collection. Any room suitable for habitation will generally be satisfactory for the preservation of this material. Never leave it in the basement or attic, where change of temperature and humidity occur regularly and can cause deterioration.[10]

If you frame your collection, include an ultraviolet filtering screen between them and bright light. Secondly, select only archival quality acid free containers for permanent storage. These can be fairly costly if purchased already made up, but with a little ingenuity, some Mylar, and double-sided adhesive tape, you can make your own custom holders at a considerable savings. Documents may be treated with acid-neutralizing chemical agents, though it is suggested that amateurs do not attempt this process as the solvents can be harmful and the results erratic. To quote a popular Sanskrit verse —'A manuscripts deserves decoration as a dear child, protection as a good wife from rogue's hand, healing treatment as a sore limb, daily care as a good friend, not so loose tightening by strong cords as a condemned prisoner and remembrance as the name of Lord Hari. If it be so, a manuscript never decays....These are the words of the teacher.'[11]

References

1. Basu, Ratna and Das, Kanunasindhu. 'Introduction', *Aspects of Manuscriptology,* The Asiatic Society, Kolkata, 2005.
2. Louis Bréhier. Transcribed by Bryan R. Johnson. The Catholic Encyclopedia, Volume IX. New York, 1910.
3. Kanjilal, Dileepkumar. Manuscriptology, *Aspects of Manuscriptology,* edited by Ratna Basu and Kanunasindhu Das, The Asiatic society, Kolkata, 2005.
4. Harper, Douglas. "Manuscript", Online Etymology Dictionary. Nov. 2001.
5. Sarkar, Jagatpati and Roy, Naba Gopal. *Jogadya Bandana*, Sanskrit Pustak Bhandar, Kolkata, 2008.
6. Ray, Ostom. Article Source: www.articleresourceindex.com
7. Vellum and Paper: a fine grade of goat, calf, or sheep skin. Fortunately for collectors, it is an extremely durable substance which generally survives the centuries well. It was an expensive material, however, and the production of a complete Bible, for example, might require years of a scribe's time, and the skins of several hundred animals, thus making books a rare and expensive commodity. The Medieval practice of autumn livestock butchering, to conserve fodder for the winter, is thought to have been the primary source of skins used in the production of books. How the skins were prepared has been recorded in a monastic account of the Twelfth century; they were alternately soaked in clear water, immersed in a strong lime solution, then scraped of hairs, and sun-dried. The process was repeated over the course of several weeks until the vellum became sufficiently clean and flexible for use. As natural animal products, old vellum leaves and documents exhibit wide variations in texture, thickness, and tone, and almost all books exhibit a few small natural flaws in the leaves, around which the copyist skillfully worked his text. One side of vellum is always darker than the other, as the "inside" side of the skin was harder to clean of flesh than the outer or "skin" side.
8. Inks exist in two major kinds. One is black encaustic, an acidic iron gall mixture that etches into the vellum and thus fixes itself ineradicably. The other and more often employed ink is a mixture of common lampblack, a fixing agent and a medium such as oil or water. It is

brown in color and, although it has a slight tendency to flake off the vellum under humid condition, MSS written in this common ink are still fully legible today. Colored inks were most often supplied in red and blue, though oils in all colors were available and used in the most sumptuous presentation volumes for royalty and the clergy. Gold accents were sometimes added to the MSS, in two forms, one of gold leaf, which still retains its flashing brilliance in extant manuscripts, and the other as gold ink, which adds a lovely highlight to the initial letter decorations.

9. 'Conservation of Books & Manuscripts (Paper) in Libraries', Das.S.K. *Aspects of Manuscriptology,* edited by Ratna Basu and Kanunasindhu Das, The Asiatic Society, Kolkata, 2005.

10. Biswas, Achintya. *Bangla Puthir katha,* Ratnabaly, Kolkata, 2003.

11. "*Sanbhusyam sadaptyavat*
parakarad rakshyam ca suksetravat...
Khalu kadapy etad gudunam vacah//"

History of the Catalogues of Sanskrit Manuscripts

23

MITALI CHATTERJEE

Manuscript is derived from the Latin 'Manuscriptum' means hand-written. It corresponds to Sanskrit 'Hastalikhita' meaning the same two component words. India has more manuscript collection than any other country in the world and there is no other world civilization which has such a proliferation of hand written literature as the Indian. As for example, one full volume of 505 pages of the new Catalogus Catalogorum: an alphabetical register of Sanskrit and other works and authors (published from Chennai : University of Madras, 1969) comprises of list of manuscripts of Sanskrit texts and authors whose names commence with the alphabet 'a' only. From this the vastness of collection of manuscript can be assumed. The religious writing of Hinduism, Buddhism and Jainism, philosophical writing, rich collection of literature form the bulk of the texts. Recording them in writing was the only means to preserve and propagate them. From the urge to preserve them for the posterity, preparation of manuscript, side by side the oral tradition, in huge scale was started in India from early times. These manuscripts are widely distributed in the form of copies and copies of copies. These manuscripts are written in various languages and in different scripts such as *Devanagari*, *Sharada*, *Grantha*, *Kannada*, *Telegu*, etc. These are recorded on a variety of materials : birch-bark, palm leaf, paper, leather, copper plate, textile, stone, clay tablet, wooden board and what not. They deal with the socio-cultural history, language and literature, science and technology, art and crafts of India. These manuscripts show the development of human knowledge in India over the past few centuries.

Sir William Jones (1746-94) the great orientalist and founder of the Asiatic Society declared in 1786, "The Sanskrit language whatever be its antiquity, is of a wonderful structure, more perfect than either; Many European Scholars turned to the study of Sanskrit which had affinity with European and Iranian languages. It opened the vista of the theory of Indo-European language group and new science of comparative languages i.e. linguistics. A. A. Macdenell, Professor of Oxford, wrote in his History of Sanskrit Literature, "Since the Renaissance there has been no event of such world wide significance in the history of culture as the discovery of Sanskrit literature in the later part of the 18th century."

Professor Gold Stucker in his 'Introduction to Panini' has proved from both internal and external evidences that letters were known to Panini, who according to him flourished about 800 B.C. Thus existence of letter is in his opinion pre-Paninian. *Siksa* is one of the *Vedangas*. This deals with vowels and consonants, accents and euphonic combinations etc. This clearly shows that the origin of script goes as far as 1400 B.C., which is supposed to be the lowest limit of the *Brahmana* period by many modern scholars.

Manuscripts repositories are found in many libraries of the world, mostly in India. Institutions and universities have holdings of Indian manuscripts, mostly Sanskrit. Moreover manuscripts are stored in monasteries, mosques, temples, etc. There are hundreds and thousands of them scattered in private collections. A large part of manuscript collection are not yet catalogued, even not yet recorded.

There are 3.5 million manuscripts in various collection in India. About 60,000 manuscripts are preserved in 20 different countries of Europe and USA including Canada. Asian countries which are outside India also have nearly 150,000 manuscripts in Indian scripts and languages. Nepal, Pakistan, Bangladesh, Sri Lanka, China, Tibet, Japan, Mynamar (Burma) have these manuscripts. Of these manuscripts 67% are in Sanskrit, 25% are in modern Indian languages and the rest in Arabic, Persian, Tibetan and other languages.

It may be mentioned that only a small percentage of these manuscripts collection have been properly catalogued. In a majority of cases only hand lists were prepared, giving some basic data., i.e. author, title, language, scripts, etc.

Catalogues are lists of a class of materials arranged in some convenient manner in order to enable any required item to be located and picked out easily to use.

We are trying to trace a history of catalogue of manuscript and describe the peculiarities and basic features of these catalogues.

It is not easy to suggest a date of the compilation of the first catalogue of Indian manuscripts. The first list of manuscripts is probably '*Brhat tippanika*' dated 1383 A.D. It provides short descriptions of approximately 600 Jain manuscripts.

Kavindacarya (17th Century A.D). a versatile scholar of Varanasi, had a rich collection of 2192 titles in his manuscript collection. His Library existed in Benares during his lifetime in the 17th Century A.D. Kavindracarya — sucipatram was edited with introduction by R. Ananta Krishna Sastri, with a foreword by Ganganatha Jha. It was published from Baroda by Central Library, 1921.

There is a *sucipatram* in the Asiatic Society, Calcutta, dated 1838. Three classified alphabetical lists in tabular form with short descriptions of about 3000 manuscripts including some printed books in Sanskrit, Bengali, Karnatabhasa, Maharashtrabhasa, etc. in the (1) College of Fort William (2) Library and College of the Asiatic Society of Bengal (3) Benares Sanskrit College. There is no index.

Sucipustakam, Phorta-Uliyam [i.e. Fort William ityakhyaya atratya—Imlandiya—pathasalayah preritapustakasahitanam Gauda-desiya Asyatikakhya—sabha sambandhi-pustakagrhasthapustakanan etad yatiriktanan catratva Sanskrtavidyamandirasya—Kasistha—Samiskrtavidyamandirasya ca pustakanam suci; tatsabhadhyaksa sriyukta—Jemsa—Prinsep [i.e. James Prinsep]—sahevanujnaya sadharanajanopakarartham Kalikata [i.e. Calcutta] akhya rajadhanyam tanmudranayantralaye mudrita, etatsabhasambandhi panditena Sri-Ramagovinda Ta[r]karatnena samgrhita samsodhita ca, sakabda 1759, [i.e.] khr 1838 Calcutta : Asiatic Society of Bengal, 1838.

Rajakiya-Varanasi-vidya-mandira-Sarasvatibhavana-vartti-pustakanam Sucipatram is a classified list in tabular form with short descriptive notices of about 3000 manuscripts. It is a list of manuscripts in the collection of Sanskrit College, Benares published during 1869-1975. It was published as a 'Supplement' at the end of the monthly issues of the journal '*Pandit*'. There was no index attached with this list.

There are several different types of catalogue format:

1. Manuscript search report: It provides general account of the availability of manuscripts in a particular area with list of titles acquired. Notice of Sanskrit manuscripts in ten volumes written by Hara Prasad Sastri and published in 1871-95, 1900-1911 is a search report.
2. Simple list: It contains author and title, sometimes only the title is listed.
   a. Ahmedabad Gujarat Vidyapith

      A hand list of 409 manuscripts in Gujarat Vidyapith, Ahmedabad. Unpublished.
   b. Aligarh. Aligarh Muslim University. Maulana Azad Library

      Handlist of 206 Sanskrit manuscripts in Sanskrit and Hindi departments of Aligarh Muslim University. Unpublished.
   c. Allahabad. Jha, Ganganath

      A handlist of the manuscripts of Ganganath Jha, Allahabad in two section.

d. Allahabad. Municipal Museum

A list of Sanskrit manuscripts in the Municipal Museum. Unpublished.

e. Amritsar. Piara Mall

A hand list of 18 birch-bark manuscripts with Piara Mall, M. D. Dhob Khaitan. Amritsar. Unpublished.

3. Alphabetical catalogue by author or title: It contains author title, commentator, script, date, extent etc. sometimes only the short title and corresponding accession number.

a. Allahabad. Uttar Pradesh State Archive

An alphabetical index of Sanskrit manuscript in the State Archives of Uttar Pradesh / edited by G. N. Saletore, compiled by S. N. Pandey. Allahabad, 1970.

4. Catalogue in tabular form: It is arranged in classified order, information are tabulated under separate column /heads.

a. Ahmedabad Gujarati Vidyapith

Hastapratisuci / ed. by Kanubhai Shah and Kirtibhai

Description in tabular form comprising 535 Sanskrit, Prakrit, Apabhramsa and Gujarati, Hindi and Marathi manuscripts, 1988.

5. Descriptive catalogue in tabular form: This type of catalogue is published in India since 1961. The Government of India Committee has devised a proforma for the descriptive catalogue of manuscripts in all Indian languages. Since the Government made the use of this proforma a condition for the grant of the expenses for the compilation and publication of manuscript catalogues, a good number of institution are using the model for compiling the catalogues of their institutions. In fact, this form of the catalogue is more easy to refer to than the old type catalogues where the information is spread out.

Column 1 - The Main and Sub headings are to be printed inside this column. The Main heading is printed at the left and right top corners of the pages, it would facilitate easy identification of the required subject.

Column 2 - This records the Accession no. of the Institution to find the manuscript easily.

Column 3 - The term 'Work' means the 'text' when there is only the text is written in the manuscript. The 'commentary' when there is only the commentary and when the 'text and commentary that means both the text and the commentary exist in it. If the commentary is titled the name of the commentary must be mentioned.

Column 4,5 - The name of the author and commentator are recorded here. If there is any alternate names of the author and identification it must be also recorded.

Column 6,8 - The Material or Substance, Script, Size, Number of folios or leaves, lines per page and number of letters per line are recorded here.

Column 9 - The extent of the work is written here for specifying actual length of the work.

Column 10 - Condition and Age of the work. If the manuscript is dated the date must be recorded here.

Column 11 - Note section, additional particulars. The specialities relating to the 'text' like the 'source' any detail about the author, etc. should be recorded first, and then the specialities of the manuscript, like illustrations, name of the scribe, owner or patron, its uniqueness, the availability of manuscripts of the work in other libraries and details of at least one edition of the work if it is available in print, should be noted.

The Note of Government of India instructs the addition of an appendix to each volume of the manuscript catalogues and states that this "Appendix on rare manuscripts which have been indicated by letter "E" under column I should include extracts of the beginnings end and colophons, as also any other extract of exceptional significance from the manuscripts, and lists of authors, works etc., cited". The above is very valuable suggestion.

a. Ahmedabad. Gujarat Vidya Sabha

A descriptive catalogue of Sanskrit manuscripts : Gujarat Vidya Sabha Collection / compiled and edited by Priyabala Shah. Ahmedabad, 1964-1987. 3 vols.

Description in tabular form of 5866 Sanskrit manuscripts with extracts.

b. Ahmedabad. L. D. Institute of Indology

Catalogue of Sanskrit and Prakrit manuscripts / compiled by Muniraja Punyavijayaji; edited by Ambalal P. Shah. Ahmedabad, 1963-1968. 4 pts.

Description in tabular form of about 10,000 manuscripts. Extracts from select manuscripts and appendices.

c. Ahmednagar. Sanatan Dharma Sabha

Catalogue of old manuscripts in Sanskrit in the collection of Sanatan Dharma Sabha / [ed. by M. N. Bopardikar]. Ahmednagar, 1962.

Description in tabular form of select 322 Sanskrit manuscripts. Arranged by subject. Various Indians. Sabha has about 5000 manuscripts.

d. Kolkata. Bangiya Sahitya Parisad

A descriptive catalogue of Sanskrit manuscripts in the Bangiya Sahitya Parisad / by Chintaharan Chakravarti. Kolkata, 1935.

Description in tabular form arranged by subject.

e. Kolkata. Sanskrit Sahitya Parisad

A descriptive catalogue of Sanskrit manuscripts in the Sanskrit Sahitya Parisad, Kolkata / compiled by Madhusudan Chakravarti, edited with an introduction and appendices by Heramba Chatterjee Sastri and Satya Ranjan Banerjee. Kolkata, 1984. 5 vols.

Description in tabular form List of titles A-Z. Extracts from select manuscripts with Index.

f. Varanasi. Nagari Pracharini Sabha

Hastalikhita Samskrita-grantha suci / edited by Sudhakar Pandey [et al]. Varanasi, [1974-78 A. D.]. 5 vols.

Description in tabular form of about 10,275 manuscripts. Arranged by subject. No index.

6. Descriptive catalogue: It provides full physical description, post colophons, select portions from the text, notes on authors and works. Descriptive catalogues of the Asiatic Society.

a. Assam. Hem Chandra Goswami.

Descriptive catalogue of Assamese manuscripts / by Hemchandra Goswami. Calcutta. 1930.

Alphabetical detailed description of 156 Assamese and 77 Sanskrit manuscripts with beginning, ending, contents, notes.

b. Calcutta, Asiatic Society of Bengal,

A descriptive catalogue of Sanskrit manuscripts in the government collection under the care of the Asiatic Society of Bengal. Calcutta : Baptist Mission Press, 1917-1955. 14 vols.

Vol. 1 published in 1917. Buddhist manuscripts, ed. by Hara Prasad Sastri.

Vol. 2 published in 1923. Vedic

Vol. 1 published in 1925. Smriti

Vol. 1 published in 1925. History and Geography.

Vol. 2-4 edited by Hara Prasad Sastri (Asutosh Tarkatirtha, Nanigopal Banerji etc.).

Vol. 5 published in 1928. Purana

Vol. 6 published in 1931. Vyakarana

Vol. 7 published in 1934. Kavya

Vol. 8 published in 1939/40. Tantra.

Vol. 5-8 under the title : A descriptive Catalogue of the Sanskrit manuscripts in the collection of the Royal Asiatic Society of Bengal. Vol. 8 revised and edited by Chintaharan Chakravarti.

Vol. 9 published in 1941. Bengali, Hindi, Oriya etc. ed. by Jogendra Nath Gupta.

Vol. 9. Supplement. Bengali and Assamese manuscripts, edited by Praphulla Chandra Pal.

Vol. 9 under the title : A descriptive Catalogue of the Vernacular Manuscripts in the collection of the Royal Asiatic Society of Bengal.

Vol. 9 supplement under the title : A descriptive catalogue of the Bengali and Assamese manuscripts.

Vol. 10, Vol. 1-2 Published in 1945-48. Astronomy edited by Prabodh Chandra Sen Gupta.

Vol. 11, Published in 1957. Philosophy edited by Haraprasada Shastri, Narendra Chandra Vedantatirtha and Chintharan Chakravarti.

Vol. 14, published in 1955. Kama Caurya Sastra edited by Hara Prasad Shastri and Chintaharan Chakravarti.

These volumes consists of detailed descriptions, mostly with beginnings, endings and notes. Each volume with separate indices; some volumes with important prefaces.

7. General register of works: It is written on the basis of the catalogues of manuscripts. It contains short information on author and title with source of availability.

   Catalogus Catalogorum (1891-1903), - New Catalogus Catalogorum (1937)- and Jinaratnakosa (1944) are well known works of this type. These are alphabetical register of works, though they refer to manuscript catalogues and collections.

After scrutinising the features of different types of catalogue format it is evident that

1. Manuscript search report is meant only for locating the manuscripts. It is important for trace the unknown location of the manuscripts. As the manuscript search report provide only general information of availability of manuscripts, it is important for locate the manuscript only. Even sometimes, it does not help to acquire particular manuscript.
2. Simple list only describes the author and title, sometime only the title is listed. So this type of list offer only bare description of the manuscripts. As it is not giving the full description of the manuscripts, it is only helping the scholars to locate the manuscripts. It is not very useful. Simple list also helps to locate the manuscript. As it does not describe the different features of one particular manuscript, it is also not very helpful to researchers.
3. Alphabetical catalogue by author or title is giving description of the manuscripts. As each manuscript is produced individually it has its own physical characteristics, length, breadth, thickness, number of folios, number of lines per page, number of letter per line in each page is varying. Alphabetical catalogue by author or title gives more information i.e. commentator, script, data, extent etc. but as it is not comprehensive. Scholars need more information of a particular manuscript.
4. Catalogue in tabular form specifies information under classified arrangement, till if requires comprehensive data which are lacking in this format.
5. The tabular description consisting of eleven vertical columns including additional particulars, i.e. beginning and ending lines, colophons of select manuscript is easy for consultation. As it is classified in specific columns the

data is easily accessible. This type of tabular catalogue will be very helpful to the scholars if the extract of the manuscript is included in the catalogue. Sometimes this extract is recorded in different volume. This is also not helpful. The extract must be noted at the time of accessioning. Extract of one manuscript must be recorded just after the tabular description. Colophonic remarks are important for socio-cultural study and for critical study of the manuscript. Generally post colophon remark, name of the scribe are neglected while preparation of catalogue of manuscripts. The catalogue of Orissa State Museum includes post colophonic remarks. In the catalogue of Nagari Pracharini Sabha, they have included the extracts in the remark column. It is ideal for retrieving data from the catalogue. It also includes authors and works cited in Smriti works compiled in Orissa, pp—1-17.

The catalogue of Bombay branch of the Royal Asiatic Society includes detailed descriptions of about 2100 manuscripts with beginning, endings, notes and subject arrangement i.e. listed according to subject. As the Government of India committee referred to above, it is used by a number of institutions.

Descriptive catalogue offers beginning and ending of the text and also other information. Detailed descriptive Cataloguing of manuscripts involve considerable time and labour. The information is spread out. It is also time consuming to search particular data. Descriptive cataloguing is important for understanding particular manuscript.

Manuscripts of texts in different languages must be catalogued in different volume. Then the catalogue must be classified under different subjects. Each descriptive catalogue followed certain subject classification. Editors of text utilize the descriptive catalogue. Critical editing of text requires first collection as many as possible numbers of copies of work. In certain case where only one copy of manuscript is available, critical edition may be prepared but it poses various problems. A critical editor requires the physical condition of the manuscript, its script, the complete or incomplete information, its age, purity of the text as well as legibility of the writing etc. The extracts of the text i.e. beginning, ending, colophon etc. will help to work with particular manuscript. When one scholar starts editing an unpublished text, he requires more detailed information as no other source to trace the information is known to him. The colophonic remark is important for socio-cultural study and critical study of the manuscript. Sometimes the descriptive catalogue does not include the index. Catalogue without index is also difficult to consult.

General register of works contains short information of author and title and the name of institution where the manuscript is deposited. This is very important for trace the manuscript, but it is not very useful to the scholars for editing the manuscript.

After studying these aspects of the catalogue of manuscript, it is clear that the tabular description of catalogue as suggested by the Government of India Committee with proper recording of extract is very useful. At the time of accessioning, extracts must be noted. Post colophonic remarks must not be neglected and proper care to record the relevant portion must be taken. In tabular form the notes must be properly recorded in 'Additional particulars' or in comment section. Extracts must be recorded in same volume. As for example, Descriptive catalogue of the Sanskrit Manuscripts in the Government Oriental Library includes detailed descriptions with beginning, endings and notes. It also includes indices. The single consolidated index where different types of information are arranged in the alphabetical sequence is user friendly. Scholar can locate any information with the least difficulty and time. In this way this type of descriptive catalogue in tabular format with well arranged index will serve the purpose of retrieving data from the catalogue.

Select Bibliography

1. An annotated bibliography of the catalogues of Indian manuscripts by Klaus Ludwig Janert. Wiesbaden, 1965.
2. Calcutta, Asiatic Society of Bengal, A descriptive catalogue of Sanskrit manuscripts in the government collection under the care of the Asiatic Society of Bengal. Calcutta : Baptist Mission Press, 1917-1955. 14 vols.
3. Bibliographic survey of Indian manuscript catalogues : being a union list of manuscript collected, edited by S. C. Biswas and M. K. Prajapati. Delhi, 1998.
4. New lights on manuscriptology; edited by Siniruddha Dash. Adyar, Chennai, 2007.
5. Kolkata. Sanskrit Sahitya Parisad A descriptive catalogue of Sanskrit manuscripts in the Sanskrit Sahitya Parisad, Kolkata / compiled by Madhusudan Chakravarti, edited with an introduction and appendices by Heramba Chatterjee Sastri and Satya Ranjan Banerjee. Kolkata, 1984. 5 vols.

Cataloguing of Manuscripts and its Difficulties

24

J. Lalitha

Introduction

According to recent survey, it is estimated that there are about 3.5. million Manuscripts of Indian origin are preserved in public and private collections in India. About 60,000 Indian manuscripts are preserved in 20 different centers of Europe and North America. Asian centers of Pakistan, Bangladesh, Nepal, Sri Lanka, Tibet, China, Japan, etc. also possess about 1.50 lakhs Indian manuscripts. It is noted that a large part of these manuscripts are yet to be catalogued, some not even recorded.

Objectives of Cataloguing of Manuscripts: The word catalogue is a Greek word of '***katalogos***'. '***Kata***' means by and '***logos***' means order/reason/word. Thus catalogue means a list of items arranged in some definite order. The systematic arrangement of a manuscript is known as cataloguing. To prepare a catalogue from the viewer point of a manuscript library, may note the special features of the library —

1. The fifth law of library science does not have much relevance for the manuscript library as the rate of growth of this library is very low.
2. There is no comparison at all between the frequency of readers visiting a printed books library and that of a manuscript library. Only specialized scholars and researchers make use of the library. The number of users is very limited.
3. The manuscripts cannot be browsed near the shelves because of the nature of manuscripts and of the care one has to take in handling them.

The manuscripts catalogue should provide a complete bibliographical information which help the researchers to distinguish each manuscript from other ones. The catalogue should be prepared for the benefit of various type of users like text finder, paleographer, artist, historian, etc.

The bibliographical details vary from those of printed books. Many works are unknown by their titles, though in some cases, there may be name of the author; some works are by anonymous authors. While preparing the catalogue, the cataloguer has to be guided by the information given in the manuscript.

Background of Catalogue: From medieval period there has been different kinds of catalogues/lists of manuscripts. In 1383 A.D. oldest known catalogue of ***Brahattipanika*** which provides information about 600 Jain manuscripts with author, title date and extent. During the 17th century A.D. a Sanskrit scholar Kavindracharya had a rich collection of Sanskrit manuscripts and its catalogue '***Kavindracharya Sucipatram***'[1,2] provides information about 2192 manuscripts.

After printing started the oldest known catalogue of Indian manuscripts is 'A Catalogue of Oriental manuscripts, chiefly Persian, Arabian and Sanskrit languages collected in the East' by James Fresher. This catalogue gives details about 165 Arabic, Persian and 35 Sanskrit manuscripts. Indian and European scholars have prepared variety of catalogues.

Form of A Manuscript Catalogue: The manuscript catalogue should not only be in the form of cards or library register but also to be printed. For the sake of uniformity, the format of the printed catalogue should be royal octavo. Every manuscripts library issues its catalogue in print. It is imperative that the catalogues of all manuscripts libraries must be available to other manuscript libraries and also to scholars and researchers. If the acquisition is low, supplement may be issued.

Types of Catalogues

1. **Card Index:** Generally custodians use cards indices.
2. **Accession Register**: This is master record of every bibliographic item in the library. The list of items by author, title or subject may be in the form of alphabetical register.
3. **Triennial Catalogue**: Details collected once in every three years in Triennial catalogue, GOML, Chennai.
4. **Descriptive Catalogue in Tabular form**: Descriptive catalogue gives the detailed description of the manuscripts. It contains serial no., subject, collection no., title, author, commentator, script, language, size, number of folios or leaves, line per page, number of letters per line, extent, condition, date, beginning, ending and colophon. Extracts of manuscripts, are also provided in GOML, Chennai.

5. **Descriptive Catalogue in descriptive form:** Providing full description as in the Descriptive catalogue tabular form and also post colophon, select portion from the text and notes on the author and work.

6. **General Register**: Containing short information on author and title with source of availability. New Catalogus Catalagorum, Dept. of Sanskrit, Univ. of Madras.

Fields of Catalogues

i. **Record No**: The serial number of manuscript of the collections starts from 1 to total number of manuscripts.

ii. **Address**: The complete postal address of the Institution or individual who owns the manuscripts.

iii. **Title**: A name given in the text.

- The title should be as written in the manuscript
- It is found either at the beginning of the text or in the colophon.
- If not able to find out the name of the text then fill '**unknown**'.
- Alternative title or parallel title, if any, must also be noted.
- If title is not available a few lines from the beginning and end of the text should be included in '**Remarks**'.

iv. **Author**: The author name may be found at the beginning or at the end or in colophon of the text.

- If the name is not found write '**unknown**'.
- Any information about the author can be written in '**Remarks**'.

v. **Joint Author**: Person/s jointly responsible for the content of the text.

vi. **Commentary**: The notes explaining or interpreting a written text/document.

- If more than one commentary it must be mentioned.

vii. **Commentator**: The person responsible for interpreting the content of the text.

viii. **Language**: Language in which text is written.

ix. **Date of Manuscript**: Date of creation of the manuscript by scribe/writer.

- Here date refers to the period when a particular manuscript was put to writing.
- The date may be available in post colophon.

- If date is not found write '**Not available**'.

x. **Scribe**: The person who has written the copy of the manuscript.

- Scribe may differ from the author.
- Scribe's name usually given in the post colophon.
- Sometimes scribe advises readers how to use the manuscript; how to protect, etc.

xi. **Subject**: Refers to the topic/theme of the text.

xii. **Colophon**: Ending part of the text.

- Contains name of the author, scribe, text, date of composition, etc.
- The purpose for which the scribe wrote, date, handling of manuscript, preservation and conservation of manuscript, etc.

xiii. **Folios**: The number of folios within a manuscript.

- Number of folios can be different from its pagination. For example if a manuscript has folios from 1 to 60, if folios 5-10 are missing, then the number of folios in the manuscript are 54 only.

xiv. **Size of manuscript**: Height x width in centimeters.

xv. **Material**: Manuscript is made of palm leaf, paper, birch-bark, etc.

xvi. **Illustration**: Pictures or diagrams that accompany the text.

xvii. **Status**: If the text is complete write '**com**' or '**complete**'.

- If incomplete '**Inc**' or '**Incomplete**'.
- If some folios are missing, but beginning and ending exist, it is also incomplete.

xviii. **Condition**: Condition of the manuscript — 'good', 'bad', 'worm eaten', brittle, etc.

Some Problems and Suggestions: General opinion among the readers is that the Indian manuscripts catalogues are inadequate in content and fail to satisfy the needs of the researchers. The catalogue should provide all types of detailed information. From the cataloguer's view, we may find several problems such as:

1. Generally poets do not provide any type of biographical information about them. Some times there is no mention of even their name as the author.
2. A number of anonymous works whose real authorship is still to be determined.

3. Severe problems in interpolation
4. Some times some portions of other text is inserted in a particular manuscript.
5. Many texts with same title, sometimes with or without authors name. Just by looking at the title one cannot determine the subject of the text. For example, text starting with the title Yoga can be on Yoga, Ayurveda, or Jyotisha. Similarly the text starting with Nyaya can be on Nyaya, Vaiseshika, Mimamsa, Advaita and so on.
6. Manuscripts are written in several scripts and also regional languages. So regional pronunciation, practices etc., have been included.
7. Number of manuscripts are composite in nature and are also incomplete. Due to lack of care, loose sheets get intermixed causing problems.
8. Like printed books, manuscripts do not contain title, author, pages. The cataloguer has to find out its author, title, commentator, etc., either from colophon, beginning of the text or from the end portion of some chapters.
9. The cataloguer should be aware of the different styles of writing.

To overcome these problems, the cataloguer should be conversant with the language, subject knowledge of various scripts and writing method, etc. Fortunately the recent years catalogues were maintain consistency and uniformity. Although there is a need for some more information like —

1. The manuscript should be furnished with beginning, ending, colophon, post colophon and some portion of the text.
2. Notes on unknown poets and works.
3. Notes on illustrations and illuminations (i.e. black and white or coloured, etc.)
4. Notes of calligraphy, insertions of some folios of some other manuscripts, if any.

Conclusion: The cataloguing of manuscript is a special type of art and requires deep knowledge. It is difficult to find particular manuscript on the basis of simple catalogue. Generally the manuscripts are not lent out; hence the catalogue is the only source in selecting a particular manuscript. The cataloguer should provide the data which should be adequate to distinguish each manuscript of the same work.

For the best utility of manuscript catalogue, the following steps are to be taken:

1. Prepare and publish manuscript catalogues of all the manuscripts preserved in India which help to identify the known, the unknown or lost work.

2. Universities, Research Institutions can get microfilm copies of all the catalogues of Indian manuscripts published in India and abroad because a number of catalogues are out of print and not available in the market and these catalogues will never get reprinted.
3. During this period of advanced technological development think about a computer based national register of Manuscripts.

Bibliography

Biswas, S, C. and Prajapati, M.K. Bibliographic survey of Indian Manuscripts collection.

Katre, S.M. Indian Textual Criticism, Poona, BORI.

Raghavan, V. Manuscripts, Catalogues, editions, Madras: Bharati Vijayam Press, 1963.

Shivaganesha Murthy, R.S. Introduction to Manuscriptology.

References

1 Kavindracharya Sucipatram, Dr.V.Raghavan, B.R.Bhandarkar Volume, p.159-65, Indian Research Institute, Calcutta, 1940.

2. A Forgotten Event of Shahjehan's Reigm, H.D.Sharma, The Kuppuswami Sastri Commemoration Volume, p.53-60, The Presidency College, Madras 600 005.

Traditional Methods of Preserving Manuscripts: An Overview

25

Aarti Sharma and Suniti Bala

Manuscripts are considered as the most important source of authenticity and constitute our national and cultural heritage. Manuscripts are the powerful medium for preservation of our literary, linguistic, artistic and cultural heritage. These are the only source of the unknown and unknowable. So every possible effort must be taken to save these treasures for the future generation. Preservation of manuscripts is a serious issue for the Librarians, Information scientists and Archivist. The problem of preservation of rare documents has continued ever since human beings acquired the knowledge of writing. In spite of the advent of suitable chemicals for preservation and their availability, traditional methods for preservation are in practice. In this paper an attempt has been made to summarize the various traditional methods of preservation.

Introduction

In India over thousand of years manuscripts have been written in a vast number of languages each in itself embodies her history. India possesses more than an estimated five million manuscripts, making her the largest repository of manuscript wealth in the world, but this tremendous pool of knowledge is under threat and manuscripts are disappearing at an alarming rate. Thousand of manuscripts lie neglected in institutions and homes around the country. They are found on materials such as birch, palm leaf, handmade paper and cloth that require specialized care and conservation. It is obligatory on our part to protect and conserve this heritage as long as possible.

Undoubtedly, the advent of technology has given rise to greater concerns of preservation of manuscripts by adopting modern technologies. Moreover, there is no dearth of modern chemical pesticides and repellants for the safe upkeep of manuscripts. Still the traditional methods of preservation are in vogue, as these methods are not hazardous for human health, they do not have any adverse effect on the materials and they do not require much expertise, equipment and money.

Traditional Storage Methods

The cause of deterioration is not only neglect or negligence but the basic factors of deterioration of the manuscripts are light, dust, heat and humidity. To protect the manuscripts from these possible factors, the different traditional methods were adopted by the custodians to safeguard manuscripts and these practices are still being practiced:-

- In order to protect the manuscripts from deterioration seasoning of the leaf by burying them under the mud or boiling them in water was done prior to writing. Finally turmeric paste was applied to save them from insects.
- Usually to fasten the manuscripts, holes are punched on the leaves and cords are passed through them, which keep the leaves intact. The bundles of manuscripts are also kept in heavy wooden chests to reduce the rigorous changing of climate.
- Wrapping the manuscripts in clothes, protect them from dust, insects and humidity. Palm leaves are usually wrapped in red or yellow colour clothes. It is believed that red is a repelling colour for the insects and yellow colour if, produced by turmeric possess some germicidal power that repel the insects from getting in contact with the manuscripts. The manuscript is wrapped in the cloth and then finally ribbon is tightly bound around the bundle to exert an even pressure on manuscript.
- Palm leaves were kept in the kitchen lofts, if there is no immediate requirements of the processed palm-leaf as the smoke particles have the capacity to repel the insects. The leaves can be preserved for a longer time without being affected by insect, fungi or mildew.
- Exposure of the leaves to the tender rays of the rising or setting Sun destroys the traces of growth of insects and micro-organisms. Manuscripts are generally exposed to the Sun in the Lunar month of Bhadraba i.e. in August as the rays of the Sun in that particular month are very favorable. By this the worms are killed under the Sun.
- When transporting a manuscript, a narrow cotton cushion with a strap is used to protect the manuscript from damage in transit.

Herbals and Natural Products

Manuscripts are old and preserve the text which is otherwise lost or readings which are forgotten. They deserve special care by reason of their importance and require the same care for the reason of their fragility. Plants are nature chemical factories, providing a wide range of phytochemical mostly aromatic essential oils, alkaloids, etc. Some of such plants and their products have been recognized by our ancestors. Since ancient times for their germicidal properties and insect repellency potentialities they are used for storage of manuscripts and to prevent them from deterioration. Some natural products, adopted by the custodians of manuscripts, are enumerated below:-

- Small packets of powder of dried leaves of aswagandha are kept with the manuscripts covered in clothes to repel insect attack.
- Dried ginger is kept along with bundles of manuscripts to save them from insect attack. In China, ginger root and stem are used as pesticides against aphids and fungal spores.
- Lemon-grass oil coatings strengthen the leaves of manuscripts and also destroy the growths of micro-organisms.
- Kumkum fruit powder is used in many repositories as it is a very good insect repellant.
- Powdered roots of dried sweet flag are filled in small bags and are kept in cup-boards of manuscripts as it has got very good medicinal value and insecticidal power.
- Powdered ajwain also acts as an insect killer and fungicide. Fumes of ajwain obtained by its burning, has often been used as a fungicide and an antiseptic in Indian homes.
- The mixture of neem leaves, karanja, nirgundi and citronella are known for their insecticidal properties for which they are used in the manuscript libraries.
- Dried tamakhu leaves are packed in small cloth bags or spread on the shelves where manuscripts are kept. The nicotinic acid of the leaves keeps the insects away.
- Naga-damani bears an essential oil whose sweet aroma and insect repellant action helps to eradicate insects from the manuscripts.
- Mint leaves in its natural form are used to repel ants and cockroaches.
- Black-Cumin commonly known as Kala Jeera is used as an insect repellant. The seeds are scattered at the manuscript storage area and strong aromatic smell keeps away insects.
- Sandal wood dust is commonly used as insect repellant. The dust is traditionally kept in cupboards used for storage of textile etc. It also act as a humidity buffer.

- Neem contains limonoids, a class of compounds that acts as anti-feedants or growth regulators in insects; they don't kill instantly but wipe out a whole generation of insects by preventing the young ones from maturing and adults from reproducing. Dried neem leaves and seeds are also useful in keeping away insects. Dried leaves from neem tree were placed between the cover of the book to deter booklice. As the wooden planks attached to the bundles of manuscripts are prone to insect attack, in some libraries the planks are made of neem wood which can ward off termite.
- Camphor is commonly used in India to protect valuable documents. A mixture of camphor and clove has also been used to repel insects from textile and manuscripts collections. Moreover, synthetic camphor oil is also used to protect palm leaf manuscripts against insect attack. The smoke produced on burning camphor oil has been found to be very effective as an insecticide and a fungicide.
- A mixture of camphor and clove has also been used to repel insects from textile and manuscript collections.
- Citronella oil was rubbed on palm-leaf manuscripts to increase flexibility and to deter attack by insect.
- Oil extracts of some natural products like black pepper, sandal wood or clove facilitate in the restoration of flexibility to the palm leaf manuscripts.
- Resin oil was applied on manuscripts as the strong aroma prevents silver fish from attacking thc folios.
- Khus roots and oil are both used as insect repellent.
- Canola oil is used to control insects. It repels insects by acting as an insect irritant.
- Garlic exhibits antibacterial, antifungal and insecticidal qualities. Garlic oil spray also has fungicidal properties.
- Combination of acorus calmus, cumin, cloves, pepper, cinnamon and camphor was used as an insect repellent for six months, though it had to be replaced after six month or so.
- Peacock feathers while attached to the peacock leave aromatic accretions, which spread throughout their feathers. when the leaves are detached the residual aroma acts as insect-repellent, therefore feathers were kept in the books to keep the insects away.
- Snake slough have often been kept in old book as the snake slough is charged with an aroma liberated by male to entice the female and the aroma has insect -repellent property.
- Nirgandi is a shrub, after being dried in sun, the leaves are inserted between the bundles of palm-leaves manuscripts to keep the insects away.

Conclusion

There are many traditional methods of storage and the natural and herbal products for the control of bio-deterioration of manuscripts which either had been or are still used in different parts of the country, but because of the availability of other ready made materials, lack of knowledge as well as lack of confidence in their long-term efficiency, they are dwindling away. These methods have been found to be effective in many cases, but they also seem to have failed in some other cases as they are not always sufficient to eradicate insects and fungal growth. It has been observed that their efficiency significantly increase by introducing some surfactant, preparing their mixture and by adding some synthetic chemicals. The natural materials should not be dismissed in favour of other synthetic materials. Efforts instead should be made to exploit their relatively non-toxic characteristics and ability to resist the development of resistance, by addition of some other non-toxic material or using their mixtures.

References

Agarwal, O.P. (1984). Conservation of manuscripts and painting of South-East Asia. London: Butterworth, pp. 36-54.

Bhattacharyya, B. (1947). Palm Leaf Manuscripts and other Preservation. Indian Archives.Vol. 1, no.3. pp. 233-34.

Gupta, K.K. (2005). An introduction to the traditional practices for the control of bio-deterioration of manuscripts. Indigenous Methods and Manuscript Preservation. Edited by Anupam Sah. New Delhi: National Mission For Manuscripts. pp.35-59.

Jeyaraj, V. (2005). Traditional practices and palm-leaf manuscripts in Tamil Nadu. *In* Indigenous Methods and Manuscript Preservation. Edited by Anupam Sah. New Delhi:National Mission For Manuscripts. pp.143-150.

Prasad, Lalan Kumar (1981-82). Role of Neem Leaves in Protecting Textile Materials and Paper Document. Conservation of Cultural Property in India, Vol. 14-15. pp.95-97

Saini, M.L. (1969). Manuscripts literature in Indian Languages. ILA Bulletin, 5(1), January-March, pp.6-21.

Subaraman, S. (2005). The use of turmeric in the preservation of manuscripts. *In* Indigenous Methods and Manuscript Preservation. Edited by Anupam Sah. New Delhi: National Mission For Manuscripts. pp.119-124.

Suri, Jina Harisagara (1947). Palm Leaf Manuscripts in Jaisalmir. Indian Archives. Vol. 1, No.3. pp. 235-36.

Preservation, Conservation and Digitization of Manuscripts: Problems & Prospects

26

RUPINDER SINGH, SANJEEV KUMAR & DEEPAK AGARWAL

Introduction

India possesses a rich and enormous cultural heritage of manuscripts since the ancient period. India probably has the largest number of manuscripts in the world. Manuscripts collections are scattered in several places all over India and stored in various types of academic and research institutions, libraries, temples, mathas and individual collections. It is roughly estimated that over 3.5 million manuscripts may be preserved and 30% of the remaining total MSS that are stored in temples, mathas and in private hands. Manuscripts provide authentic records for tracing the cultural, social, political and economic history of the people of a region or country. Libraries are social institution bestowed with the responsibility of storing, preserving the cultural heritage of accounting and making them available for use to the community. But manuscripts are in a poor state of preservation in most of the libraries and private repositories. Manuscripts throw light on the various aspects of human activities of ancient time so it is necessary to protect the cultural property through activities that minimize deterioration/damage and further prevent the loss of information content.

Digitization or Digitization in Manuscript Preservation and Conservation

Preservation refers to the totality of process and operation involved in the stabilization and protection of documents against damage or destruction and in the treatment of damaged or deteriorated documents. It is an indirect method of treatment in which the environment around an item is changed. Conservation is a direct method of treatment in which item is physically or chemically changed. This includes cleaning, deacidifying, repairing, rebinding and reformatting. Digitization or digital image technology can act as a facilitator in conserving manuscripts. It is creation of computerized representation of printed analog.

Musafir Memorial Central State Library, Patiala: Brief History

Musafir Memorial Central State Library (MMCSL) at Patiala is the state library of Punjab. Its foundation stone was laid as the Central Public Library on Feb. 1, 1955 by the then Hon'ble Chief Minister of PEPSU Sh. Brish Bhan Ji and was opened on July 23, 1956 by Hon'ble Sh. C.P.N. Singh the then Governor, Punjab. In 1978, the library was renamed as Musafir Memorial Central State Library in honour of late Giani Gurmukh Singh Musafir, the literary Chief Minister of Punjab. The total area of this library is 23 bighas and 2 biswas. M.M. Central State library works as apex library in Punjab and 14 district libraries of the state are under the administrative control of this library. The library provides not only lending and reference services but also serves as community centre for educational and cultural activities, as it has two hall attached to it. One lecture hall serves as a seminar hall and the other fully air-conditioned auditorium, which can accommodate 800 persons. The building of MMCSL has been planned in such a manner as it can be extended to meet the future needs. The registered members of this library are about 19000 in Adult Section and about 3500 in Children Section. The library provides service to its members/readers through five sections i.e. Technical Section, Lending Section, Reference Section, Children Section and Periodical Section. The library has rich collection of about 1.5 lac documents on various subjects in different sections. The State Archives Department donated about 3000 rare manuscripts in reference section.

Manuscripts Collection

The oldest manuscript available in the Reference Section of M.M. Central State Library donated by State Archives is "Skanda Puran" which is engraving on leaves. Scholars from far off places come to consult these manuscripts. These belong to a variety of subjects like history, religion, ayurveda, palmistry, literature etc. Language wise break-up of manuscripts is:

Persian	961
Sanskrit	784
Gurmukhi/ Punjabi	595
Urdu	152
Hindi	126
Arabic	102

Following is a select list of manuscripts displayed in the Reference Section of M.M.Central State Library, Patiala, Punjab:

1. Bhagvad Gita: Translation by Faizi & Raja Jai Singh Sawai Dated : 1872 A.D. There are three columns on each page. First column contains the translation in Hindi the second is the original Sanskrit in Devnagri and the third Persian translation by Faizi. There is a running commentary in margin of each page in Hindi in Persian script.
2. Masadas da madah mubark Hazrat Baba Guru Nanak Sahib. Rehmat Aliaalia Qudas. Allah Sira ulaziz. By Mohd. Ali Khushnavis.
3. Asap Namah: A Persian manuscript on the various kinds of horses, their diseases and remedies.
4. Bhagvat (Bhavad Puran) Dated : 1787 BK. Persian translation of the twelve chapters of the Bhagvad Puran.
5. Noor Audin Abdul Rehamajami Yusaf — Wa Zulikha Jami Persian (169 pages, 56 illustrations).
6. The Holy Quran By Kashid Ul Umar Dated : 1252 A.H. (1733 AD). An extremely rare manuscript on account of its calligraphy and ornamentation.
7. Bazam Afroz: Love story of one of the kings of Kanauj.
8. Tuti Nama: By Ziauldin Bakshi 170 pages & 55 illustrations.
9. Hanuman Natak: By Hirda Ram Dated : 1880 BK 342 pages & 1 illustration.
10. Bhavrattanparkash: By Fatha Singh Dated : 1877 BK (1820 AD) 173 pages & 2 illustrations.
11. Ashev Perkalunidh Granth: By Fatha Singh.
12. Skandapurana: Engraving on leaves (The oldest manuscript in the library).
13. Pothi Gurbani.
14. Shiv Puran: Translator: Kishan Singh Nishat Dated : 1929 BK (1872 AD) Persian translation in 20 adhyayas.
15. Sri Bhagwat Puran 300 pages and 261 illustrations.
16. Mahabharat: Translated by Muhammad Sultan Thanesri, Naqieb Khan & Abdul Qadir Badayuni. Dated : 1903 BK A translation into Persian of the original work in Sanskrit.
17. Shah Namah by Firdausi, A superbly illumined copy of the famous Persian epic.

18. Guldashta-i-Akhlaq Dated 1288 AH (1928 BK) (1871 AD). A beautifully transcribed manuscript on morality.

The team from NMM visited the library in September 2006 and stayed for 20 days. They went thoroughly through these manuscripts. They first classified the manuscripts according to their physical condition A - Deteriorated, B - Okay, and C - Good. Different subject experts then identified these manuscripts in different languages and subjects. Then these manuscripts were chemically treated with Thymol and Ethnol spray and wrapped in red cloth and moisture resistant white thick paper. An e-catalogue of the collection of manuscripts at the Central State Library was also prepared using software named 'Granthavali'. A hard copy was handed to the library only for Sanskrit and Hindi language medium manuscripts. These manuscripts are used by wide-ranging users like Ph.D scholars of different subjects, historians, religious and literary scholars from India and abroad, local astrologers, vaids and hakims are the frequent users. They are not allowed to get any manuscript photocopied and they have to handle the manuscripts with great care. They are allowed to use digital cameras to photograph them only. The team also sensitized the library staff about preventive and curative conservation.

Punjab State Archives Department

Besides these, Punjab State Archives, Patiala has been housing for the last 50 years manuscripts belonging to erstwhile Patiala, Nabha, Faridkot, Malerkotla, Jind, Kapurthala, Nalagarh and Kalsia states. Valuable works are decaying because of want of funds as the annual budget of Rs.50,000 of this department is very less to meet the requirements of preservation and conservation of these manuscripts. Punjab State Archives, Patiala has been the biggest repository of archival material in North India. It contains valuable records pertaining to princely states, residency records and Khalsa Durbar records, besides printed accounts of some of the important British officials in Punjab. For the past 50 years, the records were ably preserved and catalogued. Punjab owes a heavy debt of gratitude for the initiative taken by the doyen of Punjab history, Dr Ganda Singh, who was invited by Maharaja Yadavindra Singh, the Rajparmukh of PEPSU, to take over as Director of the Archives at Patiala... This repository of the records is indispensable for the writing of the history of Punjab.

The archives have illustrated and written manuscripts, including copies of *Ain-i-Akbari, Zaffarnama* of Guru Gobind Singh, an illustrated book of the Shahnama of Firdausi, *Adi Granth* of 1666, an illustrated book on Laila Majnu, rare Tibetan palm-leaf manuscripts and even a copy of the letter issued by Guru Gobind Singh to the Khalsa Sangat in 1764, asking it to arm itself for the coming conflict. Besides manuscripts, there are a number of paintings of the British era, including those of the battle of Ferozeshah Kotla, miniatures and even conferment of titles of kingship on two Maharajas' of Patiala by Mughal emperors. But somehow this treasure is decaying and due to want of funds has not been able to preserve and conserve its wealth. Rather the fate of these manuscripts has been regrettable as some of these have been dumped in Punjabi University Library, and rest in the Deputy Commissioner's office.

Problems at official level

Four major problems we can say in this group.

Finance: Finance problem is the biggest one, at least in this region. Be it a government organization, a non-government organization or an individual case. Finance for MSS collection, display, preserves the material is not available. For documentation, study, publication etc. MSS funds are needed. The existing govt. facilities are not sufficient and are not easily available. Suitable steps must be taken in this respect immediately.

Technical: Very few persons are now available for deciphering the old scripts like Modi, Takri, Nagari, etc. Even in conservation and preservation purpose technical persons needed and the laboratories are very few in India for the same purpose.

Administrative: A lot of administrative obstructions are arising in various ways. If some one needs an illustrated or unpublished MSS for research purpose, the formalities of institution are such it is difficult to get. The permission to get access to collection is not easy. There is no typing or Xeroxing arrangement in these government institutions.

Non-cooperation: Both the government and as well as common people are not co-operating. The MSS in one's collection may get spoilt due to daily offering of sandal paste, flowers, water and also by insects, he will prefer to submerge in water than to hand over to some scholar or institution. Similar is the situation in some public institution. Often it is pleaded by the officials that unless the materials, is published others are not allowed to get access to it.

Culture as Knowledge Base

Culture is multi-dimensional, multi-form representation of nature. Cultural heritage enables people to anchor themselves in a time and a place, creates a frame of reference for their actions and provides a value base for their lives. Cultural heritage underpins civilization, and its plurality must be safeguarded. Archives, libraries and museums (memory institutions) deal with and are keepers of our major resources of cultural and scientific knowledge, both as our inheritance from the past and our legacy to the future. These resources form a significant part of the intellectual capital of the Information Society where they are increasingly being made available to large communities of users in digital form.

Role of Technology in Preservation of Culture

Modern (Multimedia) Technology can play a major role in preservation and promotion of cultural heritage. Multimedia encompass all forms of materials e.g. textual, visual (still and moving) and audio all together to represent the holistic form. The WORLD-WIDE-WEB is wide reaching medium through which anything and everything could be made available to anyone and everyone around the globe.

Benefits of Digitization of Manuscripts

Preservation and Conservation: Digital reproductions are virtually immortal, Minimizes handling of originals, Reconstruction using image processing techniques, Use of life-size print reproductions for conservation.

Research: Access to images for researchers, Study of disparate images in new contexts.

Collections Management: Assistance in retrospective cataloging, Researching collection, Assistance with curatorial functions, Managing material movement, Licensed use of digital reproductions in advertising and publishing.

Dissemination and promotion: Dissemination of art via the Internet.

New Revenue Streams: Making digital reproductions at lower resolution available to scholars as a paid service, Sale of high quality posters to art patrons around the world via an e-commerce website.

Digitization of Heritage Knowledge base : India's initiative Indian Heritage

India perhaps has one of the oldest and largest collections of manuscripts in the world. These manuscripts are in different languages and in different scripts. They are written on different kinds of material like birch bark, palm leaf, cloth and paper. They are in the custody of different institutions like libraries, museums, monasteries, mutts and individuals. Only a small percentage of these manuscripts have been surveyed and catalogued. Catalogues are perhaps available for not more than 20-25% of the manuscript collections in the country. The catalogues do not follow a standard format. A significant proportion of manuscripts are not preserved scientifically. Experts estimate that almost all palm leaf manuscripts may perish due to wear and fear over the next 50 to 100 years. An estimate of heritage wealth of India is as under:

- Total number of manuscripts in India 5,000,000
- Indian manuscripts available in European countries 60,000

- Indian manuscripts in South Asia and Asian countries 150,000
- Number of manuscripts recorded in catalogues 1,000,000 (approx.)
- Percentage of manuscripts language wise Sanskrit 67%
- Other Indian Languages 25%
- Arabic/Persian/Tibetan 8%
- Indira Gandhi National Centre for the Arts (IGNCA) has covered around 2,50,000 manuscripts. Indian National
- Trust for Art and Cultural Heritage (INTACH) has already surveyed more than 300 sites in three districts and prepared an inventory of about 47,000 palm leaf and paper manuscripts.

Core Technical Issues Involved

Technologies and their scalability to manage emerging new models of distributed cultural collections and services is required. A range of technologies and tools apply to the digitization process that covers the following tasks:

Storage, manipulation, access, delivery, use, security and charging. The issue is one of availability, suitability, robustness, standards, and affordability for use of the tools in the culture sector. To deliver these services, the sector requires comprehensive *technical solutions* which are sustainable, i.e. they must be robust, have a broad applicability, take into account the abilities to handle large numbers of records be consistent across categories. The appropriate application of technical standards by those involved in digitisation activities is essential if the digitised collections are to be maintainable in a cost-effective way over time.

Quality Criteria

Quality criteria for sites delivering cultural content is a another core issue, supporting confidence and trust from the user and enabling institutions. A framework is required that describes quality in terms of the underlying technical characteristics provided by individual sites or subject gateways and in terms of the quality of service provided to the users. Quality evaluation of content and processes is also desired.

Interoperability between Digitized Collections

Data and semantic interoperability standards support the systematic exchange of data and the accessibility of the resources by world citizens in their own language in a usable and persistent way. The focus should be on the infrastructures needed to support access to and delivery of the resources. Common metadata is essential to support unified access and needs to be promoted and used. Multilingual access further enable access in citizens own language.

Legal Issues

There is need to investigate the legal position (Copyright) in relation to making digital copies of the relevant source materials. The project should comply with appropriate local legal deposit legislation. A clear policy needs to be in place on access to and use of images within the completed digital project, including, if appropriate provision of copyright disclaimer. Digital Rights Management structure needs to be further enhanced. IPR and acquisition and management of rights, on licensing Institutional assets, patents, trademarks, etc. need to be evolved.

International Cooperation

Co-operation fulfils a number of functions and is required at different levels, based on different partnerships. Given the scale of activities and the nature of the content itself, co-operation should be sought at India/Asia level. There is need to identify added-value models for cooperation, on Asian level. Models for cross domain cooperation (i.e. co-operation between archives, libraries and museums as content owners) should be explored as the means of developing complementarities between resources, creation of content and context, and delivering new digital services.

Vision 2010

By 2010 the foremost cultural heritage in museums, archives and libraries should be digitized according to prioritization plans. The materials should be universally accessible to all through information networks, providing access to and promoting knowledge of Indian civilization at the national and international levels. The cultural heritage materials should emerge to constitute an important resource for research, education and content creation.

National Mission for Manuscripts (NMM) and M.M. Central State Library, Patiala

Wealth of Knowledge

Human beings have expressed their thoughts, feelings and knowledge about various areas in writing in different languages ever since they found a medium to write on. A manuscript is a hand-written composition on paper, bark, cloth, metal, palm leaf or any other material dating back at least seventy five years, that has significant scientific, historical or aesthetic value. There are manuscripts on horse-lore, on the science of the stars, on the rule of kings, on states of being, on rituals of war, on curing ailments, on sensual aspects of life and much more. Manuscripts have knowledge value. The enormous range of languages and scripts in which manuscripts are found reflects vibrant linguistic and literary traditions over thousands years. Following is an estimation of manuscripts:

- Total Number of manuscripts in India 5,000,000
- Indian manuscripts available in European countries 60,000
- Indian manuscripts in South Asia and Asian countries 1,50,000
- Manuscripts recorded in catalogues (approx.) 1,000,000
- Percentage of manuscripts language wise-
  - Sanskrit 67%
  - Other Indian Languages 25%
  - Arabic/Persian/Tibetan 8%

There are over 77 libraries outside India where major collections of manuscripts of Indian origin exist. Some of the foreign libraries are:

Denmark: Royal Library, Copenhagen

France: Bibliotheque Nationale, Paris

Germany: Preussiche Stats Bibliothek Berlin; Universitas Bibliothek; Leipzig, Staats Bibliothek, Marburg; Bayerishe Staats Bibliothek, Munchen

United Kingdom: British Library, London; Royal Asiatic Society, London; Bodleian Library, Oxford; Indian Institute, Oxford; Cambridge University Library, Cambridge

Nepal: Darbar Library, Kathmandu

Pakistan: Punjab University Library, Lahore

Sri Lanka: Museum Library, Colombo

India's manuscripts reveal different streams of thought that cover a variety of themes reflecting on several facets of life. Today, most of this important knowledge lies neglected and on the verge of destruction by the ravages of time that have left them without readers and without people to look after them. There is an immediate need to identify, collect and preserve this wealth still scattered in many religious places or is in personal custodies and interpret the knowledge that is available in them, and provide access to those who need them. There are so many stories how these treasures of information are being identified and collected from places beyond one's imagination by those who value them. It is not possible for individuals alone to carry out this voluminous task.

National Mission for Manuscripts (NMM)

Hence, National Mission for Manuscripts (NMM), a five year project was launched on February 7, 2003 in New Delhi under the Ministry of Culture, Government of

India by the then Prime Minister Shri Atal Bihari Vajpayee to save the most valuable but less visible of our cultural inheritances. Indira Gandhi National Centre for the Arts (IGNCA) was chosen the National Nodal Agency for the implementation of the Mission, to house the National Manuscripts Library. This library is envisaged as the central repository for microfilms and digital copies of all Indian manuscripts.

Mission's Objectives

Survey and Locate: The Mission launches massive surveys around the country and abroad to locate manuscripts in the care of a variety of custodians.

Catalogue and Compile: Through extensive cataloguing we are creating a national electronic database of manuscripts.

Conserve and Preserve: By networking with the leading conservation agencies in the country, we are conserving damaged or threatened manuscripts and setting standards for manuscript conservation.

Promote Access: Through ready availability of our database in a soon-to-be-established National Manuscripts Library and eventually on the internet on our website, the Mission is improving access to the treasure of manuscripts.

Promote Scholarship: By documenting and preserving manuscripts, and with our research and publications as well as training programmes we seek to promote their use to increase knowledge and improve learning.

Public Outreach: The Mission carries out a number of public outreach programmes that seek to enlist the cooperation and assistance of all members of the public starting from school children to retired persons through series of talks, seminars, our newsletter and other programmes to ensure the future of manuscripts in India.

To achieve these objectives, there are Manuscript Resource Centres (MRCs) and Manuscript Conservation Centres (MCCs) spread all over the country, region wise. National surveys are being conducted all over India to locate, document and preserve manuscripts lying in local temple or mosque, in a big library or state archives, in the private collection of a Nawab or in the small home of a villager. To start with, a pilot survey was carried out in three states-Orissa, Bihar and Uttar Pradesh and in the following years other states were also included. The Mission has taken the task of evolving a National Electronic Database of manuscripts which integrates information pertaining to different aspects of manuscriptology such as material, script, language, subject, place of availability, no. of pages, illustrations etc. Another important function of NMM is digitization of manuscripts as experts estimate that almost all palm leaf manuscripts may perish due to wear and tear over next 50 to 100 years. Digitization means acquiring, converting, storing and providing information in a computer format that is standardized, organized and available on demand from common system. With specialized scanner's, manuscripts are converted into compressed digital signals and stored systematically for future reference. The MRCs are digitizing most important manuscripts identified by the experts.

Visveshvaranand Viswa Bandhu Institute of Sanskrit & Indological Studies, Hoshiarpur (Punjab)

The Manuscript Resource Centre (MRC) from the north-west zone of the country was started in September 2003. It has a rich collection of about 3000 manuscripts pertaining to different subjects such as Veda, Upanishads, Puranas, astrology, astronomy, and ayurveda among others. It has been collecting information on manuscripts through surveys and writing letters to different institutions and has been successful in collecting 14,000 manuscripts from different collections in places such as Chandigarh, Patiala, Ludhiana, and Hoshiarpur. This MRC identified institutional and personal collections of manuscripts in Patiala of M.M. Central Sate Library, State Language Department and personal collection of Prof. Pritam Singh, a renowned scholar. Prof. Pritam Singh wanted to handover his collection of manuscripts to the Punjabi University, Patiala but changed his mind when manuscripts of Prof. Puran Singh went missing from this library. The largest collection of manuscripts is with Central State Library. A professionally trained team of NMM visited Patiala to help in preserving these collections.

Challenges and Suggestions

The biggest challenge for the experts was to determine the subject and identify the time period. In many manuscripts time period is mentioned in the text somewhere, but sometimes it is not. In the second phase after identification, introduction and an abstract of the manuscripts is prepared. Regarding preservation of manuscripts also, in the second phase those manuscripts which are in very bad condition are identified and chemically treated. Efforts are made to preserve these manuscripts permanently by scanning and digitizing them. NMM has yet to decide on the second phase regarding manuscripts at M.M. Central State Library, Patiala. The most vital issue is of providing access to these manuscripts and ascertaining their use also. NMM is spending large sum of money on the preservation and conservation of these manuscripts. It is essential to determine the relevance of these manuscripts in the present context. There should be an overall policy in detail concerning manuscripts. There is need for training the staff of M.M. Central State Library. One or two professionally trained conservators could be attached with the Reference Section of the library to preserve and conserve these manuscripts. The library should generate resources from other agencies to scan these manuscripts and digitize them and make these available on CD's so that original ones are preserved. An e-catalogue of complete collection should be prepared and made available via the web. The M.M. Central State Library should develop its web page and put whatever information it has about its rare collection including manuscripts. Last but not the least, there should be a disaster management plan for the library to preserve these relics of past.

Conclusion

A new horizon has been opened before the library professionals and information scientists not only to conserve the library materials by using IT but also to provide better services for the fragile documents and non book material to the reading communities with this technology.

Manuscript Collections in Indian Public Libraries

27

RANI SYAMALAMBA

Introduction

India is a land of many languages. Each language has many dialects. Varieties of writings in different genres of literature have been produced in each of the Indian languages over several centuries. Each language has developed its own script, even with different regional variations. Before the advent of the printing machine the scripts of various languages remained in non-standardized varying forms changing from region to region and from era to era. Sanskrit has remained the only pan-Indian language of our ancient and medieval literature. Literary outputs in Sanskrit are found written in various scripts throughout the length and breadth of India. They are preserved in old palm leaf and birch leaf manuscripts. To decipher the varying scripts of ancient and medieval languages in India requires a special skill.

India's manuscripts spread all over the country and abroad, are composed in different Indian languages such as Sanskrit, Pali, Prakrit, Urdu, Persian and the different regional Indian languages. They are written in different scripts such as *Brahmi, Sarada, Modi, Newari, Grantha* among others. Given India's immense linguistic diversity and sophistication, many documents are inaccessible because there is little knowledge of the languages and scripts used.

History

From early times onwards, efforts have been made to collect, store and preserve the manuscripts in libraries inside and outside India. In the second half of the 18th century, a few British officers such as Sir William Jones (1746-1794), Sir Robert Chambers (1774-1779), Colin Mackenzie (1782-1806) took a deep interest in Indian culture. They tried to get acquainted with the Sanskrit language and literature, and started collecting inscriptions, epigraphs, and manuscripts privately. An institution named as "The Asiatic Society of Bengal" was established in 1781 with as one of its aims the collection and preservation of valuable manuscripts, a huge number of which was lying in the houses of scholars, in schools and patashalas, in religious matas, monasteries, temples, palace and village libraries in Bengal and different parts of India. Later on, in the latter half of the 19th century, the then Government of India took an active part and allocated funds for the collection of manuscripts. Scholars such as G. Bühler, A.C. Burnell, R.G. Bhandarkar, R.L. Mitra, F. Kielhorn, G. Oppert, G.B. Malleson and few others were deputed to tour in different provinces of India in search of manuscripts, to make a list of the available ones and to purchase the more important of them. Since then the mission of the collection, preservation, and cataloguing of manuscripts, and the preparation of critical editions of important texts conserved in them, is going on, in and outside India by scholar's world wide with an interest to protect and study this rich cultural heritage.

With the exception of a few royal or scholarly manuscript collections, most of the manuscripts in the major manuscripts depositories today are derived from individual collections of priestly or other Brahmin householders.

India perhaps has one of the oldest and largest collections of manuscripts in the world. These manuscripts are in different languages and in different scripts. They are written on different kinds of material like birch bark, palm leaf, cloth and paper. They are in the custody of different institutions like libraries, museums, monasteries, mutts and individuals. Only a small percentage of these manuscripts have been surveyed and catalogued. Catalogues are perhaps available for not more than 20-25% of the manuscript collections in the country. The catalogues do not follow a standard format. A significant proportion of manuscripts are not preserved scientifically. Experts estimate that almost all palm leaf manuscripts may perish due to wear and fear over the next 50 to 100 years. An estimate of heritage wealth of India is as under:

Total number of manuscripts in India	5,000,000
Indian manuscripts available in European countries	60,000
Indian manuscripts in South Asia and Asian countries	150,000
Number of manuscripts recorded in catalogues	1,000,000 (approx.)
Percentage of manuscripts language wise Sanskrit	67%
Other Indian Languages	25%
Arabic/Persian/Tibetan	8%

Indira Gandhi National Centre for the Arts (IGNCA) has covered around 2,50,000 manuscripts. Indian National Trust for Art and Cultural Heritage (INTACH) has already surveyed more than 300 sites in three districts and prepared an inventory of about 47,000 palm leaf and paper manuscripts.

Manuscript collection in Indian Public Libraries

India has produced a large wealth of literature in the form of manuscripts over 5000 years. These manuscripts cover a broad range of subjects relating to Astronomy, Art and Architecture, Philosophy, Music, Ayurveda, literature, medicine, Tanta etc. A brief description is given below to know about the present scenario of Manuscript Public Libraries in India.

1. Saraswathi Bhawan Library, Varanasi

Saraswathi Bhavan Library established at the time of the establishment of the Govt. Sanskrit College. The foundation stone of the building was laid on the occasion of the visit of prince and princess of Wales on 16 Nov., 1907. The building was completed in 1914 and it was named "The Prince of Wales Saraswati Bhavana". The library underwent a number of changes after the establishment of the University. Six years after the University came into its existence a large new building was constructed to accommodate printed books. The famed Saraswati Bhavan building was earmarked for manuscripts only. In 1988-89 an air-conditioned building was constructed for its preservation and maintenance. This is perhaps biggest manuscript library in India, which has collection of about 1,50,000 manuscripts in different disciplines of knowledge and in various scripts like Bengali, Devanagari, Maithili, Newari.

The library has a collection of more than one lakh manuscripts of different sanskrit texts. In its printed Section there are more than one lakh ninety thousand printed books. There is also the facility for filming and photostat of manuscripts. Since its inception the Saraswati Bhavana has been the centre of study for serious Indian and Western scholars.

2. Khuda Baksh Oriental Public Library, Patna

This Library is recognized world over for its rich collection of individual manuscripts, rare printed books, many miniatures and paintings of Hindu Gods and original paintings of Mughal, Rajput, Turkish and Iranian schools.

Close to the banks of the Ganges in Patna, stands the Khuda Bakhsh Oriental Public Library a unique repository of about 21,000 Oriental manuscripts and 2.5 lakh printed books. Though founded earlier, it was opened for public in October, 1891 by the illustrious son of Bihar Khan Bahadur Khuda Bakhsh with 4,000 manuscripts, of which he inherited 1,400 from his father Maulvi Mohammed Bakhsh.

Khuda Baksh Khan donated his entire personal collection to the people of Patna by a deed of trust. Acknowledging the immense historical and intellectual value of its rich and valued collection, the Govt. of India declared the Library an Institution of National importance by an act of Parliament in 1969. The Library is now fully funded by the Ministry of Culture, Government of India.

This autonomous institution is being governed by a Board with the Governor of Bihar as its ex-officio Chairman and the responsibility of day-to-day management of Library affairs is entrusted to Director, Khuda Bakhsh Library.

The Library specializes in Islamic Studies, Tibb (Unani Medicine), Tazkira (Biography), Tasawwuf (Islamic Mysticism), Comparative religions, Medieval History, South East Asian History, West Asian History, Central Asian History, Medieval Science, Literature on Freedom Movement and National Integration as also Urdu, Persian and Arabic Literatures.

It contains about 21,000 manuscripts in Arabic, Persian, Urdu, Turkish, Hindi and Sanskrit and Palm-Leaves. It includes splendours of arts of Iranian, Mughal, Central Asian, Kashmiri and Rajasthani schools besides Calligraphic Masterpieces.

3. The Bhandarker Oriental Research Institute, Pune

The Bhandarkar Oriental Research Institute (BORI), Pune was founded on July 06, 1917, in commemoration of the name and work of Ramakrishna Gopal Bhandarkar (1837-1925). The Institute receives grants from the Government of India, the University Grants Commission, public trusts like the Sanmati Teertha, and individual donors, for its specific projects.

For understanding the history and the cultural heritage of a country, the literary treasure enshrined in Manuscripts forms as precious a means as stone-monuments or other antiquities. In India, for nearly 4,000 years, Sanskrit with its derived (Indo-Aryan) languages and the languages of the Dravidian family have been continually active in producing an enormous (and varied) literature. Through different stages of civilisation, the material used for writing in India was quite varied, being mainly palm leaf (taala-patra), birch bark (bhuurja-patra), stone, metal (like taamrapatra), and lastly, from the 10th century A.D. onwards, paper. The Institute's library possesses a rich collection of 1,05,000 books on Orientology, and regularly receives a large number of research journals.

Apart from the gift which it received, on the very foundation day, of the personal library of Bhandarkar, which was a precious collection of about 2500 books and bound volumes of journals, the then British Government, out of confidence in the young band of the founders of the Institute, entrusted in 1918, its rare Collection of

Manuscripts (earlier housed in the then Deccan College) to the custody of the Institute for better care and preservation.

The Bombay Government's entire collection of nearly 20,000 manuscripts, which was transferred to the Institute, was earlier acquired through strenuous tours and wanderings by great Indologists and Professors like George Bühler, R.G. Bhandarkar, P. Peterson, F. Kielhorn, V.S. Ghate, and A.V. Kathavate. About 10,000 new manuscripts have been added to this original stock later through fresh acquisitions by the Institute's workers, and this activity continues till today to enrich the total collection.

These manuscripts (on birch bark, palm leaf, and paper) cover a wide variety of subjects and branches like: religious works in the Devanagari script in Sanskrit, Pali and Prakrit languages from the Hindus, the Buddhas and the Jainas, Muslim religious works in the Arabic and Farsi scripts, literary works in the Sharada, Devanagari, Malayalam, Tamil, Telegu and Kannada scripts, Vedic literature, Puraanic texts, and works on grammar, music, drama, stotras, tantra, medicine, and philosophical systems. The Institute feels proud of possessing some old and unique MSS on paper, palm-leaf and birch-bark.

The Institute's Archives have a separate section of about 400 manuscripts in Farsi and Arabic. This section contains copies of Farsi translation of the Gita and the Yogavaasishtha, made by Dara Shukoh 340 years ago, a copy of the Vishnu Puraana translated into Persian by a Kashmiri Pandit, a manuscript relating to horse-breeding written by Qazi Hasan Iftakhan 390 years ago, and an original manuscript bearing the seal of the royal library of Emperor Jahangir. The Archives also contain two clay tablets of 600 B.C., similar to those found in Egypt, Assyria and Babylon.

4. Thanjavur Maharaja Serfoji's Saraswathi Mahal Library, Thanjavur

The Thanjavur Maharaja Serfoji's Sarasvati Mahal Library is one among a few medieval libraries existing in the world. It is an unparalleled repository of culture and an inexhaustible treasure house of knowledge built up by successive dynasties of Nayaks and the Marathas of Thanjavur. It contains very rare and valuable collections of manuscripts, books, maps and paintings on all aspects of Art, Culture and Literature.

The Major parts of the manuscripts are in Sanskrit language, which exceed 39,300 and written in Grantha, Devanagari, Nandinagari, Telugu scripts. The total number of Tamil manuscripts is 3780 comprising titles of literature and medicine. This Library has a collection of 3076 Marathi manuscripts of South Indian Maharastrian of the 17th, 18th, and 19th centuries and the hierarchy of the Saints of Maharashtra belonging to Sri Ramadasi and Dattatreya Mutts. The Marathi manuscripts are mostly on paper and a few in palm-leaf, written in Telugu script. There are 846 Telugu manuscripts in this Library, which are mostly on palm leaf and a few in papers.

Apart from these manuscripts there are 1342 bundles of Maratha Raj records available at the Library. The Raj records were written in the Modi script (fast script for Devanagari) of the Marathi language. These records encompass the information of the political, cultural and social administration of the Maratha kings of Thanjavur. The Manuscripts have been classified as–

Palm Leaf Manuscripts: Palm leaves were commonly used as writing material in ancient India and were known as tada patra, tala patra or panna. The leaves of the palm tree, available all over India, were collected and dried and cut into the same convenient length. Two holes were made to pass a string, which tied the leaves together.

Paper Manuscripts: Paper was introduced quite late in India, but had appeared by the time Ekoji I took over Thanjavur. It was made by hand from cellulose vegetable material; masi or mela was the ink used for writing, available in red, black, gold and silver. The permanent black ink was prepared by mixing the lamp soot of sesame (Sesamum indicum) oil with the gum of acacia and rainwater. The pens were made of either wood, bamboo or goose quill. The papers were dipped in turmeric water for protection from insects.

Sanskrit Manuscripts: The Sanskrit Collection of the Sarasvati Mahal, which is largest in the collection, contains not only the major works of Sanskrit literature beginning with the Vedas but is also especially noteworthy for the history of later Sanskrit literature and copies of works which were produced directly under the patronage of the Telugu and Maratha Rajas of Thanjavur. The manuscripts are in palm leaf and paper form which are written in Devanagari, Nandinagari, Grantha and Telugu scripts.

A few outstanding works whose manuscripts are unique to the Sarasvati Mahal are rare and short lexicons, the grammar of the rare dialect called Bhandira-bhasha, the play Jambavatiparinaya of King Krishnadevaraya, Vivaranadarpana of Rangaraja, father of the great Appayya Dikshita, the prose work of Krishna Charita of Agastyapandita, the allegorical play Bhavanapurushottama of Ratnakheta Srinivasa Dikshitar, some rare works of the great Appayya Dikshitar, Tattvachintamanivyakhya (logic) by Dharmarajadhvarin, poetess Ramabhadramba's biographical poem on her patron King Raghunatha Nayak, Vatttikabharana (mimamsa) of Venkatamakhin and works of Ramabhadra Dikshita and Sadasiva Brahmendra Sarasvati. Short Advaita-Prakaranas in large number are also available in Sarasvati Mahal. One branch of literature in which the Sarasvati Mahal is especially rich in namely the Puranic accounts of the sanctity and legends of the great shrines and sacred villages and towns in which the Cauvery delta abounds. The oldest manuscripts in the Library are perhaps the Adwaita work, Bhamati of Vachaspatimisra, which was copied in Banaras in 1468 A.D. There is also a manuscript, attributed to the great Appayya Dikshitar. The post scripts in several manuscripts carry very interesting historical, biographical and other information relating to owners, copyists, date of copying, etc. One of these contains precious information about the great Sadasiva Brahmendra Sarasvati and his blessings to the King of Tanjore.

The Sanskrit Manuscript Collection of this Library dates back to 16th century A.D. The Manuscripts used by the Poets and Kings during the Nayak and Maratha period are preserved even today

Marathi Manuscripts: The Marathi Paper Manuscripts collected during the reign of Marathas of Thanjavur i.e., from 1676 to 1855 A.D. are preserved in this Library. They are 1856 in number. They are all the works of the saint poets of Ramadasi and Dattatreya Mutts. Later on, when the Library was opened for public in 1919 A.D., Marathi Manuscripts from Pandits and Scholars besides those of the Mutts, were received as donation and even now preserved well. They are 1220 in number. The total number of 3076 Marathi Paper Manuscripts are compiled in 6 volumes of catalogues called "The Descriptive Catalogue of Marathi Manuscripts" and classified into many subjects like Philosophy, Literature, Drama, Music, Lexicon, Medicine, Science, etc. The Marathi Manuscripts in palm leaf are written in Telugu script. They deal with Marathi musical dance dramas.

The works composed by the poets of Thanjavur are not available in Maharashtra. So they are rare manuscripts. "The Ramayana" and "Mahabharata" by Madhava Swami, "Avadhuta Gita Tika" and "Ramasohala" by Meru Swami, "Sri Ramakrupa vilas" by Mukunda Swami, "Aatmabodha" by Raghava Swami and "Bhagvat Gita" by Ananta Mouni are some of the note worthy works.

Tamil Manuscripts

The Tamil Manuscript Section comprises of 3780 manuscripts of which 2083 are Literary and the rest are Medical. All these are in palm leaf and are of the following categories:

a. Rare Works like Kambaramayana, Kalingathu Bharani, Moovarula, etc., are available in palm leaf manuscripts.

b. Unpublished portions of classics.

c. Saiva, Vaishnava and Jain works.

d. Later poetry of all descriptions.

So far, 20 volumes of Descriptive Catalogues are published. Some of the rare works belonging to the Imperial Chola period are written in manipravala style. The medical manuscripts written by the Tamil scholars like Kottaiyur Sivakolundu Desikar were based on the process made in the Dhanvantri Mahal Hospital. Sivarahasyam, which was written during Serfoji I, is one of the oldest Tamil manuscripts, Kumbakonap-puranam, Sarabhendra Bhoopala Kuravanchi are the notable manuscripts. The 18th century "Kambaramayanam" palm leaf manuscript with 537 leaves and seven khandas is also a typical one. In 'Thiruvaimozhi vacaka malai' the line drawing of Lord Renganatha with his consorts can be seen.

Dhanvantari Mahal: Sage Dhanvantri was the father of Indian medicine. To honour the memory of Dhanvantri Raja Serfoji ran a medical institution called "Dhanvantri Mahal" besides research on many ailments, excellent work was done on diseases like cancer, polio, diabetes and tuberculosis by the Institution of Ayurvedic and Siddha medicines. Raja devoted himself to the progress of research in Dhanvantri Mahal by bringing together Siddha, Ayurveda and Unani physicians of repute. As a result of physicians discussion, the best among tried and effective remedies are embodied in the series of works named Sarabhendra Vaidhya Muraigal. These works are composed in lucid Tamil verse form to facilitate easy memorisation. This Library has published many of them. The Dhanvantri Mahal also had a wing of research for animal husbandry. Many prescriptions for the disease of domestic as well as wild animals and birds show the broad scope of interests supported by the Rajah and implemented by the Dhanvantri Mahal. The concept of research, especially of a clinical nature is comparatively modern. Some modern systems carry out research only on rabbits and other animals. But at a comparatively early period Rajah Serfoji's doctors were confident enough to use their drugs on human beings.

Telugu Manuscripts: The Tanjore Telugu manuscripts collection is unique and it represented the home productions of royal patrons of art, their court Pandits and other scholars domiciled in the Tanjore country. It may be said that the collection represents the southern school of Telugu literature.

The Telugu Manuscript section deal with Padya Kavyas, Dvipada Kavyas, Satakas, Yakshaganas, Astrology, Medical, etc. The works of Nannaiya, Tikkanna, Bodanna, Krishnadevaraya, and Vijayaraghava Nayak are also available. These are the most valuable collection of manuscripts particularly relating to the Southern School of Telugu Literature. These manuscripts are catalogued in two volumes. The Bhagavata mela tradition of dramas was first written in Telugu language and lot of dramas is available in palm leaf manuscripts.

Persian and Urdu: This Library has 22 Persian and Urdu manuscripts mostly of 19th century. Some of the manuscripts have illustrations. Important manuscripts in this collection are:

1. Firdausi's Shahnamah
2. Life of Gajni Mohammed.

Hindi Manuscripts: This Library also has more than 100 Hindi manuscripts, which deal with dramatic and historical subjects.

Other Manuscripts: Along with the above, manuscripts in Sanskrit, Tamil, Telugu and Marathi languages written in various scripts like Grantha, Devanagari, Nandinagari, Tamil, Telugu, Malayalam, Oriya, Bengali, Burmese are also in this Library.

5. Adyar Library, Chennai

The Adyar Library and Research Centre was founded in 1886 by Colonel Olcott with a small but valuable collection of the Founders' books. Originally situated in the Headquarters building, it was shifted in 1968 to a more spacious one, better suited to its growing needs. It has always been one of the important aspects of the work at Adyar, both for members and for the public; moreover, today it is one of the most important oriental libraries in the world, dedicated to research and publication in the field of eastern civilization, philosophy and religion. It contains over 250,000 printed volumes and nearly 20,000 palm-leaf manuscripts from India, Sri Lanka, China, and other places, a few of which are kept on display for visitors. The printed books include rare indological publications in several languages and a fine collection of works on different religions, philosophies and cultures. Several rare and previously unpublished works in the manuscript collection have been edited and brought out in print; a staff of pundits and scholars is continually engaged on this task. The Library has had a series of distinguished scholars as its Director and is recognized as a Research Centre for a Ph.D. in Sanskrit and Indology by the University of Madras.

6. The Government Oriental Manuscript Library, Chennai

The Government Oriental Manuscripts Library is one of the world's largest and best manuscript library. It was established in 1867 in the western wing of the first floor of the Madras University. It has mainly three important collections.

1. The Colonel Colin Mackenzie's Collection (1754-1821)
2. East India House Dr. Leyden's Collection (1803-1811) and
3. The C.P. Brown's Collection (1798-1814)

The Col. Mackenzie's precious Dravidian Collection consists of 1500 manuscripts. There are total 50,000 palm leaf manuscripts, 20,000 paper manuscripts and 20,000 books in the library. Most of the manuscripts are not decoded yet. It also contains the manuscripts of works in literature, history, philosophy and science, which are written in South Indian and Oriental languages as well as in Kaifiyats. The inscriptions found in many places belong to different periods.

Colonel Colin Mackenzie came to India in 1783 as a cadet of Engineers on the Madras Establishment of the East India Company. He was interested in the study of ancient mathematics, logarithm in particular and in Oriental languages. He had a collection of numerous manuscripts, coins, inscriptions, maps, etc. These had information on the literature, religion, history, manners and customs of the people not only from different parts of India but also from Ceylon and Java. During his service as Surveyor-General of India in 1818, Colonel Mackenzie he brought all the precious collections with him to Calcutta and went on adding more to them till he died in 1821. The East India Company bought these collections from Mrs Mackenzie in 1821 for 10,000 pounds. They parted into three divisions of which one part was retained in London, the other parts were sent to Calcutta and Madras.

A collection of manuscripts in Tamil, Telugu and Kannada characters was noticed by C.P. Brown in the India Office Library, London. These were the collection of Dr. Leyden, who was a notable linguist and traveller. These were kept at the India House, London by East India Company. Later, CP Brown, who was in Indian Civil Service brought them to India. He gifted these valuable collections of paper manuscripts of Sanskrit and Telugu works to the East India Company in 1855. In 1869 a full blown library was set up. In 1870, all the collections were taken to the Presidency College. Almost 7,000 manuscripts in Telugu, Kannada and Malayalam were transferred to Andhra Pradesh, Karnataka and Kerala respectively. Besides this, 22,887 printed books are available for reference in the Government Oriental Manuscripts library. It now consists of 71180 manuscripts in Telugu (2150), Sanskrit (48884), Tamil (16398), Kannada (250), Marathi (956), Urdu (184), Arabic (407), Persian (1390), other Oriental languages (127) and local records (434).

The Government Oriental Manuscripts Library has numerous rare and valuable palm-leaf manuscripts, which are very carefully preserved by manual and chemical methods. The damaged paper manuscripts are repaired with chiffon cloth and preserved carefully. The Oriental Manuscripts Library publishes multilingual bulletin annually, which consists of rare and unpublished manuscripts in various languages. Till today, total 21 volumes of this bulletin have been published. The library has published total 350 publications till now, which includes descriptive and triennial catalogues of its manuscripts in various languages. These are published under two categories named—the Government Oriental manuscripts series and Government Oriental Series.

The Government Oriental Manuscripts Library is a government institution headed by the Curator under the control of the Director of Archaeology, Government of Tamilnadu.

7. Anup Sanskrit Library, Bikaner

Anup Sanskrit Library is housed in a wing of the Lalgarh Palace called Sadul Niwas. This historical and cultural attraction at Bikaner, Rajasthan preserves a priceless collection of rare Sanskrit manuscripts. The texts in the library were brought from Deccan by Raja Anup Singh in the 17th century. This rare specimen, counted among the best, are inscribed on parchments or engraved on copper, gold and silver plaques. Visitors are admitted to the library during the day for a nominal fee. It has got a collection of 11,000 manuscripts.

8. Rampur Raza Library, Rampur

The Rampur Raza Library is a treasure house of Indo Islamic learning and Art. It was founded by Nawab Faizullah Khan in 1774 AD. His descendants continued to enrich the collection. After the independence and merger of Rampur State in the Union of India, the library was brought under the management of a Trust till the Government of India took over the library on 1st July 1975 under the Act of Parliament which declared it as an institution of National importance. Its affairs are managed by the Rampur Raza Library Board whose Chairman is the Governor of Uttar Pradesh.

Famous for its varied collection of manuscripts, the library has 17,000 such specimens of artistic creation which include 150 illustrated ones with 4413 paintings in them. The subjects of the manuscripts are related to History, Philosophy, religions, sciences, art, literature, medicine, astronomy, astrology, mathematics, geology, fine arts, etc.

In addition to them, there are 205 hand-written palm-leaves, 5000 miniature paintings, nearly 3000 specimens of Islamic Calligraphy. The miniature paintings represent the Turko-Mongol, Mughal, Persian, Rajput, Pahari, Awadh and Indo-European schools of art which are of great value for the researchers. The rich collection also includes art objects and astronomical instruments.

The Library has a collection of about 75,000 printed books. The printed book section has a unique importance as thousands of rare Arabic, Persian, Hindi, Urdu and English books which are now out of print, may be treated as an important material for research work.

9. Rajasthan Oriental Research Institute, Jodhpur

Rajasthan Oriental Research Institute is an initiative of the Government of Rajasthan. The Institute was established as Sanskrit Mandal in 1950 and extended as a full-fledged department in 1954 with a view to explore, collect, preserve, edit and publish ancient literature of Rajasthan and adjacent areas available in Sanskrit, Prakrit,

Apbhramsa and Hindi-Rajasthani. It has a large reference library comprising of 26,713 rare titles and 6,000 periodicals. With seven branch repositories at Bikaner, Jaipur, Bharatpur, Kota, Chittorgarh, Udaipur, Alwar having a collection of 1,19,830 manuscripts including 1011 illustrated manuscripts on different subjects like the Vedas, dharmashastra, itihasa, purana, tantra, mantra, darshana, jyotisha and ayurveda, the Institute has published 130 Descriptive Catalogues and published critical editions of more than 200 important texts.

The rich manuscripts in the collection of the Rajasthan Oriental Institute include miniature versions with Pala, Western Indian, Rajput, Kangra and Jammu and Kashmir schools of painting on palm, birch-bark, paper, wood and cloth. There is an excellent calligraphy text called Dvipath, Tripath and Panchpath. Some unique specimens are Arsha-Ramayana, Gita Govinda (Mewar school), illuminated Kalpasutra of VS 1485, Buddhist manuscript Arya Mahavidya, illustrated Bhagwata among others. An authenticated manuscript of Prithviraj Raso from Dharnoj village of Gujrat and a number of manuscripts written profusely in gold ink are also worth mentioning.

Rajasthan Oriental Research Institute started functioning as a Manuscript Resource Centre in September 2003. With the active participation of the affiliate branches spread across Rajasthan, the MRC has been able to document 61,732 manuscripts so far. The MRC has enriched the Mission database by producing electronic data for 39,277 manuscripts. The Institute explored thirteen districts including Dholpur, Alwar, Jaipur, Kota and Bikaner and managed to cover sixty-eight institutions and eighteen private collections during survey. The seven awareness campaigns conducted by the MRC have unearthed information on fresh data concerning manuscripts.

10. National Library, Calcutta

The National Library, India is the largest library in the country. It is an institution of National importance under the 'Department of Culture, Ministry of Tourism & Culture, and Government of India'. The library is designated to collect, disseminate and preserve the printed material produced in the country. The library is situated on a scenic 30 acres Belvedere Estate, in Kolkata, formerly Calcutta City.

The National Library has innumerable number of rare books and other reading materials. Earlier, these items were stacked with other books. But, in 1973, a separate Rare Books Division was established to take care of the rare books. At present the books published prior to 1860 are considered as rare books. Along with such materials, manuscripts and microfilms of the library are also stacked in this division.

National Library has about 3600 rare and historically important manuscripts in different languages. These manuscripts are preserved separately along with other important and rare books in the Rare Books Division. The xylographs presented by H.E. the Dalai Lama are also preserved in this collection.

The library has a rich collection of maps. The collection ranges from 17th century onwards. Indian topographical sheets of earlier days (at scale of one inch, half inch and quarter inch to a mile) and maps of natural resources, population, transport and communication systems, agricultural production, Soil, Vegetation and Geology of India form the major part of the collection. At present the library has 85, 000 printed maps, 54 cartographic manuscripts and 280 atlases.

11. Oriental Research Institute, Sri Venkateswara University, Tirupati

The Oriental Research Institute in Sri Venkateswara University, Tirupati was established by Tirumala Tirupati Devasthanam in 1939 and was handed over to Sri Venkateshwara University in 1956. Set up with the objectives of furthering Indological research and propagating Indian culture and heritage, the Institute has become a nucleus for advanced research in the area.

Oriental Research Institute has a rich collection of 50,000 palm-leaf and paper manuscripts and 75,000 rare printed books in its library. The Institute has published one tabular alphabetical catalogue covering all the subjects. The manuscripts in the collection cover a wide range from philosophy, religion, epic, language, grammar to poetics and horoscopy.

The Manuscript Resource Centre (MRC) at Oriental Research Institute, Tirupati has been working together with the National Manuscript Mission (NMM) since September 2003. The MRC has so far documented 20,000 manuscripts in Telugu and Sanskrit manuscripts. Data pertaining to 3556 manuscripts have been entered in to e-granthavali data base. The survey taken up by the Institute has extended to eighteen institutions and nine private collections covering three districts of the State. It has held two awareness campaigns and sensitization programmes through newspaper and TV channels. This created a good response in the area, especially in research scholars, teachers and manuscript holders.

In order to step up the efforts at locating, documenting and preserving India's manuscripts, the Mission has launched a pilot survey in three states - Orissa, Bihar and Uttar Pradesh. As with any pilot project, the Mission has experimented with formats and programmes and finally evolved a model for future surveys of this scale with the cooperation and inputs of our partners in the three states.

In Orissa, the Survey has been conducted in all 30 districts, while in Bihar, in 10 districts and in Uttar Pradesh, in 13 districts. In these 53 districts, approximately

2700 surveyors have been employed for a period of 5 days, resulting in the unearthing of information on 6,50,000 manuscripts and about 35, 000 repositories. During the survey itself, about 1,00,000 manuscripts have documented.

To create new networks of survey, documentation, cataloguing and awareness among the people and to help the stakeholders of manuscripts, the Mission has set up twenty-seven Manuscript Resource Centres (MRC-s) across the country. The Manuscript Resource Centres are mostly established in universities, renowned research institutions and established non-governmental organizations engaged in work relating to manuscripts.

12. State Central Library, Hyderabad

State Central library was established during 1891 by name 'Asifia Library' by Nizams. It has a collection of 4,41,600 books in different languages. This library is having the rich collection of 17,000 manuscripts written in various south Indian scripts such as Telugu, Malayalam, Tamil and Kannada scripts. Scanning centre has been established here to scan rare books as a pilot project. In 1975, the Andhra Pradesh State Central Library transferre its Arabic script manuscript collection to the newly formed Oriental Manuscripts Library and Research Centre (OMLRI). In April 1997, it is moved to a purpose-built building on the Osmania University Campus.

Following are the other places where we can see manuscript collection in Andhra Pradesh:

Andhra Pradesh Government Oriental Manuscripts Library and Research Institute (OMLRI), Osmania University Campus, Hyderabad

In 1975, the Andhra Pradesh State Central Library, formerly known as the Asafiya Library, transferred its Arabic script manuscript collection to the newly formed OMLRI. In April 1997, it moved to a purpose-built building on the Osmania University Campus. The total number of manuscripts available here are 23,000.

Andhra Pradesh State Archives, Tarnaka, Hyderabad

The State Archives was established in the 18th century in the Nizam's Dominion through the merger of various departmental depositories. It has a large collection of state papers in Persian and Urdu, but fewer manuscripts. The present institution and building dates from1956 and 1965 respectively.

Andhra Pradesh State Museum, Public Gardens, Hyderabad

The Museum was established in 1930 as the Hyderabad State Museum. The name was changed in 1956 to the present name. There are 117 Manuscripts are available in this museum.

Idarah-yi Ihya al-Maarif al-Numaniya, Jalal Kucha, Hyderabad

It was established by Abu al-Wafa al-Afghani, a scholar from Afghanistan domiciled in Hyderabad. He passed away in 1976. This institution contains several manuscripts, as yet uncataloged or listed.

Idarah-i Adabiyat-i Urdu, Iwan-i Urdu, Panjagutta, P.O. Somajiguda, Hyderabad

The Idarah was established in 1931 by Sayyid Muhi al-Din Qadiri Zor and his colleagues. Besides Urdu, it has manuscripts in Arabic and Persian. Manuscript collection is 1426.

Kutub Khanah-i Rawdat al-Hadith, Rain Bazaar, Hyderabad

It is under the control of Muslim Waqf Board. The collection of 800 manuscripts is housed in a building inappropriate for the purpose.

Osmania University Library, Osmania University Campus, Hyderabad

The University was established in 1918, and the library was located in the College of Arts. Since 1963, it is housed in the present purpose-built facility. There are 3418 manuscripts in this library.

Saidiya Library, 5-6-175 Aghapura, Hyderabad

The library was founded by Mufti Muhammad Said Khan, (1831-95), a judge of Hyderabad High Court. It was opened in 1935 by members of the Mufti Said Khan's family. It used to be located in the Jam Bagh/Troop Bazaar in the heart of the city. However, on 9 September 1984, a mob of crazed fanatics burned down a portion of the library, destroying a number of precious manuscripts. Since then it is located in the private home of Mr. Ahmad Ataullah. There are 3141 manuscripts available here.

Salar Jang Museum and Library, Hyderabad

The museum and the library rich in Arabic script manuscripts is the collection of Nawab Mir Yusuf Ali Khan Salar Jang III, (1888-1949) an important nobleman and diwan of Hyderabad. Some of the collection had began long before Salar Jang III, in fact it started at least with his grandfather, Salar Jang I, better known to Hdyerabadis as Mukhtar al-Mulk. The collection is 10000.

Urdu Research Center, Sundarayya Vignana Kendram, Bagh Lingampalli Hyderabad

This is a library and research center founded by Muhammad Abdussamad Khan, a bibliophile and automobile mechanic who started collecting since 1965. After various locations, the collection called Urdu Research Center moved to Sundarayya Vignana

Kendram, a research center named after a Communist Party (Marxist) of India leader. There are more than 250 Manuscripts are available here.

Indian Institute of History of Medicine, Hyderabad

The Institute which is only one of its kind in the whole of South East Asia has of late been recognized as a national historical archives and resource centre in literary research in ISM. The Institute's Library housed in Osmania Medical College Building Campus is one of the richest Libraries on History of Medicine and now possesses some of the antique and rare manuscripts on Indian Medicine. Although presently it has around 200 original manuscripts and another 100 manuscripts on microfilms yet in the years to come the Institute envisages to procure huge manuscripts wealth as soon as it acquire its own building.

The Institute has compiled a checklist of Sanskrit Medical Manuscripts containing details of 108 manuscripts held in 25 repositories/collection, which presently is under revision. The revised version is expected to cover the details of around 4000 manuscripts titles. Of late preparation of the descriptive catalogue of manuscripts held in the Institute's archive has also been initiated.

Dr. V.S. Krishna Library, Andhra University

There are nearly 2,500 manuscripts with the AU library, the oldest being a 17th century manuscript. A Manuscripts Conservation Partner Centre at which a team of officials from the Salar Jung Museum led by Chief Curator Md. Ali started a two-month training programme for the staff of the AU library on preservation of paper, palm leaf and cloth manuscripts in October 2006.

Conclusion

India has the largest collection of manuscripts in the world. They are spread all over the country and also abroad in different libraries, academic institutions, museums, temples and monasteries and in private collections. The rich manuscript wealth of India today faces a threat of survival. The invaluable heritage of India in the form of manuscripts has to be documented, preserved and made accessible to us and to succeeding generations.

Bibliography

1. Prof. Sasikala, C & Anuradha, R. Preserving and Accessing the Manuscript collections effectively through Digital Initiatives. Conference papers of National Conference on Reorientation of Library Services in India, APLA, 2007, Vijavawada. pp. 351-359.

2. http://www.jamianizamia.org/jamiaa.htm
3. http://kblibrary.bih.nic.in/
4. http://www.sarasvatimahallibrary.tn.nic.in
5. http://www.ts-adyar.org/library.html
6. http://namami.nic.in
7. http://rori.nic.in
8. http://razalibrary.gov.in
9. http://namami.nic.in/National Survey of Manuscripts. htm
10. http://varanasi.nic.in
11. http://www.nlindia.org
12. http://business.vsn.com/netcity/sayeedia.htm
13. http://www.salarjungmuseum.com/
14. http://ccras.nic.in
15. http://asiaitsummit.nic.in/Digitisation

Manuscript Collections of South India

28

M.N. KRISHNAKUMAR

Indian Manuscript tradition shows an astonishing permanence and its immensity surpasses that of any other country. Manuscripts were an entity of high esteem. The offering of a manuscript was acknowledged as the best of gifts. There were an object of reverence and they were stored in the best room in the house; they were ornamented and well cared for. In the *Āgama* texts of south, there are detailed directions for the structure of the *Sarasvati Bhavana* an integral part of temples.

Collection of Manuscripts

One of the most vital tasks for who involved in the field of manuscript is to bring together the manuscripts from places where they are not set aside with sufficient care. If not, they may be lost for ever. Most of the private collections are of this kind. Palm-leaf manuscripts are found even now in many of the ancient families and in centers of devotion. Except in a few cases they are on the brink of total ruin. For the safety of the manuscripts and for their wider use by the scholarly world, such manuscripts need to be kept in the reputed manuscript libraries. The collection of manuscripts is not an easy task. Rules or procedures commonly applicable cannot be formulated since each case is different from the other. The places where manuscripts are found are termed as manuscript locations. The person who is engaged in the identification of manuscript locations and the collection of manuscripts can be called 'manuscript collector'. The people who inform the manuscript locations can be termed as 'informants'. The informants also act as connecting bridge between the manuscript collector and manuscript custodians.

The Past of Manuscript Collections

Before the beginning of printing and the successive establishment of libraries of printed books, manuscripts were foremost source for the diffusion and progression of knowledge. There were large collections of manuscripts in places like palaces, residences of Zamindars, temples and monasteries. In addition, manuscripts are found in the families of priests, scholars and professionals like traditional architects, astrologers, practitioners of Indian medicine etc.

Some of the European scholars and British officials of India took effort in collecting possessions from India. They showed particular interest in securing ancient manuscripts. British government gave ample support to them. These Europeans took away the manuscripts and other curios collected by them to their home lands. The European scholars and academicians show keen interest in the literatures of Sanskrit including the technical works. This resulted in frequent demands on India Government for ancient manuscripts of this country from different parts of the western world. Due to such tremendous pressure from various corners, the Government encouraged the collection and preservation of ancient Indian records and literary works.

The interest shown by the Indian government and the western scholars had a catalytic effect on the Indian scholars too in the field of manuscript collection. The attempts for collecting manuscripts and publishing them in India itself were started by the Indian and European scholars. In this regard, the services of Burnell, Bühler, F.Keilhorn, R.L.Mitra, R.G.Bhandarkar and Hara Prasad Shastri, are to be gratefully acknowledged. The efforts in this direction in the early part of 20th century by people like T. Ganapati Shastry, Sambasiva Shastry, R.A. Shastry, and U.V. Swaminatha Iyer are also to be remembered. The Provincial Governments gave enormous support to the efforts of collection and publication of manuscripts. For the reason that of the enthusiastic efforts of scholars and their accomplishment in these field, separate libraries for manuscripts came into existence at different places in India. The Governments of Bombay, Bengal, and Madras gave the lead in establishing manuscript libraries. Other provinces and princely states followed them. Sarfoji Maharaja's Sarasvati Mahal Library-Thanjavoor, Government Oriental Manuscripts Library-Chennai, Oriental Research Institute-Mysore, Oriental Research Institute and Manuscripts Library Thiruvananthapuram are a few such examples to mention. These Institutions were established not only for the collection of manuscripts but also for the publication of important manuscripts.

In this connection it is to be bear in mind that some of the kings of the princely states of India had taken keen interest and were models for others in collecting manuscripts from different sources. For instance, the king of Travancore had shown great interest in the collection and preservation of manuscripts. It can be seen that Shri Ayilyam Thirunal Ramavarm Maharaja (1860-1880) issued an order for collecting the manuscripts from private possessions and to keep them in the Palace Library. Shri Karthika Thirunal Ramavarama Maharaja (1758-1795) as a Yuvaraja had taken possession of all, the manuscripts from the principality of Ambalapuzha when that territory was conquered and added to Travancore. It was during the period of Shri Moolam Thirunal Maharaja (1885-1924) the Trivandrum Sanskrit series commenced in 1903 under the editorship of Dr. T. Ganapati Sastri. Like the Travancore kings some other rulers of the princely states too had taken much interest in the collection and preservation of manuscripts. An important name to be mentioned in this regard is Sarfoji Maharaja of Thanjavoor.

Extraordinary Centers of Manuscript Collections

I would like to share my experience in the field of manuscripts. I could find amazing manuscript collections in South India, which are very significant, usually not very much known to general public as well as scholars and researchers in this field. Most of these collections are private and having at least one rare manuscript with each libraries.

1. **Institute Francais de Pondicherry**: Collection of manuscripts at the French Institute of Pondicherry (IFP) began in 1955 at the instigation of its founder-director of the Ecole Francaise d'Extrême-Orient. His objective was to explain the Hindu temple and what happens in it. He focused his attention on collecting manuscripts of Śaiva texts, particularly those of Śaiva Siddhanta.

   Two large collections of palm-leaf and paper manuscripts are preserved in the French institutions of research in the South Indian Town of Pondicherry. The major collection is that of the French Institute, which comprises 8187 palm-leaf bundles 360 paper codices. These manuscripts are collected from the Tamil-speaking parts of South India. Nearly half of the material relates to one of the major theistic traditions of India that concerned with the worship of the God Śiva. It is in fact the largest collection in the world of manuscripts of texts of the Śaiva Siddhanta. Most of these codices are written in Grantha script, the script used by Tamilian Brahmins for writing Sanskrit; others are in Malayalam, Telugu, Nandinagari, Oriya and Tulu scripts.

   The Āgamas, the scriptures of Śaiva Siddhanta, were in the 1950s neglected and virtually unknown to most scholars of Sanskrit in India as well as in the West. It is the publications of the French Institutions of research in Pondicherry that have brought them to the attention of the scholarly world.

2. **Kilvezlur Balasubramnia Sivacariyar's Collection:** This is a traditional private collection owned from the forefathers by Śri Balasubramania Śivacariyar of Kilvelur, Nagapattinam district of Tamil Nadu. In this collection there are 57 bundles of palm-leaf manuscripts, most of them are belongs to the Śaiva Āgama subject, which is a part of Śaiva Siddhanta. This is the only manuscript collection

having all important texts of ritual part of Śaiva Āgama. Out of twenty eight Śaiva Āgama texts twenty one are available with this collection. These Grantha script texts are copied by French Institute of Pondicherry for their Āgama series publication.

Almost all manuscripts have been digitized by some institutions for their research purposes and also for preservation. Presently the owner has the digitized copies as well as the original form of palm leaf manuscripts which have to be preserved in a well manner.

3. **Sridurga Indological Research Institute:** This is a newly established (in 2006) private institute situated in a village called Nainaragaram near Tenkasi in Tirunelveli district of Tamil Nadu. This Institute is run by a trust named P.S. Krishna Iyer Memorial Trust. This institute's manuscript library is having a collection 1192 palm-leaf manuscripts. Large part of this collection is made by late Sri. P.S. Krishna Iyer. This Institute has been declared as 'Manuscript Partner Center' (MPC) by the National Mission for Manuscripts (NMM).

   Most of the manuscripts in this collection is belongs to the Vedic rituals such as Prayogā and Mantra Vādā. In this group there is one important manuscript named '*Vīrasimhāvalokanam*', which is a blend of Jyotiṣa, Mantra and Vaidya is available intact. This is also known as *Maṇi Mantra Auṣadha*. Some peculiar illustrated manuscripts also seen in this gathering.

   The present authorities of this institute are planning to preserve the whole collection by way of digitization. They are also trying to publish the rare manuscripts after a high end research and edit made by the renowned scholars.

4. **Nedumpilly Mana:** This is a famous Namputiri (Kerala Brahmin) home in a village near Irinjalakuda town of Trichur district in Kerala. This is the only family existing with Śrauta and Tantra in Vātūla branch. Here there is a manuscript collection as inheritance. Altogether 270 manuscripts are kept in this collection. Manuscripts on Vātūla śrauta rituals and Vātūla Tantra (Temple rituals of Malayalam region) are very rare. Prof Yashiki Ikkari from Japan has made some researches on these Malayalam scripted manuscripts. The present condition of these manuscripts is very pathetic. The owners are trying to get some grant from government authorities to preserve the precious manuscript legacy.

5. **Thaikkatuu Mana:** This is also a home collection situated in a village near Vattamkulam of Malappuram District in Kerala. There is a total collection of 235 manuscripts in this center. Most of them are belongs to ritual parts of both Śrauta and Grhya.

6. **Andaladi Maṇa:** This is one of the famous Tantric families in Kerala. This center located near Pattambi town in Palakkad district of Kerala. They are having a total collection 67 manuscripts and most of them are Tantra rituals which are using in the temples of central and northern part of Kerala. In this collection there is a unique manuscript named *Parameśvarānuṣthānam*, this is one and only available in total Manalayam Tantra manuscript collections.
7. **Vezhaparambu Mana**: This is also another huge Tantra manuscript collection placed near North Parur of Ernakulam district in Kerala. Here more than 320 manuscripts are available. Most of them are belongs to Tantra rituals of temples in middle and southern part of Kerala. Most of the bundles are in Malayalam script, some Grantha manuscript also available.
8. **Joglekar Family**: This is a fine Ṛg Vedic collection situated in the west coastal town called Gokarna in North Canara district of Karnataka. A total of 127 paper manuscripts are available with this collection. Some important and rare Ṛg Vedic texts are also obtainable. *Aśvalāyana Śrauta Prayoga* is an important one.

The above said centers are only a little among the hundreds of private manuscript collection centers in the southern part of India. Here this is highlighted because of their uniqueness in subjects and number of manuscript bundles they are having. Moreover they are very much co-operative towards the manuscript researchers and well wishers.

Select Bibliography

Muller, J.P & Goodall, Dominic (2006). The Shaiva Manuscripts of Pondicherry, pp.1-3.

Murthy, R. S., Sivaganesa, (1996). Introduction to Manuscriptology, pp.67-71.

Nair, K. Mahesvaran (1998), Manuscriptology, pp 95-98.

Thakur, M.M. Anantalal (1998). Manuscriptology from Indian Sources, pp.1-4.

Visalakshy, P., (2003).The Fundamentals of Manuscriptology, pp.40-44.